URALIC AND ALTAIC SERIES

Volume 43

Routledge
Taylor & Francis Group
LONDON AND NEW YORK

The Uralic and Altaic Series
Volumes 1–150, 1960–1990

First published 1997 by Curzon Press Ltd

Published 2022 by Routledge
2 Park Square, Milton Park, Abingdon, Oxon OX14 4RN
605 Third Avenue, New York, NY 10017

Routledge is an imprint of the Taylor & Francis Group, an informa business

Publisher's Note

The publisher has gone to great lengths to ensure the quality of this reprint but points out that some imperfections in the original copies may be apparent.

ISBN 978-0-7007-0380-7
ISBN 978-0-700-70843-7 (hbk)

FUNDAMENTAL PRINCIPLES

OF

MONGOL LAW

FUNDAMENTAL PRINCIPLES OF
MONGOL LAW

by Valentin A. Riasanovsky

INDIANA UNIVERSITY PUBLICATIONS
Uralic and Altaic Series, Vol. 43

Published by
Indiana University, Bloomington
Mouton & Co., The Hague, The Netherlands
1965

INDIANA UNIVERSITY PUBLICATIONS

Graduate School

URALIC AND ALTAIC SERIES

Volume 43

Originally published: *Fundamental Principles of Mongol Law,*
by Professor V. A. Riasanovsky, Tientsin, 1937.

All orders from the United States of America and from
Canada should be addressed to the
Editor, Uralic and Altaic Series, Patton House,
Indiana University, Bloomington, Indiana

Orders from all other countries should be sent to
Mouton & Co., Publishers, The Hague, The Netherlands

Library of Congress Catalog Card Number: 65-63020

VALENTIN A. RIASANOVSKY
SAN FRANCISCO, 1964

FOREWORD TO THE 1965 EDITION*

Professor Valentin Aleksandrovich Riasanovsky was born in Kostroma, Russia, in 1884. He received his secondary education at the classical gymnasia in Kostroma, and then enrolled in the Faculty of Law, Moscow University. Following his graduation in 1908, he was invited to remain at the University, but declined owing to ill-health. He settled instead in Nizhnii-Novgorod, and having overcome his illness, he entered private legal practice. In 1911, he went abroad. After spending a year in Germany, where he continued his legal studies, he returned to Russia.

Professor Riasanovsky's teaching career began in 1915, when he accepted an appointment as *Privatdocent* at the Demidov Juridical Lyceum, in Jaroslavl'. After successfully defending his dissertation in 1917, he was awarded an advanced degree in civil law by Donskoi University. The same year, he was promoted to the rank of Professor Extraordinarius of Civil Law. Along with his teaching duties at the Lyceum, he continued to practice law; he became a recognized authority on questions of inheritance and succession. In Jaroslavl', where he remained until 1918, he was also elected to a number of honorary civil and judicial positions.

Between the years 1911 and 1918, Riasanovsky's scholarly interests centered largely on Russian civil law and juridical procedure. The numerous contributions he made to Russian legal studies, published during this period and later, are listed in Section I, A-B (pp. 339-403) of "Valentin A. Riasanovsky: Bibliography". The bibliography was prepared especially for the present volume.

The Russian Revolution was the decisive political event in the lives of Professor Riasanovsky's generation of Russian scholars. The road of exile, which he chose, led first to Siberia, then to Manchuria, to China, and finally, to the United States. From 1918 to 1922, he lived, practiced law, and taught at universities in Tomsk, Irkutsk, and Vladivostok. He

* The Foreword is a slightly revised version of Alexander V. Riasanovsky. "The Contribution of V. A. Riasanovsky to Oriental Studies: An Appreciation on His Eightieth Birthday," paper presented at the One Hundred and Seventy-Fourth Meeting of the *American Oriental Society,* New York, 1964. This paper was based in part on the following secondary sources: unsigned article, "Prof. V. A. Rjazanovskii. K dvadtsatipjatiletiju uchenoi i prakticheskoi dejatel'nosti (1908-1933 gg.)", *Izvestija Juridicheskogo Fakul'teta v g. Kharbine,* X, 1933; B. S. Roomiantseff, "Scientific Works of Professor V. A. Riasanovsky in the Sphere of the Laws of Oriental Peoples," *The Chinese Social and Political Science Review,* XXII, 1, 1938; published comments and book-reviews.

spent the years 1923-1934 in Harbin, Manchuria, where he married Antonina Fedorovna Podgorinova. Their two sons, Nicholas and Alexander, were born in Harbin.

While in Harbin, Riasanovsky was instrumental in organizing the Faculty of Law, an institute for legal and related studies. He taught in the Faculty for twelve years, and was Dean for five years. Student enrollment, drawn mostly from the Russian *émigré* community, reached one thousand, and special classes were also established for training Chinese students. The Faculty sponsored a number of scholarly publications, including the journal *Izvestija Juridicheskogo Fakul'teta v gorode Kharbine (Proceedings of the Faculty of Law in Harbin)*, which printed articles on Russian, Soviet, and Oriental law, on legal theory, comparative jurisprudence, and allied subjects. In Harbin, he continued private practice as an attorney, and served as the head of the Legal Department of the Chinese Eastern Railway.

In 1934, following the Japanese occupation of Manchuria, Professor Riasanovsky and his family emigrated to Tientsin, China. They settled on the British Concession. His career as attorney and teacher ended at this point. Consequently, during the four years he spent in Tientsin, he devoted himself largely to scholarly research and writing.

His major contributions to the study of Oriental law were made in the period 1918-1938. His works in this field, published in Russian, English, French, and Japanese are listed in Section II, A-G (pp. 340-42) of the bibliography.

In 1938, when a major war seemed imminent, Professor Riasanovsky and his family emigrated to the United States, first to Eugene, Oregon, and then to San Francisco, California, where he now lives. Soon after his arrival in the United States, Riasanovsky was striken with paralysis, at the height of which, he lost the use of his arms and legs. He was completely bed-ridden for several years. After five major operations, and protracted convalescent periods, he succeeded in partially conquering the paralysis, but he is still forced to spend most of his time in bed or in a sedentary position.

Despite the great physical handicap, Professor Riasanovsky managed to continue his scholarly activity. Between 1947 and 1949, he published in Russian the three volume study *Obzor russkoi kul'tury (Survey of Russian Culture)*, and the companion volume *Razvitie russkoi nauchnoi mysli v XVIII-XX st. st. (The Development of Russian Scientific Thought in the XVIII-XX Centuries)*. These and other works in the field of Russian history and culture are listed in Section III, A-C (p. 340) of the bibliography. At present, he is preparing for publication two separate studies; the one, a collection of essays on mediaeval Russian history, and the other, a historical survey of Soviet science from 1918 to 1963.

Among the many scholarly and honorary societies which have elected Professor Riasanovsky to membership, the following may be mentioned: *Société de Législation Comparée* (Paris), *The Chinese Social and Political Science Association* (Peking), *Istituto di Studi Legislativi* (Rome), the *Royal Asiatic Society* (London), the *American Academy of Political and Social Sciences,* and the *American Oriental Society.*

His international reputation as a legal scholar rests primarily on his work in Oriental law. His contributions to this field may be conveniently divided into three major areas and discussed under the following headings: 1) Chinese Law, 2) Mongol Law, and 3) Law of the Siberian Tribes.

1) *Chinese Law*

Professor Riasanovsky, Jean Escarra, and a handful of other scholars may be regarded as pioneer investigators in the field of Chinese civil law. It should be noted, that while pre-Republican China had a well-elaborated criminal code, applicable to the entire country, no general civil code had been promulgated. Thus, Old Chinese Civil Law varied considerably from region to region and according to local customs and usages.

The article "Osnovnye instituty kitaiskogo grazhdanskogo prava" (also published in English as a separate monograph *Fundamental Institutions of Chinese Civil Law,* 1926) is particularly noteworthy, therefore, as one of the first systematic attempts to penetrate beyond the confusion of local peculiarities which seemed to characterize the Old Civil Law of China. In "Osnovnye instituty", Professor Riasanovsky employs meticulous juridical analysis to uncover a number of basic elements common to the Old Civil Law of China in such spheres as law of ownership, family law, the law of inheritance and succession, and others. The analysis is enriched and broadened in scope by careful comparisons drawn between certain aspects of Chinese and European legal thought. Significant conceptual differences are noted and discussed.

The two volume study *Sovremennoe grazhdanskoe pravo Kitaja,* 1926-1927 (published in English as *The Modern Civil Law of China,* 1927-1928), was originally intended by Riasanovsky to serve a practical as well as a scholarly purpose. This work offers a systematic treatment of Chinese civil law in the so-called "transitional period", that is after the Republican Revolution, but before the promulgation of the Civil Code of the Republic of China in 1929-1931. Used widely in its time by European lawyers practicing in China, the contemporary value of the study is primarily historical. It gives a cogent picture of the juridical-institutional background from which the Civil Code of the Republic of China emerged.

The book *Chinese Civil Law,* 1938, presents, first of all, a theoretical discussion of civil law in general, and then places the Civil Code of the Republic of China within the conceptual framework thus established. It contains a close analysis and explanation of the various provisions of the newly promulgated Chinese Civil Code. Finally, these provisions are compared and contrasted, in several instances, with analogous provisions in three European civil codes then in effect—the French, the German, and the Swiss. *Chinese Civil Law,* therefore, makes an important contribution not only to Chinese legal scholarship, but also to legal theory and comparative jurisprudence.

In addition to the works mentioned already, Professor Riasanovsky published a number of monographs and articles dealing with specific aspects of Chinese civil law. He was also editor of two major projects—the translations into Russian of the Draft Civil Code of the Republic of China, and of the Civil Code of the Republic of China. These were the first full translations into any European language.

2) *Mongol Law*

Prior to the appearance of Professor Riasanovsky's works in this field, the study of Mongol law was in a comparatively low state of development. With few exceptions, Mongol law was approached, heretofore, either from the historical or the philological points of view. He was one of the first scholars to undertake an examination of Mongol law from the vantage point of a trained jurist.

The Yassa of Genghiz-Khan was perhaps the most important Mongol code of laws. Historians and philologists such as Howorth, Purgstall, Erdmann, de Sacy, and Berezin had already written on some aspects of the Yassa. But it was Riasanovsky, in his article "Velikaja Jasa Chingiz-Khana" ("The Great Yassa of Genghiz-Khan"), 1933, who was the first to subject the Yassa to a searching juridical-legal analysis. He established that the Yassa was promulgated in 1206-1218, ascertained its major internal and external sources, described them, determined that the norms of the Yassa were divided into five basic groups, and indicated the influence of the Yassa and the sphere of its application.

The second important Mongol code, known as the Mongol-Oirat Regulations of 1640, had already been subjected to legal analysis by Leontovich. Riasanovsky's work on this code was confined largely to an explanation of its provisions and of its historical significance.

The third major compilation of Mongol law, the Khalkha Djirum Code of 1709, was described in 1923 by Jamtsarano. Riasanovsky, however, greatly amplified and supplemented the findings of his personal friend and colleague. Working with a different transcription than the one used by Jamtsarano, he determined that the Khalkha Djirum consisted of twenty-three parts, and contained seventeen different records. He published a systematic analysis of the Code and of its sources. In connection with his investigation of the Khalkha Djirum, he established the existence of yet another and earlier Mongol code—the Great Seven-Hoshuns Regulations of Northern Mongolia.

Professor Riasanovsky also established the existence of three separate Chinese Regulations for Mongolia. The first of these was promulgated by Emperor K'ang-hsi in *ca.* 1696; it applied to Inner Mongolia. The second was issued by the Chinese Yuan for Foreign Relations in 1789, and the third, by the Chinese Yuan for Foreign Relations in 1815.

His interest in comparative jurisprudence led him to examine the influence exercised by Mongol law upon other nations. He concluded that Mongol law, owing primarily to the basic differences in the social, economic, and cultural background from which it developed, had very little effect upon the legal systems of the Chinese, the Persians, and the Russians. His article "Mongol Law and Chinese Law in the Yuan Dynasty", 1936, for example, upset the previously held opinion that Mongol law had a fundamental impact on Chinese law at the time in question. On the other hand, Riasanovsky demonstrated convincingly that Mongol law profoundly influenced the law of various nomadic tribes in Eastern Asia, which, generally speaking, had social and economic institutions similar to those of the Mongols.

Professor Riasanovsky's book *Fundamental Principles of Mongol Law,* 1937, may be regarded as his single most important contribution to this field of study. Incorporating the findings derived from his earlier research on more specialized problems, it presents a comprehensive examination of the essential features of Mongol law in their historical development together with a tightly reasoned appraisal of their significance. Some of the conclusions reached in this book may be summarized as follows.

In continental Eastern Asia, until modern times, there existed two fundamental and independent systems of law—the Chinese and the Mongol. Chinese law reflected primarily the legal relations of a settled, agrarian people, with an extraordinarily rich cultural heritage. Mongol law reflected the needs of a basically nomadic society of hunters and cattle-breeders, with a comparatively poorer cultural inheritance. The two systems, therefore, were basically different, since each arose under vastly different economic, social, and cultural conditions.

Mongol law, according to Professor Riasanovsky, was chiefly customary law, based on clan-organization, clan-administration, and the clan court. The patriarchal, nomadic, clan nature of Mongol society found clear expression in Mongol law, in the basic recognition of relationship through the father, in the powers given to the father and husband in a family, in the recognition of polygamy, as well as in the relatively weak development of state principles and of civil jurisprudence. Mongol law, however, exhibited also certain matriarchal institutions, for example, in the survival of levirate, of avanculate, and of heterism, and in the special recognition and respect accorded to the mother's or wife's clan. These and other considerations rooted in the historical development of Mongol law, led him to propose that Mongol society was originally matriarchal, and that the patriarchal system was a later development.

3) *Law of the Siberian Tribes*

Commentators and reviewers of Professor Riasanovsky's work in this field have credited him with placing the investigation of the customary law of the Siberian nomads on a solid, scholarly, and systematic basis. Beginning with his book *Obychnoe pravo burjat (Customary Law of the Buriats)*, 1921, Riasanovsky undertook separate studies of the law of the Buriats, the Kirghiz, the Voguls, the Ostyaks, the Kalmuks, the Samoyeds, the Altais, the Teleuts, the Tunguses, the Yakuts, and of other primarily Eastern Siberian tribes. He determined that in addition to indigenous factors, the legal relations of these various tribes were influenced by Mongol law, by Muslim law—especially among the Kirghiz and the Ostyaks, by Lamaist law—among the Southern Buriats, and by Russian law. It may be mentioned that he also published several heretofore unavailable records of Buriat law: the Zaadza of 1759, the Heb, 1763, the Hip-Toktogol, 1800, the Steppe Code of 1808, and the Decisions of 1817 and 1818.

From these separate studies, Riasanovsky reached the following general conclusion. Owing to the fact that the life of the Siberian tribes in question was governed by similar socio-economic conditions implicit in nomadic, clan, and patriarchal based cultures, the principles underlying their legal institutions, despite local differences in customs and traditions, were fundamentally similar. He also concluded, as he did from his examination of Mongol law, that the patriarchal system which characterized these tribal societies had developed from an earlier matriarchal stage.

The preceding, then, has been a brief description of Professor Riasanovsky's contributions to the study of Oriental law. He brought to this field a breadth of approach, a technical erudition, and an ability for analysis and synthesis rarely equaled by others. The world of scholarship should welcome, therefore, the republication of his *Fundamental Principles of Mongol Law*. This book, like many of Riasanovsky's other writings, has been too long out of print. A debt of gratitude is owed to Indiana University for undertaking the project. Special acknowledgements must be made to Professor Denis Sinor, Chairman of the Program in Uralic and Altaic Studies, Indiana University, whose scholarly sensitivity and practical enthusiasm made this volume, marking Professor Riasanovsky's eightieth birthday, a reality. In the near future the Indiana University Uralic and Altaic Series will republish Riasanovsky's *Customary Law of the Nomadic Tribes of Siberia*.

ERRATA

page	*line*	*reads*	*should read*
57	5 down	existing	delete
57	9 up (foot-note)	with some changes	delete
259	1 up (foot-note)	of children	delete
272	last line (foot-note)	Dukes	Princes
276	6 up (foot-note)	Grand-Ducal	Grand-Princely

CONTENTS

PREFACE.

The study of Mongol law is of considerable scientific interest, especially from the historical point of view, the point of view of the history of law. Mongol law is a manifestation of the juristic creativeness of a people which has its own glorious history, and once exercised great influence on the progress of the history of many peoples of three continents, and upon the laws of some of these people. The law of the Mongol tribes, based on a nomadic pastoral culture, represented the second great system of law in Eastern Asia, the first being Chinese law, which was based on a settled agricultural way of life. Moreover, apart from this, the study of Mongol law is interesting from the point of view of comparative jurisprudence. In the life of the Mongol tribes, we meet expressions of a type of legal organization long obsolete among European and American peoples (with a few exceptions) and rich in materials for comparative study.

The Author of the present work has occupied himself with the study of Mongol law for a period of more than 15 years. One of his first essays was an outline in the Russian language "Obychnoe pravo buriat" (Customary Law of the Buriats), published in 1921. Continuing with his study of Mongol law, the Author came to the conclusion that the works of his predecessors on separate aspects of Mongol law, and also his own works dealing with this subject, had made it possible to write a general outline of the law of the Mongol tribes in its historical development, an outline which did not previously exist in scientific literature. The Author's first attempt in this direction was an outline, "Obichnoe pravo Mongolskikh plemen (Mongolov, Buriat i Kalmykov)" (Customary Law of the Mongol Tribes—Mongols, Buriats, and Kalmucks) which appeared in the "Vestnik Azii" (Messenger of Asia), a Russian language publication in Harbin, in the years 1923-4. This outline was translated into English and published in book form under the title of "The Customary Law of the Mongol Tribes" in the year 1929. Subsequently, the Author revised and enlarged this work, re-publishing it in 1931 in the Russian language, under the title of "Mongolskoie pravo, preimuschestvenno obychnoe" (Mongol Law, With

Special Reference to Customary Law). After publishing this book the Author continued to occupy himself with the study of different questions of Mongol law (see further) and prepared the present work.

In this historical work the survey and analysis of Mongol Law is brought up to 1924.[1] Brief information about the Mongol law of the present time (1924-1936) is given in the introduction.

The Author wishes here to record his gratitude to Mr. Ts. J. Jamtsarano, who placed at his disposal a transcription of the Code of Northern Mongolia, "Khalkha-Djirom", which made it possible for him to acquaint himself in detail with the contents of this important juridical record and to use it in the present volume and in a separate special article devoted to this Code.

He also wishes to thank Mr. I. Epstein for his help in translating the present volume.

The following works of the Author were used in the writing of this book:

"Customary Law of the Mongol Tribes", 1929; "Dva pamiatnika obychnogo prava mongolskikh plemen" (Two Records of the Customary Law of the Mongol Tribes), an article in "Vestnik Mandjurii", 1930-1; "O vlianii mongolskoi kultury i prava na russkuiu kulturu i pravo" (On the Influence of Mongol Culture and Law on Russian Culture and Law), Graduation Day speech, in the Memoirs of the Faculty of Law in Harbin, Vol. IX (1931); "Mongolskoie pravo, preimuschestvenno obychnoe" (Mongol Law, with Special Reference to Customary Law), 1931; "The Influence of Chinese Law Upon the Mongolian Law", article in the "Chinese Political and Social Science Review", 1931, No. 3; "Nekotorye cherty obychnogo prava altaiev i teleutov" (Some Features of

1 In the present work (Chapter II) the Author reproduces the contents of the records of Mongol law, because the contents of some of these records (e.g. the Khalkha-Djirum and the law of Autonomous Mongolia) were not incorporated in the corresponding sections of his previous work: "Customary Law of the Mongol Tribes". Other records, such as the Maxims of Jenghiz Khan, are here presented in more complete form, while in the case of the Great Yassa and the Ancient Tsaadjin Bichik the Author has in some respects corrected the previous translation. These reasons have prompted the Author, in Chapter II of the present work, to repeat the contents of the records of Mongol law.

As for the records of Buriat and Kalmuck law, the contents of these were given in detail in "Customary Law of the Mongol Tribes" (and in the later "Mongolskoe pravo") and the Author has not since obtained any important material which might supplement or amend the historical summary there given. For this reason, the contents of Buriat and Kalmuck law are not repeated in the present volume.

the Customary Law of the Altais and Teleuts), article in the "Monitor of Chinese Law", Harbin, 1931, No. 3; "Mongol Law and Comparative Jurisprudence", a paper submitted to the 1st International Congress of Comparative Jurisprudence, 1932; "Les monuments de droit mongol", in the "Bulletin de la Société de Législation Comparée", 1932, No. 7-12; "Iavliaetsia li mongolskoie pravo pravom obychnym?" (Is Mongol Law Customary Law?), a sketch, 1932; "Velikaia Yassa Chingis-hana" (The Great Yassa of Jenghiz Khan), an outline, 1933; "Mongol Law and Chinese Law in the Yuan Dynasty", in the "Chinese Social and Political Science Review", 1936, No. 2; "The Code of Northern Mongolia—Khalkha-Djirom", Report submitted to the annual (1936) meeting of International Academy of Comparative Law, *Ibidem,* 1936, No. 3, "The Fundamental Institutions of Chinese Civil Law", 1926; "The Modern Civil Law of China", Part I, 1927; "The Modern Civil Law of China", Part II, 1928.

V. RIASANOVSKY.

Tientsin, China, March 1, 1937.

INTRODUCTION.

Historical Note.—The origin of the Mongols is not exactly known. Their appearance on the stage of world history dates from the second half of the XII-th century when a great leader and organizer appeared among the Mongol tribes scattered through Eastern Asia—the celebrated Temuchin of the tribe of Tadjiut, better known under the name of Jenghiz Khan.

This conqueror of half the world, who lived from 1155 to 1227 A.D., created, with the aid of the conquered Uigurs and Chinese, the vast Mongol Empire which embraced Mongolia, Southern Siberia, the greater part of Northern China, Tangut, Bokhara, Samarkand, Khorassan, Koohistan and several other countries. His immediate successors, the Khans Ogodai (1229-1241), Kuyuk (1246-1248) and Mangu (Munké) (1251-1259) considerably extended the limits of this Empire, conquering all Northern and a large part of Southern China, Korea, the Ussuri and Amur regions, Armenia, Georgia, Azerbaijan, Greater Bulgaria, Russia, Persia, Siberia, Mesopotamia and parts of Tibet and India.

Kublai Khan (1260-1294), who completed the conquest of South China, Tibet, and India, established his residence in Peking (Kambalu) and in the year 1271 founded the Mongol (Yuan) dynasty in China. It was at the time of his proclamation as Khan without a legally convened Kurultai that the great Mongol Empire began to disintegrate.

Its size, the diversity of the races peopling it, and the absence of any economic and cultural ties between the tribes, peoples and countries that composed it, made it impossible for the world empire of the Mongols to exist as a unit for any length of time. At the time of Kublai Khan it had already begun to disintegrate, and thus lasted for only forty years after the death of Jenghiz Khan, its founder.

At first China and the countries adjacent to it were the base of the rule of the Jenghizids. But, in time, independent states came into existence in the West: in Iran—Persia, in Turkestan—the State of Djagatai, and in the plains of Western Siberia and Eastern Europe—the Kipchak State of the Golden Horde. All these States were also short-lived.

In China proper, the Mongol dynasty reigned from 1271 to 1368 A.D. In the latter year, the last Emperor of the House of Jenghiz Khan, Toghon Temur, was compelled to leave China and retire to the

Mongolian border. In Persia, the Mongol dynasty ruled from 1256 to 1344 over the united State, and until 1380 over a series of small domains which were finally conquered by Tamerlane. In Bokhara and Turkestan, the Mongols governed from 1242 until 1370. The Golden Horde suffered a decisive defeat at the hands of the Russians in 1380, and as a result of this it fell apart into separate territories (Crimea, Kazan, Astrakhan, etc.), lost its power over Russia in the middle of the XVth century, and ceased to exist as a State in about the year 1500.

The later history of Mongolia is occupied on the one hand by the almost constant struggle with China, and on the other by the internal dissensions of the Mongol tribes themselves. The Mongols fell apart into three parts, Northern Mongolia (Khalkha); Southern (Inner) Mongolia; and Western Mongolia (Djungaria) all of which were hostile to each other and were themselves far from internal solidarity.

The Western Mongols were chiefly settled in Djungaria. At the end of the XIVth century they formed a political union (Oirat) the chief members of which were the Choros, Torgod, Khoshout and Khoit tribes (the "Derben Oirat" or Quadruple Union). At the end of the XIVth century, the warlike Kontaishas (Khans) of the Oirat—Mahmud, Toghon and especially Essen (Yissun), succeeded in subduing and unifying the whole of Mongolia, and inflicting a series of severe defeats on China. But after the death of Essen (1453 A.D.), the Oirat union broke up and leadership again passed to the Eastern Mongols. In the first half of the XVIth century, Dayan Khan not only succeeded in resisting Chinese encroachments but decisively defeated the invaders in a number of engagements and united the whole of Mongolia under his rule. After his death, (1544 A.D.) however, the country again broke up into independent aimaks and it has never since been completely re-united. Dayan Khan divided Mongolia into eleven appanages which he gave to his sons, South Mongolia going to the eldest and the 13 Otoks of Khalkha to Gherescenza, one of his younger sons.

At first the leadership rested with South Mongolia, the camping ground of the senior descendants of Dayan Khan. These produced several conspicuous leaders, such as Altan Khan of Tumed (died 1585) and Lingdan (Lekdan) Khan of Chahar (d. 1634). The growth of the power of the Manchus, however, reduced many of the Southern Mongol tribes to the status of their dependents; and after the Manchus had conquered China, they completely subdued Southern Mongolia. Lingdan Khan's attempt to resist met with utter defeat (in 1633), and from that time on Southern Mongolia fall entirely under Chinese influence and was later incorporated into the territory of China (as "Inner Mongolia.")

Northern Mongolia (Khalkha) was the camping and pasture ground of the clans of Gherescenza (over 10,000 kibitakas or households), the progenitor of the present princely families of Khalkha. Before his death, Gherescenza divided his Aimak into 7 Hoshuns over which he set his sons.

Among the subsequent ruling princes of Khalkha, the most prominent were the descendants of three of the sons of Gherescenza, Ashihay, Nunuhu and Amin. The great-grandson of Ashihay, Subudi, was granted the title of Djasaktu Khan by the Dalai Lama, while the great-grandson of Nunuhu, Gombo, was given the title of Tushetu Khan, and Sholoi, the grandson of Amin, that of Tsetsen Khan. Around these senior potentates, the lesser Hoshun princes of their tribe grouped themselves. In this way Northern Mongolia (Khalkha) was divided into the three aimaks of Djasaktu Khan, Tushetu Khan, and Tsetsen Khan.

In Western Mongolia in the beginning of the XVIIth century, the energetic Khans of Choros, Khara-Khula and his son Batur, again united the Oirat tribes under their leadership. As a consequence of this, some prominent Taishas with their clans left Djungaria and migrated in different directions. One of them, Kho-Urluk, first went to Eastern Siberia and thence to the steppes of the Lower Volga, founding the settlements of the Russian Kalmucks.

The growth of the Manchu power, the defeat of Lingdan Khan in South Mongolia and the consequent capitulation of that territory, and the ever increasing pressure of the conquerors on North Mongolia were accompanied by the weakening of the Oirats as a result of the emigration of part of their number to various neighbouring countries. These circumstances induced the princes of Northern and Western Mongolia to undertake the establishment of internal peace and protection against the external foe. In 1640 the Khans and Princes of Northern and Western Mongolia, of Kokonor, and even of Russia, met at a Congress of forty-four Mongol tribes at which, as a consequence of the great influence of Batur Khan, a new alliance was concluded and a code of law, the socalled Mongol-Oirat Regulations of 1640, was framed and approved. The Mongol-Oirat Federation then established and the internal peace which it engendered were not, however, long-lived, lasting only about forty years.

Batur Khun-Taidji died in 1654. He left eleven sons of whom nine were by one wife and two (Senghe and Galdan) by another.

The energetic Galdan united the Oirats under his leadership, (1677-8), subdued Eastern Turkestan, and extended his dominion to include Khalkha in his attempt to unite the whole of Mongolia under his rule. To this end, he undertook an expedition against the princes of Khalkha which ended in the complete defeat of the latter in 1688. Galdan Khan gave the whole country over to devastation as a result of which a part of the Northern Mongols (as many as 1,000 families) emigrated North with their entire households and settled on the river Selenga in Russia, being henceforth known as the Selenga Buriats. The greater part of the population, however, consisting of about 20,000 families, moved South and submitted to Chinese rule. At the middle of the XVIIth century (1757-8) Djungaria was subdued by Chinese arms, after a fierce and bloody struggle.

After the Chinese conquered the whole of Mongolia, they gradually organized it into several administrative units. The country was divided into Inner (Southern) and Outer (Northern and Western) Mongolia and reorganized on military principles. Both these territories were divided into Aimaks (provinces) and Hoshuns (Djassaks, principalities). Inner Mongolia comprised 24 Aimaks and 49 Hoshuns which were grouped in six Leagues (Jerim, Josotu, Ju-Uda, Silin-gol, Ulan-Tsab, and Yeke-Tsu) and were, in their turn, divided into Somuns. Besides this, a part of the Mongol tribes, such as the Barguts, Chahars and Tumeds, were placed under a special administration. Militarily the Djassaks of Inner Mongolia included six Army Corps or Chulhans (corresponding to the number of Leagues), and 49 Divisions (Gussa), one for each Hoshun. Outer Mongolia consisted of four Aimaks—Djasaktu Khan, Tushetu Khan, Tsetsen Khan and Sain Noyon-Khan—which in their turn were divided into 86 appanages (principalities, Hoshuns). These were grouped into four Leagues to conform with the number of Aimaks (the Khan Ula, Bara-Khoto, Tsetserlik, and Binduria-Nor Leagues). Over and above these, there were some appanages of Hubilgans. As regards administration, the provinces of Kokonor, Ili and Altai were joined to Outer Mongolia. Militarily the Outer Mongolian Djassaks were divided into 7 Army Corps; four for the four Aimaks of Khalkha, one from Kokonor, one from Ili and one formed of the tribes of the Altai region. These seven Corps were split up into 149 divisions.

The internal administration under the control of the Tuchun of Uliassutai and the Ambans of Kobdo and Urga was concentrated (from 1727) in the hands of the presidents of the Seims (Leagues), who were elected from among the Seim princes and the Hoshun Princes with their civil and military establishments.

Mongolia in the XXth Century. At the beginning of the XXth century Mongolia represented a strange anachronism in the family of European and Asiatic nations. In an epoch of exceptional development of private property Mongolia did not yet know private property in immovables. In an era of industrial prosperity, social crises, and finance capital, this country had no industry of its own, no labour question, and no national currency system. While elsewhere the period was remarkable for the flight of population from village to town, Mongolia had almost no towns at all; and in those few that did exist the population was chiefly made up of foreigners. More than this, even the house was unknown in Mongolia. The inhabitants of the country were nomads, just as they had been a thousand years ago, with hardly a notion of agriculture or settled life. (The weakly developed trade of Mongolia was in foreign hands). The people, which had once been noted for its military prowess, conquered half the world, and filled the then known Earth with its name, lived under foreign sovereignty, passive, weak and disunited; without any army of its own or any idea of modern armaments or methods of attack and defence. Subject to foreign domination which split them into 150 small principalities, each under its own hereditary prince wielding medieval power over his subjects, feeding a huge class of Lamas, and forced to pay a multitude of levies in kind to support these princes and priests (and in Inner Mongolia pushed deeper and deeper into the steppe by the advance of Chinese colonization), the Mongols led an unenviable existence as small herdsmen, just as in the epoch of Jenghiz Khan, and, in the mass, with almost the same absence of culture and even literacy as had then obtained.

Precarious economic conditions in Mongolia and the Chinese revolution of 1911 led to an uprising in that year in Northern Mongolia, with Urga as its centre. As a result of this revolt, Northern Mongolia proclaimed its independence under the supreme authority of the Bogdo Gegen Khutukhtu, the Pontiff of Urga. In 1912 the revolution spread over the whole of Outer Mongolia as well as a part of Manchuria (the Barguts) involving an area from the Khingan range to the Altai. The Chinese strongholds of Uliassutai and Kobdo fell, and the Chinese authorities (the Tu-chun and Ambans) were driven from Khalkha where a national government was established. It was at this time that the Manchu dynasty was overthrown in China and this led further to the recognition of the authority of the Urga Khutukhtu by a part of South Mongolia (the Silin-Gol, Ulan-Tsab and Yekedzu Leagues) and also by Barga. Russia recognised the autonomy of Mongolia in 1912, and in 1913 a Sino-Russian Treaty concerning Mongolia was signed, followed in 1915 by the conclusion of a tripartite agreement (between China, Russia and Mongolia). According to this instrument, Outer Mongolia (but not Inner Mongolia and Barga) was recognized as an autonomous State under the suzerainty of China and the protectorate of Russia. China had no right to interfere in questions of internal administration, or to station troops in Outer Mongolia, but retained the right to appoint a special Commissioner to Urga with three assistant commissioners in Kobdo, Uliassutai and Maimachen. Outer Mongolia was defined as consisting of Khalkha (four Aimaks) and Kobdo (two Aimaks).

The supreme power in the State was vested in the Bogdo Gegen Khutukhtu of Urga, who was assisted by a Council of Ministers consisting of a Minister-President and the Ministers of Foreign Affairs, the Interior, Finance, War and Justice. There also existed the special Shabin department (great yamen). Matters of great importance were decided by a Congress of the Hoshun princes (the Huruldan). The decisions of the Huruldan and Council of Ministers were subject to the approval of the Head of the State. Local administration remained in the hands of the Hoshun princes and of the Seims of the Aimaks, while in remote localities (Kobdo) special government agents were appointed. Generally speaking, the revolution put an end to Chinese influence and increased the power of the clergy and the princes, contributing very little to the improvement of the condition of the Mongol people.

The condition of national economy was extremely difficult.[1] The Mongols engaged in agriculture to only a very small extent, and almost exclusively in border territories close to Russian or Chinese settlements. In 1917 the Bogdo-Gegen promulgated a decree concerning the compulsory sowing of grain, but the order did not have much effect. The Chinese rented land in Mongolia for agricultural purposes, and according to Posdneev they sowed crops over an area of about 70,000 dessiatines before the Revolution of 1911/12. But in the epoch of Autonomous Mongolia this sown area shrank by more than half and the area cultivated by Mongols grew very little.

Industry was almost completely undeveloped. There were State coal-mines in Nalaiho, where about 100,000 poods of anthracite were mined every year, and in some places a primitive method of obtaining salt from the lakes was practiced. The Russians established about a score of small tanneries, some casing and animal oil plants, and about 100 small wool-washeries to prepare the product for export to Russia. There were also three corporations of moderate means engaged in mineral development, the largest ("Mongolor", founded 1907) being a gold mining enterprise. Crafts were almost entirely in the hands of the Chinese, who maintained over 300 manufactories (sheepskin, leather, carpentries, smithies etc.) employing a total of about 4,000 workers.

---

1 The figures given here, as well as the data concerning the national economy of Autonomous Outer Mongolia are taken from Maisky's "Modern Mongolia" 1921. (*v.* pp. 123-126, 221, 225, 284-5, 307, etc.) They are based on a census of the population and cattle in Outer Mongolia in 1918 (the data of this census being given in the form of an appendix in the work named) as well as on a special investigation of the country during 1919-20.

The Mongols themselves hardly engaged in trade, which was from ancient times concentrated in the hands of the Chinese. After the revolution of 1911/12 much of this trade passed over into the hands of Russian merchants, but the European war again gradually opened the door to Chinese commercial firms. The trade turnover was from 40,000,000 to 50,000,000 roubles annually, and the indebtedness of the Mongols to foreign merchants, under conditions of the mutual responsibility of Hoshuns for their members, as well as the exploitation of the native populations, was extremely great.

Transportation was most primitive. There were no railroads or any roads at all maintained by the State or communities for the facilitation of communications. In Autonomous Outer Mongolia, only the most primitive avenues of communication existed, only "directions" along which men rode on horses during the summer, while freight was carried on bullock-carts during the warm weather and on camels in the winter. There were no bridges on these roads (in 1919 there were only 10 bridges in all Autonomous Mongolia). For the maintenance of communications a heavy levy in kind (Urton) was imposed, having both State (along the main avenues) and local (within the Hoshun) significance, this duty being borne by specially designated families within each Hoshun which lived at the Urton stations. These families were obliged to supply the necessary number of horses, bullocks, and camels to travellers entitled to make use of Urton facilities. Private persons travelled over the country on their own or hired horses and camels, while cargo was usually transported by caravans (of camels or bullocks).

Mongolia had no currency of its own. Before the Revolution of 1911/12 Chinese silver weight units (Lan) served as money, being supplanted after that year by the Russian silver, or more often paper, rouble. After the Russian revolution of 1917, the Chinese silver (Mexican) dollar and Chinese paper currency replaced the Russian. Due to the shortage of such money, however, sheep, brick-tea etc. were used as currency, especially in the interior.

The Mongols' chief means of livelihood was cattle-breeding, supplemented by hunting. The main forms of cattle were horses, bullocks, camels, sheep, and goats. Cattle-breeding in Mongolia was extensive and primitive in character. The cattle were kept in pastures under the open sky throughout the year without any supervision, and were forced to find their own food. Livestock (and especially the young) perished in tens of thousands from cold, hunger, storms, wolves and epizootics. Only in some places, under the influence of the Russians, the Mongols began to mow grass and stock hay for the cattle in winter, while winter shelters (Hashans) were also built. No steps were taken for the improvement of stock and almost nothing was done to prevent epizootics. The natural increase of cattle was therefore extremely small.

On the basis of the census of 1918, Maisky estimated the number of cattle in Outer Mongolia as follows: Horses—1,500,000; camels—300,000; horned cattle—1,400,000; sheep and goats—9,500,000; totalling 12,700,000. Of these 77.5% belonged to the tributary classes, 19.1% to the Church, and 3.4% to the princes and hereditary nobility. On the average, the economy of a prince consisted of 2,370 head of cattle; of a monastery—662 head; and of a tributary—60 head. From the figures quoted it is clear that Mongolia was a land of petty pastorial economy.

Hunting, generally speaking, was little developed among the Mongols, and the chief article of export in this connection was the skin of the tarabagan or marmot. Fishing was not practised at all.

The annual national income of Autonomous Mongolia was put at 74,500,000 roubles by Maisky. The income from cattle was 14,000,000 roubles; from pastoral products—42,500,000; from carting—10,000,000; coal and salt—5,000,000; personal labour—2,500,000; trapping products—500,000 roubles. The annual expenditure was 73,500,000 (food—51,000,000; clothing—8,500,000; dwellings and domestic utensils—5,500,000; working equipment—2,000,000; religious needs, 1,500,-000; and State needs—5,000,000). He estimated the entire national wealth of Mongolia at 250,000,000 roubles (not counting the mineral wealth). Thus the amount of national wealth per capita was 461 roubles, of national income—137 roubles, per capita expenditure—135 roubles.

The income of the Central Government comprised less that 2,000,-000 roubles, being composed chiefly of the income from indirect taxation; while the budget expenditures slightly exceeded the sum of 2,000,000 annually. The difference was covered by loans from the Russian Government (altogether 5,000,000 roubles).

The budgets of Aimak and Hoshun administrations totalled about 5,000,000 roubles per annum and were coverd chiefly by Alba, i.e. levies and taxes paid by the population. The indebtedness of the Hoshuns to the Chinese was very great—about 15,000,000 roubles.

From the data given above the economic backwardness of the country and poverty of the population should be sufficiently evident.[2]

2 According to the figures of the 1918 census, the Mongol population of Outer Mongolia, numbered about 550,000.

To the above figures we may add that, except for two special schools founded by the Russians, there were in Mongolia no secular schools. There was also no secular medicine.

The Russian revolution of 1917, and the civil war of 1918-1920 deprived Autonomous Mongolia of her foreign support and as a direct result of this Chinese troops (under General "Little Hsu") were again moved into Urga in 1919. Under the pressure of this armed force, and with the connivance of some Mongol princes and lamas, autonomy was renounced (by a decree of the President of the Republic of China dated November 22, 1919); and as from January 1, 1920, General Hsu was appointed Pacification Commissioner for Outer Mongolia, at the head of three administrative department—Military Affairs, Finance, and General Affairs. In accordance with the temporary Regulations relating to the administration of Outer Mongolia (promulgated at the end of 1920), the Pacification Commissioner headed the administration, being assisted by three Ambans at Uliassutai, Kobdo, and in the Uriankhai region respectively. All these reforms had not been carried out or placed on a sound footing, when, at the beginning of 1921, Outer Mongolia (with the assistance of White Russian military detachments under Baron Ungern-Sternberg) again proclaimed her independence under the sovereignty of the Urga Gegen. After a series of battles, the Chinese troops were compelled to withdraw from the country.

In 1919 the Mongolian People's Party appeared on the scene, and in 1921 (March 13) it elected a Provisional People's Government of Mongolia headed by Bodo which called upon Soviet Russia for help. The White Russian detachments, were shortly afterwards defeated by the Soviet armies (July 1921), and the People's Government assumed power. By virtue of his high religious authority, the Bogdo Gegen Khutukhtu remained (with a limited power of *veto*) the head of the State, which thus assumed the aspect of a constitutional monarchy. The power was in the hands of the Mongolian People's Party and the government appointed by it (under the perceptible influence of Soviet Russia). At this time (Outer) Mongolia declared its independence from China. In 1921 an agreement was concluded with Soviet Russia in accordance with which that country renounced all the privileges of Czarist times and recognized Mongolia (and was in turn recognized by Mongolia) as an independent State (5th November, 1921).[3]

The Provisional People's Government, even during the lifetime of the Urga Gegen, carried through a number of important reforms, such as the abolition of the condition of dependence (serfdom), the abolition of the hereditary power of the princes, the separation of Church and

3 In 1924, in the Peking Treaty concluded with China in that year (31st May), the U.S.S.R. recognized that Mongolia was a part of China.

State, abolition of torture and corporal punishment, institution of a standing army, etc. The Urga Gegen died in May of 1924 and the Provisional People's Government proclaimed the Republic in Mongolia, on June 13, 1924. In November of that year there took place the Great Huruldan or Hural (Constituent Congress) of the peoples of Mongolia, which adopted the new constitution of Mongolia.

Since 1921, and especially from 1924 until the present time (end of 1936), Mongolia has been passing through a second revolution, a revolution deeper than that of 1911-12.

The ruling People's Revolutionary Party, at its third and fourth Congresses (1924 and 1925), described the tasks of the Government and Party at the present time approximately as follows: to liquidate the remnants of feudalism, encourage the development of the productive forces of the country, and to concentrate political, financial and economic activity in the hands of the State, and to prepare the country for a transition to non-capitalist paths of development with a view to the eventual establishment of a Communist order in social relations.

It is natural that these aims influenced the contents of the legislation of the Mongolian People's Republic and the nature of the enterprises undertaken by the Government.

In November 1924, the Great Hural adopted a new Constitution for Outer Mongolia.

Mongolia was proclaimed an independent People's Republic (without a President), in which the entire power was vested in the toiling people and exercised through the Great People's Huruldan and the government elected by this body. In the periods between the sessions of the Great Huruldan, the supreme power was exercised by the Lesser Huruldan, and in the intervals between the sessions of the latter by the Praesidium of the Hural and the Government (Council of Ministers). The land with its waters and mineral and plant wealth was nationalised and private property in land was not permitted. The monopoly of foreign trade was not complete. The Church and State were divided. The ranks, privileges and titles of Khans, princes and nobles were abolished. The ballot (for the Great, Lesser and local Hurals) was given to all persons over the age of 18 years earning their own living, and to soldiers of the People's Revolutionary Army.

(The territory of Mongolia was divided into the former Aimaks the names of these being changed as follows: Tushetu Khan—Bagda-Khana-Ula, Tsetsen Khan—Khan-Tu-Tei-Ula; Djasaktu Khan—Khan-Nai-Inner-Ula; and Sain Noyon—Tsetserlik Mandalon. The Shabin department (of the tributaries of the Khutukhtu) was reorganized into a special Aimak and Kobdo (the Kobdo region) was divided into two Aimaks (later one). Besides these, several separate Hoshuns were included in the territory of the Republic).

Among other provisions and enterprises undertaken by the Government during the period we are considering it is necessary to note the following:

At the end of 1925 the Great Shabi Department was abolished and an elective organ (composed of Lamas) was instituted to deal with the administration of the monasteries, while the levies previously payable by the Shabinars to the monasteries were abolished. The separation of religion from the State was accomplished and the titles of Hubilgan, Hutukhtu, etc. were abolished in 1926. Furthermore, monastery property was taxed and the monasteries were forbidden to receive (as Lamas or novices) persons under 18 years of age. In 1934 the building of new monasteries and monastery trade were forbidden, while Lamas under 48 years of age were obliged to pay a special military tax. In 1936 the first and second sons of Mongol families were forbidden to enter monasteries.

Reform of the judiciary was carried out in 1925-6 and a new system of courts was established (Regulations Concerning Courts.) In the years which followed, criminal and civil codes and necessary laws of procedure were promulgated. The State Bank was founded in 1925, and in 1926 monetary reforms were decreed and a national unit of value (the Tuhrik, divisible into 100 Mungro) was introduced. Finally, in 1928, the currency was changed from the silver to the gold standard. A unified State Treasury and a State monopoly of foreign trade were fully instituted (1929) and the bases of the taxation policy of the Government were changed. Internal customs duties and taxes in kind were abolished, etc.

In 1930 the Hoshuns and Horins were abolished and the country was divided into 12 Aimaks, 309 Somuns, and 2930 Baks.

After the VIIth congress of the R.M.P. Party and the Vth Great Hural (1929), at which more Left tendencies triumphed, the confiscation of cattle belonging to "feudals" was carried out (1929-31).[4] During the same period strong pressure was applied to individual cattle economies to induce them to accept collectivisation, this being also the case in the spheres of private trade and transportation (cartage). However, in 1932 the Lesser Hural branded this policy as erroneous and discontinued it.

---

4 According to the report of the Chairman of the 21st session of the Lesser Hural in July 1936 "in 1929 there were confiscated the estates of 427 black and 302 yellow fendals. In 1931-32, the estates of 205 yellow and 622 black fendals were confiscated."—"Tikhi Okean" (The Pacific Ocean), 1936, No. 3 (9), pg. 87.

Thus, the Government retained the monopoly of foreign trade, a part of the internal (wholesale) trade, a large section of industry, the credit structure, and a part of transportation (automobile transport). The greater part of the retail trade and a section of industry were in the hands of co-operatives. Individual property and control continued to prevail in the majority of cattle-breeding economies, the larger part of transportation (cartage) and partly in trade.

At the VIIth Great Hural, held in 1934, it was stated that "private economy dominates in quantity and lies at the basis of the economy of the entire country."

It is necessary to add that a series of measures were undertaken towards the development of the national economy (agriculture, hay production, cattle-breeding, hunting, co-operation, national industry, and transport), medicine and veterinary science, popular education (schools, a national theatre, printing presses), etc.

Although in 1925 Soviet troops were withdrawn from Outer Mongolia, where the Mongolian army had been organized by this time, the connections between the M.P.R. and the U.S.S.R. and the influence of the latter upon the former did not in any way weaken. On March 12, 1936 a pact of mutual assistance in case of attack by a third Power was concluded (for a period of 10 years) between the two countries.

Let us consider some figures concerning the position of national economy in Outer Mongolia:[5]

The number of cattle in 1924 was as follows: Horses—1,350,-000; camels—275,000; horned cattle—1,512,000; sheep and goats—10,649,000, the total being 13,776,000 head. In 1935 there were 1,773,290 horses, 557,320 camels, 2,351,220 head of horned cattle, and 17,693,650 sheep and goats, totalling 22,375,480 head.

The cultivated area in 1924 was 4,383 hectares, in 1935—24,000 hectares; while the area of haymows, which was 1,551 ha. in 1924 had risen to 81,660 ha. in 1935.

In 1935, an industrial plant for the finishing and manufacture of raw materials was organized with 1,300 workers. This plant consists of a leather tannery, shoe factory, factory for the production of sheep-skin coats, weaving plant, felt factory, steam wool-washery, electric power station, and workers' settlement. Besides this a number of small plants were organized. Altogether, the number of industrial

5 These figures, and some other data, are taken mainly from an article by Mr. Ryzhik, "Economic and Cultural Construction in the Mongol People's Republic" in "Planovoe Hoziaistvo" (Planned Economy), 1936, No. 6, and also from the article "Lessons of 15 years of the Revolution" (Report by the chairman of the 21st session of the Lesser Hural), "Tikhi Okean", 1936, No. 3(9).

workers in State-owned industry in 1935 was 3,500 (90% of them being Mongols). Apart from this there is some small, co-operative industry (about 1,000 workers) and craft industries.

The hunting of fur-bearing animals is being developed, the tarbagan (marmot), squirrel, badger, fox and wolf being its main objects. In 1935 furs and skins comprised 15% of the country's exports.

The turnover of foreign trade with the U.S.S.R. in 1932 comprised 60,673,000 Tuhriks, while the turnover of co-operative trade in 1934 exceeded 40,000,000 Tuhriks.

In the sphere of transportation, an automobile mail and passenger service was established over the main regions, with repair of highways, construction of bridges, etc. Transportation of freight is also partly handled by trucks, but the greater part is still carried by carts. An air service, including air mail, has been established between the chief centres of population, as has shipping along the Selenga and Orkhon rivers and on Lake Kosogol.

The State budget in 1934 was 35,117,000 Tuhriks, of which about 10,000,000 Tuhriks were assigned to expenditures on national economy and 5,000,000 Tuhriks for cultural needs.

As regards cultural needs, in 1935, besides points for the liquidation of illiteracy, there were 70 primary schools, 6 middle schools, and a few special schools: a medical school, veterinary school, pedagogical school, technical school, and various courses. The medical personnel in the country in 1924 consisted of 7 doctors and trained assistants and a total of 88 persons serving the medical needs of the population; and the veterinary personnel in the same year consisted of 24 surgeons and trained assistants. In 1935 there were 139 medical doctors and trained assistants in the country, and the total medical personnel was 753, while there were 91 veterinary practicians in 52 points.[6]

Inner Mongolia.—Inner Mongolia represented the territory occupied by the Silingol (10 Hoshuns), Ulantsab (6 Hoshuns), Jerim (10 Hosh.), Jo-sotu (5 Hosh.), Yeke-Tsu (7 Hosh.), Ju-Uda (11 H.) Leagues; Chahars (8 banners) and Tumets (2 H.). The colonisation of

---

6 According to figures for 1930, the Mongol population of Outer Mongolia was about 700,000 including 2% nobility, 13% clergy, and 85% peasant Arats ("Concise Soviet Encyclopaedia," Vol. V, 1931, ppg. 336 338).

According to the latest data (second half of 1936) there are 75 primary school, 8 middle schools, and 73 institutions for medical instruction or treatment on the territory of the M.P.R.

Inner Mongolia by Chinese became especially pronounced after the abolition in 1878 of the prohibition previously in force against it, and a large Chinese population settled in these territories.[7] The Mongols were gradually pushed away into the Northern parts of Inner Mongolia, and large sections of it were occupied by Chinese populations which brought with them Chinese administration and administrative divisions.

Thus, in 1914, Inner Mongolia was divided into three special regions, Jehol, Chahar and Suiyuan, and the district of Taochan in Fengtien (Liaoning) province. In 1928 these regions were transformed into the provinces of Jehol, Chahar, Suiyuan, and Ninghsia (Alashan) and the Taochan district, besides which numbers of Mongols lived in the provinces of Kirin and Heilungkiang. These provinces had the same status as all other Chinese provinces and the same system of administration (a governor—Tuchun, Taotais—heads of several districts, Chi Hsiens—district magistrates; and their administrative offices). However, in the parts of these provinces inhabited by nomadic Mongols the division into League and Hoshuns was retained as was the power of the hereditary princes, the Djassaks (the Aimaks were abolished). These Djassaks were subject not only to the President of the League but also to the Tuchuns. The highest administrative organ was and is the Commission for Mongolian and Tibetan Affairs of the National Government at Nanking. Thus Inner Mongolia does not represent a unit. It is divided into several provinces and special administrations (the Chahars and Tumets).

After the appearance under the influence of the Japanese in 1932, of a new State organization in Manchuria—Manchukuo, this division was still further intensified. The Mongols of the three Manchurian provinces and of Jehol entered into the composition of the new State which by 1935 had also absorbed 6 districts of the province of Chahar.

In 1932, the Chinese Government organized a Political Council for the Mongols of Chahar and Suiyuan provinces, composed of Mongol princes and subject to the Commission for Mongolian and Tibetan Affairs.[8]

A part of these Mongols have gone over to a settled form of life, engage in agriculture, or live in cities, and have become Sinocized (*e.g.* the Harachins and a part of the Tumets), but the majority are still nomads, engaging in cattle-breeding under the leadership of their Ho-

7 According to Skachkov's estimate, Inner Mongolia has 11-12 millions of inhabitants, of whom 1,500,000 are Mongols (*v.* Skachkov, "Inner Mongolia", 1933, pg. 12).

8 In 1936 a separate P.C. was organized for the Mongols of Suiyuan Province.

shun princes. The administrative power is centred in the Tamgas of the Hoshun princes and bears the same medieval character as before. The indebtedness of the Mongols is very great.

Mongol Tribes in Russia (U.S.S.R.)—In their advance to the Pacific Ocean in the first half of the XVIIth century, the Russians conquered the Buriat tribes of Siberia: the Bulahats who inhabited the valley of the Angara river, the Echirites who lived on the Lena; and the Hori tribe of the Transbaikal region. In the Transbaikal region there were also groups of clans (emigrants from Mongolia) along the river Selenga (the Selenga Buriats), etc. The Bulahats and Echirites (comprising the Northern Buriats) were included in the former province of Irkutsk; the Horins and Selenguins in the Transbaikal Region. At the beginning of the XXth century the number of these Buriats, most of whom were engaged in nomadic pastoral economy, was estimated at about 300,000. They are at present (since 1923) organized into the Buriat-Mongol Autonomous Soviet Socialist Republic with its capital at Verkhne-Udinsk.

In the first half of the XVIIth century a number of Taishas with the tribes and clans subject to them, emigrated from Djungaria to Tibet, Kokonor, and Siberia. In about the year 1630 the Taisha of the Torgout tribe, Kho-Urluk, with 50,000 kibitkas (200,000 to 250,000 souls) crossed the Urals and settled along the lower regions of the Volga from Astrakhan to Samara, becoming the Russian Kalmucks. The son of Kho-Urluk, Shukur-Daichin, first took the Shert (oath) of allegiance to Russia, but this oath was repeatedly broken and reaffirmed by his militant son, Puntzuk, and by Ayuka, his grandson. The latter received the title of Khan from the Dalai Lama and was the most powerful of the Kalmuck Khans. After his death, in 1724, the Kalmucks finally recognized the Russian rule. In 1771 the large group headed by Khan Ubashi, containing about 40,000 Kibitkas (175,000 souls), began its migration to the ancestral land of the Kalmucks, Djungaria, which it reached with great difficulty. After reaching Djungaria, these Kalmucks acknowledged the sovereignty of China.

About 15,000 Kibitkas of Kalmucks remained in Russia, where they were mainly concentrated in the province of Astrakhan (the Kalmuck Steppe) and the Don Cossack region. At the beginning of the XXth century there were in Russia some 180,000 Kalmucks, living a nomadic pastoral life. They now comprise the Kalmuck Autonomous Soviet Socialist Republic.

It is necessary to note here that both the Buriat and Kalmuck tribes, in their internal life, were guided by law of common Mongol origin. There were, however, certain distinguishing features between the development of these two branches. Buriat law was more independent than that of the Kalmucks. The Buriat tribes broke away early from the common Mongol root and independently developed their legal customs which were, of course, based on the common nomadic cattle-breeding economy and clan-patriarchal organization. They also created their own codes and statutes which were collections of their legal customs. The Kalmucks, on the other hand, broke off from the common Mongol root only recently (in the XVII-th century) and for long after this maintained close connections with the Mongols. They appeared in the South Russian steppe with fully developed laws and customs, and brought with them for guidance the Mongol-Oirat Regulations of 1640. The entire subsequent development of Kalmuck law represented only variations of the provisions of the Code, introduced under the stress of slow changes in the life of this people.

CHAPTER I.
RECORDS OF MONGOL LAW (DESCRIPTION).

The General Law of the Epoch of Jenghiz Khan and His Successors.

1. The Great Yassa of Jenghiz Khan.

The Great Yassa of Jenghiz Khan is the best known and most ancient of the records of Mongol law that have come down to us. Its origin may be described as follows.

At first the scattered Mongol tribes regulated their internal life according to local customs. With the union of the Mongol tribes under the sovereignty of Jenghiz Khan at the beginning of the XIII-th century came the union of Mongol customary law and the creation of a pan-Mongol written law, the Great Yassa of Jenghiz Khan.

The world "Yassa" may be interpreted as meaning "prohibition" "regulation" or "law". According to the prevailing scientific opinion, based on the testimony of the chroniclers and annalists of the XIII-th and XIV-th centuries, the Great Yassa was a written legislative document promulgated by Jenghiz Khan. It was described as "Great" because it was the law common to all the Mongol tribes, as distinct from the small or tribal Yassas which existed independently, of and possibly contemporaneously with, the Great Yassa.

But the Great Yassa has not come down to us in its entirety, either in the original or in copy. We know only fragments of it which have been transmitted by ancient Arab, Persian, and Armenian historians—Makrizi, Mirhond, Ibn-Batuta, Vartang and Mahakia. Although this opinion predominates among historians, other points of view exist.

The well known Russian sinologist, Academician Vasiliev thought it impossible to consider the Yassa a collection of laws. In his opinion, the Yassa was not a legislative document, but a collection of Jenghiz Khan's maxims like those of the Chinese Emperors, which were published posthumously (*e.g.* the maxims of K'ang-hsi.)[1]

Another sinologist, Professor Popov, also denied that the Yassa was a legislative record. He pointed out that if it had been, the Yassa would have been included in the legislative records of the Mongol (Yuan) dynasty in China, the direct successor of the House of Jenghiz

1 Proceedings of the Oriental Section of the Russian Archeol. Society, v. IV, 381.

Khan. At the same time he found only three references to the Great Yassa of Jenghiz Khan in the Code of the Yuan Dynasty (promulgated 1320) only one of which corresponded to a fragment quoted by Makrizi. Popov, therefore, supposed that the Yassa represented only the instructions given by Jenghiz Khan, which did not then exist in a written form, and were preserved only by oral transmission. Therefore they reached the Arabian chroniclers in a distorted form.[2]

The above mentioned opinion, denying that the Yassa was either a written law or a collection of legislative rules, contradicts a series of historical records—Mongolian, Arabian, Persian, Armenian, Russian and Chinese.

One of the Mongol records states: "After having expelled the Chinese Altan Khan, and after the majority of the Chinese, Tibetans, and Mongols had submitted to his authority, Jenghiz Khan, then the ruler of a great kingdom, thought the laws and regulations of the Chinese strong, subtle, and unchangeable; so he invited a great teacher of letters with eighteen of his clever pupils from China and ordered them to draft laws (Yosson) which should contribute to the peace and welfare of all his subjects, and especially a code of laws (Khuli-Yessonu-bichik) for the protection of his rule. When these laws had been drafted and examined by Jenghiz Khan, he found that they corresponded to his ideas and rewarded the authors thereof with titles, promotions and praise."[3]

This tale-tradition and others have direct relevance to the point in question, and are interesting on account of their general tendency (they point to the Chinese influence upon the Yassa).

Precise information on the subject is given by the Arab and Persian historians.

Thus, the conscientious Arabian chronicler, Djuveini, who lived during the time of the united Mongol Empire and once visited it, stated in his "History of the World-Conquerors" (written in 1260), that the laws of the Yassa were traced out on sheets, which were kept in the treasury of the chief princes. On especially important occasions the sheets were brought out and served as the basis on which cases were decided[4]).

The information given by Rashid-Ed-din (d.1318) is worthy of our special attention. Having served as vizier at the time of the Persian

2 Ibidem, v. XVII, sect. IV, page 0151-2.

3 Cindamani-yin-erike, v. Golstounsky "Mongol-Oirat Laws of 1640", p. 11, 103.

4 Barthold—"Turkestan at the Time of the Mongolian Invasion", II, page 42. (There is also an English edition), P. Pelliot—"Notes sur le "Turkestan de M. Barthold"—T'oung Pao, XXVII, 1930.

Hulagids (the direct descendants of Jenghis Khan) and received instructions from Khan Ghazan to write the history of the Mongols, Rashid-Ed-din made use of a great quantity of official and private materials and oral traditions. He knew many maxims (bilig) and orders of Jenghiz Khan, which had reached his time by careful oral transmission, and translated their contents in detail. Nevertheless, he discriminated between them and the Yassa, which latter he considered to be a (written) legislative record.

Rashid-Ed-din wrote that after his victory over Wang Khan (1206) Jenghiz Khan "convoked a great assembly and in gratitude for his great success ordered wise and strong yassaks and happily ascended the throne of the Khans" (History of Jenghis Khan, 1,47). In another passage of his work Rashid-Ed-din spoke more definitely "When the year of the hare came, which fell on the 614th year of Zul-ka'da (1218?) Jenghiz Khan convoked an assembly, organized the Kurultai, *laid the foundation of the yassak which had been composed of innovations and ancient rules,* and undertook a military expedition in the country of Khoresmshah" (*Ibid.* 11,42). It is evident that, in the second case, reference was made to the law, or more exactly Code of Laws compiled from ancient provisions and innovations introduced by Jenghiz Khan and approved by the Kurultai. It is possible that the resolution to issue a code of Laws was first adopted in 1206, and that its fundamental rules were confirmed by the Kurultai in 1218 A.D.[5]

The third author, the Egyptian-Arab historian Makrizi (d.1441), who, according to the opinion of the Russian academician Krimsky, was the most accurate in his information, wrote as followes: "When Jenghiz Khan, the founder of the Tartar power in the countries of the Orient, vanquished King Wang Khan and seized the supreme power, he established some fundamental rules and punishments and outlined them in a book, the proper name of which was "Yassa", although it was also called "Yassak". When the draft of that book was finished, he ordered laws to be engraved on steel tablets and to be considered as the Code of his nation. This was done until the Lord annihilated that nation. The Yassa was regarded by his posterity as an unbreakable law and they never departed from its commandments."[6]

5 "When Jenghiz Khan's fortune appeared, they (the Mongols) came under his power; and he governed them by means of a firmly established Yassak", *Ibid.*, 121; also 77, 97, etc.

6 Berezin—"Outline of the Inner Organisation of the Ooloos of Juchi", p. 23 (Rus.)

In the Shemsul-mun-shi manuscript of the XIV Century we find the information that in Persia, at least a part of the disputes between Mongols was decided by the Mongol judges, on the basis of the Yassa[7]; and similar indications concerning Egypt and Syria were given by Makrizi.[8]

The Armenian writers Vartang and Mahakia also considered the Yassa of Jenghiz Khan to be a legislative record[9]. Some information about the Yassa may likewise be obtained from the Russian and Chinese records (chronicles, etc.).

References to the Yassa of Jenghiz Khan are found in the "Yarliks" given by the Khans of the Golden Horde to the metropolitans of the Russian church for the defence and protection of the latter. We know the yarliks of the Khans Munké-Timur, Uzbek, Berdibeg, Tulunbeg (Atuliak) and three Yarliks of the Khana Taidula. The Yarlik of Janibeg has not come down to our times, but it is mentioned in the Yarlik of Taidula, seven Yarliks thus being known.

In the first Yarlik of Munké-Timur (evidently of the year 1279) we find the following statement: "As the former Kings protected priests and monks and all paupers, and we do not mean to change their charters, we also protect them . . . and he who would rob them—be he Baskak or princes' scribe, or tax gatherer or customs-officer, will not be forgiven, but in accordance with the Great Yassa, punished with death".[10] Khan Uzbeg and other khans also made references to the Yarliks of the "first and former Kings."

If we, together with Prof. Grigoriev[11], reject all doubt concerning the authenticity of these Yarliks, we cannot deny that these references to the Yassa confirm: 1) the effectiveness of the Yassa in Ooloos of Juchi; and 2) its operation not as an oral regulation, but a general common law, the penalty for violation of which was death.

Some references to the Yassa may be found in the Chinese annals. Prof. Popov, the investigator of the Code of the Yuan dynasty—Yuan Ch'ao Tien Chang (1320) points out that three references to Jenghiz

---

7 Melioransky—"About the Koudatkou Bilig of Jenghiz Khan", The Proceedings of the Or. S, XIII, 1,019.

8 Berezin—"The Outline of the Inner Organization of the Ooloos of Juchi"—Works of the Or. S, 1863,421.

9 Patkanov—"The History of the Mongols Based on the Armenian Annals".

10 The Academician Golubinsky understands the "former Kings" to be Jenghiz Khan and his nearest successors—"The History of the Russian Church" v. II, sec. I, 1900,33. As Jenghiz Khan put forth the idea of religion toleration in his Yassa and also released the clergy from taxes, the above mentioned supposition is veracious.

11 "On the Authenticity of the Yarliks, given by the Khans of the Golden Horde to the Russian clergy", 1842. The text of the Yarliks is also given there. See also his book "Russia and Asia".

Khan's Yassa were found in the above mentioned Code, and that one of the three was identical with a fragment given by Makrizi.[12]

In another ancient Chinese treatise 續文獻通考 Wen Hsiang T'ung Kao "The Study of the History of Culture" published at the beginning of the reign of Emperor Tsiang Lun it is written:" Yuan T'ai-tzu (another name of Jenghiz Khan)[13] published the rules for capital crimes and prisons, according to which only the very important transgressions were punished by death, and other offenses were punished by flogging in compliance with the circumstances of the case [14]. That proves that the Chinese long ago recognized the fact, that Jenghiz Khan published a criminal code.

In a modern treatise 新元史 "Hsin Yuan Shih"—"The New Yuan Shih", written in 1920 by the State historiographer, Mr. Kuo Shao-min, on the subject of the ancient documents in order to complete the records of the "Yuan Shih" we find the following story: "During the 6th year of the reign of T'ai Tzu (Jenghiz Khan) the Mongols were at war with the Chin-people in the place of U-sha-pu and routed them totally. Go-Bao-yui, the commander-in-chief of the Chin army surrendered. He advised T'ai-tzu (i.e. Jenghiz Khan) to publish new rules on the organization of the new state. T'ai-tzu consented. In consequence the five sections of rules (Tiao-hua) were published. In these it was said for instance that during the campaign one could not put the guiltless to death, only heavy crimes were to be so punished; the other offenses were punished with bamboos according to the circumstances of the case. This presents the beginning of the legislation of that dynasty."[15]

This treatise also ascribes the promulgation of the code to Jenghiz Khan and marks the Chinese influence upon it.

The circumstance that the full text of the Yassa has not come down to us is satisfactorily explained in general by the non-existence of printing at the time and particularly by the absence of a Mongolian written language.[16] The non-inclusion of the Great Yassa in the codification of the Yuan dynasty is fully explained by fact that Jenghiz Khan neither was nor had ever been a Chinese emperor, nor was the

---

12 See Prof. Popov "The Yassa of Jenghiz Khan and the Code of the Yuan dynasty, Yuan C'hao Tien Chang," Proceedings of the Orient. Sect. of the Russian Archeol. Society" v. XVII, IV, 0150-0163. Compare the indications of arch. Palladius—"The Secret Chronicle of Jenghiz Khan", note 576.

13 Kublai Khan bore the name of Shih-tzû.

14 See the chapter (book) 135, page 28.

15 See the chapter (book) 102, page 1.

16 At that time the Mongols used Uigur and Chinese graphic signs. From the 1269 they used square characters, and only from 1911—the modern writing. See Laufer—"Outline of Mongolian Literature", 1927, p.19.

Yassa a collection of Chinese law. The contradiction with regard to the Yassa met in the works of foreign authors may be elucidated by the fact, that, printing being unknown, all the information about it was obtained through oral transmission, often at second and even third hand, the only written copies of the Yassa being kept in the state archives or in the record offices of princes which were generally not easily accessible, and quite inaccessible to foreigners.[17]

To the aforesaid one must add that many fragments of the Yassa cannot in any way be considered as oral instructions. As we shall see further, the majority of the provisions of the Yassa are reproductions of customs, of the customary law of the Mongols. Such reproduction is well understood in a primary code, and it would be out of place in oral instructions. Why, for instance, should Jenghiz Khan have given a special instruction to the effect that one had to pay nine horses for one stolen horse; that a Mongol could have several wives, one of them being the chief; that the junior son inherited the household goods, etc., if all these customs had long been ancient institutions of Mongol common law? But from the point of view of the legislative codification of the institutes of customary law such extensive reproduction of the latter is quite comprehensible and appropriate.

Undoubtedly Jenghiz Khan left some oral instructions and orders (Bilig) to his posterity, these being kept in the court archives and read at the feasts of the Emperors of the Yuan dynasty[18]. They have come down to us chiefly through Rashid-Ed-din. But one must not confuse them with the provisions of the Yassa. The very word "Yassa" means prohibition, rule, or law, not instruction or maxim (Bilig). Moreover, in these maxims (Bilig) we find references to the Yassa, as a special ratified statute (cf. Maxim 23.[19]), which could not be applied to a simple oral instruction. Equally the commission given to Jagatai to supervise the application of the Yassa was better suited to a publicly ratified statute than to an oral instruction.

Incidentally, the same Arab, Persian, and other writers have given cause for the confusion of the maxims of Jenghiz Khan with his Yassa. For instance, Rashid-Ed-din attributed the sentence about drunkenness to the maxims (Maxim 20) while other authors attributed the same phrase to the Yassa (33rd fragment).

---

17 The Mongols generally considered the Law as a thing to be disclosed to the initiated but hidden from the masses (*v.* further the example of the Khalkha Djirom).

18 See Palladius "Secret Chronicle", Works, IV, note 576.

19 See also the aforementioned quotations from Rashid Ed-din.

Similar confusion undoubtedly had a place in the works of Vartang and Mahakia (see fragm. 30 and 31) and in many other cases (see further) and was later carried on by professors Vasiliev and Popov.

The above-mentioned testimony from Arabian, Persian, Armenian, Russian and Chinese sources and the aforesaid considerations lead us to share the opinion, that the Yassa of Jenghiz Khan was a legislative document, and not a mere collection of his oral instructions.

As we have seen, the Yassa has come down to us only in fragments which were transmitted chiefly by Arabian and Persian writers. The most extensive of the fragments was quoted by Makrizi.

The fragments that have come down to us and the information given by the ancient writers about the Yassa are compared in the following works: Hammer-Purgstall—"Geschichte der goldenen Horde in Kiptschak", 1840; Erdmann—"Temudschin der Unerschutterliehe", 1862; Howorth—"History of the Mongols", 1876 (88), in Russian—Prof. Berezin, "Outline of the Inner Organization of the Ooloos of Juchi". In our works we have used the text of the Yassa which was adopted by Prof. Berezin.[20]

It is necessary to acknowledge that the text of the Yassa, composed of fragments quoted by different authors, is not complete. The following considerations may prove this statement.

In the 29th fragment, punishment is imposed for the stealing of a horse, but there is no statement on theft in general, whilst in the concise exposition of the statements of the Yassa written by Vartang and Mahakia (see 30 and 31 fr. of the Yassa) it is pointed out, that the Yassa forbade theft in general. Plano-Carpini informs us that death was the penalty for larceny or open stealing[21]; Rubruquis—death for a considerable theft (for an insignificant one—the bastinado)[22]. Marco Polo also mentioned the bastinado and death as punishments for larceny[23]. Evidently the corresponding paragraph of the Yassa either has not come down to us or was not reproduced in full. The 28th fragment says that ransom was permitted in cases of murder, and Marco Polo also tells of ransom for theft[24]. In the 23rd maxim of Jenghiz Khan, some punishments are named, which are not mentioned in the fragments known to us, viz. exile and prison with fetters (irons). Plano Carpini

---

20 In French the fragments of the Yassa are given by de Sacy "Chrestomathie Arabe", II, 1828; there are also translations into French of Arabian and Persian writers who have written about the Yassa.

21 "History of Mongols", 1911, page 15 (in Russian).

22 "A Voyage to the Orient", 1911, p. 79 (in Russian).

23 "The Journey of Marco Polo" (in Russian) Minaev, 1902,91.

24 *Ibidem.*

also writes about punishment by whipping.[25] In the known fragments of the Yassa there is nothing about maihem—wounds, maiming etc. Plano Carpini[26] and Rubruquis[27] quote a number of transgressions and crimes which were punished by severe penalties and about which we find nothing in the fragments of the Yassa known to us. Similar information may be found in the other works[28]. Certainly the Great Yassa could not have foreseen all the crimes, and some of them might have been controlled by customary law. But a part of the latter may also have been mentioned in those fragments of the Yassa which have not survived, as we can see from the comparison of the 29th, 30th, and 31st fragments of the Yassa.

The maxims of Jenghiz Khan (Bilig) may be of services as a supplement to the Yassa; they explain the general spirit of Jenghiz Khan's legislation and fill some gaps of the Code. These maxims are most fully quoted by Rashid-Ed-din, whence we have drawn them[29] The testimony of contemporaries who wrote about the Mongols can also be of use as a supplement[30].

Now it is necessary to turn to the question of the period of time when Yassa was promulgated, and also of the sphere and time of its application.

Historians hold the opinion that the Yassa was created during the period of time which followed the victory over Wang Khan, when Temuchin was elected Khan of all the Mongolian tribes and the nomad peoples of Central Asia which joined the Mongolian State. This took place at the Kurultai of 1206.[31] But it does not mean that the Yassa was necessarily accepted at the Kurultai of 1206. It is probable that from the moment of Jenghiz Khan's election as Great Khan till the promulgation of the Yassa, several years passed, during which the Code was prepared. It is even more probable that Jenghiz Khan entered upon the organization of his state, and the creation of the code, only after his public election as the Great Khan—as Makrizi wrote (see previous quotation).

From the passages from Rashid Ed-din quoted above it is possible to determine approximately the time of the creation of the Great Yassa as between 1206 and 1218 A.D.

---

25 *Ibid.* p. 15.
26 *Ibid.* 9, 10, 15.
27 *Ibid.* 79.
28 Cf. Grum-Grzimailo—"Western Mongolia and the Country of Uriankhai", 1926, p. 439.
29 History of J. Kh.—II, 120 sqq. (Works of the East Sect. of the Rus. Arch. Socty., v. XV).
30 Cf. especially information of Meng Hun, Plano Carpini, Rubruquis, M. Polo, Rashid-Ed-din and others.
31 See Yuan-Ch'ao-Mi-Shih, translated by Palladius. The works of the members of Russian Orthodox Mission in Peking, IV, p. 55, note 430, and others.

At the same time, one may infer on the basis of the 23rd fragment that the Yassa was ratified by the Kurultai (v. above, also the information given by Rashid Ed-din).

According to its contents the Great Yassa was created with the purpose of controlling the life of the nomadic Mongol tribes as well as the Turki, Tungus and others, who joined the Mongols and comprised part of the Mongol Empire of that time. But it was not devised to guide the Empire in the future, in the years to come when such cultured countries as China, Persia, Armenia Russia and others became part of it. The difference of cultures prevented complete unification. This applied in particular to the absence among the Mongol tribes of the right to immovable property and land tenure (lease, tenancy, mortgage etc.), the absence of agriculture, the wandering mode of life, etc. All this and many other things made the Yassa inapplicable to the countries with a settled agricultural life. This was the reason that the Mongols, after their conquest, allowed Chinese law to continue to function in China, Persian law in Persia, and Russian law in Russia.

It should be noted that the Great Yassa of Jenghiz Khan, like any other primitive code, did not regulate all sides of the life of the nomadic Mongol tribes. It seems that it was chiefly meant to improve the relations among the allied Mongol tribes of which the Kingdom of Jenghiz Khan was composed, to amalgamate them through the general character of some tribal customs in a common legislation. Thus there was left a vast field in which the inner tribal customary law prevailed. Small tribal Yassas may have existed side by side with the Great Yassa. Probably there was such co-existence at the time of the rule of the Jenghizids. Such at least is the opinion of Leontovich with references to Pallas and Rashid Ed-din.[32]

The effectiveness of the Great Yassa, as a general compulsory Code for all the tribes did not continue long. At the end of the thirteenth century, its importance began to decline, this process being precipitated by the collapse of the Mongol State, and by the fact that some of the Mongolian tribes later adopted Buddhism or Mohammedanism. However, as the common customs of the Mongolian tribes survived for a long time, and owing to the authority of Jenghiz Khan, the Great Yassa did not completely lose its significance and exerted a certain influence on the legislation of the nomadic tribes long after the collapse of the Great Mongolian kingdom.

---

32 Comp. Leontovich, op. cit. 198-199.

The fundamental source of the Great Yassa was the customary law of the Mongol tribes, while the supplementary sources were the legislative provisions (legislative innovations) of Jenghiz Khan, and Chinese law.

In reading the Yassa we see that its provisions fall into five main groups, viz. 1. Rules relating to civil organization and internal administration (State and administrative law); 2. Provisions of a military character (organization and management of military affairs); 3. Provisions of Criminal law; 4. Provisions of Private law; 5. Special rules pertaining to the customs of the Steppes.

The Yassa confirmed the absolute power of the Khan. Kuyuk Khan's maxim that his subjects "carry out my will, to come wherever I shall call him, to go wheresover I shall order and to put to death whomsoever I shall name", found full support in its provisions. Thus Fragment 23 ordered even the highest of the princes to deliver themselves resignedly into the power of even the lowest servant if the latter were sent by the Khan to inflict punishment upon them, even if the punishment was death. Fragment 21 prescribed that Mongols show their daughters to the Khan every year that he might pick out any of them for himself or his sons. Fragment 26 imposed on Jagatai, the austerest of the sons of Jenghiz, the duty of specially supervising the observance of the Yassa. Violators of the Yassa were subjected to severe penalties, no exception being made in the case of the Khans and their relatives (Maxim 23).

Plano Carpini, a contemporary of the epoch, who accomplished a journey to the Mongol Empire in 1246 and the following years, wrote of the authority of the Khan as follows:

"The Emperor of the Tartars has an amazing power over his subjects. No one has the right to stay in the country unless permitted by the Khan to be there. He orders chiefs where they shall live; the chiefs fix the habitation of the commanders of a thousand; the commanders of a thousand—those of the commanders of a hundred; the commanders of a hundred—those of the commanders of ten. Moreover, whenever, whatever and whoever he orders, be it war, life or death, they obey him without contradiction."

The Yassa maintained the principle of religious toleration (Fragment 11) and forbade preference to be shown to any sect. It forbade the division of things into clean and unclean (Fr. 16), imposed taxes (Fr. 20), exempted from taxation the clergy of different faiths as well as learned men (Fr. 10), and established the organization of permanent postal communications (Fr. 25).

Provisions concerning military organization and administration were contained in the seven fragments of the Yassa considered below, as well as in certain of the Maxims.

Fragment 22 explained the organization of the troops and their division into tens, hundreds and thousands. Maxim 3 and others also mentioned the division of troops into detachments of ten thousand (tümens). Maxim 24 ordered the Beks of the hundreds, thousands and tümens to keep their troops in order, in full battle array, in constant readiness for the campaign. Fragment 18 ordered the successors of Jenghiz Khan to personally review their troops before giving battle.—Fragment 19 ordered women accompanying the troops to assume the duties of the men at such times as the latter were away fighting. Fragment 19 regulated mutual assistance during battles. Fragment 24 prohibited the changing of one's post without permission on pain of death. Fragment 27 ordered the punishment of soldiers for negligence. Fragment 6 forbade anyone to give food to a prisoner without the permission of his captor. Maxim 17 pointed out who was and who was not fit to be appointed a Bek, and Maxim 6 stated that the Beks, with their wives and children, were to be held responsible for any disorders among the troops in their charge. Maxim 18 ordered that boys be trained to shoot and ride.

The majority of the provisions of the Yassa had to do with punitive measures. The greater part of the regulations we have here placed in other categories likewise provided for punishments. The Yassa may therefore be called a record of Criminal law, a Code of primarily criminal regulations. It may here be pointed out that it did not contain many crimes of a personal character or against property in the strict sense, the ones provided for being murder, adultery, sodomy, false witness, theft and a few others. The majority of the penal provisions of the Yassa aimed at ensuring the execution of the orders of the Khan, the observance of the Yassa, the carrying out of military orders and the maintenance of Mongol custom.

Severe penal provisions comprise the greater part of the surviving fragments of the Great Yassa. Of the 36 that have come down to us, fourteen provided for the infliction of capital punishment (*v.* Frs. 1-9, 24, 27, 29, 31 and 32) for a series of crimes and offences. Capital punishment was inflicted for adultery, deliberate lying, witchcraft, spying upon the behaviour of others, helping one of two quarreling parties against the other, urinating into water or ashes, triple bankruptcy, charity to captives (providing them with food and clothing without the permission of their captor), withholding a slave or fugitive prisoner and not returning him to his owner or captor, killing animals in the Mohammedan manner in violation of the established rite, omitting to give help during battle, for Emirs addressing themselves to anyone except the sovereign, for leaving a post without permission, for negligence on the part of soldiers and hunters, for possession of a stolen horse in the case of persons having no property out of which to pay the established fine and no wives or children to be enslaved in lieu of payment, for theft, for false witness, for treachery, for want of respect for elders and beggars, for gluttony, and for stepping upon the threshold of the tent of a military chief. Some of the offences treated were very characteristic and depicted the mode of life of the people. Thus the infliction of capital punishment for deliberate lies, false witness, theft, want of respect, and gluttony show the simplicity and moderation of Mongol life at the time. The penalty for urinating into water or ashes reflected the religious superstitions of shamanism, and that for slaughtering animals in the Mohammedan manner characterised a species of fanaticism and superstition which throve side by side with religious toleration.

The death penalty was very widely inflicted, sometimes for what seem to us trifling offences. Human life was held to be of no more value than that of a domestic animal. Thus, when a man was unable to pay a fine (for theft) in livestock his children were enslaved, and if there were no children the Yassa ordered the culprit himself to be killed like a sheep (Fr. 29). All these features are vividly characteristic of a warlike nomadic people, a predatory nation of cattlebreeders.

Besides capital punishment, there was in the Yassa another penalty which was often inflicted for minor offences—flogging with rods (cf. Fr. 27.) In addition, there were references to exile and imprisonment (Maxim 23). Plano-Carpini also wrote of punishment by flogging with the Knout.

The Yassa also contained provisions of a prohibitive character which were not supplied with punitive sanctions. For instance, it was forbidden to eat food taken from the hands of another before the giver himself tasted the food; to take food in the presence of another without inviting him to share the meal; to stride over a fire over which food was being prepared and dishes from which food was eaten; to dip one's hands in water; to wash clothes, etc. (Frs. 12-15, 17). Evidently these offences were also punished by various penalties, this being suggested by the general spirit of the accompanying legislation and by some known facts of history. However, in such cases the punishment was not death but flogging or the bastinado.

The 6th Maxim of Jenghiz Khan recognized the responsibility of an entire family for a crime committed by one of its members.

The Yassa permitted the payment of ransom instead of punishment for murder (Fr. 28), and, according to Marco Polo, ("Travels", pg. 91; cf. Fr. 29) the same practice obtained in the case of theft.

In the writings of contemporaries we find the following information on the laws and customs of the Mongols with regard to Criminal law.

Plano Carpini (1246) wrote: "It is further a law or custom to kill any man or woman caught in the very act of adultery. If a maiden commit fornication with anyone, she or both are killed. If they catch anyone on their land in the act of robbery or theft he is killed without mercy. If anyone discloses their plans, especially when they are going to war, he is given a hundred strokes on the back as hard as a peasant can give them with a big stick. When young men insult anyone, their elders do not spare them but subject them to severe flogging."[33]

According to Rubruquis (1253-1256): "Manslaughter is punished by death as is cohabitation with another man's woman. Under another man's woman I include both a wife and a maidservant because one is permitted to make any use one likes of a female slave. Considerable thefts are also punished by death. For petty theft, as, for instance, the theft of a sheep, they beat the thief severely, and when they sentence a man to 100 strokes it means that he receives a hundred strokes with the stick."[34]

And from Marco Polo, who spent twenty years (1272-1292) in China, we have the following: "They administer justice in the following manner: Whoever steals even a trifle is given seven strokes with a stick, or seventeen strokes, or twenty-seven, or thirty-seven, or forty-seven, and so forth up to three hundred and seven, adding ten each time, according to the thing stolen. These beatings cause many deaths. Whoever steals a horse or anything of value is put to death, being cut to pieces with a sword; but whoever can pay ransom amounting to ten times the value of the stolen property, (nine times according to other versions) is not killed."[35]

Provisions of Private law were not numerous in the Fragments of the Yassa that have come down to our times. As we can see from Fragment 5, commercial relations were fairly well developed at the time of Jenghiz Khan. This fragment was aimed against third bankruptcy on the part of merchants (cf. also Maxim 18.)

---

33 Op. cit., pg. 15.

34 Op. cit., pg. 79.

35 Minayev: "Travels of Marco Polo", 1902, pg. 91 (in Russ.)

In the sphere of Family law, the Yassa permitted the institutions of polygamy and concubinage so characteristic of nomadic peoples (cf. the lives of the Biblical patriarchs). Children born of concubines were considered legitimate. After the father's death, the son was at liberty to dispose of his wives, with the exception of his own mother. The seniority of children derived from the status of the wives of whom they were born, the wife first taken in marriage by the deceased father usually being considered the senior. As regards inheritance, the Yassa made the following provisions. Property remaining after the father's death was divided in such a way that the eldest son received more than the youngest,[36] but the latter inherited the household of the father (cf. the similar provision in the ancient Russian code, "Ruskaya Pravda".) Children of concubines also received a share in the inheritance, in accordance with the instructions of the father (or with custom). It was strictly forbidden to anyone save the legitimate heirs to make use of any articles belonging to the deceased.

Some additional information on the subject of Private law is derived from the works of Plano Carpini (1246) and Rubruquis who in 1253-56 travelled to the Mongol Empire, and also from Marco Polo who sojourned in China about from 1272 to 1292 A. D.

Plano-Carpini wrote of the marriage customs of the contemporary Mongols as follows: "Any Mongol has as many wives as he can afford to keep; one has a hundred, the other—fifty; some have more, and some have less, and they may marry any of their kinswomen except their mothers, daughters and sisters born of the same mother. They may marry their half-sisters and their father's wives after the father's death. They are even bound to marry the wives of their brothers after their death. As for other women, the Mongols take them in marriage without any discrimination and buy them from their parents at a very high price. After the death of a husband, it is not an easy matter to marry again unless the heir is willing to marry his stepmother."[37]

"As regards their marriages", wrote Rubruquis, "know that nobody there has a wife unless he buys one; and in consequence many maids reach a very mature age before being married, their parents keeping them until they happen to sell them. They observe the first and second degrees of kinship but do not recognize connections by marriage of any degree. For instance they may marry two sisters consecutively or simultaneously. No widow ever marries again because they believe that all those who serve them in this life will also serve them in the next

36 An ancient Mongol proverb stated: "Ten to the elder and four to the younger." (Rashid Ed-din).

37 Plano Carpini, pg. 78.

world, hence their belief is that the widow will always return to her first husband in the hereafter. As a consequence, they practise a disgraceful custom, a son sometimes taking all the wives of his father with the exception of his own mother. The household of the father and mother always falls to the share of the youngest son, and for this reason, he must provide for all the wives of his father who descend to him with all his father's household. He therefore uses them as his wives, because it will not hurt him if after death the wives go back to his father."[38]

Marco Polo wrote as follows: "As a condescension, men are permitted as many wives as they wish. The expense to the husband is not too considerable and, on the other hand, there is always a good profit derived from the knowledge and labour of their wives because they are always busy. That is the reason why a man has to pay for a girl to her mother. The wife who was first taken has the privilege of special attention and is considered to be the most legitimate, as are the children born of her. As a result of this the Mongols have an unlimited number of wives and their posterity is more numerous than that of other peoples. After a father's death, his son may take the wives he leaves for himself, with the exception of his own mother. They are forbidden to take their own sisters in marriage, but after the death of a brother they are permitted to marry his wives. Every marriage is celebrated with great ceremony."[39]

Rashid Ed-din wrote: "The Mongol custom is such that the junior son is called Edgen, because he stays at home; and the property, lands and household are allotted to him."[40]

The above quotations show that polygamy was widely practised among the Mongols, that marriages were concluded by purchase of wives, and that vestiges of the matriarchate may easily be traced in Mongol custom (the reckoning of degrees of kinship with respect to marriage through the maternal line, and marriage to stepmothers). The levirate (marriage to the wife of a deceased brother) was also practised.

In addition to the above, it is necessary to point out several prohibitive provisions dealing with steppe life. Among these were the prohibition against eating food offered by another unless it was previously tasted by the host, against eating in the presence of another without first inviting him to partake of the meal, eating more than one's table companions, striding over a fire over which food was being prepared or over

---

38 Rubruquis, "A Journey to the Oriental Countries", ppg. 78-79.
39 "The Travels of Marco Polo", by M. Komroff, 1918, ppg. 91-92.
40 Proceedings of the O.S. R. A. S., v.XIV, pg. 207.

a dish from which food was eaten (12), dipping the hand in water and drinking from the hollow of the hand (14), washing clothes before they fell to pieces from wear (15), etc.

Generally speaking it must be confessed that the contents of the Yassa were poor, that it was a code depicting the primitive life of the nomadic Mongols. The fundamental portion of the Code represented a recapitulation of the customs of the Mongols, which were primitive, superstitious, and often cruel.

The opinion has occasionally been expressed that the Yassa was too cruel a code, some scientists even claiming that its cruelty surpassed that of other analogous codes.[41] This, however, is an exaggeration

There is no doubt that the Great Yassa was cruel. Of its 36 discovered fragments, fourteen provided for the death penalty. But its severity was no greater than that of the codes of other Oriental countries (e.g. China, Babylonia, Judaea, the Mohammedan lands)[42] and of the criminal law of mediaeval Europe.

2. The question of the Code "Koudatkou Bilig" ascribed to Jenghiz Khan.

Certain men of science ascribe to Jenghiz Khan the compilation of a special collection of laws concerning legal procedure, the "Koudatkou-Bilig".

Hammer von Purgstall was the first to mention the existence of this code, quoting a Persian manuscript of the third quarter of the XIVth century, composed by a certain Mahomet-Hindu-Shah whose surname was Shemsu-l-Munshi. The Russian professor P. M. Melioransky investigated this question. He studied the Leyden copy of Shemsu-l-Munshi's manuscript and compared it with that in the British Museum. He made the conclusion that beside the Yassa of Jenghiz Khan, there existed also a separate book "Koudatkou Bilig" (the royal tale), which contained regulations concerning the order of inquiry and legal proceedings, and which was created either by Jenghiz Khan or by some of his associates.[43]

After an examination of the quotations, upon which Hammer von Purgstall and Melioransky based their opinion, and also taking into consideration the existence of other facts, we come to the conclusion

41 Cf., for instance, the opinion of Professor Telberg in the "Proceedings of the Harbin Faculty of Law", Harbin, 1931, vol. IX, pg. 279 (in Russian).

42 *v.* the writer's "The Great Yassa of Jenhiz Khan", (in Russian), pg. 22.

43 Proceedings of the O.S. Russ. Arch. Soc., vol. XIII, I, pg. 015-023.

that the above mentioned opinion of these two investigators was erroneous. No special code such as the "Koudatkou Bilig" was created in the epoch of Jenghiz Khan.

In the second part of the manuscript of Shemsu-l-Munshi, there is a concise description of the offices that existed in the state of the Persian Ilkhans in the second half of the XIVth century. Here we find three quotations concerning the "Koudatkou Bilig" of Jenghiz Khan. Let us quote in English the respective fragments, which were translated from Persian into Russian by Prof. Melioransky.

The first fragment runs as follows:

"Since Emir Bayan surpasses all the Emirs of the present time in his numerous talents and activity and knowledge of the customs and laws of the Mongol Sultans and Emirs, and also in his deep knowledge of their 'jassaks' (i.e. procedure) and 'tore' (i.e. norms of customary law), therefore the performance of the duties of 'emir-i-yargu' and the inquiry into those cases among the Mongols which by their nature and substance pertain thereto, is entrusted to him in order that he may examine disputes between Mongols in accordance with examples which he has seen and read (about) in the *Kudatkou Bilig of Jenghiz Khan* and observed (in practice) among the great Yargutchees (judges); and at the same time he must not violate (the principles of) justice and equity even by a hair's breadth, and he must decide the cases between parties on the basis of the rules of the Yassak. The justice of one party being proved, he must give him 'yargu-name', that is, a written decision of the case (the charter of justification) in order that he may keep it carefully. Then, if the adversary (who lost the case) will a second time disturb (the judge), the judge must insist upon a solution on the basis of the (previously given) 'yargu-name' and know that it is right to refuse him (the plantiff or accuser).

"For this reason the present decree is published, so that, beginning to-day, he (the Emir Bayan) may be esteemed as the Yargutchee of the capital town ('emir-i-yargu-i-hordu-i-muazzam'); and concerning the things which are within his competence, one must address one's self only to him and not thwart his opinion and his judgment. The Mongol Emirs have no right to renew and make inquiry into cases that have been (once) examined by him and decided on the basis of the Yassa and Yassak (and Kudatkou-Bilig ?)[44] of Jenghiz-Khan. The litigants present before the session (of the court) of the yargu are bound to answer everything both to him (the judge) and to his assistants (servants) and

44 Query by Melioransky.

the scribe of the yargu-name, so that he, after having examined all to his satisfaction (i.e. having taken into consideration all the evidence and testimony of the witnesses) may decide the case."

The second fragment, given below, also casts light on the point in question.

"Let all the Mongol warriors consider Bayan-temur Bahshi as the Yargutchee of the capital town, and as to those Mongols who will trust him with the decision of (their) cases, let them never thwart his opinions and judgments which he (makes) on the basis of the laws of *Kudatkou Bilig* (the M.S. kept in London gives it: 'on the basis of the law of Jenghiz Khan and the decrees of the Khaan'—i.e. of Ogadai) and let them neither consider anybody else (as having the right) to take part (in the legal proceedings) nor contest it."

The third fragment:

"As Sheik Ali of yore held discourse and acquaintance with the Mongol Emirs and Yargutchees, and actually acquired knowledge of the Yargutchee regulations and studied the *Koudatkou Bilig of Jenghiz Khan* and the decrees of the Khaan (i.e. of Ogadai)."

Here, then, are all the quotations on the basis of which the two above mentioned investigators concluded the existence of a special code of the regulations of Jenghiz Khan, dealing with judicial procedure. In the opinion of the writer, the fragments quoted do not provide any solid basis for such an assertion.

The words "Koudatkou-Bilig" cannot be translated as "royal knowledge" or "royal science", as Professor Melioransky states. They mean "royal bilig" or "royal maxims", i.e. the Maxims of Jenghiz Khan. As we know, not only the Yassa of Jenghiz Khan but also his maxims were highly esteemed among the Mongols. These maxims were written down and kept in the archives of the state, being sometimes read at the feasts of the Emperors of the Yuan dynasty.

The references of the author to the Yassa, Yassak and Koudatkou Bilig (i.e. the royal bilig) are definitely allusions to the Yassa and Maxims of Jenghiz Khan. The appointment of the Emir Bayan to the office of Emir-i-yargu meant that the Emir Bayan was appointed chief judge (of Persia). The office of the chief judge was established by Jenghiz Khan. In the performance of his duties, the Emir Bayan was obliged to follow the Yassa, the Maxims of Jenghiz Khan, customs and the decisions of previous judges.

Moreover, it must be taken into consideration that had a special code, the "Koudatkou Bilig", been created by Jenghiz Khan, it would have been no less known in the XIIIth century than the Yassa or Maxims (bilig) of Jenghiz Khan, and its contents would have come down to us, if only in fragmentary form, because everything that stemmed from Jenghiz Khan was highly esteemed by the Mongols. In actual fact, however, the Koudatkou Bilig is mentioned only in the MS. of the second half of the XIVth century which we have quoted above. Besides the fact that any such omission is extremely improbable, there was no necessity for a special code of the kind mentioned in view of the fact that the judiciary system existed only in embryo during the reign of Jenghiz Khan.[45] Plano-Carpini, a contemporary of the epoch, testifies: "everything is performed there without the noise of legal proceedings, according to the will of the Emperor."

The absence of any necessity for such a code, the silence of authors who were generally well informed on the deeds of Jenghiz Khan and his successors (Rashid Ed-din, Djuveini, Makrizi, etc.), the complete darkness as to its contents and the possibility of explaining the above-quoted fragments from the MS. of Shemsu-l-Munshi in a way that is both simpler and in more comprehensible correspondence with historical fact—all these factors support us in discarding the version of the creation by Jenghiz Khan of a special code of legal procedure, the "Koudatkou Bilig."

3. Yarliks, Defters and P'ai-tzes.

Among the state documents of the epoch which have come down to us, the most important are the Yarliks, Defters, and P'ai-tzes.

A *Yarlik* was an edict (decree) which expressed the will of the Khan as the wielder of the supreme power and dealt with certain administrative and legislative questions. As legislative acts, or acts of the supreme ruler, the Yarliks were necessarily publicly proclaimed. In accordance with the manner in which such proclamation was made, the Yarliks were divided into notification (Suan) and dispositions (Chai.) The former were proclaimed orally, while the latter were issued in the form of a kind of charter of the Khan, written on small tablets of stone or wood, single leaves (palm leaves, and later paper), or engraved on rocks, cliffs, etc. When the Yarliks were to be brought to public

---

45 *v.* further, chap IV.

knowledge, they were written in several languages for the respective nations composing the empire, to which end special scribes were attached to the Courts of the Khans. Instead of a seal, the *tamga* (coat of arms) of the Khan was attached to the Yarliks. As regards their contents, the Yarliks may be classified as follows: (1) Edicts of a legislative character, laws decreed by the Khan, (2) Administrative orders and dispositions; (3) Decrees conferring privileges, offices, etc.

The following edict of Jenghiz Khan, given in the name of a Taoist teacher (Tzu Shen Hsien), the monk Chan Chun, can serve as an example. "The holy commandment. The commandment of Khan Jenghiz to the chiefs of all districts: Whatever hermitages and ascetic retreats pertain to the Tzu Shen Hsien, let those who daily read these holy scriptures and pray to Heaven, pray also for the longevity of the Khan; let them be free from all great and small tributes, taxes and duties; let all the hermitages and abodes of monks belonging to the Tzu Shen Hsien in all places be freed of tribute, taxes and duties; and further, if anyone refuse to pay taxes on the false pretence of being a monk, let him be denounced to the authorities and punished accordingly. After the receipt of this order, let no one dare to contradict it. For this reason the present decree is given. . . ."[46]

In addition to the Yarlik the person who was to publish it was given a special order (*P'ai-tze*) which confirmed the will of the Khan and attested the authenticity of the Yarlik. Thus, the edict of Berdibeg-Khan (of the Gold Horde) to the Russian Metropolitan Alexis states: "We gave you a Baisa (P'ai-tze) and Yarlik with a scarlet Tamga to confirm it (your appointment)."[47]

The P'ai tze were used[48]: (1) to confirm the Yarliks of the Khans; (2) as briefs of some ranks such as ambassador, courtier, attendant, etc.; and (3) as a safeguard for those who had submitted to the Khan.

A Defter (Debter—roll, scroll) was an act of the Khans dealing with internal administration, which it was not permitted to make public. Defters were documents of an administrative and financial character (e.g. relating to taxes). They were, for instance, given to the Baskaks (tax-collectors) and later to the Russian princes for the collection of tribute paid to the Horde.

---

45 Description of a Journey to the West or Hsi Yu Tze, by the monk Chan Chun, translated by Palladius—Works of the Russ. Orth. Mission, v. IV, ppg. 375-6 (in Russian).

47 Bulletin of the Siberian Sect. of the Russ. Geog. Soc. v. V, p. 89 (in Russian).

48 *v.* Men Hun (Vasiliev, Op. cit. pg. 229); Rashid Ed-din, op. cit. v. II, p. 128, No. 24, cf. No. 26.

The Local Law of Mongolia.

A. WESTERN MONGOLIA OR DJUNGARIA.

THE ANCIENT TSAADJIN-BICHIK.

The formation of the Oirat Federation at the end of the XIVth century soon necessitated the creation of a common code for the allied tribes to regulate their mutual relations. Academician Pallas informs us of the existence of such an ancient Oirat Code, unfortunately without details.[49] Apparently Academician Pallas possessed a copy of these ancient regulations (in whole or in part) of the Tsadjin-Bichik because he quotes a number of fragments not as his own paraphrase, but as a literal transcription (in some parts) of the text, which differs from that of the Yassa of Jenghiz Khan and the Oirat Regulations of 1640. Pallas referred the Ancient Tsaadjin-Bichik to the laws of the Mongol tribes which were the basis of the customary law of the Western Mongols (Kalmucks) of his time, i.e. he considered it to have been the code not of a separate tribe but of all the Western Tribes. Professor Leontovich, with good reason, refers the appearance of the ancient Mongol Code to the early stages of the formation of the Oirat Federation and considers it to have been the emblem of the political compromise on which the fourfold Oirat Federation was based, just as the subsequent Tsaadjin-Bichik of 1640 was the juristic emblem of the greater federation of forty-four Mongol tribes. This conclusion was based on a study of the ancient regulations. The first fragment of the latter stated that adultery committed by priests (Pfaffen—as Pallas called them) was not punishable. Yet, beginning with the second half of the XVIth century, Lamaism penetrated into Mongolia with its strict demands of chastity for the lamas and penalties for violations of this rule. Consequently the ancient Tsaadjin-Bichik must have come into existence prior to the establishment of Buddhism in Mongolia and Djungaria, i.e. not later than the first half of the XVIth century. Professor Leontovich dates its origin from the XVth century.

The ancient Tsaadjin-Bichik has not survived, but eight fragments of it have been quoted in German by Pallas, in his Sammlungen (Part I, pg. 193 *sqq.*) A Russian translation of these has been published

49 Sammlungen historicher Nachrichten, I, 192 sqq.

by Spassky in the appendix to Igoumnoff's article, "A Survey of Mongolia",[50] and reproduced by Gourland in his article, "Legislation of the Steppes from Ancient Times to the XVIIth Century."[51]

These fragments of the ancient Oirat Code dealt with adultery (1-4), the endowment of sons (5), insulting actions (6) and the condition of women (7, 8).[52]

This ancient code differed considerably from the Great Yassa. If we compare its first four articles relating to adultery and providing for lenient penalties for this offence with the corresponding provisions of the Yassa (which prescribes capital punishment for adultery) it immediately becomes evident that the ancient Tsaadjin Bichik was neither a part of the Yassa nor based upon the latter, but represented a separate collection (of customary law). In general the punitive provisions of the Tsaadjin Bichik were considerably less severe than those of the Yassa (cf. Frs. 1-4) and such parts of the Code as have come down to us seem to indicate the entire collection was permeated with more humanitarian principles. The treatment of women in the Tsaadjin Bichik was characteristic. She enjoyed consideration and respect. As mistress of the household, she was inviolable and insults offered to her were more severely punished (7, 8). Of the remaining provisions of the Tsaadjin Bichik one more is worth noting: a grown son capable of earning his living had the right to demand a share of his father's property and to form a separate household (5).

Customary law may be considered to have been the fundamental source of the ancient Tsaadjin Bichik.

The Mongol-Oirat Regulations of 1640.

After the collapse of the great Mongol Empire and the formation of the Derben-Oirat federation in Djungaria, the disorders in Mongolia did not cease. But the danger from without, as well as dissension within, led the Eastern and Western Mongol Princes of the first half of the XVIIth century to consider the necessity of establishing internal peace and creating a solid union among the Mongol tribes in order to resist

50 "Siberian Messenger", 1819, vol. V.

51 Journal of the Society for Archaeology, History and Ethnography at the University of Kazan, XX, ppg. 79-98, 1904.

52 Incidentally, Academician Vladimirtzov considered the information about the ancient Tsaadjin Bichik given by Pallas to have been due to a misunderstanding, since Pallas knew neither the Mongol nor Oirat languages and did not mention the sources of his information on the subject (*v.* Social Organisation of the Mongols, p. 177). However, there are no serious proofs of such a grave error having been committed by Pallas. And in the Regulations of 1640 we find references to "the ancient laws" (para. 142). It is quite possible that Pallas, in the XVIIIth century, discovered fragments of the latter. And their contents do not contradict the assertions of Pallas.

foreign invasion and put an end to internecine strife. In 1640, the Mongol princes and Taishas of Khalkha, Djungaria and Kokonor, Siberia and the Volga steppes gathered for a Seim or conference, which took place, apparently, in Djungaria. One can conclude, on the basis of certain facts, that this Seim, under the influence of Batur Khan, confirmed the new union and created the new Mongol-Oirat Regulations. The purpose of this great union, which included not only the tribes of Djungaria but also those of Northern Mongolia, Kokonor, and Russia, forty-four in all, was the establishment of inter-tribal peace and defence against outside enemies. These aims had their influence on the contents of the Code.

Thus, while they were not a Code for all the Mongol tribes, (not being effective, for example, in Inner Mongolia) the Regulations of 1640 undoubtedly represented the effective law of a considrable number, if not the greater part, of the Mongol tribes, and were after the Great Yassa of Jenghiz Khan, the most widely applied Mongol Code of purely Mongol origin.

A reservation must, however, be made. The Regulations of 1640 undoubtedly enjoyed a long period of effectiveness among the Western Mongols, including the Russian Kalmucks. As regards the extension of their influence over Northern Mongolia, it must be recognized that here their effect was not of long duration and they left no deep traces. This was due to the fact that during the same epoch, Northern Mongolia had its own codes, e.g. the Great Code of the Seven Hoshuns and the Khalkha Djirum. Moreover, the Mongol-Oirat Federation was soon afterwards dissolved.[53]

The Kalmuck text of the Mongol-Oirat Regulations of 1640 has been published by Professor Golstounsky under the title of "Mongol-Oirat Laws of 1640 (1880)[54] A German translation is included in Academician Pallas's "Sammlungen historischer Nachrichten uber die mongolischen Volkerschaften", 1801, Part I, ppg. 194 *sqq.* and reproduced by Professor Leontovich in his "Ancient Mongol-Kalmuck or Oirat Regulations on Punishments", 1879, ppg. 65 *sqq.* There are several Russian translations of the Code. According to the Sheremetieff copy, the first such edition was published in 1776 in the third part of the "Essays of the Private Russian Society at Moscow University", under the title, "Translation of the Laws of the Mongol and Kalmuck

53 For the attitude of the Khalkha Mongols towards the Regulations of 1640, cf. Professor Pozdneyev—"The Mongol Annals—Erdemjin Erihe", ppg. 131-137.

54 No Mongol text of the Regulations of 1640 is known to us. On the copies of the Regulations in Kalmuck and translations from them, see Prof. Kotwich, "Russian Archive-Records Concerning Intercourse with the Oirats in the XVIIth and XVIIIth Centuries"—Memoirs of the Russian Academy of Sciences, 1919, ppg. 795-797.

Peoples". The second edition was published in 1828, in the "Northern Archives" and "Son of the Fatherland", under the heading, "Laws of the Mongols and Kalmucks". The third version was provided by Professor Leontovich in his work, "The Ancient Mongol-Kalmuck or Oirat Regulations on Punishments (Tsaadjin-Bichik)", 1879; and the fourth by Professor Golstounsky in his "Mongol-Oirat Laws of 1640", published in 1880.

According to Pallas, the Regulations of 1640 (excluding supplements) contained 130 articles; according to Leontovich's version, 150, and according to Golstounsky, 121. Since the Russian text given by Professor Golstounsky is a translation from the Kalmuck made and verified by himself, while the origin of the texts given by Leontovich and Pallas is unknown, we shall use the first mentioned edition in this study (with some references to Leontovich's edition.)

Contrary to the opinion of some scholars (Kostenkov, Rovinsky, Mulov), Djungaria or Khalkha, but in no wise Russia, must be considered as the venue of the Seim which sanctioned the Regulations of 1640. At that time only the tribe of Kho-Urluk, together with a part of the Torguts, were wandering in Russia. All the other tribes were elsewhere and neither the supposed author of the Regulations, Batur-Khun-Taidji, nor the proved author of the supplements thereto, his son Galdan, ever set foot on Russian territory.

In the biography of Zaya-Pandita, the Aimak of Djasaktu-Khan in Khalkha is mentioned as the venue of the Seim (meeting).[55] In their contents, however, the Regulations mainly concerned the life of the Western Mongol tribes, and in actual fact they were in force for a long time among the Western Mongols (Oirats and Kalmucks) and not among those of Khalkha. From this, it may be concluded that the author of the Code was an Oirat and that the Seim took place most probably in Djungaria.

The fundamental aims of the Regulations may be clearly seen even from the first articles, they were: to consolidate the intertribal federation, secure peace and order in the internal relations of the union, and organize defence against external aggression. These aims were placed in the foreground and it is therefore natural that the Code dealt first of all with the intertribal relations of the Mongols. A series of provisions here found, arose from the military aspect of the union and dealt with the relations of attack and defence. A further series outlined the social

55 *v.* Acad. Vladimirtzov, "Social Organization of the Mongols", 1934, p. 177, ftn. 2 (in Russian).

structure of Mongol society, and a third regulated the principal occupations of the Mongols—cattlebreeding and hunting. Some twenty articles pertained to the sphere of private law, and a considerable number (about a half of the whole) contained provisions of criminal law.

The Regulations of 1640 were based on the clan life and clan organization of the Mongol tribes. Each family camped in a fixed location, with its Aoul, Khoton, Aimak and Otok, from which it was forbidden to wander into others inhabited by near or distant kinsmen. These units were under the command of their chiefs of ten, Shulengas, Demchis, Zaisans, Otok chiefs, tribal princes etc. But at the period with which we are dealing, the clan form of life had already undergone certain changes. Instead of the primitive clan communism, private (not only family but also individual) movable property in cattle and implements had appeared, with its attending considerable social differentiation.

We find in the Regulations the division of the Mongols into nobles and commoners, into members of the upper, middle, and lower classes. To the nobles, or the "white bone" belonged: (1) the Princes (arts. 10,11,20,21,26,35), who were in turn divided into those of chief (Khans, Kon-taidjis, Taishas), intermediate (princely officials who headed the Oolooses and Tabunang-princes) and minor (non-official princes and noyons) rank. These princes received their income (in kind) from their subjects (26); they (or at least the officials among them) were entitled to a share of the judicial fees (128); their inviolability was safeguarded by severe penalties (20,59). (2) The Tabunangs (those who were not princes) and (administrative) officials (10-11); and (3) Administrators, clan chiefs, Zaisans and courtiers (10,11,20,21,35). The middle class consisted of the minor clan chiefs, such as Demchis, Shulengas and Tarkhans (tax-exempt), bannermen and soldiers (11,20,55). To the lower classes belonged the tradesmen, cattlebreeders, husbandmen and slaves (11,15,39,59,44,46,69,100.)

Members of the lower classes were in all cases less valued than those of the middle class, who were in turn considered as of less account than those of the higher class. Thus they paid smaller ransoms and fines, were less severely punished for insults, less weight was attached to their testimony in court, etc. Generally speaking, juristic importance was in proportion to social standing according to the Regulations. Slaves stood on the lowest rung of the social scale and were mostly recruited from prisoners of war. These slaves were, however, by no means devoid of rights before the law. For example, for the killing of his own male slave the offender was fairly heavily fined, viz. five times nine animals; for the killing of a female slave, thrice nine (32); a female slave who presented *corpus delicti* was permitted to bear witness in court (101) while a male slave was permitted to do so even without the *corpus delicti*. For the rape of a female slave, the culprit was fined a horse (69), etc. Generally, the number of slaves was not very great.

The right to real property was unknown but private property in movables existed. Relations arising out of obligations were not satisfactorily developed. The family preserved its patriarchal character, the power of the head of the household (husband and father) was great, polygamy existed and marriage was concluded by the ransoming (Kalim) of the bride.

The system of punishments was based chiefly upon property-fines reckoned in nines of cattle. Punishments were adapted to separate cases and bore a customary character. Besides the code of punishments, there also existed a system of rewards for help rendered in danger and in need.

The Regulations of 1640 differed widely from the Great Yassa of Jenghiz Khan. Thus, in the religious sphere, the Yassa adopted the principle of toleration, taught respect for all creeds and forbade the giving of preference to any sect. The Regulations, on the other hand, proclaimed Lamaism as the only true and supreme religion and persecuted Shamanism. In the sphere of morals, the Yassa punished adultery with death; while the Regulations imposed only a small fine upon men and married women guilty of this offence, and let maidens go completely unpunished. The repressive penalties for criminal offences were considerably milder in the Regulations than in the Yassa. In the latter, capital punishment was lavishly prescribed, often for trifling offences, while in the Regulations it was a rare exception, the whole system of punishments being based on property fines, etc. But alongside of these important differences between the Yassa and the Regulations, common traits were also present. Fines in kind, so commonly met with in the Regulations in the form chiefly of fines in cattle, were also met with in the Yassa (Frs. 28,29). The Yassa prescribed that any man who choked on his food was to be dragged outdoors through a hole under the Yurt and put to death (31). The Regulations likewise emphasised that there was no crime in killing a man who choked on his food in the house of another, although such killing was fined by 5 times nine animals (49).[56] The Yassa punished with death anyone who urinated on fire (4) and forbade stepping over a fire on which food was being cooked (12). The

56 Art. 49 : "If a man, who in another person's house chokes on his food or becomes drunk, be killed, though it shall not be considered a crime nevertheless five times nine must be taken from the killer."

Regulations inflicted a heavy fine upon anyone throwing a block of wood on the fire (so as to put it out) (90). Both the Yassa and the Regulations forbade anyone to help either of the parties in a brawl or fight (Fr. 3 and Art. 71). Hospitality was prescribed equally by the Yassa and the Regulations (Fr. 12,13 and Arts. 24.87, and others respectively.)

In their contents the Regulations seemed to approach far more closely the Ancient Tsaadjin-Bichik. To become assured of this it is sufficient to compare the treatment of adultery, women, and the allotmont of part of the family property to sons. This circumstance is quite comprehensible because these Codes were closer to each other in time, besides being mainly codes of the Oirat federation.

The sources of the Regulations of 1640 were chiefly the customary law of the Mongol tribes, and, to a certain extent, the ancient Tsaadjin-Bichik, the canon law of the Lamaists and some legislative provisions.

The contents of the Regulations which comprise the most important available record of Mongol law are of great scientific interest. The Yassa of Jenghiz Khan has survived only in fragments and in inexact interpretations. The Regulations of 1640, on the other hand, have come down to us in their complete form. For a time they served as the fundamental source of our knowledge of Mongol law, and even now only the recently discovered Code of Northern Mongolia, the Khalkha Djirum, can compare with them in importance. Moreover, the discovery of the latter code has in no way diminished the scientific value of the former, not only because it represented the legislation of the Western Mongols as the Khalkha Djirum did that of Northern Mongolia but also because of the independent interest of its contents. Although the Khalkha Djirum contained more records and was richer in the quantity of its articles, some of these records dealt with the same subjects. If the Khalkha Djirum, as we shall see further, gives more detailed information on certain aspects of the customary law of the Mongol tribes, there are others which are better elucidated in the Regulations. This applies, for instance, to the clan life and clan relations of the Mongols which are better described in the Regulations, evidently because clan life was better preserved among the Western Mongols in the XVIIth century than among their North Mongolian kinsmen in the XVIIIth. The Regulations also give more details concerning hunting, which occupied a more prominent place as a means of subsistence among the contemporary Western Mongols than among those of the North a century later. In the supplementary decrees added to the Regulations by Khan Galdan, the organization of the judiciary was set forth in greater detail than in the Khalkha Djirum. On specific questions of private and criminal law, the Regulations also contained a certain amount of information not included in the later code. Of course, owing to the incompleteness of both codes, we find other questions treated in greater detail in the Khalkha Djirum. The above has, however, been sufficient to show that the Mongol-Oirat Regulations of 1640 continue to preserve their scientific value at the present time.

Supplementary Decrees of Galdan-Khun-Taidji.

Galdan, the son of Batur, was the head (Khun-Taidji) of the Oirat Federation from 1677 to 1697 and issued two decrees serving as supplements to the Regulations of 1640.

In Professor Leontovich's edition, only one supplementary decree of Galdan-Khan is quoted, while Pallas and Golstounsky given both. Buler refers the issue of the first supplementary decree to the year 1654, while Leontovich inclines towards 1687, in which year a meeting of Mongol princes took place in Khalkha. Both these suppositions seem erroneous to the writer. As a matter of fact, neither in the edition of Leontovich, nor in that of Pallas was the time of the promulgation of the supplementary decrees indicated. But in Golstounsky's edition, the second decree was dated 1678. Moreover, since in Golstounsky's original text, as in that of Pallas, the legislative acts were apparently reproduced in chronological order, beginning with the Regulations of 1640 and ending with the complementary provisions of Khan Donduk-Dashi (1741-1761), it is reasonable to suppose that the first of the decrees of Galdan Khan to be listed was also the first in point of time, which would make the date of its issue 1677 or 1678.[57]

The first decree of Galdan, in the edition of Leontovich, contained 16 articles; in the Pallas and Golstounsky editions—12. The second decree, if we are to follow Pallas, contained three articles, while as presented by Golstounsky it was not divided into articles at all.

The first decree contained provisions for the relief of the poor (Art. 122 in Golstounsky's edition); on theft (123-124); on the formation of new Otoks and Aimaks comprising people living in different Hoshuns (125); on courts (126,128,129); on deserters and fugitives from otoks and Aimaks (131,133).

The second decree dealt exclusively with the courts.

57 Galdan Khan became the head of the Oirat federation only in 1677 and both decrees are attributed to him as the Khun-Taidji. Indeed, only the head of the federation could supplement the Regulations of the entire federation.

YARLIKS—INSCRIPTIONS.

Yarliks, separate legislative and administrative acts, were issued also at the time of the Oirat federation. The decrees of Galdan Khan described above may serve as an example. Another example may be found in the "Inscription of Abakansk", so called from its nature and the place where it was found.

Certain special acts of the Oirat Khans (and especially their decrees) were proclaimed by means of inscriptions on rocks, and the decrees and ordinances of the Khans were often hewn out or written in colours on rocks and cliffs.

This was a primitive and convenient way for a nomad people to publish its laws. "To the ancient nomads", says Professor Leontovich, "the rocks and cliffs were like books always open and accessible to all. Engraved in huge letters on the cliffs and rocks by which the nomads passed, the ordinances of the Khans involuntarily attracted attention and were thus made accessible to all literate people."

The Inscription of Abakansk. This inscription was written in black on a cliff of red sandstone on Perevoznaya mountain, on the bank of the Yenisei river, opposite the village of Abakansk. It occupied a conspicuous and picturesque place by the ancient ford the nomads used to cross the Yenisei. The words were written in regular lines on three of the rocks comprising the cliff, and were protected by an overhanging projection. Pallas was the first to notice the inscription (in 1771) and he copied a part of it. In 1817-1818 Spassky did the same, being followed by Kastren in 1847 and Titov and Kostrov in the fifties. In 1857 Spassky published the text of the inscription in the Proceedings of the Geographic Society (Vol. XII). Attempts to translate the inscription were made by the orientalists, Fren, Klaprot, Igoumnov and Berezin. Owing, however, to the deterioration of the inscription and the defective nature of the copies, the two last named scientists could decipher only a few words. Even the learned Lamas of Urga were unable to give a translation, and the only person able to do so turned out to be Father A. Orlov, who taught the Mongol language at the Theological Seminary in Irkutsk. The inscription was in the ancient Mongol language and the first part was missing, this being probably due either to the weather-worn condition of the rock or to non-inclusion in the copy. It apparently contained an order of the Khan to the troops and Lamas prescribing how captives were to be dealt with and the proper behaviour in the country of the enemy.[58] Popov reterred the origin of the inscription to the XVIIth century, the epoch of the expeditions of Irden Khan and other rulers to Siberia (in 1642, 1652, 1657 and 1676). In 1642 and 1652 Irden Khan reached Abakansk and camped by the ford across the Yenisei.

The translation of the inscription follows.

(1) "............... because of the wild animals on the roads, do not abandon or kill submissive and inoffensive captives from the Kibitkas and Oolooses. Until peace (is concluded) you, the Lamas (appointed) for burying the dead .... speak loudly of tombs (because) relationship (intercourse) with captives is association with infidels.

(2) Bury, therefore, men and women as a sacrifice to the illustrious (wrathful) dragons for the sake of a great abundance of honey, curds, meat and milk.

(3) When you have shot and buried (them) throw branches on the tomb-mound for each of the dragons, and for the sake of remembrance sow seeds on it (on all sides).

(4) Above the flowers (seeds) inter the mares (that belonged to the slaughtered captives) but barren female camels take by the bridle and do not inter, as they may be destined to become mothers. Bury men by the hundreds. Women, of course, must not be tortured or maimed as men (may be born of the). Should others, perhaps, be annihilated? (Then) bury them.

(5) Do not maim old fathers and mothers. And is it necessary to destroy herds of cattle?

Then shoot and bury all of them."

Thus we see that religious fanaticism was here emphasised. Intercourse with captives was considered tantamount to association with infidels, and in a war the Lamas were instructed to speak loudly of tombs, i.e. to demand the massacre of resisting infidels, though not of the meek and submissive. The order was given not to throw away slain captives like carrion but rather to bury them as a kind of sacrifice to the dragons. The killed were to be buried by hundreds together with their mares (but not with female camels which were rare and necessary in the household) according to Mongol custom, and the seeds of flowers and trees were to be sown on the tombs. Captives who offered no resistance

58 Popov explains that only a Khan could give orders to Lamas.

were to be spared and subsequently enslaved, women were not to be maimed because they might become mothers of a new generation, and the maiming of old fathers and mothers was likewise prohibited. We see that in this military ordinance, as in the Mongol-Oirat Regulations of 1640, women were dealt with much more leniently than men. This passage provides additional proof that the inscription of Abakansk belongs to the XVIIth century, the epoch of the Oirat federation. As for other person (i.e. those who did not belong to the categories specified) and their herds, they could be dealt with as it pleased their captors, i.e. made slaves or annihilated.

Thus the entire ordinance was permeated with the spirit of merciless annihilation of enemies who offered resistance, of mercy to old people and women and indifference, or rather cruelty, to the others. The same duality of character marked the Mongol-Oirat Regulations of 1640.

The Inscription of Shalabolinsk. This inscription was situated on the right bank of the river Tuba, a tributary of the Yenisei, within three kilometres of the village of Shalabolinsk.

It was painted on a rock consisting of eleven layers of sandstone divided into separate rocks. On some of these rocks pictures of various animals and lettering were painted.

As translated by Father Orlov the inscription of Shalabolinsk read: "Having consented to conclude (literally—to promote) peace, I affix the seal (Tamga) of the black (red) ox (the seal of the year of the black ox)[59] saying—peace and tranquillity." And lower down: "On the seventh day of the seventh month of the (this, the current) year. (Be it) true (or: the Lama of Galdan Khan.)" From its contents the inscription seems to be a treaty of peace concluded by an envoy of Galdan (since Galdan Khan himself never visited the Yenisei) with some princeling of Tubinsk, the treaty being signed (and probably also drafted) on behalf of the Khan by his envoy, a Lama, while the local prince affixed to it his seal of the black ox. The translation is corroborated by the picture on the rock. Thus, we see that the Shalabolinsk inscription also pertains to the period of the reign of Galdan Khan. N. J. Popov gives 1691 as the date of the inscription, because, in accordance with historical data, a Lama[60] envoy was in that year sent by Boshoktu (Galdan) Khan to the people of Tubinsk.[61]

---

59 Painted on the left side of the rock.

60 Popov, *op. cit.*

61 There also exists the Inscription of Tessi, but it has been almost completely erased by time.

B. NORTHERN MONGOLIA OR KHALKHA.

THE GREAT CODE OF THE SEVEN HOSHUNS.

Northern Mongolia, like its Western counterpart, had its own collection of customs, regulations and codes, based upon local customary law and serving as a guide for the solution of disputes. The Great Code of the Seven Hoshuns was the most ancient of such collections or codes of Khalkha, information concerning which has come down to us. In the first article of the first chapter of the Khalkha Djirum (1709), the following statement appeared: "Wherever the Hutukhtu Gegen may go, let him have horses and victuals without limitation, *as was settled by the seven Hoshuns some time ago.*" In the same chapter we read: "If an Elchi commit theft, it is necessary to act according to the *Great Code.*"[62] The Regulations of 1718, which are included in the Khalkha Djirum, prescribed action according to "*the Ancient Code.*"[63] Another record, also forming part of the Khalkha Djirum, stated: "The messengers of our seven Hoshuns, going on our errands, must not make use of the cartage of the Shabinars tributaries of the Hutukhtu (High) except on the affairs of The High and military affairs, and if they do make such use of them, they must be punished in accordance with the *fundamental statute.*"[64] One can see from this and other indications that a separate ancient Code of the Seven Hoshuns existed before the Khalkha Djirum.

Khalkha was divided into seven hoshuns after the death of Gherescenza (in the second half of the XVIth century). The Code of the Seven Hoshuns, incidentally regulated the duty of supplying cartage to the High Hutukhtu of Urga, a post which appeared in Mongolia in the XVIIth century. Thus the creation of such a Code of seven Hoshuns might very well also have taken place during the XVIIth century, though some of its provisions might have originated at an earlier date. The text of the Code of the Seven Hoshuns is unknown.

---

62 Khalkha-Djirum, MS., I-1, 8.
63 *Ibid.* XIV.
64 *Ibid.* II, 2.

"KHALKHA DJIRUM."

The *Yamenu Khalkha Djirum-un-durim,* or *Khalkha Djirum* (Djirom) as it is more briefly known, is an unpublished code of the customary laws of the Northern Mongols (*Khalkhas*). It is otherwise called the "Great Statute of the Three Hoshuns" (of Khalkha). In accordance with the ancient Mongol custom, the only existing copy of this record was kept in the Shanzotbin Yamen (on the Ibingol River not far from Kiakhta), and ordinary mortals were strictly forbidden to make or possess transcriptions of it. From the ancient manuscript kept in the Yamen a copy was made in 1914 by the well known expert on Mongolia, Ts. J. Jamtsarano who sent it to the Asiatic Museum of the Academy of Sciences in St. Petersburg (Leningrad). Two other transcriptions were made, one of which (the Urga copy) served as the basis on which Messrs. Jamtsarano and Turunov gave a description of the *Khalkha Djirom.*[65]

It is evident from this description that the Code was compiled at different times. It consists, in all, of eight sections. Its fundamental parts were composed by the Mongols of the Aimak of Tushetu Khan, with the latter at their head, in the year 1709. This code of customary law was effective in the whole of Northern Mongolia, in all its three (later four) Aimaks (*v.* heading of Record I and end of Record VI).

At the present time there exist two basic transcription of the Code: the Urga and Barun-Kuren copies which differ from each other mainly in the arrangement and quantity of their contents, the latter being fuller.[66] As stated above, a description of the Code according to the Urga transcript has been compiled by Messrs. Jamtsarano and Turunov and repeated by the Author. The description of the Code which follows below is based on the Barun-Kuren transcript, (a copy of which is in the Author's possession.[67])

The Barun-Kuren copy of the Khalkha Djirum contains the following items (records):

I. "The Great Statute of the Three Hoshuns" of 1709. This is the first and fundamental record of the Code. It is preceded by an

65 Ts. Jamtsarano and A. Turnov, "*Khalkha Djirom*" (a description), 1923. Separate reprint from the "Collection of Works of the Professors and Teachers of the Irkutsk Government University." No. 6. This description, with some changes, was given in the Author's works: "Customary Law of the Mongol Tribes" (in English), 1929, on ppg. 39-51; and "Mongolskoe Pravo" (Mongol Law) (in Russian), 1931, on ppg. 71-81.

66 There is also the copy of the Academy of Sciences of the U.S.S.R. (manuscript No. 196), which contains a part of the Code. (v. Vladimirtzov, "Social Organisation of the Mongols", 1934, ppg. 20 *sqq.*)

67 This MS. was translated into Russian by Ts. J. Jamtsarano who also annotated it. To Mr. Jamtsarano also the Author is grateful for furnishing his copy. Fragmentary excerpts from it are given in the Appendix of the present work.

introduction containing expressions of religious piety and a list of participants in the compilation of the Statute.

The Statute contains three chapters entitled as follows: "On the Elchis (Messengers) of the Hutukhtu-Gegen"; "On the Elchis of the Khan and Other Matters"; and "On Insults" (to the Elchis). These three chapters are further divided into 15 Articles dealing with the regulation of requisitions (compulsory cartage). Only these 15 Articles come directly under the heading of "The Great Statute of the Three Hoshuns" 1709. Undoubtedly, however, the Statute cannot have been so short or so poor in content. If it had been, it would not have been called "The Great Statute" or carried a special introduction. In fact, we find in the Code, its further continuation (see below, IV, VIII, XI, XIII, (v. also XXII and XXIII). These items undoubedly represent an extension of the provisions of the "Great Statute" of 1709 relating to compulsory cartage.

II. After these three chapters come the "Regulations of the Middle Autumn Month", of 1722, relating also to compulsory cartage (two Articles).[68]

III. Then follow the "Regulations of the Last Autumn Month", 1722, the first Article of which also fixes relations arising from the duty of compulsory cartage serving as a further extension of the "Great Statute" of 1709.

IV. All other articles (over 40) placed under the former heading deal with theft from the herds of the Gegen, trespassing on the Gegen's Kuren, (cloister), and with theft in general. These serve as the natural continuation of the "Great Statute" of 1709. This circumstance led the investigator and translator of the Khalkha Djirum, Mr. Jamtsarano, to believe that the last articles were originally part of the "Great Statute of 1709"[69]. Briefly, the contents of these articles are as follows: On Various Thefts; On Robbery; On Ransom; On Court Costs; On Fines; On the Oath; On Compensation for Things Stolen; On Search and Removal of Landmarks; On Court Decisions and their Execution; and On the Operation of the Right of Sanctuary at the Gegen's.

V. "The Great Statute" of 1728. It is not stated that this Great Statute applies to three Hoshuns. This Statute begins with expressions of piety and contains one long article dealing with theft. Here again we encounter the question of the brevity and poorness of

68 The second Article of these Regulations evidently repeats a more ancient rule. It deals with the messengers of Seven Hoshuns and provides for penalties "in accordance with the fundamental Statute."

69 We may note here the reference to the mother of the Khan, the Dowager Khanna (see the Chapter: "On Thieves in General"), as in the Statute of 1709, Art. 6.

this item, and this Great Statute also has extensions which may be found in further sections of the Code, (see below IX and XV.)

VI. The Regulations of 1746, comprising one Article on Robbery (with references to "The Great Statute of His Majesty", i.e. the Mongol Statute of the Emperor K'ang Hsi, 1696.)

VII. The Regulations of 1736 (in Mr. Jamtsarano's opinion 1676) on the theft of cattle and other property of the monasteries and lamas (privileges of the clergy).[70]

VIII. Articles of 1709 on marriage, inheritance and fugitives. These articles evidently constitute a continuation of the "Great Statute" of 1709, because the second Article refers to the "participants in the compilation of the Great Statute of the Three Hoshuns" (The Great Statute of 1709). Moreover, in a Court judgment handed down in 1770 (see XXII) reference is made to them as the Mongolian (i.e. All-Mongolian) Statute.

IX. Conclusion of the said Articles of the Great Statue of 1709, dealing with theft and the concealment of thieves, which is considered as an extension of the Statute of 1728.

X. Agreement of the Shabin Department with the Khotogoid Tusalakchi, dated 1746, on the compensation for persons unintentionally killed.

XI. Articles of 1709. These likewise represent an extension of "The Great Statute of the Three Hoshuns" of which they form a part in the Urga transcript. They contain resolutions on relations with the Urga Gegen, the building of monasteries and prohibitions of the killing of certain animals.

XII. Regulations governing the relations between the clergy and laity, dated 1746. This item comprises an introduction, an invocation to Buddha, and a series of articles defining the position of the clergy in Mongolia (privileges of the clergy.)

XIII. The previous Regulations contain an article on the killing by a Noyon of a subject of himself or some other dignitary. This article, as can be seen from its content, belongs with the following items which represent an extension of the Great Statute of 1709, or possibly some more ancient law. This extension consists of approximately 25 articles and deals with murder, wounding, mad camels, libel, insults, stray cattle, theft of a man, mad dogs and madmen, crossbows and traps.

---

70 Both the above mentioned Articles of the Great Statute of 1728 (V) as well as the Regulations of 1746 (VI) and 1676 (VII) serve, in their contents, as extensions of the final chapters of the Great Statute of 1709 dealing with various kinds of theft.

XIV. Regulations of 1729, on horse-racing.

XV. Statute of Vachirai Tushetu Khan V, (1728). This Statute consists of 20 articles and a conclusion, and deals with the exile of prominent criminals, wrecking of graves, saving of rams, night lodgers, articles found, wells, the duties of an Uteg, taking of merchandise on credit, steppe fires, the duty of Somuns to acquire 10 suits of armour, on debt, witnesses, and grant charters.

The Statute has an eloquent conclusion containing expressions of religious piety and ending with the following indication of the identity of the compilers and the time of compilation. "On the Northern side of Zambutib, the first of the four Tibs (continents) the King of the Mongol peoples, blessed by the Tengri (spirits), of the golden clan of Jenghiz-Khan,[71] in a (his) country which has great power, in the fifth generation of the Great Ancestor Vachirai Khan, (his descendent) Tushetu Khan, in order to spread the Buddhist faith and Government, compiled this (Statute) in accordance with the Teaching, in the year of Kalika (i.e. the year of the Earthen Monkey—1728), in the month of Abidzi, on the 18th day, finishing it on a propitious day for the accomplishment of this writing. Let it be well."

Evidently these Articles represent an extension of the Great Statute of 1728.

XVI. The Regulations of 1718 on arms, on branded camels, on horses and persons liable to military service (two articles).

XVII. Regulations of 1724, on loans and the collection of debts (one article).

XVIII. The Regulations of 1724, forbidding monks to drink wine (two articles).

XIX. An extension of the above, dated 1726, on the wine trade and speculation.

XX. The Regulations of 1726, on trade (three articles), and aid against thieves (one article).

XXI. Regulations of 1759, forbidding the clergy to drink wine, one article (with the permission of the Gegen.)

XXII. A Judicial Decision of 1770, on the seduction of the wife of another, recognized as an article of the Statute. (This decision was handed down on the basis of the Great Statute of 1709.)

XXIII. A Judicial Decision, dated 1770, on the infection of cattle belonging to another, an amendment to the Mongolian Statute.

---

71 An expression of piety with respect to the clan of Jenghiz.

These are the contents of the Code of the Northern Mongols, the Khalkha Djirum, according to the Barun Kuren copy. According to the Author's reckoning the Code contains 17 different records, the main one being "The Great Statute of the Three Hoshuns" of 1709. One, or perhaps two, items of the Code belong to an earlier period, to the XVIIth Century, but the majority were written after 1709. The basic and most comprehensive record is the "Great Statute of the Three Hoshuns" of 1709.

The Khalkha Djirum, like the Mongol-Oirat Regulations of 1640, was based on a clan, nomadic way of life and a pastoral economy; the concept of real property was absent, the land being administered by some particular Hoshun (principality) for the purposes of pastoral economy. Movable property was developed, the family bore a patriarchal character, wives were bought for Kalim, and polygamy existed. The system of punishment was based on property fines, reckoned mainly in nines of cattle. From the Khalkha Djirum we see that the Northern Mongols were divided into the nobility (persons of Khan rank, Noyon-princes, Noyons who were not princes, Tabunans and Taijis), the middle class (lower tribal functionaries, Tarkhans), members of the subject classes (commoners, serfs and slaves), and the clergy.

The importance of this record of Mongol law is very great. Before its discovery, our knowledge of the laws of the Mongols was derived from two main sources: the Yassa of Jenghiz Khan and the Mongol-Oirat Regulation of 1640. The Khalkha Djirum represents the third great record of Mongol law. The Oirat Code applied chiefly to the Western Mongols, the Khalkha Djirum to those of the North. Finally, the Khalkha Djirum remained until very recently the effective law in the Shabin department (the Shabinars-tributaries) of the Urga Gegen, in whose yamen the manuscript was preserved. This invests its provisions with particular importance and makes it possible to judge from them the legal consciousness of the Mongols in the first quarter of the XXth century.

The sources of the Khalkha Djirum were the Customary Law of the Northern Mongols, the Canon Law of the Lamaists, and the previous Great Statute of the Seven Hoshuns of Khalkha. Some influence was further exercised upon it by the Mongol Statute of the Emperor K'ang Hsi of the year 1696 (punishment of Taijis for theft, punishments for robbery and adultery) and the provisions of various Edicts.

Of the period of effectiveness of the Khalkha Djirum it may be said that it was applied as the general Code of Northern Mongolia from the beginning to the end of the XVIIIth century (evidently one or two of the provisions contained in this copy of the Code appertain to the end of the XVIIth century) and the latest of the items contained in it is dated

1770. The Mongol Statute of 1789, promulgated by the Chinese Board of Foreign Relations and effective all over Mongolia, (evidently) superseded it as the all-Mongolian Code. But in the jurisdiction of the Urga Gegen, where Chinese influence hardly penetrated, in matters relating to the Shabinars (tributaries), the Khalkha Djirum retained its effectiveness until 1925.

As regards the relation of the Khalkha Djirum to the Mongol-Oirat Code of 1640 and the tribal statutes of the Buriats, the writer is of the opinion that the Regulations of 1640 did not exercise any direct influence on the Khalkha Djirum, although the common culture which gave rise to both expressed itself in a number of similar provisions.

On some questions of the legal life of the Mongols, the Khalkha Djirum gives more detailed information than the Mongol-Oirat Regulations of 1640. The Khalkha Djirum sheds much light on the legal position of the Lamaist church and clergy in Mongolia, and gives a remarkably detailed account of the articles in common household and military use among the Northern Mongols as the objects of theft. It treats in detail the question of remuneratory agreements, the making good of damages, and trade—all this testifying to more highly developed civil relations. Various problems of private and criminal law are also treated in greater detail than in the Mongol-Oirat Regulation of 1640. But, as has already been stated above, the Mongol-Oirat Regulations give more detailed consideration to some sides of the legal life of the Mongols. Neither Code can replace the other. Both are full of omissions and devoid of system. The discovery of the Khalkha Djirum, has greatly enriched the study of the social organisation and legal life of the Mongols just as the discovery of Buriat Statutes gave much to the study, of the legal life of the Mongol tribes as a whole, and of Mongol law in its broader aspects.

Chinese Legislation for Mongolia.

At the end of the XVIIth century, Northern Mongolia (Khalkha) fell wholly under the rule of the Chinese, who brought with them their own administration. Already in 1696, the Emperor K'ang Hsi promulgated a special Statute for Mongolia. In the middle of the XVIIIth century Djungaria also fell prey to Chinese conquest. At that time the conqueror of Djungaria, the Emperor Ch'ien Lung, promulgated a code effective in all Mongolia, the socalled Regulations of the Chinese Board of Foreign Relations (1789) to which Mongolia, and later also Djungaria, was subject. These Regulations were soon afterwards revised and reissued (in 1815).

1. The Statute of 1696.

Besides the two codes known to science as having been promulgated by the Chinese authorities for Mongolia (those of 1789 and 1815), there are indications[72] of the existence of a third and more ancient similar body of law relating to the epoch of the Emperor K'ang Hsi. The manuscript of this Code was recently found in Mongolia.

The Code represented a collection of the laws dealing with Mongolian affairs issued by the Manchu T'ai Tsung and the Chinese emperors during the period from 1629 to 1695, and was issued, evidently after final revision by the Emperor K'ang Hsi, in 1696. The collection contains 152 articles. The following dates are contained in this record: the reign of T'ai Tsung, 1627-1644; the reign of Shun Chih, 1644-1662; and the reign of K'ang Hsi: 1667, 1668, 1672, 1676, 1687, 1690, 1691 and 1695.

No system or order is perceptible in the arrangement of the records of this collection.

The identity of this code with that of 1789 as quoted by Father Hyachinth (see further), points to the supposition that most of the articles in the Code of K'ang Hsi were repeated in that of 1789 (though not in that of 1815). Consequently, the earlier collection of laws served as the foundation of the fuller code of 1789 which contained 210 articles.

It is necessary to note further that the Code of K'ang Hsi was to a large extent itself based on Mongol laws and customs,[73] as well as on Chinese law.

From the data given above it may be concluded that the fundamental legal provisions included in the Code of 1696 dealt with the region known as Inner Mongolia and were obligatory only with respect to that region. As regards Khalkha, it had its own native Code, the Khalkha Djirum.

2. The Regulations (Code) of 1789.

The Regulations published for Mongolia by the Chinese Board of Foreign Relations in 1789 were compiled on the basis of the Statute of the Emperor K'ang Hsi (1696) which in turn was based on Chinese law and Mongol custom. These Regulations were effective for the whole of Mongolia.

---

72 Timkovsky—"A Journey to China Through Mongolia", v. III; ppg. 222, 243, and after him by Leontovich and Dareste.

73 The information concerning the Code of 1696 given above was supplied by Mr. Ts. J. Jamtsarano at the writer's special request.

The Regulations of 1789 were translated into Russian by Father Hyacinth, comprising Part IV of his "Notes on Mongolia", 1828, which were translated into German by von der Borg in 1832.

The contents of the Regulations, in Father Hyacinth's translation, were divided into 12 sections containing 210 articles. The sections were as follows: Section I—On Ranks (24 arts.); II. On Revision and Obligations (23 art.), III—On Visiting the Court and Bringing Tribute (8 or 9 art.); IV—On Meeting for the Seim and Going to War (13 art.); V—On Paths and Guards (17 art.); VI—On Robbery and Theft (35 art.); VII—On Homicide (10 art.); VII—On Complaints (5 art.); IX—On Lamas (6 art.); and XII—On the Decision of Litigations (29 art.)

3. The Regulations (Code) of 1815.

This Code, promulgated by the Chinese Board of Foreign Relations in 1789, was based on the Code of 1696 and the slowly-changing customs of the nomadic tribes. These, naturally, could not satisfy the demands of the considerably more advanced Chinese and had little in common with the general problems of administration occupying the Chinese courts. As early as 1811, the Chairman of the Board of Foreign Relations and the Prime Minister, Ch'ing Hui, submitted to Emperor Chia Ch'ing a report dealing with the Mongol Code. An excerpt from this report read as follows:

"As regards the civil organization and criminal jurisprudence of Mongolia, the Board follows the existing Code which contains 209 articles. This Code, in the Manchu, Mongol and Chinese languages, was drafted in the year 54 Abkai Vosekhe (1789), over 20 years ago. During this period, a great many criminal offences have been committed among the Mongols which, not being provided for by any articles of the effective Code, had to be submitted to the Emperor for his decision. In consequence, a number of ministerial reports had to be submitted and as many decrees were issued; but these decrees have so far not been included in the general Regulations and remain therefore unpromulgated."

Ch'ing Hui therefore requested permission "to collect the decrees and rules that might have the power of laws, beginning with the 34th year of the present reign, and to include them in the Code as supplementary articles. . . " This permission was given and a commission was appointed to carry out the work, three years being fixed as the time at the end of which it was to be completed. Having studied the Code, however, the Commission found that it did not correspond to its aim and they proceeded to draft a new Code, asking for an extension of the three year period to four years. When the Commission completed its work, the new Chairman of the Board of Foreign Relations wrote in his report: "Each article of the former Code having been examined, we found twenty of them which might have had the force of laws in former times but are now recognized as useless for the new Code. These were therefore excluded from the general plan. Of the remaining 189 articles, 178 had to be completely revised, this being duly done. After having put in order the abovementioned articles of the former Code, we proceeded to examine the former files of the Board, beginning with the reign of Ch'iskhun Dasan (1644-1662) and ending with the present year, and to translate these from the Manchu into Chinese in order to better judge which of them could be included in the new Code. From the material thus examined we drafted 516 articles, etc. . . ."[74]

It is thus more correct to consider the Code drafted in 1815[75] not merely as an amended edition of that of 1789 but as a new and separate body of law.

In its original form (in Manchu) the Code was not divided into sections and had neither an index nor numbered articles. Physically it consisted of 67 separate paper books, completely independent of, and unconnected with each other. Their translator, Mr. Lipovtzev, arranged the articles of the Code in systematic order, numbered them, and divided them into sections and chapters.

The contents of the Code consisted of an introduction and six parts. Each of these parts was divided by the translator into chapters, and the chapters into sections, which were in turn split up into paragraphs and articles.

Introduction: Constitution of the Board of Foreign Relations, containing 6 chapters and 56 articles; Part I—Civil Law (properly speaking, the administrative organization and rule of Mongolia), containing 21 chapters and 494 articles; Part II—Military Regulations, containing 6 chapters and 88 articles; Part III—Criminal Law, containing 20 chapters and 191 articles; Part IV—Provisions Relating to the Lamaist Religion, 11 chapters and 117 articles; Part V—Provisions Relating to Tibet, 13 chapters and 66 articles; Part VI—Relations with Russia, 6 chapters and 28 articles.

The Mongol Code of 1815 (1817) had several editions (e.g. 1826, 1832, etc.)[76]

---

74 Lipovtzev—"Code of the Chinese Board of Foreign Relations," 1828, ppg. xii, xvi.

75 Acad. Vladimirtzov indicated that this Code was published in 1817 ("Social Organization of the Mongols", 1934, pg. 20, ftn. 3). This is quite possible.

76 See *e.g.* Dr. Laufer, "Outline of Mongol Literature", pg. 84 (in Russian).

The Codes of 1789 and 1815 were greatly under the influence of Chinese law, especially as regards administrative law (provisions for the organization and administration of Mongolia.)

Apart from administrative law, Chinese influence also made itself felt in the sphere of criminal law. In place of the lenient punitive provisions of the Regulations of 1640, we find here cruel punishments not always corresponding with the mode of life of the nomadic Mongols, such as, for example, deprivation of liberty, as well as frequent recourse to capital punishment, (cutting to pieces, strangulation), the cangue, various forms of banishment, the exhibition of the heads of the executed, etc. At the same time some institutions of Mongol law found clear expression, e.g. the fine in cattle reckoned in nines, which, already met with in the Yassa, was often applied in the regulations of 1640 and in the customary law of the Buriat tribes; severe punishment for the theft of cattle, consideration of death as a result of maiming or wounding in a hand-to-hand fight as the equivalent of murder if such death occured within 50 days of the wound (as in Buriat customary law.) Naturally enough, the Chinese conquerors were forced to give still more place to custom in the sphere of private law. There were, however, few provisions in either code relating to private law (the fixed rate of Kalim, adoption, inheritance, etc.) The Mongols continued to apply in the sphere of private law the practice of their customs and ancient codes.

The Law of Autonomous Outer Mongolia.

AUTONOMOUS MONGOLIA.

In the so-called "Autonomous Mongolia" (1911-1924) the publication was begun of "The Laws of the Mongol Government". Thirty-four books (debters) of this Code were issued but publication was not completed. Criminal and Civil Codes were also compiled, but these were not published up to the date of the demise of "Autonomous Mongolia".

During this period the Code of the Northern Mongols, the Khalkha Djirum, continued to be applied among the Shabinars of the Urga Gegen. Among the rest of the population local customary law continued to rule in the sphere of private-legal relations. The provisions of the Regulations of 1815 as well as Mongol custom ruled in the sphere of Criminal law.

A special agreement concluded on November 21, 1921 defined the status of the Bogdo Gegen as the head of the State, and according to this instrument he assumed the position of a constitutional monarch with a limited power of veto.

The text of this agreement follows:

AGREEMENT UNDER OATH CONCLUDED BETWEEN THE BOGDO-KHAKAN AND THE GOVERNMENT FOR THE PURPOSE OF DEFINING THEIR MUTUAL RELATIONS.

Article 1. The Bogdo Khakan of the Mongol State, Djebtsun-Damba Hutukhtu, being the holy head of the Yellow Religion[77] must not concern himself with affairs of State; but in all matters dealing with religion he is to wield unlimited powers.

Article 2. The Bogdo Djebtsun-Damba Hutukhtu Gegen, being the head (Khakan) of the Mongol People's State, the government of which is on the lines of a constitutional monarchy, will carry out all his State functions through the President (Premier) of the People's Government.

Article 3. The People's Government may not promulgate new laws without a preliminary report to the Bogdo-Khakan. Moreover, it must also report to the Bogdo-Khakan on all orders issued by it in any important affairs.

Article 4. Legislative acts issued on the initiative of the Government for strengthening and improving the bases of the Mongol People's State[78] and also for the common welfare may be enforced only after being reported to the Bogdo-Khakan. Such laws can neither be rejected nor annulled by him. Projects of laws[79] of some other nature may, after being reported to the Bogdo-Khakan, be returned by him for reconsideration, but not more than one time. After second consideration by the Government the project reported to the Khakan becomes law.[80]

Article 5. On all new legislation and also orders issued by the Government on important problems, a report must be made to the Bogdo-Khakan by the Premier of the Government (in the text: "State") alone or jointly with the Sait of another Yamen.

Article 6. In case of a coup d'etat or internal rebellion, the Government may, dispensing with the procedure in times of peace, undertake important action or promulgate laws (Haoli) without reporting to the Bogdo-Khakan.

77 The "Yellow Hat" sect founded by the famous evangelist of Tibetan Buddhism, Tsonhava (1355-1417 A.D.)

78 Literally "of the People's State the Government of which is limited in its powers."

79 In the Mongol text: "provisions of law."

80 Literally: "The above mentioned laws, after a second consideration and report, are brought into force."

Article 7. The awarding of distinctions, although depending upon the discretion of the Bogdo-Khakan, will be effected through the Government. First and second Saits, and also the Commander in Chief and second Commander in Chief will be appointed by the Government after a (preliminary) report has been made to the Bogdo-Khakan. Other officials will be appointed by the Government.

Article 8. The present agreement will come into force before the convocation of the Great People's Hural.[81]

Article 9. The present agreement is written with the aim of strengthening the People's State, promoting the spread of religion, internal co-operation, external glory and the well-being of the people.

The non-violation and proper observance of the present agreement on the part of the Bogdo-Khakan and the Government is guaranteed by the sacred oath.

After this, towards the end of the existence of the Autonomous *regime* (November 1921-May 1924), several important laws were issued and applied, e.g. the separation of Church and State, the abolition of serfdom, abolition of the hereditary power of the princes, of corporal punishment and torture, the institution of a standing army, the proclamation of the land as the property of the State, the declaration nullifying the foreign indebtedness of Mongolia and the Mongols, an income tax, etc.

Records of Buriat Law.

The records of Buriat law may be divided into two main groups: (1) Records of the law of the Southern Buriats; and (2) Records of the law of the Northern Buriats. The legal provisions of both possessed certain peculiar traits, and even within the groups there might have been observed a certain particularism of legal provisions (the Hori and Selenga Buriats, the Buriats of Verkholensk and Balagansk, etc.). It is necessary to note further that the records of Buriat law represented the written customs of the tribes, produced by the Buriats for their own needs or at the demand of the Russian authorities.

81 In the Mongol text the word in this text is "Huraldagan." In modern legislation and in the official correspondence of this institution the designation "Hural" is employed.

A. THE SOUTHERN BURIATS.

THE HORI TRIBE.

The known records of the Hori tribe are as follows:

Heb (Regulations) of the Year of the Ram (1763), of the 10th day of the mid-autumn month, composed by the Taishas and Saitas of eleven Hori clans at the Seim of Allan, and relating to the apportionment of taxes and dues. This record contained three articles: 1) On Marriage; 2) On Hunting; and 3) On Measures Against Intoxication. A Russian translation of the Mongol MS. is reproduced in the writer's, "Mongol Law, With Special Reference to Customary Law" 1931 (in Russian) (*v.* Appendix 2.)

The Ancient Steppe Code of the Hori Buriats (1781). The Russian investigators of the life of the Buriats, A.R., Professor Leontovich and Professor Gourland, shared the opinion that the first Code of the Hori Buriats was represented by the Mongol-Oirat Regulations of 1640, or generally some Code compiled in Mongolia. However, an investigation of this question by the writer has convinced him that neither the Regulations of 1640 nor the Khalkha Djirum, nor any other Mongolian Code was effective among the Buriats, and that the first code of the Hori Buriats was that composed by themselves in the Mongol language in the year 1781.[82] In the surviving Steppe Code of 1808, it is stated that this code represented only an amendment and supplement to the Code of 1780 (see Introduction). In a decision handed down in May 1818 (see below) there was also a reference to the previous Code of 1781 as well as to the then effective Code of 1808 (Art. 1). In information dated May 30, 1823, we find similar indications (introduction, decision). The Code of 1781 has not been published and has evidently been lost. Some fragments of this Code were, however, quoted by A. R. in his article, "On the Laws of Some Siberian Natives," in the "Siberian Messenger", 1823, No. 1, and reproduced by the present writer in his "Customary Law of the Mongol Tribes", 1929, p. 156 and also in "Mongol Law, with Special Reference to Customary Law" (in Russian), 1931, p. 137. The provisions contained in these fragments (with some changes) were repeated in succeeding Codes of the Buriats.

Dzakia. These were instructions given by the chief Taisha of the eleven Hori clans, Shiral-Dambo-Doogar Rinchino, to Arslan

---

82 *v.* "Customary Law of the Mongol Tribes", ppg. 153 *sqq.*

Mordain, Zaisan of the Golstun clan, and his companions in the year 1793, on the 25th day of the mid-summer month. The Dzakia bore the character of an administrative decision and was divided into 9 articles, eight of which contained measures against gambling with cards and dice and against intoxication, while the ninth was directed against abuses in the requisitioning of carts. For a Russian translation of the Mongol MS. see *Ibid.*, No. 4.

Hipp-Toktogol. These were conciliatory regulations relating to trade in the steppes among the eleven Horin clans, issued on the 20th day of the 1-st summer month in the year 1800. They were submitted to the chief Taisha, Dambo-Doogar Rinchino who was then in St. Petersburg, with a covering report of the Taishas, Zaisans, Shulengas, etc. of the eleven Horin clans. It contained 11 articles regulating trade among the Horins and dealt with the payment of debts and the lending of money on interest. For a Russian translation of the Mongol MS. see *Ibid.*, No. 5.

The Steppe Code (Hipp) of the Eleven Horin Clans (1808). This code was otherwise known as the Statute of 1808. It represented an amended version of the Code of 1781 and contained 131 articles. This is avery important record. The MS. was in Mongol (for a Russian translation, see *Ibid.* No. 6) and was accompanied by an index of the contents of the Code (41 paragraphs) as follows: 1. On Verbal Insults and Assault (Arts. 1-8, 38); 2. On Mutilation and Injury in Brawls (Arts. 9, 10, 3); 3. On the Behaviour of Intoxicated Persons (Arts. 11, 4); 4. On Customary Match-making and "Anda" (Mutual) Match-making (Arts. 12-14, 28); 5. On Disputes Between Husband and Wife and On Divorce (Arts. 15, 88, 116, 117), etc.

The Communal Decision of the Eleven Horin Clans (December 18, 1817). This record dealt with the manner of administration of the eleven Horin clans. In its 22 articles it depicted the administrative organization of the Hori Buriats prior to the epoch of the Regulations of 1822 relating to the administration of the native tribes of Siberia. For a Russian translation of the Mongol MS. see *Ibid.* No. 7.

The Decision of the Eleven Horin Clans (May 1818). This decision dealt with the administration of the Hori Buriats and was adopted at a Seim of the 11 clans. It contained six articles on internal administration, on the collection and distribution of taxes and on Courts, etc. Article 4 contained the history of the origin of the three Taishas of the Horin clans and the order of succession to these offices. A Russian translation of the Mongol MS. may be found in *Ibid.* No. 8.

Communal Decision of the Eleven Horin Clans (October 27, 1820). This item was divided into 7 articles or points dealing with the collection of taxes and dues. Mongol manuscript.[83]

Statute of the Hori Buriats (March 30, 1823). This record was produced by a Seim of the best men of the 11 Horin clans on March 30, 1823 and related to the trade, mode of life, and jurisdiction of the Hori Buriats. It was published in the "Collection of the Customary Laws of the Siberian Natives", by Professor Samokvasov, in 1876.

The record was divided into 12 chapters and 144 articles. The first chapter dealt with temples, the Bourkhans and the Lamas; the second with the way in which disputes were settled which arose between Lamas, officials and commoners; Chapter III with the various lists, the Yassak and other taxes and their payment; Chapter IV with the discharge of official duties; Chapter V with the collection of local dues, rewards, and the upkeep of local and district postal stations, as well as the repairing of roads; Chapter VI. Matchmaking and litigations between husbands and wives; Chapter VII. Debts; Chapter VIII. Control of the consumption of alcoholic liquors and the playing of cards; Chapter IX. Theft and searches; Chapter X. Trespassing on pastures, the allotment of hay and corn fields and the purchase and sale of corn; Chapter XI Precaution against fire, incendiarism in forests, and the supply of carts to Oolooses; Chapter XII. Miscellaneous matters.

The Horin Statute of 1851. This was composed at the plenary Seim of the "Horin Steppe Administration", in December 1851. The Statute consisted of 197 articles and 19 sections. The contents of the section were as follows: The first eight sections dealt with the clergy and their needs. 9. On the Duties of Officials of the Administration of the Hori Buriats; 10. On the Safeguarding of Fields and Meadows; 11. On Carts Kept for Government and Public Use in the Horin Region; 12. On the Construction and Upkeep of Roads and Bridges; 13. On Betrothals and Weddings; 14. On the Decision of Lawsuits; 15. On Measures against Drunkenness, and Cards and Other Gambling Games; 16. On Searches for Stolen Property and Judgment in Such Cases; 17. On Measures Against Fire and Relief to Sufferers from Fire and Flood; 18. Miscellaneous; 19. On Outrages and Slanders.[84]

The Buriats of Selenga.

The Ancient Code of the Selenguins. From the resolution of June 5, 1823 (see below) it is evident that the first Steppe Code was

---

83 *v.* the article by Jamtsarano and Turunov; "Review of Records of the Written Law of the Mongol Tribes", Proceedings of Irkutsk University, I.

84 *v.* the already mentioned articles of Jamtsarano and Turunov.

adopted by the Buriats of Selenga (the Selenga river) between 1765 and 1818.[85] And indeed, information has recently come into the possession of the writer, to the effect that the ancient code of the Selenga Buriats (dated 1775) has been found.[86]

The Statute of the Selenga Buriats (March 30, 1823.) This record of the customary law of the Buriats of Selenga is contained in the collection compiled by Samokvasov, on ppg. 149-197 of the work. It represented a supplement to the resolution of the eighteen Selenguin clans adopted on June 5, 1823, and was compiled in pursuance of Order No. 863 of Zeidler, Governor of Irkutsk, which advised the Buriats "to supply information concerning the laws of the steppes and to describe the manner in which cases are examined on the spot, as far as can be ascertained from tradition."

The record was divided into 9 chapters and 180 articles. The chapters were as follows: I. On the Theft of Cattle, etc.; II. On Discord between Husband and Wife, and On Cattle given as "Kalim"; III. On Verbal Disputes and Fights; IV. On Medical Treatment and the Reading of the (sacred) Books; V. On Debts and Lawsuits; VI. On Inherited Estates; VII. On the Care of Fields and Meadows; IX. On the Election of Elders, etc.

The Selenguin Code of 1818. In the resolution of June 5, 1823, already quoted mention was made of the fact that in 1818 the Buriats of Selenga assembled for a Seim in accordance with the order (inquiry) of the authorities, and adopted a code similar in content to a former one composed on the basis of certain traditions, i.e. they apparently altered and completed the code already in force. This amended code is not known to us but it does not seem to have differed much from the Statute of 1823 and probably served as the basis for the latter.

Records of Customary Law Common to the Horins and Selenguins.

The following written collections of the Juristic customs common to the Selenga and Hori Buriats contained data relating to the customary law of the Transbaikal Buriats as a whole.

The Tzaadza (Law, Decree, Prohibition) of 1759 was a record purely religious in character. It was produced as a result of an inquiry by Frontier Commissioner Jacobi into the religious life of the Buriats. Enquiries were addressed to both the Horins and Seleguins who gave a

85 *v.* Riasanovsky, "Customary Law of the Mongol Tribes", pg. 160.

86 The author has at his disposal some articles of this Code. From their contents one may suppose that the Code of 1775 served as the basis for the Statute of 1823.

common reply. A Russian translation of the Mongol MS. was published in the writer's "Mongol Law, With Special Reference to Customary Law", Appendix I.

The Conciliatory Regulations (Hipp-Toktogol) of 1788. These applied both to the Hori and Selenga Buriats, and contained ten articles dealing with the law of marriage. For the Russian translation of the Mongol MS., see *Ibid.* Appendix 3.

The New Rules (Shine Toktogol), regulating life and behaviour, were composed by the spiritual and lay Saitas of Selenga and Hori in 1841. This work contained 54 articles divided into three parts as follows: I. On the Lama Priesthood; II. On the Insignia and Uniforms of Chiefs and Honorary or Public Officials; III. On Wedding Banquets, and supplementary articles.[87]

B. THE NORTHERN BURIATS.

The Buriats of Balagansk.

On April 1,1818, the 17 clans of the Balagansk Buriats unanimously adopted a resolution expressing the desire that their former rights with regard to local administration be maintained without any alteration. To this resolution was attached a document entitled: "Information received from the Buriat Community of the Department of Balagansk of the District of Irkutsk Under the Chief Taisha of the Twelfth Class Andrei Nazarov, Drawn Up By a Meeting of All 17 Clans in Accordance with the Order of the Local Court of Irkutsk Dated March 21, 1818 (No. 4696) Issued to the Noble of the Ninth Class, Michael Ivanovich on March 29,1818."

This memorandum comprised six questions with their answers, as follows: 1. What cases do the Buriats consider to have been left within the competence of the native courts? The reply contained a list of cases which "in accordance with the ancient customs of the Buriats and the instructions issued by Savva Vladislavovich, Count Illyriisky, former Ambassador Plenipotentiary on the Chinese Frontier" (1728) and other decisions, the Buriats considered as coming under the jurisdiction of their native courts, as well as a list of cases considered "capital and criminal" by the authorities, 4 articles in all. Question 2: How does the procedure in the examination of cases begin and when and how does such examination end?; Question 3: What rules do the native chiefs follow in the

---

87 *v.* the previously mentioned article by Jamtsarano and Turunov.

examination of cases? The replies to these questions, comprising 13 articles, gave information on the manner in which justice was administered. Question 4 inquired about the penalties dealt out for each separate crime. The reply recapitulated the provisions of the criminal law of the Buriats of Selenga (15 articles, of which art. 14 contained provisions of private law relating to the payment of debts). Question 5 concerned marriages and matters relating to the Kalim (ransom for the bride). The answer contained the provisions relating to family, and partly to marriage law, three articles in all. Question 6: What is the power of the native chiefs? The reply enumerated the rights and duties of the chief Taisha and the heads of the clans (1 art.)

The resolution and information annexed to it have been published in the article by Hangalov which has been previously mentioned, on pg. 101, etc.

The Buriats of Balagansk, Idinsk, Tunkinsk and Kudinsk.

Information concerning the customs of this section of the Buriats is contained in ppg. 87-105 of Samokvasov's book. The material is divided into eight chapters: I. On Religion; II. Cases Judged by Chiefs of Clans; III. Judicial Procedure; IV. On Regulations Applied by the Natives to Various Crimes; VI. On Marriages and Disputes Concerning the Kalim; VII. On the Extent of the Power of the Native Chiefs; VIII. On the Rights of the Natives.

The Buriats of Verkholensk.

Materials referring to the juristic customs of the Buriats of the District of Verkholensk are given on ppg. 77-85 of Professor Samokvasov's collection. They comprise the information (resolution) signed by the Taisha Alexander Yeringarov and his assistant, Hurugan Oubugurov, as well as 27 clan chiefs and 42 honourable Buriats. The material is divided into ten chapters as follows: I. The Chiefs and System of Administration (15 articles, comprising provisions relating to procedure and punishment); On Native Marriages (13 arts.); III. On Wives Deserting Their Husbands and On Wives and Husbands Who Have Been Baptised (5 arts.); IV. On the Customs of the Steppes (Land Ownership) (7 arts.); V. On the Damage Caused to Fields by Cattle Grazing on Them (4 arts.); VI. On Taxes (3 arts.); VII. On Public Revenues (2 arts.); VIII. Explanations Governing the Customs and Laws of the Steppes (2 arts.); IX. On the Election of Native Chiefs; and X. Supplementary Articles to the Preceding Chapters (6 articles, on the Courts, On Insults and On Marriage.)

Generally speaking the law of the Buriats presents the same aspects as the law of the Mongols, supplementing and developing it in some respects.

The social structure was patriarchal and tribal in character, and the administration and judiciary were constructed on clan lines; kinship was recognized only in the male line; the family was strong and based on exogamous marriage, the purchase (ransoming) of wives and the supreme power of the husband and father in the family. Polygamy was permitted and divorce was simple. The character of economic life was primarily nomadic and pastoral. The utilisation of land was partly family and partly clan in character (though individual land ownership was also met with in the case of specially tilled plots.) The crimes treated were not complex, the chief among them being personal insults and the theft of cattle. Penalties were notably mild: flogging and property fines (in cattle and money).

The customary law of the Buriats comprised many provisions of private law. The concept of private property in movables was well developed, and the embryo of private real property was present. The concept of compensation for damages and losses was considerably advanced. A whole series of legal transactions, including credit transactions, were dealt with. Family law and the law of inheritance were treated in sufficient detail, and bequests of property to spiritual institutions were recognized. All these features indicate that civil life was quite well developed.

Particularly worthy of attention are the peculiar provisions dealing with the utilisation of water (irrigation), and also some provisions of Buriat marriage law. In the latter we find, especially among the Northern Buriats, institutions of great interest from the standpoint of comparative jurisprudence. Among these were marriage with ransom (and exchange), the giving of brides for labour service rendered, levitary marriage, marriage accompanied by the abduction of the bride, fixed indications concerning the amount (and composition) of the Kalim and dowry and some others.

It is necessary also to note certain divergencies (particularism) of the legal customs of the Northern Buriats from that of their southern kinsmen. These divergencies were expressed, for instance in the provisions regulating compensation for damages (in certain cases), the allowed rate of interest, some provisions concerning marriage, the rights of a wife leaving her husband to the children and property, etc.

C. THE CODE OF STEPPE LAWS OF THE NATIVE NOMADS OF EASTERN SIBERIA.

This collection of laws represented the draft of a Code created by the Russian authorities for the native peoples of Eastern Siberia (the Buriats, Yakuts, Tunguses, etc.) The draft was printed in 1841 but was not confirmed by legislation. The need for systematisation of the customary law of the native peoples inhabiting Siberia was, however, so great, that in spite of its not having received legislative confirmation, the draft became the effective law within its province, being applied in judicial practice pertaining to the Siberian peoples not only by the native courts but sometimes also by the government judges. The present writer is in possession of exact data concerning the application of this Code among the Buriats from its inception until the most recent times. It may be noted in this connection that in 1918 the Buriat National Congress created the National Buriat Courts, consisting of Hoshun (first instance) and Aimak (second instance) courts, which functioned on the basis of a special Statute (Novel No. 3) and rules of procedure. Article 38 of the Novel and 65 of the Rules of Procedure confirmed the application of the Steppe Code as the effective code of law. The writer was personally shown a resolution of the conference of Buriat judges (held in 1918) recommending that each Hoshun judge keep for his guidance a copy of the Code of Steppe Laws of 1841. The Code was translated into the Mongol language for practical application among the Buriats, among whom it spread in both Mongol and Russian versions and was applied by the judicial and administrative organs.

The Code of Steppe Laws was divided into six sections and 35 chapters, containing 802 articles. The sections were as follows: I. On Family Rights and Duties (3 chapters); II. On the Property Rights of the Natives (5 chaps.); III. On Contractual Obligations (2 chaps.), IV. On Good Behaviour in Native Camping Grounds (8 ch.); V. On Fines and Punishments (5 chaps.); VI. On Judicial Procedure (5 ch.)

The sources of the Code were the customary law of the native tribes and, in the event of omissions or inadequacies in the former, the common law of Russia (vol. X, Part I, Code of Laws.)[88]

---

88 For further details *v.* the writer's article "Two Records of the Customary Law of the Mongol Tribes", *Vestnik Mandjurii* (Manch. Messenger), 1930, 1.

Records of Kalmuck Law.

The Mongol-Oirat Regulations of 1640 were the fundamental source of the customary law of the Kalmucks.

While the application of these Regulations among the Buriats remains, in spite of the opinion to the contrary of A. R., Leontovich and Gourland, not only unproved but even extremely doubtful it is absolutely certain that the Regulations were applied in the remote Kalmuck steppes where attempts were made to supplement them and adapt them to the demands of changed times and conditions.

The first Kalmuck Khans, Kho-Urluk and his son Shukur-Daichin, participated in the promulgation of the Regulations to which their signatures were appended. It is certain that they brought the Tsaadjin-Bichik (the Oirat designation of the Regulations) with them to the steppes of the Volga. In the beginning of XVIIIth century the Russian government (through the Collegium of Foreign Affairs) had already secured a copy of the Regulations in the Kalmuck language, and in or about the year 1724 Bakunin, a councillor of the Collegium, undertook their translation into Russian. In 1742 Bakunin's translation was sent by the Collegium of Foreign Affairs to the Director of the Commission for Kalmuck Affairs, V. N. Tatischev. In 1821 a similar translation was sent by the Foreign Ministry to Khakanov, Chief Commissar of the Kalmucks, with instructions that the Kalmuck Noyons, Zaisans and clergy were to complete and amend them in accordance with the exigencies of their life. This was accordingly done at the Diet of Zinzili. Russian editions of the Oirat Regulations (translated by Sheremetiev, Bentkovsky and Buler) were found among the Russian Kalmucks. At the time of Khan Donduk-Dashi, provisions supplementing the Regulations were drawn up in which reference was made to the ancient Code.[89] All these facts prove conclusively that the Mongol-Oirat Regulations of 1640 were effective among the Kalmucks.

Complementary Provisions to the Regulations of 1640 Drafted in the Reign of Donduk-Dashi.

The new conditions of life to which the Kalmucks were subject in Russia, so different from those of Djungaria, gave rise to new requirements and customs and made it necessary to amend and supplement the ancient Oirat Regulations. This was done in the reign of the Kalmuck Khan Donduk-Dashi 1741-1761 when complementary provisions were drafted.

89 *Cf.* 62-4, 69-1, 4.

A German translation of the text of these provisions was published by Pallas (Sammlungen, I, ppg. 214-218) and reproduced by Leontovich under the title of "New Supplement to the Code of Laws Drafted with the Concurrence of the Six High Ecclesiastics" in his "Ancient Mongol-Oirat Regulations on Punishments," (1879), ppg. 145-150. The original Kalmuck text, with a Russian translation, was later published by Professor Golstounsky, in his "Mongol-Oirat Laws", (1880) under the title of, "Supplement to the Regulations Drafted at the Time of the Kalmuck Donduk-Dashi."

Professor Leontovich defined these provisions as "the local laws of the Ooloos of Derbet"[90] finding support for this in the German text in which occurred the words "unter uns Derbet", (among us Derbets.[91]) In fact, however, the provisions were drafted by Khan Donduk-Dashi, who was ruler of the whole Kalmuck people, with the participation of representatives of the higher clergy and the whole people ("all lay and clerical persons"); and their title and contents bore a general character in no way justifying the assumption that they were local provisions, meant for a single Ooloos, but on the contrary confirming that they represented general legislation applicable to the entire people. Moreover, Professor Golstounsky has since supplied us with an exact translation of the provision containing these words,[92] which run as follows: "When a man is permitted to leave who belongs to the Derbets or other people having houses in the vicinity of the Russian villages......". Here mention of the Derbets was undoubtedly prompted solely by the fact that they lived in the vicinity of Russian villages in the province of Stavropol and the Cossack villages of the Don. All this goes to confirm the opinion commonly held, and to refute the supposition of Professor Leontovich.

Exclusive of the introduction, which was religious in character and thus reminiscent of the introduction to the Mongol-Oirat Regulations of 1640, these provisions comprised 54 articles. They contained laws on the clergy which aimed at the maintenance of religious discipline and the purity of Lamaism in the Russian steppes; rules governing offensive and defensive measures under the new conditions of life; rules relating to the clan organization, to the internal relations of the Kalmucks, the duty of compulsory cartage, stray cattle and other and more elaborate provisions dealing with criminal law and procedure.

90 "Kalmuck Laws", ppg. 167 *sqq.*

91 Pallas, "Sammlungen", I, pg. 217; Leontovich, *Op. cit.*, pg. 148, art. 158.

92 "Mongol-Oirat Laws", *cf.* art. 65 on "night's lodging".

All the provisions represented amendments, substitutions and extensions of the Mongol-Oirat Regulations of 1640 made necessary by the requirements of the new conditions of life facing the Kalmucks in Russia.

CODE (DIGEST) OF KALMUCK LAWS (1822-1827.)

("The laws of the Mungal and Kalmuck peoples, amended and extended at the Congress of the Kalmuck Noyons, Zaisans, Lamas and Gelungs at Zinzili.", i.e. the Mongol-Oirat Regulations of 1640, the Zinzili Resolutions, the Opinion of the Two "owners" (Ooloos Noyons) and the advice of the Kalmuck Commission.)

As time went on, the provisions of the Regulations of 1640 became, in spite of the additions and amendments made by Khan Donduk-Dashi, more and more inadequate in the face of the requirements of the life of the Kalmucks. The southern marches of Russia were pacified, the nomadic tribes began to lose their military-predatory character and gradually adopted a purely pastoral and in some places agricultural mode of life; and the Kalmuck people entered into closer contact with the Russian State and fell under the influence of its laws and culture. On the other hand, the provisions of Russian legislation were often out of harmony with the customs of the Kalmucks. All this made it necessary to promulgate clear and definite legal provisions satisfying both the requirements of Kalmuck life and the exigencies of Russian legislation. On the insistence of the Kalmuck Lamas and Noyons, Lieutenant (Regent) Chuchei Tundutov petitioned the Government for the revision of the Mongol-Oirat Regulations of 1640. As a result of this petition, in 1802 the Collegium of Foreign Affairs was instructed to take the matter in hand and ordered the Chief Comissar of the Kalmucks, Strahov, to send it a translation of the Regulations. The correspondence dragged on and it was only in 1821 that the Ministry of Foreign Affairs sent a copy of the Regulations to Chief Comissar Khakanov instructing him to submit it to the inspection of the "owners" and the clergy in order to discover which of the Regulations required amendment and extension. In 1822 a congress of Kalmuck Noyons, Zaisans, and Zamas and other members of the clergy was convoked at Zinzili (within 100 Km. of Astrakhan). The Congress examined the Regulations and amended and extended the provisions contained therein in conformity with the demands of the changed times and the customs of the Kalmucks which still remained in force. The resolutions of this Congress were called the Zinzili Resolutions. They were submitted to the Russian government for confirmation in 1825 whereupon the Special Commission for Kalmuck Affairs was instructed to compare the resolutions adopted at Zinzili, the provisions of the Regulations of 1640, and the opinions of the "owners" on the Zinzili Resolutions with the Russian legislation of the time. This work the Commission completed in 1827, but neither its work nor the Zinzili Resolutions ever received legislative sanction. Nevertheless, the Zinzili Resolutions, which were based on the customary law of the Kalmucks, are of great importance to us as a source in the study of the latter. Moreover, the Regulations of 1827 authorised the Ooloos Zargos to apply "the ancient Kalmuck Regulations" (under which may be understood the Regulations of 1640 as amended by the Congress of Zinzili) in cases concerning property.

In 1880, Professor Leontovich published a "Digest of Kalmuck Laws" on the basis of a list obtained by Baron Buler. This digest contained four records of Kalmuck law. In the first column of each page were printed the articles of the Oirat Regulations, in the second column the corresponding resolutions of the Zinzili Congress, in the third—the separate opinion of the two "owners" on the Zinzili Resolutions, and in the fourth the opinion of the Commission for Kalmuck Affairs on the material incorporated in the three preceding columns. Professor Leontovich published this digest with some alterations. He omitted the first column, i.e. the text of the Oirat Regulations and only referred to the numbers of the articles in his edition; and he did not repeat such of the Zinzili Resolutions as were quoted in the Digest several times in different articles, merely noting such repetitions. We shall use this unique printed edition of the Digest for the purposes of the present work.

The basis of the Digest was supplied by the Zinzili Resolutions which were in turn based on the Regulations of 1640, the laws of Donduk-Dashi, Kalmuck customary law and the canonical law of the Lamaists. The opinions of the Commission bore the influence of provisions of Russian law.

The Digest was divided into five sections, 28 chapters and 224 articles. Some chapters were also divided into paragraphs.

Section I, dealing with personal rights, contained three chapters: 1. On Priests (18 arts.); 2. On "Owners"; Officials and Zaisans (24 arts.); 3. On Parents, Children and Relations (10 arts.)

Section II. On Courts, contained two chapters: 1. On Courts in General and On Judges (51 arts.); 2. On Witnesses, the Oath, etc. (10 arts.)

Section III. On Public Order. Six chapters: 1. On Civil Order (12 arts.); 2. On Charitable Institutions (1 art.); 3. On Public Instruction (2 arts.); IV. On Compulsory Service (5 arts.); 5. On Carts, Carters and Travellers (7 arts.); 6. On Delegates (2 arts.)

Section IV, on Military Institutions, contained 10 articles.

Section V. On Religious Matters.[93] Sixteen chapters: 1. On Matters Relating to Religion (3 arts.); 2. On Marriage (11 arts.); 3. On Inheritance (3 arts.); 4. On Debts (1 art.); 5. On Cattle Breeding (4 arts.); 6. On Hunting and Trading (4 arts.); 7. On Games and Feasts (1 art.); 8. On Medical Matters (2 arts.); 8. On Premeditated Murder (9 arts.); 10. On Manslaughter and Self-defence (10 arts.); 11. On Theft and Robbery (4 arts.); 12. On Fugitives and Concealers of Fugitives (6 arts.); 13. On Theft (16 arts.); 14. On Swindling and Deceit (4 arts.); 15. On Rape, Insults, etc. (11 arts.); 16. Miscellaneous Matters (9 arts).

In making a survey of the Digest of Kalmuck Laws, we must first of all remember that it was based on the Mongol-Oirat Regulations of 1640, a great many of whose provisions (60 or 61) remained effective in the Digest. Among these were a number of provisions of criminal law and marriage law, some provisions relating to procedure (on tracking, search, etc.), to intercourse among the Kalmucks (succour to perishing people ,rescue of cattle, assistance to the thirsty, etc.) and to cattlebreeding and hunting.

A considerable part of the provisions of the Regulations was amended and extended. Some provisions were completely eliminated and new ones introduced in their place. All these alterations were effected by the Congress of Zinzili which adapted them to the requirements, customs and mode of life of the Kalmucks at the beginning of the XVIIIth century, while the Commission for Kalmuck Affairs co-ordinated them with Russian laws and culture.

In criminal law, in particular, considerable changes were effected in the system of punishments. In the Regulations the principal type of punishment was the heavy fine in cattle, graded in proportion to the size of the Kalmuck family fined. This was now mitigated to (in most cases) corporal punishment with the whip or rods, which became the principal penalty among the Kalmucks. Imprisonment and the institution of third theft were introduced, the punishments for personal insults and offences altered, and more important cases were tried by the Russian courts. Some, though minor, alterations were made in private law which comprised the stablest institutions of customary law. Thus the minimum marriage age and the provisions concerning the adoption of children were

---

93 This designation is misleading as it does not cover all the contents of the Section, which, in addition to matters having to do with religion contained provisions pertaining to civil and criminal law and other subjects.

altered. The provisions relating to succession in the line of descent received more detailed treatment and threw much light on this question which was insufficiently elucidated in the Regulations.

The system of courts was, of course, also altered.

The articles in the Regulations which concerned the relations of the tribes comprising the Oirat Federation were eliminated (by the Commission) as were all the military provisions, some of the punishments for personal insults and offences, and the ancient rulings of the Yassa of Jenghiz Khan and the Regulations providing for severe punishment (death) of gluttons who choked through over-eating and persons committing nuisances in the homes of others. In the sphere of private law, a few provisions were also eliminated, e.g. one relating to the redemption, by her relations, of a wife repudiated by her husband.

With the exception of the abovementioned amendments and extensions, the Digest as a whole, and especially its principal part—the Zinzili Resolutions, retained the fundamental features of Mongol customary law which was based on a common nomadic culture. Among such features were the prohibitions against separate (individual) migration, obligatory marriages for the continuation of the family, and the provisions relating to the use of land, particularly for cattlebreeding and its requirements, and the consequent absence or feeble development of the right of immovable property, the patriarchal character of clan and communal relations, etc. All these contributed to the common character of most of the provisions of the civil, criminal, and procedural provisions in the customary law of the Mongols, Buriats and Kalmucks.

CHAPTER II.

CONTENTS OF THE RECORDS OF MONGOL LAW.

The Great Yassa of Jenghiz Khan.

The fragments of the Great Yassa of Jenghiz Khan which have come down to us through Makrizi read as follows:

1. An adulterer is to be put to death without any regard as to whether he is married or not.

2. Whoever is guilty of sodomy is also to be put to death.

3. Whoever intentionally lies, or practises sorcery, or spies upon the behaviour of others, or intervenes between the two parties in a quarrel to help the one against the other is also to be put to death.

4. Whoever urinates into water or ashes is also to be put to death.

5. Whoever takes goods (on credit) and becomes bankrupt, then again takes goods and again becomes bankrupt, then takes goods again and yet again becomes bankrupt is to be put to death after the third time.

6. Whoever gives food or clothing to a captive without the permission of his captor is to be put to death.

7. Whoever finds a runaway slave or captive and does not return him to the person to whom he belongs is to be put to death.

8. When an animal is to be eaten, its feet must be tied, its belly ripped open and its heart squeezed in the hand until the animal dies; then its meat may be eaten; but if anyone slaughter an animal after the Mohammedan fashion, he is to be himself slaughtered.

9. If in battle, during an attack or a retreat, anyone let fall his pack, or bow, or any luggage, the man behind him must alight and return the thing fallen to its owner; if he does not so alight and return the thing fallen, he is to be put to death.

10. He (Jenghiz Khan) decided that no taxes or duties should be imposed upon the descendants of Ali-Bek, Abu-Ta-leb, without exception, as well as upon fakirs, readers of the Al-Koran, lawyers, physicians, scholars, people who devote themselves to prayer and asceticism, muezzins and those who wash the bodies of the dead.

11. He ordered that all religions were to be respected and that no preference was to be shown to any of them. All this he commanded in order that it might be agreeable to God.

12. He forbade his people to eat food offered by another until the one offering the food tasted of it himself, even though one be a prince (Emir) and the other a captive; he forbade them to eat anything in the presence of another without having invited him to partake of the food; he forbade any man to eat more than his comrades, and to step over a fire on which food was being cooked or a dish from which people were eating.

13. When a wayfarer passes by people eating, he must alight and eat with them without asking for permission, and they must not forbid him this.

14. He forbade them to dip their hands into water and ordered them to use some vessel for the drawing of water.

15. He forbade them to wash their clothes until they were completely worn out.

16. He forbade them to say of anything that it was unclean, and insisted that all things were clean and made no distinction between the clean and unclean.

17. He forbade them to show preference for any sect, to pronounce words with emphasis, to use honorary titles; when speaking to the Sultan or anyone else simply his name was to be used.

18. He ordered his successors to personally examine the troops and their armament before going to battle, to supply the troops with everything they needed for the campaign and to survey everything even to needle and thread, and if any of the soldiers lacked a necessary thing that soldier was to be punished.

19. He ordered women accompanying the troops to do the work and perform the duties of the men, while the latter were absent fighting.

20. He ordered the warriors, on their return from the campaign (battle) to carry out certain duties in the service of the Sultan.

21. He ordered them to present all their daughters to the Sultan at the beginning of each year that he might choose some of them for himself and his children.

22. He put Emirs at the head of the troops and appointed Emirs of thousands, of hundreds, and of tens.

23. He ordered that the oldest of the Emirs, if he had committed some offence, was to give himself up to the messenger sent by the

sovereign to punish him, even if he was the lowest of his servants; and prostrate himself before him until he had carried out the punishment prescribed by the sovereign, even if it be to put him to death.

24. He forbade Emirs to address themselves to anyone except the sovereign. Whoever addressed himself to anyone but the sovereign was to be put to death, and anyone changing his post without permission was also to be put to death.

25. He ordered the Sultan to establish permanent postal communications in order that he might be informed in good time of all the events in the country.

26. He ordered his son, Jagatai-ben-Jenghiz Khan to see that the Yassa was observed.

From Mirhond (or Mirhovend)

27. He ordered that soldiers be punished for negligence; and hunters who let an animal escape during a community hunt he ordered to be beaten with sticks and in some cases to be put to death.

28. In cases of murder (punishment for murder) one could ransom himself by paying fines which were: for a Mohammedan—40 golden coins (Balysh); and for a Chinese—one donkey.

From Ibn—Batuta.

29. The man in whose possession a stolen horse is found must return it to its owner and add nine horses of the same kind: if he is unable to pay this fine, his children must be taken instead of the horses, and if he have no children, he himself shall be slaughtered like a sheep.

From Vartang:

30. The Yassa of Jenghiz Khan forbids lies, theft and adultery and prescribes love of one's neighbour as one's self; it orders men not to hurt each other and to forget offences completely, to spare countries and cities which submit voluntarily, to free from taxes temples consecrated to God, and to respect the temples of God and their servants.

From Mahakia:

31. (The Yassa prescribes these rules:) to love one another, not to commit adultery, not to steal, not to give false witness, not to be a traitor, and to respect old people and beggars. Whoever violates these commands is put to death.

From various sources.

32. (The Yassa of Jenghiz Khan prescribes that) a man who chokes on food must be driven out of the camp and immediately killed; and whosoever puts his foot on the threshold of the tent of the commander of an army shall also be put to death.

33. If unable to abstain from drinking, a man may get drunk three times a month; if he does it more than three times he is culpable; if he gets drunk twice a month it is better; if once a month, this is still more laudable; and if one does not drink at all what can be better? But where can such a man be found? If such a man were found he would be worthy of the highest esteem.[1]

34. Children born of a concubine are to be considered as legitimate, and receive their share of the heritage according to the disposition of it made by the father. The distribution of property is to be carried out on the basis of the senior son receiving more than the junior, the younger son inheriting the household of the father. The seniority of children depends upon the rank of their mother; one of the wives must always be the senior, this being determined chiefly by the time of her marriage.

35. After the death of his father, a son may dispose of the father's wives, all except his mother; he may marry them or give them in marriage to others.

36. All except the legal heirs are strictly forbidden to make use of any of the property of the deceased.[2]

The Maxims of Jenghiz Khan.[3]

1. From the goodness of severity the stability of the government.

2. If the Grandees, Knights and Beks of the children of the many sovereigns to come will not strictly observe the Yassa, the state will be shaken and collapse. People will again eagerly look for a Jenghiz Khan but will not find him.

3. He also said: "The Beks of a tümen (10,000 kibitkas), of a thousand and of hundred who come to hear our thoughts at the beginning and at the end of the year and then return may command the troops; the state of those who sit in their yurts and do not hear these thoughts is like that of a stone that falls into deep water or an arrow shot into the reeds—they disappear. It is not fit for such men to command."

1 We consider this fragment to belong to the Maxims of Jenghiz-Khan (*v.* Maxim 20).

2 On ppg. 214-216 of his "Jenghiz Khan, Emperor of All Men", Harold Lamb quotes 22 rules of the Yassa taken from the "Abbregé Chronologique de l'Histoire Ottomane" of Pétis de la Croix (1768). These twenty two rules do not correspond to those quoted here. Upon investigation the present writer has ascertained that the author took some tales of the customs of the Mongols, gave them the form of rules, and presented them as "fragments of the Yassa" No doubt Makrizi was unknown to him.

3 *v.* Rashid Ed-din, "History of Jenghiz Khan", II, ppg. 120-131. Maxims 1, 15, 20, 21, 26 and 30 are given in the present work in abbreviated form.

4. He also said: "Whoever can manage his own house well can also manage an estate, whoever can keep ten men in order in accordance with conditions may be given a thousand and a tumen and he will also keep them in order."

5. He also said: "Whoever can clean his own house can rid the country of thieves."

6. He also said: "Any Bek who cannot keep his ten men in order will, with his wife and children, be considered by us as guilty, and another man from his ten will be chosen and appointed Bek. In the same manner Beks of a hundred, a thousand and a tumen shall be dealt with."

7. He also said: "Any word on which three well-informed men are agreed may be spoken anywhere, otherwise it cannot be relied upon. Compare your words and the words of others with those of well-informed men, and if they agree you may speak them, otherwise you should by no means say them."

8. He also said: "Whoever goes to a senior must not say a word until the senior has addressed him; then let him answer according to the question. If he speaks first and is listened to it is well; otherwise he is like a man forging cold iron."

9. He also said: "Any horse that runs well when it is fat will also run well when it is fairly stout or fairly thin. Such a horse can be said to be a good one. But no horse can be said to be good that runs well in only one of these conditions."

10. He also said: "The senior Beks who will command, and also all warriors, must, in the same way as they distinguish themselves when they occupy themselves with hunting, each distinguish his name and glory in war; and let each one always, praying fervently to Almighty God and keeping a meek heart, wish for the decoration of eight sides so that, by the power of the Lord ancient in days, it will be possible to take four limits in one place."

11. He also said: "Amongst people one must be like a calf, small and silent; but in the time of war one must be as a hungry falcon when it is hunting; he must go into battle shouting."

12. He also said: "As word that is said is considered to have been said seriously; if it is said jokingly it must not be carried out."

13. He also said: "As a man knows himself so should he know others."

14. He also said: "A man is not like the sun and therefore cannot appear everywhere before people; when the master is away

hunting, or at war, the wife must keep the household in good condition and order so that if a messenger or a guest should happen to enter the house he may see that everything is in order; and she must prepare a good meal so that the guest may not want for anything. Thus she will win a good reputation for her husband and exalt his name in the assemblies like a mountain that rears its peak. Good husbands are known by their good wives. If a wife be stupid and dull, wanting in reason and orderliness, she makes obvious the badness of her husband. There is an adage-verse: 'In a house everything resembles its master.' "

15. In affairs caution is necessary.

16. He also said: "We go hunting and kill many mountain bulls. We go to war and kill many enemes. When Almighty God makes the ways smooth and work easy, men forget themselves and change."

17. He also said: "There is no hero equal to Yesun-Bey, and no man as skilful as he is. But not knowing fatigue and hardships in the campaign he thinks that everyone can have his endurance. Yet others cannot stand so much. Therefore Yesun-Bey is not fit to be chief over his troops. Only a man who feels hunger and thirst and by this estimates the feelings of others is fit to be a commander of troops, as he will see that the warriors do not suffer from hunger and thirst and that the four-legged beasts do not starve. The meaning of this is that the campaign and its hardships must be in proportion with the strength of the weakest of the warriors."

18. He also said: "As our merchants who import brocade garments and other good wares, expecting to make a profit, become very experienced in these goods and garments, so the Beks must teach boys to shoot arrows well and to ride well and must train the boys in warlike deeds in order to make them as fearless and daring as the merchants are cunning in their trade."

19. He also said: "After us the descendants of our clan will wear gold embroidered garments, eat rich and sweet food, ride fine horses, and embrace beautiful women but they will not say that they owe all this to their fathers and elder brothers, and they will forget us and those great times."

20. He also said: "If unable to abstain from drinking, a man may get drunk three times a month; if he does it more than three times he is culpable; if he gets drunk twice a month it is better; if once a month, this is still more laudable; and if one does not drink at all what can be better? But where can such a man be found? If such a man were found he would be worthy of the highest esteem."

21. He also said: ". . . . Lord ancient in days! You know and are aware that formerly Altan Khan raised a rebellion and that he began the enmity. He slew the innocent Ukin-Barchach and Ambagai-Kaan whom the tribe of Tatars seized and sent to him and who were the elder brothers of my sire and grandsire. I am athirst for their blood in retribution and vengeance. If you know that my intention is just, send me power and victory from above and order that your angels, men, peris and spirits above give me their aid. . ."

22. He also said: "My bowmen and warriors loom like thick forests: their wives, sweethearts and maidens shine like red flames. My task and intention is to sweeten their mouths with gifts of sweet sugar, to decorate their breasts, backs and shoulders with garments of brocade, to seat them on good geldings, give them to drink from pure and sweet rivers, provide their beasts with good and abundant pastures, and to order that the great roads and highways that serve as ways for the people be cleared of garbage, tree-stumps and all bad things; and not to allow dirt and thorns in the tents."

23. He also said: "If anyone of our clan act in violation of the approved Yassa let him be admonished verbally; if he do it again, let him be persuaded by eloquence; if he does it a third time, let him be sent to the remote place Baljuin-Khuljur. When he returns thence, he will be attentive. But if he be not brought to his senses, let him be put in irons and imprisoned. If he come out of imprisonment good-tempered and reasonable, well and good. If not, let his relations assemble and deliberate as to what is to be done with him."

24. He also said: "The commanders of a tümen, of a thousand and of a hundred must each keep their troops in readiness and in order; so that whenever a decree or order reaches them, they may mount their horses without delay, even at night."

25. He also said: "Every boy born in Bargudjin Tukum, on the Onon and Kerulen, will be wise, manly and heroic without guidance, instruction or experience: he will be knowing and comely; and every maiden born there will, without combing or adornment, be handsome and beautiful."

26. He also said: "After the return of the messenger (he had sent) Muhuli-Govan asked: 'When you came to pay your respects to Jenghiz Khan and reported my speech to him what did he do?' The other replied: 'He bent his thumb.' He asked: 'Did he also put out a finger for me.'—He answered: 'He did.' Then Muhuli said: 'For this reason it is not in vain that I serve to the very death and demonstrate the greatest energy and eagerness.' He asked also: 'For whom

else did he put out a finger?' The putting out of a finger is on the road to exaltation. He said: 'He put out a finger for Burji, Burgul, Kublai, Jilogen, Harajar, Jadai, Badai and Kyshlyk, to them all, and said: 'They all served, before and behind me, skilfully with aid and reinforcement, they shot arrows well and kept pedigreed horses on the lead, hunting birds on their hands, and hunting dogs on the leash.' "

27. He also said: "Once Bala-Halaja, who was one of the honoured Beks, asked him: 'You are called the master of power and a hero: what signs of conquest and victory are there to be seen on your hand?' Jenghiz Khan condescended to answer: 'Before I assumed the throne of the kingdom I was once riding along one of the roads. Six men who had laid an ambush at the bridge-passage made an attempt upon me. When I heard them I drew my sabre and rushed to the attack. They rained arrows upon me, but none of the arrows reached their target and not a single one touched me. I put them to death with my sabre and rode on unharmed. On my return it was necessary for me to pass by these slain. Their six geldings wandered masterless. I led away all six geldings.' "

28. He also said: "Once I was riding with Burji. Twelve men sat in ambush on a peak of the mountain range. Burji rode behind. I did not await him and, relying on my own power and strength, rushed to attack them. Suddenly all twelve of them shot off arrows and their arrows flew by me on all sides, but I proceeded to the attack when suddenly one arrow struck me in the mouth. I fell and was rendered senseless by this severe wound. At this moment Burji sped up and saw me and the fact that the wound had rendered me like a man in agony, jerking my legs and rolling over like a ball. He immediately warmed some water and brought it. I washed my throat and spat out the clotted blood. My soul, which had left my body, once more returned to it and I recovered feeling and motion. I rose and rushed to the attack. They were frightened by my hardiness, threw themselves down from that mountain, and gave up the ghost. The reason for the status of Tarkhan awarded to Burji-Noyon is that at such a time he made a laudable effort."

29. He also said: "During his youth Jenghiz Khan rose one morning extremely early. Several of the dark hairs in his locks became white. Those near him asked: 'O King! Your age is youthfully happy and you have not yet reached the beginning of old age. How is it that a trace of greyness has appeared in your locks?' He said in reply: 'Since the Almighty God has willed to make me the elder and

chief of tümens and thousands and to raise through me the banner of well-doing, he has also put on me the sign of old age (greyness) which is also the sign of seniority.' "

30. He also said: "It is delightful and felicitous for a man to subdue rebels and conquer and extirpate his enemies, to take all they possess, to cause their servants to cry out, to make tears run down their faces and noses, to ride their pleasant-paced geldings, to make the bellies and navels of their wives his bed and bedding, to admire their rosy cheeks, to kiss them and to suck their red lips."

Maxims of the Jenghizids.

Guyuk Khan:

The duty of a Mongol is "to carry out my will, to come wherever I shall call him, to go wheresoever I shall order, and to put to death whomsoever I shall name."

Batu:

"Whoever violates the Yassa shall lose his head."

The Ancient Tsaadjin Bichik.

The fragments of this ancient record that have come down to us are very scanty.

Their contents are as follows:

1. According to the Tsaadjin Bichik, adultery committed with the mistresses (concubines) of clerics (priests) was not punishable.

2. Whoever commits adultery with the wife of a prince must, in sign of repentance, offer a goat and its kid.

3. Whoever commits ordinary adultery must give to the "Hörnerträger" (deceived husband)[4] a four year old horse; and the adultress must present a three year old to the judge.

4. Whoever finds another man with his female slave may take everything from him, his horse, his money and all that he has about him and turn him out naked; but he must not punish the slave.

---

4 The expression "Hornertrager" was understood, and translated, by Spassky as "bearer of the trumpet" (*Sibirsky Vestnik*, 1819, VI). Alinge, however, understands it to mean "a deceived husband" ("Mongolische Gesetze", 1934, pg. 53). The latter version seems to us to be the more correct.

Incidentally, in the work referred to above, Mr. Alinge often made use of information contained in the Author's "Mongol Law", 1931 (in Russian), unfortunately not always acknowledging its direct source. (*v.* ppg. 31-33, 37-38, 111-112, etc.). Even where Mr. Alinge did make acknowledgment, the Author's name was garbled ("Riaz" instead of Riasanovsky).

5. As soon as an adolescent is grown and can work for himself he leaves the tutelage of his father and may, if he wishes, demand that a part of the herd be given to him, and leave his father in order to become an independent subject of the legitimate prince.

6. When two Kalmucks fight and one of them tears the other's queue, or even tears it completely off, it is a punishable crime because the queue belongs to the prince and serves as a sign of subjecton; but if a man has other loose hair on his head, anyone can pull it with impunity, because this is considered to be his own hair not belonging to the prince.

7. When a woman sits in her usual place in the Yurt on the right of the entrance near the hearth, at the foot of her husband's bed, nobody can touch her; but she can abuse a stranger and even throw a log of wood or any utensil at him if she likes. But if in the quarrel she dares leave her place or step outside the yurt, she loses her rights and may be punished for insult.

8. If a woman go to the prince and ask him to remit a fine imposed upon her or her people, small fines are usually remitted out of respect for her sex, and large ones reduced by half.

The Kalmucks spared women and all insults to women were more severely punished.[5]

The Mongol-Oirat Regulations of 1640 and the Supplementary Provisions of Galdan Khun Taidji.

Attitude Towards Religion and the Clergy.

Provisions relating to religion and the clergy were not numerous in the Regulations and were all aimed at the protection of the faith and its servants.

Thus the law prescribed that Ongons (idols) be removed and that persons resisting such removal be fined (111). Persons inviting a male or female shaman were fined one horse and the shaman also had to pay a fine of a horse (111). A shaman was fined five horses for casting a spell over the house of a noble and two horses if he bewitched the habitation of a commer. For killing a widgeon, a sparrow and a dog for ritual purposes, the offender was fined a horse (112). The Regulations ruled that "the clergy have the right to take one of ten men", i.e. of every ten males in a family one had to be consecrated to God, but his

5 In arts. 6 and 8 mention is made of the Kalmucks, a modern designation. The reason for this is that Pallas considered these provisions as still effective among the Kalmucks of his time.

relations could ransom the person so dedicated by paying 5 animals if he were a prince and 3 if a commoner (9). For arbitrary violation of the monastic vows and renunciation of the clerical dignity a heavy fine was collected—a half of the offender's cattle and other property (18). Messengers (Elchis) travelling on the affairs of religion and government had the preference above all others (16). Anyone who took carts from the Lamas and Bandis (novices) was fined a cow, and whoever took a horse consecrated to Buddha for his cart was fined a horse (19). Insults by word or deed offered to the clergy were severely punished (art. 17, *cf.* art. 20). The looting of an Aimak belonging to the clergy was punished with a heavy fine (5). It was forbidden to kill red wild ducks, sparrows and dogs, the fine for doing so being one horse (Leont. Ed., art. 142).

Intertribal Relations, Organization of Attack and Defence.

In the first place the Regulations served to adjust the mutual relations of the tribes comprising the Oirat military alliance. They forbade the respective princes to pillage the tribes forming the federation and ordered the Mongols and Oirats to punish those guilty of such pillage with their united forces (art. 1, 2). They also provided for the distribution of the deserters from the Bargu-Buriat and Khoit tribes among the Mongols and Oirats (3), and the repelling of enemies by the united forces (4), established severe punishments for those not reporting the appearance of an enemy or failing to sally forth when the alarm was given (4,13). They forbade anyone to harbour deserters from other tribes or to kill them (6, 8,99) and fixed penalties for the violation of the Regulations (10).

The military and predatory character of the Federation, and indeed of the whole mode of life of the nomadic Mongol tribes, was made sufficiently evident by the provisions quoted above, and was further emphasised by a series of other regulations dealing with the organization of attack and defence against enemies.

Thus forty Kibitkas (households) were obliged to provide two cuirasses (art. 37). When the alarm was given, all were to appear before their princes, anyone failing to do so being punished with a heavy fine. Persons running away from battle were subjected to ignominy, being dressed in a woman's sleeveless jacket (11). For not reporting the approach of a considerable enemy a penalty of extreme severity was imposed—death, complete confiscation of property, and banishment of the descendants of the culprit (13). If an enemy looted a camp or drove away a herd, anyone seing this, or hearing of it, was bound to pursue the enemy and rescue the cattle, failure to do this being punished by the confiscation of half his property; while whoever rescued a herd was rewarded with half the rescued cattle or property. If a rescuer died (was killed, or injured), compensation was paid to his family in accordance with the established rule (15). Persons rescuing cattle from a thief by fighting received a reward of a stallion for every five animals so saved, or for 4 or 3 animals, a three year old mare. If cattle were rescued without fighting, a reward was also given but of less value (130). For saving the lives of princes, high officials and others in wartime, the rescuer was given the rank of Tarkhan; for abandoning a prince in distress the punishment was death and confiscation of property (12). Whoever killed an enemy in battle received his cuirass, while those who assisted him in the killing received the armour, helmet and other equipment of the slain enemy (50). For the rescue of a person fleeing from the enemy, the reward was two horses and a cuirass; for the rescue of one who went too far into the enemy's lines, nine animals from the spoils of battle (51). For unintentionally killing an ally in wartime the punishment was a fine of nine animals (54); for a similar killing during a hunt the fine was half that imposed for ordinary homicide (55).

Cattle Breeding and Hunting.

Apart from wars and raids the chief occupations of the Mongols which served them as a means of sustenance were cattle-breeding and hunting. Cattle, being the main source of wealth among the Mongols, served as a unit of exchange (instead of money), and a medium for the payment of fines, etc. In the records of Mongol law, the idea of property was usually expressed by the words "cattle and property", *e.g.* "to deprive of cattle and property" (confiscate all property), "take half of the cattle and property" (*cf.* Art. 15 of the Regulations and Part III, art. 183 of the Code of the Chinese Board of Foreign Relations, 1815.) It is therefore natural that the Regulations of 1640 contained a series of provisions dealing with cattle-breeding. Theft of cattle was severely punished (see further.)

When stray cattle joined a herd, the owner of the herd was obliged to give due notice of this fact within 24 hours. After this the stray animals could be ridden, sheared and branded on the ears, but a person appropriating stray cattle without notification was forced to pay fines to the owner (for riding the stray—a three year old mare; for shearing—5 animals; for branding—nine animals) (66).

For accidentally killing the animals of another, the fine was the replacement of the cattle killed with the addition of a horse (92); while intentional killing of another's cattle was punished in the same way as theft (102). The rescuer of cattle that were being driven away was specially rewarded; while anyone who failed to report the driving away of cattle or to pursue the perpetrator was severely punished (15). For the rescue of cattle that were being driven away, as well as for saving cattle from wild animals, fire or drowning, rewards were prescribed (57,80,82,134). The carcass of an animal was considered the property of the animal's owner because it could be used for food, and its appropriation by others was punished by a fine (68,81,113).

Hunting was the second peaceful pursuit of the nomads, who hunted by driving (beating) or stalking the game. During a drive, order was strictly observed. Whoever, during beating, passed or stood by the side of another hunter was fined 5 animals. A person who got out of line and advanced three bowshots ahead of the others was fined a horse; two bowshots—a sheep; and one bowshot—5 arrows. When the escape of an animal with an arrow in it was announced and someone then caught it and concealed the fact, he was fined 5 animals. If anyone concealed an animal wounded but not bearing an arrow, he was fined also (103). For killing the hunting bird of another, the horse was taken (103). For killing the hunting bird of another, the offender was fined one horse. For accidentally killing a man during a hunt, a half of the fine for ordinary homicide was imposed (55). If anyone was killed or maimed by an automatic crossbow, the installation of which had been announced, the owner of the crossbow was bound to pay compensation; while if no notification had been given, he was also forced to pay an additional fine (79).

The Regulations contained no special provisions concerning fishing, but in article 107 nets and snares for fishing were mentioned; it being prescribed that for the theft of these, the culprit have his finger cut off or pay a fine of five animals.

Postal Communications and Compulsory Cartage.

Permanent postal communications were established in Mongolia by Jenghiz Khan (Fr. 25 of the Yassa) and systematised by the Mongol-Oirat Regulations of 1640. Owing to the absence of good roads, the necessity of fulfilling the duty of messengers and the obligatory supply of carts for the conveying of state and communal messages were a rather heavy burden on the population.[6]

The population was by law required to supply the fixed three carts. Messengers sent on religious and administrative affairs had the preference over other messengers with respect to the supply of carts and forage. Messengers travelling in connection with the illness of the chief prince or his wife, or the attack of a strong enemy, were to be

6 The Regulations of the Chinese Board of Foreign Relations (1789 and 1815) even provided for special penal deportation to certain provinces for hard labour at the postal stations.

supplied with carts even if it was not the turn of the person called upon to do so to supply these; and failure to conform with this ordinance was punished by the heavy fine of nine nines of animals (16). Messengers on unimportant (communal) business could take carts only from their Aimaks; if one took a cart from another Aimak he was fined a three year old mare. Anyone pulling a messenger off his horse was fined 5 animals. Anyone refusing to give a cart, or taking one by force and beating the carter, was fined a horse. Anyone fraudulently taking a cart under the pretence of being a messenger, and received forage, was fined nine animals or punished with five strokes and fined nine animals; if he committed only one of these offences, he was fined 5 animals (23). Anyone conniving with an ill-intentioned person and giving him a cart and forage was fined seven times nine animals (77).

Clan Life and Mutual Relations.

The Kibitkas (yurts, households) of the Western Mongols were organized into Aouls or Hoshuns (15-125—Khotons in the Kalmuck language), the Aouls into Aimaks (23), the Aimaks into Otoks (122—Oolooses), the Otoks into tribes and the tribes into the Oirat Federation. The nomadic Mongols lived a clan life. The Aoul (camp) represented a large family whose nearest kinsmen lived in the neighbouring Aouls which together with it formed the Aimak; an Otok united several Aimaks and formed a clan (of several clans) which was part of the tribe. A tribe was usually organized as a principality. For the maintenance of the clans the Regulations prescribed obligatory marriages: of every forty kibitkas four had to marry their sons annually and ten people united to support one who was being married (art. 37). The Regulations forbade anyone to wander in Hoshuns not his own, and ruled that unattached persons so wandering be collected and organized into new Aimaks and Otoks (125). It was forbidden not only for individuals but also to whole Aimaks to change their habitations, and fugitives were to be returned to their Aimaks (112,133). The organization of the family was strictly patriarchal, the whole family being subordinated to its head, the master, the lord of the house. The power of the master was very great. If a husband killed a wife whom he had rejected he was fined 5 nines of animals, the same fine as that imposed for the killing of a slave (32,33). The brothers and Aimak-brothers (relatives) of a deserted wife had the right to redeem her (116). The penalties for insults offered to elder relatives and for beating and killing them were more severe than those for similar offences against others (17—30). Property, as a rule, belonged to the entire family but, as appears from the ancient Tsaadjin Bichik, a son able to provide for himself (*i.e.* who had come of age) could demand his share of the property and found his own family,[7] and individual property also existed (see further). Kinship was recognized only in the male line but certain bonds of relationship with the family of the mother also existed. Thus debt obligations between maternal uncles and their nephews were not recognized and theft from relations on the mother's side was not considered a crime, being compensated for only by payment of the amount stolen or a gift to the victim (118). The Regulations recognized the common responsibility of the clan for the deeds of any of its members, *e.g.* article 13 provided for the deportation of the offspring of anyone failing to report the approach of a strong enemy, while article 15 imposed payment of damages upon an offender's brothers.

In the matter of mutual relations, the legislation of the epoch of the Oirat Federation prescribed mutual aid and benevolence. A decree of Galdan Khan ordered the administrative heads of Otoks, under threat of severe punishment, to see that the Demchis of 50 Kibitkas took care of the poor and homeless. When the means for this were lacking, the Demchi was bound to inform the supervisor of the cattle, whose duty it then became to look after the indigent, and if he too was unable to do so, the higher authorities were to be informed. If, through the negligence of anyone entrusted with their care, any of the poor died, the punishment was the same as that for ordinary homicide (122). Whoever failed to offer Koumiss (fermented mare's milk) to a thirsty person was fined a sheep (87). Anyone refusing hospitality for the night was fined a three year old mare (24). The Regulations prescribed that assistance be given to couples about to be married (37). Rewards were given for the rescue of perishing people, cattle and property generally, for the rescue of a man from fire or water (5 animals); for rescuing a slave—a horse; for saving a suit of armour or a cuirass—a horse or a horse and a sheep; for saving a yurt with property—a horse and a cow (57). For curing a sick person, attending a woman in labour, or reviving a man from a swoon, payment was made in accordance with previous arrangement, and if no arrangement had been made it was fixed at one horse (83). For assistance given to a child who had got under a horse a sheep was to be given (114).

The treatment of women could be divided into two categories, within and outside the home. The patriarchal mode of life brought with it the subordinate position of the woman in the family. Not only a daughter, but also a female pupil, was dealt with at the discretion of the head of a family (40). A husband killing a wife he had rejected paid a fine equal to that imposed for the killing of a slave (33). A rejected

---

7 This was apparently confirmed by Art. 34 of the Regulations of 1640.

wife could be redeeemed (by her relatives) for a few head of cattle—the required number ranging from a horse and a camel for a person of low rank to nine head for the wife of a noble (100). Whoever killed a husband in battle received his wife as a reward (50), etc. With respect to the position of the woman outside her family, however, we observe here the same humane principles as those followed by the ancient Tsaadjin Bichik. For instance, if a woman took some of the wine and mutton she was carrying to others, it was overlooked (*i.e.* she was not made responsible for it); and if she took a great deal, she had to make good only a half of the missing quantity (65). Anyone tearing the hair of a woman or the tassel off her hat was fined nine animals. Anyone causing the abortion (a miscarriage) of a child was fined as many nines of animals as the child was months old. Freedom of behaviour with women and girls was punished: for kissing a girl over ten years old or for touching her breasts punishment and fines were inflicted (73).

Private Law.

Property Law.—Among the Mongol tribes of the XVII-th century, the primitive clan communism which had previously obtained had evolved considerably, undergoing great changes in the process. Individual property was beginning to be recognized. Although some of the provisions of the Regulations related to common family property and to the collective responsibility of the clan (13,15,116), they did not exclude the possession of private property, not only among the townspeople but also among the rural population.

The right to immovable property did not as yet exist. Land was apportioned for use to tribes or clans (Otoks); and entire Aimaks, as well as individuals, were forbidden to change their camp-sites within the Otoks (132). Each clan and each family had to camp on the land allotted to it, which was regarded as the common property of the whole clan. The right to individual moveable property did, however, exist. The conception of the individual proprietor, the owner of property, meets us at every step in the Regulations: the master of a thing had the right to its use, damage done to property was made good to its master by the person causing it. An animal killed by the projectile from an automatic crossbow was the property of the owner of the crossbow (79). If anyone took possession of a stray head of cattle on the false pretence that it belonged to him, he had to pay 5 head to the rightful owner upon discovery (92). Anyone killing a man wearing a cuirass was entitled to the cuirass (50). Anyone giving a helmet to another was entitled to receive for it five animals (58).

Article 119 established the principle of reclamation of movable property as follows: the owner of stray cattle had the right to reclaim it (in the presence of reliable witnesses), but if the cattle were found in the possession of one who had come by them by *bona fide* purchase, the original owner was entitled to only the forepart, the better part of the carcass, while the buyer was given the rump, the inferior part.

The above provisions and other similar ones were, of course, consistent with the institution of common family property in which the head of the household often acted as the representative of the interests of the family in which the real property rights were vested. This was, undoubtedly, to a certain extent the state of affairs among the Mongols in the XVII-th century. On the other hand, the owner of a thing and the personal liability of individuals for damages were constantly mentioned while common family liability and the common rights and obligations of the clan were met with comparatively rarely (13,15,116). We meet also individual rewards for military valour (50,51) which were set apart from the common booty and could hardly be considered family property, and such facts as the possession by sons of property separated from that of the father (27-30) and the division of the inheritance. All these facts lead us to the conclusion that in the epoch with which we are dealing individual right to movable property was already considerably developed and property acquired by the labour and trade of the individual existed alongside of the elements of clan life and family property.

Obligations.—Relations arising from obligations were not satisfactorily developed and the Regulations contained only a few provisions dealing with them. Article 38 provided for idemnification for a thing borrowed and lost, article 119 mentioned purchase and sale, and debts were also dealt with (63,127). The Regulations also contained certain cases of *negotiorum gestio.* With respect to the recovery of debts the following provisions obtained: a creditor wanting repayment of his loan was bound to declare such desire to the debtor thrice in the presence of witness and to inform the Shulenga,[8] after which he had the right to seize the amount owed (in cattle or property). If the Shulenga was not informed the creditor was fined a horse. If the creditor, without previous declaration, seized the debtor's property in broad daylight, he lost his right to repayment of the loan, and if he seized the property at night, he was fined nine head of cattle (63). The Regulations did not fix a prescription for debts but one of the supplementary decrees of Galdan Khan declared all debts incurred previous to the death of Galdan's

---

8 The Shulenga was the chief of 20 Kibitkas.

father, Batur Khun-Taidji (1654) to have lapsed, while debts contracted after that year were recognized (*i.e.* their repayment could be claimed) only if they had been contracted in the presence of witnesses (127).

Family Law.—The M. O. Regulations recognized polygamy (art. 33). As stated above, the Regulations instituted obligatory marriage in the interests of the perpetuation of the clan, four of every forty kibitkas being compelled to marry their sons yearly and ten persons (Kibitkas) obliged to support the sons so married (37).[9] The marriage age for a girl was fixed at 15 years (or, more exactly "above 15 years"—art. 36). When a girl was to be married an idemnity (ransom) was paid to her parents or guardians (this was called Kalim among the Buriats) and a dowry was given her. The amounts of the Kalim and dowry depended upon the social standing of the parties to the marriage (35,40). For instances, in cases of betrothal among Tabunang princes the Kalim for the bride consisted of 30 'precious things", 150 head of cattle and 400 sheep. Among commoners only 2 camels, 10 head of cattle and 15 sheep were required. The dowry generally corresponded to the Kalim in amount, this being commanded by the Regulations in the case of princes, but the dowry could be diminished by mutual consent of the parties. The son in law was bound to make a gift equal in value to the dowry (in accordance with the rule concerning the betrothals of Shulengas and members of the middle classes.)

The dowry of the daughter of a Demchi was to consist of 10 sewed gowns, 20 unsewed gowns, a saddle, a bridle, a fur coat, a sleeveless jacket, and two horses. For a Shulenga's daughter five sewn and 15 unsewn gowns were required, as well as a camel and a horse. For persons of the middle and lower classes the amounts fixed were 4 sewn and 10 unsewn gowns, a camel and a horse; and a horse, camel, fur coat, sleeveless jacket, saddle and bridle respectively (ar. 35). When the betrothed maiden reached the age of 20, the father of the fiancé (the future father-in-law) was to be notified; and if the marriage did not thereafter take place, the prince was to be informed, and the girl could be given in marriage to someone else. Whoever gave a daughter in marriage without informing the prince had to return the cattle paid him as Kalim, and was in addition dealt with according to the law. If a girl whose betrothal feast had already been arranged happened to die, her dowry still went to the bridegroom; but if the feast had not yet taken place the bridegroom had the right to ask for repayment of half the Kalim (37). Parents marrying a betrothed daughter to a man other than her fiancé were fined in accordance with their rank, the amount of

9 According to article 47 in Leontovich's edition "if anyone failed to marry through lack of support (means), the ten Kibitkas to which he belonged were fined."

the fine being five nines of cattle for a noblemen; three nines and a camel for middle-class persons; and nine head of cattle and a camel for persons of low degree. The original fiancé had, moreover, the right to claim the bride with Kalim paid for her, and if the marriage was contracted without the consent of the girl's parents, the second bridegroom (husband) not only lost the bride but also paid her parents a triple fine as an idemnity (39). The fines for persons persuading a betrothed girl to elope with them were as follows: for nobles—7 head of cattle, for middle-class persons—5 head, and for members of the lower classes a camel (41). Polygamy was permitted (33). Owing to the patriarchal structure of the family, the power of the husband and father was extremely great. Anyone killing a man in war had the right to take his wife as a reward (50). A man killing his rejected wife was fined only five nines of cattle (33). Whoever wished to redeem a wife rejected by her husband could do so by paying nine head of cattle and a precious thing for the wife of a nobleman, 5 head for the wife of a member of the middle class, and a horse and a camel for the wife of a low class commoner (100). If anyone seduced the wife of another without any resistance on the latter's part, the husband had the right to seize his wife and the abductor's cattle. Also the wife's brothers could redeem her by paying an amount equal to the Kalim given for her, and if the brothers were unable to do this, her Aimak-brothers (kinsmen) could pay nine head of cattle for her. If the latter also were too poor to do this, the matter came up before the prince for decision (116).

The Regulations permitted adoption, or more exactly the taking of a child for the purpose of bringing it up. A girl brought up by persons other than her parents was at the disposal of her foster-parents (41). If parents wished to return to their house a daughter reared by others, and if such a daughter was above 9 and under 15 years old, they were obliged to pay compensation of nine head of cattle, and if the girl had been badly reared, they were to pay only half of this. If the daughter was over 15 years old, redemption could not be effected and she was bound to remain with those who had brought her up. When such a girl was married, the father and foster-parents received equal parts of her Kalim and were jointly responsible for providing her with a dowry. A foster-son could leave his foster-parents and take his sons with him, but was obliged to pay idemnity for his wife and daughters (40,117).

The Regulations permitted correctional punishment within the home but limited it. If a father beat his son or his daughter-in-law to correct a fault, it was not considered an offence, but if he beat them unjustly, he was fined nine head of cattle if the beating was severe, 5 head for one less severe, and a horse for a light chastisement. If a father beat his daughter-in-law badly, he was fined two nines, if he beat her lightly, 5 head (29). The property of a father who killed his son was confiscated (31). Crimes and offences committed by children against their parents and by juniors against their seniors generally were much more severely punished (27).

Law of Inheritance.—The Regulations contained only one short provision relating to inheritance: the father was to divide the inheritance among his children in accordance with the established rule and if the father became impoverished he could take (retain) one animal out of every five (34).

Only sons could inherit property. The daughters did not have any part in legacies but received their dowries. The manner in which the inheritance was divided among the sons was not indicated in the Regulations, but it seems to have been done in accordance with established rules and customs. Article 34 seems to have provided for not only the division of the legacy after death but also the allotment of part of the inheritance to sons during the lifetime of the father (cf. the anticipated inheritance of old Russian law, vol. X, part I) as appears from the conclusion of the article which stated that if the father became impoverished he could take for himself one animal out of each five. This provision would have been meaningless if the inheritance was only divided after death and only makes sense if the inheritance was apportioned during the father's life. Moreover the ancient Tsaadjin Bichik dealt with the right of a grown son to claim his share of the inheritance.

CRIMINAL LAW.

The System of Punishments.—The penal provisions of the Mongol-Oirat Regulations of 1640 were considerably milder than those of the Great Yassa. Capital punishment, so often prescribed by the Yassa, was almost completely lacking in the latter Code (it was applied in only three cases in connection with the defence of the State). All investigators of the Regulations have attributed this fact to the mitigating influence of Buddhism (Lamaism) which rejects capital punishment. Without denying this benficent influence, we must point out that the penal provisions of the ancient Tsaadjin Bichik were already considerably milder than those of the Great Yassa, although promulgated before the Mongols had adopted Buddhism. Punishment by maihem occurred more often but could usually be commuted to a fine. Imprisonment, or any kind of confinement or deprivation of liberty generally, was seldom applied by the nomad peoples as a punishment because it was totally out of harmony with their character and mode of life. Indeed, we find punishment by confinement mentioned only once in the entire Regulations (art. 123, ". . . . put in irons"). Confiscation of property was in some cases practised. But the chief punishment used in the Regulations was the fine which varied greatly according to the offence and the social status of the offender and victim. With respect to severity, the penalties provided for in the Regulations may be classified as follows:

1. Capital punishment with confiscation of all property (ruin) and expulsion of offspring—inflicted upon persons who failed to report to the prince the approach of a considerable enemy of which they had knowledge (13), or who, having heard the alarm, did not come to the assistance of the prince (14).

2. Capital punishment—inflicted on persons abandoning a prince in danger (12).

3. Severing of the limbs—for failing to report a theft in his jurisdiction a chief of ten Kibitkas was liable to have his hands cut off.[10] For the theft of a series of specified household articles and of hunting equipment, the culprit lost a finger although this punishment could be commuted to a fine of five animals ("if he grudges the finger, take from him five animals"—art. 107). If one wife killed another wife, her husband was obliged to pay a heavy fine (as for homicide) to the relatives of the victim, or cut off the ears of the killer and give her in marriage to another at his discretion (33).

4. Flogging with the knout[11]—for fraudulently posing as a messenger and making use of the carts and forage provided for such persons (23); for the beating of a father-in-law by a daughter-in-law (28).

5. Confinement in irons. For concealing a theft committed in a group of ten Kibitkas all the members of the group were put in irons (123).

6. Ruin (full confiscation of property).[12]—This penalty was inflicted upon chiefs who violated the Regulations by beating people and looting a large Aimak (1), or by insulting superior princes (2); and also on sons who killed their fathers or mothers (30), on fathers killing their sons (31), for the killing of a nobleman accompanied by arson (59), and for three consecutive thefts (124).

---

10 According to the Leontovich edition, his fingers (art. 155).

11 In Golstounsky's edition only flogging was mentioned, while Leontovich specified flogging with the knout (art. 41) as did also Pallas (art. 35).

12 It is not apparent from the text of the Regulations what is meant by the term "ruin"—the looting of the offender's property (the "potok" and "razgrablenie" of ancient Russian law) or its confiscation. If we compare art. 13 with arts. 1 and 5 of the Regulations, the latter interpretation will appear the most probable.

7. Dismissal from service—Demchis and administrators of Otoks were dismissed for negligence (122), judges for wrongful and unjust decisions (129,135).

8. Subjection to ignominy—inflicted, in addition to a heavy fine, for flight from the enemy. In such cases the coward was dressed in a woman's sleeveless jacket (11). For frivolous behaviour towards a girl, in addition to the fine the offender received a rap on the genitalia (73).

9. Fines (predominantly in nines of cattle) comprised the main punishment.

10. The handing over of the culprit to his victim (for enslavement) in case of inability to pay the fine (*e.g.* in cases of theft, art. 86).

11. Fines in human beings (art. 12 in Leontovich's Ed.).

The punishable crimes and offences under the Regulations could be divided into the following categories: Crimes against religion and the clergy, crimes against the State and the Government, crimes committed by officials, crimes against the community, against individuals, and against property.

Crimes against religion and the clergy.—In the section dealing with religion and the clergy we have already touched upon this question and shall therefore not dwell on it here, apart from noting the severity of the penalties inflicted for insults, injury and damage to the clergy.

Crimes against the State and the established government.—To this category of crimes may be referred failure to report the appearance of a formidable enemy, for which the offender was punished by death, ruin and expulsion of his offspring (art. 13); failure to come forward when the alarm was sounded (punished in the same way—art. 14); the abandonment of a prince in danger, punishment by death and ruin of the criminal (11); massacre of the population and looting of a large Aimak, punished by ruin of the criminal (art. 1); looting of a small Aimak, punishable by a fine of 100 cuirasses, 100 camels and 1,000 horses with an additional fine of 5 precious things if the culprit was an official and one if he was not, besides which he had to make good all damage done (2). For refusing to render assistance against the enemy chief princes were fined 100 curirasses, 100 camels and 100 horses and minor princes 10 cuirasses, 10 camels, and 100 horses (4). If a prince did not deliver up many (fugitives from other tribes) he was fined 100 cuirasses, 100 camels and 1,000 horses (art. 8). For violating the Regulations chief princes were fined 10 camels and 100 horses, secondary princes—5 camels and 50 horses, minor princes—a camel and 3 nines of cattle. Tabunangs and the four chief officials—1 camel and twice nine head of cattle, and Ooloos officials—1 camel and nine head (10).

Crimes comitted by officials.—The beating of a man by chiefs or minor princes, high officials, Demchis or Shulengas was not punished if its aim was to promote the observance of the instructions, orders and laws of the sovereign, even though the culprit died under the punishment. Beating out of sheer arrogance, however, was punished by fines: for strong blows—nine head of cattle, for moderate ones—5 head, and for light ones a horse (21). Anyone who was the cause of the shortage of supplies of a prince was fined five nines of cattle; if he subjected a high official to such shortage—one nine; if a minor prince—a horse (26). Village headmen were fined a nine for not keeping order (60). A messenger entrusted with an errand but failing to set out upon it was fined a nine (98). Demchis and administrators of Otoks were fined a nine and dismissed from service if they neglected to provide for the poor, and if any person died as a result of such neglect, the responsible officials were punished as for ordinary homicide (122). For concealing that a theft had been committed chiefs of ten Kibitkas had their hands cut off (according to the Leontovich edition—the fingers) while other persons were put in irons (25). Judges who thrice handed down wrongful decisions were deprived of office (129). For arbitrary and dishonest judgments judges were dismissed and the bribes given them confiscated (133). If an entire Aimak changed its camp-site, the head of the Aimak was fined a nine of cattle (132). Desertion in the face of the enemy was punished by fines as follows: for chief princes,—100 cuirasses, 100 camels, 50 Kibitkas (households) and 1,000 head of cattle; for minor princes—10 cuirasses, 10 camels and 100 horse; for officials of Oolooses —3 precious things, 3 Kibitkas and 30 horses; for common men in armour—4 horses and armour; soldiers—a quiver and a horse, etc. (11).

Crimes against the community.—Punishable crimes against the common mode of life and public morals were numerous in the Regulations. Thus adultery between a married woman and another man was punished with a fine, the woman being obliged to pay 4 and the man 5 animals; a maiden who committed adultery was not punished but the man paid nine animals (69). Cohabitation with animals was punished with a fine of 5 head of cattle (70). For refusal to exchange an exhausted horse or give a traveller shelter for the night a fine of a three year old mare was imposed; for refusal to give shelter for the night, a childless woman was fined one sleeveless jacket, "and if the culprit try to exculpate herself she shall be given the oath."[13] For refusal to offer mare's milk ("koumiss") to the thirsty the fine was a sheep (87). Handling the breasts of a girl over 10 years old and kissing her was punished and fined (73). Anyone thrusting a stick into a burning fire

13 Leontovich assumes from this provision the existence among the Mongols of hospitable prostitution.

in the hearth was fined 9 nines of cattle if the hearth was that of a prince, and nine head if it belonged to a commoner (90).

Crimes Against the Person.—Murder. For the murder (with arson) of a nobleman, the punishment was ruin; of a man of the middle class—a fine of 300 animals and 30 precious things; of a man of the lower class—15 nines of cattle ond one precious thing (59); for the murder of a father or mother by a son—complete confiscation of property (30,31); for the murder of a rejected wife—5 nines of cattle (33); of a male slave —5 nines; of a female slave—3 nines (32). For the killing of a deserter a fine was imposed (99) and for the killing of a man who choked on his food or, while in a state of intoxication, defecated in the house of another the fine was fixed at 5 nines of cattle.[14] The penalty was reduced in the presence of the following circumstances: for killing a man in a hand to hand encounter the fine was nine head of cattle and one precious thing (71); for killing in course of a game in which only two persons participated, nine head, while if there were several players as many nines were paid as there were persons participating; and if the person killed was a grown man a precious thing was added to the fine (75). For the unintentional killing of an ally in war a fine of nine head of cattle was paid, and for accidental killing during a hunt the fine was generally fixed at half this amount (55). If an insane person killed a man, half of his property was confiscated (44) and no punishment was inflicted for the killing of a raging madman who was constantly causing damage to others (45). The owner was punished for deaths caused by his cattle or domestic animals. If, while in the personal charge of the owner, (or his herdsman), the cattle killed a nobleman a fine of nine head of cattle and a precious thing was paid; in cases where the victim was a member of the middle class—5 head; of the lowest class—a precious thing. If the cattle by which a man was killed were wandering about freely without a herdsman, the fine was one animal (46,48). If a man was killed by a horse on which someone was riding at the time, the rider was fined in the same measure as that applied to killings by animals under the charge of a herdsman (48). If a man died from the bite of a rabid dog the owner of the animal was fined nine head of cattle if the victim was a nobleman, seven head if he was a man of the middle class and 5 head for a victim of the lower class (44).

Maiming and Wounding.—For depriving anyone of six fingers the fine was 5 nines of cattle and a precious thing; for loss of the thumb or index finger—2 nines and 5 head; of the third finger—nine head; of the fourth—5 head; and of the little finger—three head (55). For a

14 The Mongols considered this a bad omen and the Yassa of Jenghiz Khan provided for capital punishment for such offences.

wound from which the victim recovered a fine of 9 head of cattle and a precious thing was imposed. For a light wound it was 5 head and when the dress only was shot through—one horse (55). For inflicting a large wound with a sharp weapon the fine was 5 nines of cattle; for a wound of medium size—3 nines; for a small wound—nine head; for merely pricking a person with a sharp weapon—a horse. For unsheathing a weapon for a blow the weapon itself was forfeited and a fine of one horse imposed, the horse going to the person seizing and arresting (retaining) the unsheathed weapon (71).

Rape.—For the rape of a married woman the culprit was fined nine head of cattle; of a maiden—two nines; of a slave—a horse (69).

Insult by Word and Deed.—For verbally insulting a chief prince the penalty was ruin; for insults offered to a prince of medium rank the culprit was fined as follows: for verbal insult—nine head of cattle, for insult by deed—5 nines. In the case of minor princes these punishments were 5 animals for verbal insult and 2 nines and 3 nines of cattle respectively for severe and slight beatings (20). For verbal insults to a courtier or Shulenga, the fine was a horse and a sheep, for a slight beating—5 head, and for a severe beating—nine head of cattle (20). For a severe beating administered to the offender's teacher, father, or mother the fine was 3 nines of cattle, for a beating of medium severity —2 nines, and for a slight beating—nine head (27). Daughters-in-law who beat their fathers-in-law were similarly fined, in addition to which the culprit was flogged with the knout, being given 30, 20 or 10 strokes in proportion to the severity of the original beating (28). A father who unjustly chastised his son was compelled to pay 9 head, 5 head or a horse depending upon the degree of severity of the original beating, and for similar chastisement inflicted by a mother-in-law upon her daughter-in-law the respective fines were 2 nines, 9 head and 4 head of cattle respectively (29). For severe beating of one man by another with a stick or stone the fine was 9 head of cattle and a precious thing, for a less severe beating—a horse and a sheep, and for a slight beating—a three year old mare. When the fist or a whip was used the respective fines were fixed at 5 head of cattle, a horse and a sheep, and a three year old colt (72). Anyone tearing the clothes of another was fined a two year old colt. For tearing off a beard—a horse and a sheep (12).

Anyone tearing hair off the head of a woman or the tassel off her hat paid a fine of 9 head of cattle (73). For insulting or ridiculing a man who rode well the fine was a horse (22).

Calumny.—For falsely accusing another man of theft the offender was fined and the cattle he received as a result of his calumny was taken from him (93).

Crimes Relating to Property.—Theft. Theft was severely punished under the Oirat laws, this severity of punishment being especially evident in the case of third theft the punishment for which was the ruining of the offender. "Whoever commits theft for the third time shall be dispersed and ruined", was the text of art. 24. Second in degree of severity was the punishment accorded for the theft of cattle, the basic property and means of livelihood of the nomadic Mongols. For the theft of a camel the fine was 15 nines of cattle; of a gelding or stallion—10 nines; of a mare—8 nines; a cow, a two year old colt or a sheep—6 nines, and article 60 provided that "that which has been stolen shall be many times taken from the thief." For concealing stray cattle a man living nearly was fined 9 head of cattle, and one whose habitation was distant was punished as for theft (66,67). Anyone taking possession of stray cattle on the pretext that they belonged to him was fined 5 head of cattle (92).

For the theft of military equipment the following punishments were inflicted: For the theft of armour, a cuirass, or a good bow with a quiver of ten arrows the fine was 3 nines of cattle; of a helmet, a gun, a good sword or sabre or a mediocre bow and quiver—9 head; of an inferior sword or sabre—5 head; and of inferior bows and quivers—a goat with a kid (38). Fines were also inflicted for the theft of valuable household effects. For stealing a silk-covered sheepskin coat, a rug of tiger, leopard or other skin, a sable coat, a silk padded jacket or an ermine coat, as well as for a good silver-mounted saddle and bridle and Pahvey (stirrups) the fine was 5 nines of cattle; for a coat of wolf, fox, glutton or beaver fur, or rug—3 nines of cattle, for a good sheepskin coat or the skin of a tiger or leopard, good woollen cloth, morocco leather, any other hide, or a good hammer— 9 head; for a wolf, lynx, glutton, or beaver skin, a cotton gown, a saddle of medium quality, a bridle and Pahvey—7 head; for the skin of a sable, fox, squirrel, jackal wild cat or ermine, a three year old mare for large skins and a sheep for those of smaller size. For the theft of a wild animal caught in the trap of another the fine was the same as that imposed for the theft of the animal's skin (78). For the theft of less valuable household effects the following fines were imposed: For the theft of a piece of steel, knife, arrow, smooth-file, rope, a good hat, boots, trousers, scissors, a felt cloak, shovel, axe, meat (the carcass of a sheep), inferior sheepskin coat, saw, snares and nets for catching birds or fish, traps and similar devices the law prescribed the amputation of a finger, the offender having the option of paying a fine of five head of cattle (197). For the theft of small household articles such as a bridle, lasso, needle, awl, buttons, cup, rug, trough, hat, boots, stockings, a sheepskin, strap, etc., the thief paid a sheep with a lamb if the articles were of good quality and a goat with a kid if their quality was inferior (108).

Swindling. For the fraudulent use of provisions intended for a prince the fine was a horse; while for fraudulently passing one's self off as a messenger and making use of carts and forage under this pretence the penalty was a fine of five animals and 5 strokes with the knout, or, if only one of these offences had been committed, a fine of 5 animals (23).

Arson. Arson was severely punished, and art. 58 read as follows: "Whoever sets fire (to another man's property) shall be very severely dealt with."

Concealment of a malefactor or helping him to escape from justice was punished with a fine of seven nines of cattle, while concealers of a malefactor's property were fined three nines (77).

Such, in the main, was the criminal law of the Oirats. As is apparent from the provisions quoted above, it lacked general principles and bore a purely concrete, casual character, as a consequence of which it fell short in its comprehensiveness. Penalties varied not only with the object, but also with the subject of the crime and there was no equality before the law.

The Judicial System and Jurisdiction.

The scanty provisions of the Regulations relating to the judicial system and jurisdiction were supplemented by a special (the second) decree of Galdan Khan which was wholly devoted to this subject (art. 134 in Golstounsky's edition). From it we may gather the following facts concerning the organization of the courts and administration of justice according to Oirat legislation.

"Right and wrong between the Olets and inhabitants of Turkestan must be dealt with by every means of investigation," i.e. through the courts, ruled the decree of Galdan Khun-taidji. Cases involving Khotons were to be decided by their own Khoton judges but cases which concerned the whole people came under the jurisdiction of the Supreme Court (judge). Thus the relations between the Olet and Turki tribes came into this category (134). It was forbidden to sell and buy law-suits and the plaintiff (accuser) had to plead his own case (134). Examination of cases was carried out at fixed places in the presence of the parties, no trial taking place if any of them were absent (128,109). The plaintiff (accuser) was bound to thrice serve a summons on the defendant in the presence of witnesses and, likewise in the presence of witnesses, notify the court that the summons had been served. If, in spite of the threefold summons, the defendant (accused) failed to put in an appearance he was called to Court by a messenger and fined a horse for failing to appear irrespective of whether he won or lost the case (109,126). The principal proofs considered were *corpus delicti* and the evidence of witnesses. The latter were divided into good (i.e. reliable) witnesses, such as, for example, noblemen, and unreliable witnesses (e.g. slaves) (62,109). Female slaves were not permitted to testify but if, as evidence of a theft, they brought to court the bones and flesh of the stolen animal, their testimony was taken into consideration (101). Witnesses were rewarded for aiding in the doing of justice and received nine animals from the inflicted fine and some part of the other property in proportion to the quantity adjudged by the court (106). Thefts were investigated by means of tracking. If such tracking was brought to a conclusion in the presence of noble witnesses, the case was tried according to the law (on theft), but in the absence of noble witnesses, the case was investigated by the court; and if the plaintiff alone had tracked the thief, the elder of the village was to be put on oath to find the thief who, after his guilt had been proved, was fined (62). Even though the elder himself might be exonerated, he was nevertheless fined nine head of cattle for neglecting to maintain order (62). If necessary, searches were effected and anyone refusing to submit to search was fined (110). Taxes were levied in favour of the court of the prince (128). The Regulations admitted set-off of criminal acts on both sides but did not define the institution in sufficient detail. "If two culprits state in court that there have been reciprocal offences, this shall be disregarded unless there have been witnesses of the reciprocal offence, in which case the matter shall be investigated" (art. 85).

We may gather from the above that according to Oirat legislation, the administration of justice was placed in the hands of the State and the court of justice had become a government institution. Courts were divided into local (Khoton) and Supreme courts, measures were taken by the State to ensure the carrying out of judicial decisions, and there were provisions relating to procedure (fees, taxes in favour of the prince, etc.) At the same time vestiges of the preceding period were preserved in the organisation of courts of justice in the Oirat epoch, vestiges of a time when the taking of the law into one's own hands was permitted. For instance the plaintiff (accuser) played an immediate and leading part in the initiation of a lawsuit. The suit began with the immediate summoning of the defendant to court (*in jus vocatio* of Roman and ancient Russian law) and notice to the court that such summons had been made. The presence of the parties was obligatory and witnesses were rewarded for their assistance in the administration of justice. Some cases could be settled out of court by the plaintiff taking the law into his own hands. Thus, article 62 ruled: "As regards the debt (the creditor) must serve notice thrice in the presence of witnesses and thereafter seize (the defendant's property). When serving notice he must inform the Shulenga". In accordance with the same article, if the tracking was brought to a conclusion in the presence of noble witnesses, the law (relating to theft) was to be applied, and if there were no noble witnesses, the case was to be investigated (by the court). It followed that in the first case the matter was settled without an appeal to court.

From the above evidence we may regard the period under examination as one which saw the transition from the system of private jurisdiction to the organization of jurisdiction by the State.[15]

Khalkha-Djirum.

Attitude Towards Religion and the Clergy.

The introduction to the Great Statute of 1709 contains expressions of great piety with regard to the Buddhist religion and its representatives. Such expressions are met with frequently in the contents of the Code.

Khalkha was the seat of one of the three Buddhist Pontiffs, the *Hubilgan* (Reincarnation) of *Bodhisatva Djebtzun Dambu* (*Daranata*), *Bogdo Gegen Hu-tukhtu* of Urga. The Khalkha Djirum is filled with pious respect for the Urga Gegen. Thus, the Statute of 1676, or 1736, on the theft of monastery property, begins with the following words: "We bow to the Teacher Daranata. Filled with reverence and the power of the person of the Hutukhtu-Gegen, we, Vachirai Tushetu Khan, Dalai Setsen Khan and other great and lesser Noyons, ... have discussed among ourselves a Statute on the Monasteries." The Khalkha Djirum refers to the Urga Gegen as "The High" (The consent of The High, the *kuren* (monastery, lodging) of The High, the flocks of The High, etc.) The *Kuren* of the Urga Gegen was sanctuary for criminals (III and following articles, XI—3)[16] and a person seeing a fugitive seek-

15 In the book, "The Mission of Captain Y. J. Ounkovsky to the Khan of Djungaria, Zevan Rabtan" (1722-1724), ed. by Prof. Veselovsky a description of court procedure is given as follows: "In the court (which among them is known as "zargo") ten or more Zaisans hold sittings. They announce their decisions not in writing but verbally. In cases where important criminals are sentenced to capital punishment, some are put on their knees and lashed to death, others are tied by their arms and legs to horses which are then forced to run fast until the legs and arms of the criminals are torn out. But such executions are rare among them." (Proceedings of the R.A.S., vol. X, 2, pg. 194, *cf.* ppg. 94-95).

16 Since, in accordance with Mongol custom, the Khalkha Djirum is not subdivided into articles and there is as yet no published edition of the code containing a standardized subdivision, we shall here cite as follows: Roman numerals to indicate the record according to the list given above, and, where possible, Arabic numerals indicating the Article, e.g. I—1, 2, 6 means "The Great Statute of 1709", art. 1, 2 and 6.

ing the High Hutukhtu was not only not permitted to place any obstacles in his way, but was even required to help him (VIII—"On Fugitives"). Violation of the will of the Gegen was punishable by fines of from 2 to 5 nines of cattle, or the accomplishment of 100 circumambulations around his *Kuren* and 1000 obeisances (XI—2.) Refusal to give transportation to the Gegen was punished by confiscation of all the offender's property, and refusal to transport the Khan by a fine of half one's cattle. For the same crime a Noyon was fined 300 head of cattle in the case of the Gegen, and 150 in that of the Khan (I—1, 2,6). The elchis (messengers) of the Urga Gegen had the right to 10 carts, those of the Khan and Khanna to 8 (I—3,6). Anyone touching the Gegen's envoy with a sharp weapon was fined 9 nines of cattle, an envoy of the Khan, 4 nines of cattle (I—13). If anyone killed a man seeking sanctuary at the seat of the Gegen, he paid *andzo* (a type of fine) for the killing, a fine for violating the will of the Gegen, and was forever deprived of the right of obeisance to the Gegen (XI—3). Noyons and Tarkhans (those free from payment of tribute) were not obliged to provide transport, except in the affairs of The High and the "Three Important Affairs"[17] (I—8, 9, 11). Theft from the herds of the Gegen and the monasteries was punished by confiscation of all the offender's property, 80 strokes of the knout and a penance of 300 circumambulations and 9,000 obeisances (II—2, IV, 1—5). *Shabinars,* the tributaries of the Gegen, and monastery guards were permitted to camp anywhere except in the headquarters of the Noyons and forbidden places (VII).

Theft from the temples was held equivalent to theft from the treasury or herds of the Gegen (III—4) and theft from the herds of the monasteries was likewise punished by complete confiscation of property (VII—1). For theft from the herds of monks the fine was 12 nines of male and 14 of female cattle (VII—1). For attacks on monasteries culprits of the rank of Khan were punished by exile and deprivation of their subjects; commoners by death and confiscation of their property. Khans accessory to such attacks were fined 50 families (of serfs), 100 suits of armour, 100 camels and 1,000 horses, while commoners were liable to confiscation of all their property.

Anyone wishing to become a monk had first to obtain the permission of his parents and Noyon, but if he sincerely wished to dedicate himself the Noyon was not to oppose his desire. Monks did not pay any

---

17 The "three important affairs" were enemy invasion, illness of a high-ranking dignitary, and the reconciliation of quarrelling Noyons.

taxes or tribute, being "free from all levies and compulsory cartage" except in the "three important affairs" (XII). They were obliged to observe the regulations of their monasteries and, if attached to them, had not the right to leave of their own free will. In civil affairs the monks were subject to the laws of the Hoshun (XII). The penalties for insulting monks were severe (an insult to a spiritual Noyon, for instance, was equivalent to an insult to the Khan, and insults offered to to a Gelung were punishable by a fine of 9 nines of cattle. In the case of a temporal Noyon the offender paid only 5 nines.) Punishments were provided for conduct unbecoming to a monk, fines for drinking wine, monks guilty of theft were fined three nines of cattle (but exempted from punishment in the stocks) and unfrocked. It was forbidden to kill healthy stallions, some varieties of geese, snakes, frogs, widgeons, wild goat kids, skylarks, and dogs on pain of punishment and a fine of one horse. All killing was forbidden on the 8th, 13th, 15th, 25th, and 30th day of each month (XI-last articules).

Clan and Tribal Life and Relations.

The Northern Mongols, like those of the West, lived under a clan and tribal order, under the rule of clan and tribal chiefs. The Western Mongols (Djungars) were organized in clan units—*auls, hotons, aimaks, otoks* and *tribes,* under the leadership chiefs of tens, *shulengs, demchis, zaisans* and *noyon*-princes, and we see the same conditons among the Northern, Khalkha, Mongols. The Khalkha Djirum speaks of hotons or oolooses, sumuns, otoks and hoshuns and the corresponding tribal chiefs.[18] Thus, in the Great Statute of 1709 we find the following: "If he lives in another hoton and there has his yurt, the hoton chief must pay a *baa* (type of fine) of one five-year-old stallion." (IV—1.) The Regulations of 1724, state, on the subject of the collection of debts: "In villages suits must be discontinued if people of the same sumun and the same otok have not declared to their Taiji of their somun and the ooloos (hoton, settlement) Tsangin, or the Daruga of the otok (XVII). In the Regulations of 1718 it is stated that: "On a journey of less than 20 days' duration, one may travel with the consent of the Daruga, Shulenga, Demchi and chief of ten." (XVI) The ancient division into tens had also been retained and in the Regulations of 1718 it is provided that "over every ten men one shall be appointed Daruga."

It was further forbidden to live in a hoton other than one's own or to leave the camp of one's ten without the permisson of the Daruga, Shulenga and chief of ten. (IV--1, XVI). The Khalkha Djirum con-

---

18 Even if we consider the *somun* and *hoshun* to be purely administrative units, the hotons (ooloos) were the ancient clan subdivisions of the Mongols; the otoks were connected with clan organization.

demns persons deserting their Noyons and rewards those returning to their allegiance (VIII—"On Fugitives.") Family life was strictly patriarchal. In former times the power of a father over his children had included that of life and death. At the time of the effectiveness of the Khalkha Djirum this had already been modified and the Statute of 1728 considers it necessary to make the reservation that : "Generally a father is not lord of the life of his son." (XV—final article.) Children were obliged to honour their fathers and mothers and the penalty for insults to parents was made more severe (XIII). There existed also the family responsibility of relatives (V—end, I—2, XIII.)

Relationship was traced through the male line but the Khalkha Djirum notes the existence of a special legal relationship to maternal grandparents: this was effective in the case of the grandfather, but in case of his death if he left sons (the maternal uncles) the grandchildren (nephews) were not held responsible (e.g. for theft), and did not pay yal (a type of fine) (VIII).

In the mutual relations of the Mongols the Khalkha Djirum provides for goodwill and mutual aid. Travellers leaving a sick comrade in an unpopulated place were punished with fines, while anyone staying with the sick person to render aid was rewarded (XII.) If a Khan or commoner drove a stranger asking for a night's lodging from his door and the latter died (e.g. froze to death), he had to make recompense with a serf or a camel and pay andzo (a type of fine) of 3 nines heads of cattle; if cattle perished a similar compensation had to be paid; if the person refused a night's lodging had his hands or feet frostbitten the refuser also paid a fine, and refusal of hospitality for the night generally was punished by a fine of one three-year-old stallion (XV—5). Rescue of cattle being driven away by a thief was rewarded and refusal to pursue the thief in like case punished (VII, X.) The saving of dying or stampeding cattle was rewarded, as was the saving of sheep from wolves and bad weather (XV—3) and of the young of a maddened she-camel (XIII). The Code also contains a general provision as follows: "If at the time of a robbery or theft anyone commit an especially good deed, then let the Noyon reward him." (IV—23).

Cattle Breeding.

Cattle-breeding is the main means of livelihood and chief occupation of the Mongols. As we have already stated, cattle were the basic property value among the Mongols, and served as a medium of exchange (instead of money) and a medium for the payment of fines, etc. The concept of property among the Northern Mongols, as among those of the

West, is represented by the term "cattle and property" (e.g. "to confiscate half of the cattle and property of anyone telling lies".—VIII—10.)

With particular severity the Khalkha Djirum punishes the theft and driving away of cattle; theft from the herds of monasteries, for instance, being punished by confiscation of all the property of the offender and the theft of coal, lime, firewood and other monastery property by a fine of 5 nines of cattle (VII—1). Recovery of stolen property by force was rewarded (IV, VII).

Lost animals were to be detained by the finder who was obliged to announce that he had found them. For three days the finder could not ride on them; after three days, the Noyons and Saits (clan-chiefs) having been notified, this was permitted. If such cattle were lost or died, it was necessary to make due declaration to the Sait. If within three years lost cattle were not claimed by their owner, he had (upon recovery after more than three years) to pay the person in whose possession they were the hind part of their carcasses. All natural increase of such lost cattle were the property of the person detaining them, except young still suckling at the time of recovery. Anyone illegally taking possession of lost cattle paid a fine of 1 nine of cattle, besides compensation for the cattle seized (XIII). The Khalkha Djirum provides for measures to be taken against the spread of infectious diseases among the cattle and epidemics among the human population.

Compulsory Cartage.

Among the levies it deals with, the Khalkha Djirum regulates in detail requisitions of transportation or the duty of compulsory cartage. The Hutukhtu Gegen and the Khans had the right to requisition carts and provisions without limitation (I-1,6). Refusal to supply cartage to the Gegen was punished by confiscation of the refuser's property, to the Khan by a fine of half the offender's cattle. If the person refusing to supply transportation was a Noyon he paid a fine of 300 and 150 head of cattle respectively. The messengers of the High Hutukhtu had the right to 10 carts and 2 sheep, messengers of the Khan could requisition 8 carts and 2 sheep, refusal to supply these to the former was punished by a fine of 3 nines of cattle, the latter by 2 head. The princes had the right to 10 carts and 3 sheep and refusal was punished by a fine of three nines of cattle. The Jassaks (Hoshun chiefs) had a right to 6 carts and 2 sheep and refusal was punished by a fine of 3 nines of cattle and their messengers could requisition 2 carts and one sheep (I-7). The personal herds of the Noyons were released from the duty of compulsory cartage except on the business of the Gegen and in the "three important affairs"

(I-8). The same applied to the herds of the Tarkhans (I-11). For refusing cartage to messengers travelling on the "three important affairs" commoners were punished by confiscation of property and Noyons paid 50 Boda (a type of fine in large cattle) and 50 sheep, and a Sait, 50 Boda (I-10). For refusing cartage to messengers of a Noyon the fine was one nine of cattle (*ibid.*) Various punishments were instituted for insults offered to messengers, these being severest in the case of messengers of the Gegen, then of the Khan (I-13,14,15.) Messengers were obliged to present written credentials, duly sealed, indicating the quantity and type of transportation desired (II-1).

Private Law.

Property Law.—The law of private property in real estate did not exist in the epoch of the Khalkha Djirum. Land used for the purposes of nomadic pastoral economy was at the disposal of the tribal unions such as hotons, auls, and otoks under the administration of tribal chieftains or Noyons. "A Uteg will be regarded as occupied if a yurt is put up; and if two persons argue over its occupation the preference will be given to the one who came first, or if they came simultaneously, to the one who first loosed an arrow or struck (the earth) with the knout." (XV-8). Although traces of family property are found, as for instance in the form of the responsibility of children for their parents, it is impossible to doubt the existence also of individual property in movables, especially where these were the products of the owner's labour or hunting. Thus, the young of cattle belonged to their master, and lost and wandering animals to the person finding and caring for them (XIII). A person taking possession of lost cattle was obliged to pay compensation and a fine of one head of cattle to the owner (*ibid.*) A fox, cornered in a hunt, belonged to the person first catching up with it. Dead game found within 500 *aldans* of a crossbow was considered to be the property of the owner of the weapon. (*ibidem.*) The owner of a mad dog was obliged to pay for all damage caused by it (*ibid.*) Notification of things found was to be made to the saits and published to the people. If the owner was found, the thing was returned to him but the finder was entitled to one third of its value. (XV-6).[19] If anyone took possession of any part of the carcass of stolen cattle, he was liable for the full value (to the owner) (XV). Anyone digging a well had first rights to water his cattle there, and was obliged to give water to others only for the saddle horses of travellers. If however, after having watered his livestock, he did not give water for this purpose, he was fined a stallion

19 Evidently, if the owner could not be found the thing became the property of the finder.

(XV-7).[20] Insults to parents where common family property existed was punished more severely than in its absence. (XIII). This points to the possibility of children demanding partition before their parents' death, *i.e.* the weakening of the strict family life formerly obtaining (*v.* ancient Tsaadjin Bichik) and the disintegration of family property.

Obligations.—The treatment of relations issuing from obligations was more developed in the Khalkha Djirum than in the Regulations of 1640, but was nevertheless not remarkable for intensiveness. Thus the Khalkha Djirum treated of purchase and sale but forbade riding out to meet merchants and the buying of cattle and other property for speculative purposes (XIX-3). It recognised trade as a profession and compelled merchants to take out annual licenses to trade in Urga. It was decreed that trade could be carried on only during daylight, and the secret sale of wine was forbidden (XX). The Khalkha Djirum also provided for the hiring of livestock and forbade the renting of camels to Chinese and Russians (end of XVI, XX). It also treated of loans and buying and selling on credit and regulated debt relations arising from it. By the Regulations of 1724 if a loan was given in Urga without the permission of the Khan, the Shantzotba (head of the Gegen's Shabi yamen) and the Wangs (superior princes), its collection was forbidden. It was also forbidden to collect debts in cases where a loan was concluded in a village without declaration to the Ooloos Tsangins and Otok Darugas of both parties (XVII). But in the Statute of 1728 it was stated that if goods were taken on credit from Russians or Chinese without the approval of the Noyon, the offenders were liable to a fine of a five-year-old stallion, but the debt had to be paid (XV-9). It was forbidden to recover a debt by compulsion. If force was employed during daylight the debt was annulled, if at night it was regarded as robbery (XV-14).

Among moneyless transactions the most widespread were gifts, for which, according to Mongol custom, return gifts were required. If, however, the matter concerned the Khan's gift to a commoner or a commoner's gift to the Khan, no return was necessary (VIII). Similarly, gifts to Naiden (middlemen) were not subject to return (VIII).

The Khalkha Djirum also provides for concrete cases of responsibility for costs and damages. Thus, if a fugitive wounded a man he was obliged to feed him (from his own herds) until he recovered and pay him one stallion and andzo for the wound. Besides this he had to pay a stallion and a camel to the local official. If the fugitive did not himself possess livestock, payment had to be made by his Noyon within 3 days

20 The duties of hospitality and mutual help dictated this but so that these would not overtax the owner of the well it was provided that he was not obliged to supply water for more than one saddle horse.

of his flight (VIII-"On Fugitives"). If anyone died from the bite of a mad dog, the dog's master had to pay compensation, plus a fine of three nines of cattle if he had previous knowledge of the dog's madness. In the latter case the master was also answerable for any livestock perishing from the dog's bite (XIII). If a madman (a man who has run amok) killed a man, the fine was half andzo, if he wounded a man this was considered equivalent to accidental wounding, if he killed cattle or broke anything he was obliged to pay its value. If the man's master or Noyon knew of his madness and let him run loose, not arrresting him, he paid a fine of 9 head of large cattle (XIII). If anyone was killed by a crossbow shot off in an uninhabited place, compensation was required in the measure of a camel or a man and 100 andzo. If the victim was wounded the owner of the crossbow was compelled to feed and heal him and, upon his recovery, pay him compensation of a horse (to a commoner) or a camel (to an official). It was forbidden to shoot crossbows on highways, and if a man perished from such action the crime was considered equivalent to accidental homicide. If cattle perished it had to be replaced with the addition of an extra head (XIII). If during the pursuit of a fugitive or cattle-thief a man was killed, it was necessary to pay 5 boda, and if a horse perished it had to be replaced (VII). Besides this, the Khalkha Djirum provides for compensation for damages incurred as a result of crimes or through the action of criminals.

Family Law.—Marriage relations. If the ruling Noyon gave a princess in marriage to a Tabunan already married to a princess, he was fined 15 camels and 150 horses; and a non-ruling Noyon in similar case was fined 10 camels and 100 horses. A Tabunan was fined 5 nines of cattle which were paid to the first princess, and his marriage to her was dissolved, both she and her dowry returning to her parents (VIII-1,2). If the princess married a Tabunan already married to another princess, was taken away and the Tabunan fined 5 nines of cattle (VIII-3). If a Tabunan married to a princess took a second wife who was a commoner, the second marriage was dissolved, the father of the second wife ruined (by the confiscation of all his property), the Tabunan punished with 50 strokes of the knout, and the offended princess (his first wife) given the option of divorcing him (VIII-4). Thus we see here a limitation of polygamy in the interests of princesses.

A Noyon taking a pre-betrothed wife from another was fined three families of serfs and 300 head of cattle andzo and parted from his bride (VIII-5). If, however, a Noyon took to himself the affianced bride of a commoner he was compelled to pay the latter one camel and give him in marriage any unbetrothed maid he might chose. (VIII-6). If a Noyon, after the horim (banquet, marriage feast) for his daughter, gave her in marriage to another Tabunan, he was fined 55 andzo and 5 rare things. If he gave her in marriage before the horim he had to return all cattle previously received, the kalim. (VIII-9). If a Noyon gave away a woman commoner (after the horim), to another, without warning the Noyon of her first affianced husband, he had to return her to her first husband or pay 100 head of cattle andzo. (VIII-10). If anyone took to himself a betrothed maid, stating to the Noyon that she was not betrothed, he was liable to confiscation of half his property and the maid was returned to her betrothed (*ibid*). If a commoner took a princess of the rank of Khan in marriage, the agreement was recognized as valid only if the betrothal gifts consisted of a white camel with silver plate on its nose, a white stallion with a sable neck decoration, a silver bowl full of wine and a flawless pearl. If Noyons took in marriage the daughter of a Tabunan, the agreement was valid if the gifts were a silver bowl, a pearl, and wine. If two commoners became engaged to be married the agreement was valid if there were witnesses to it and if a gift was made of wine and a ram's entrails, hooves and horns (VIII-11,12,13). If the person conluding the berothal agreement did not give his daughter in marriage for several years afterwards and then demanded the dissolution of the betrothal, he had to return all cattle received during the previous year, and half that received during the year before, with young. If more than three years passed he had to return all cattle received with their young. If the agreement was cancelled at the instance of the father of the groom, he was entitled to recover only the cattle given away (without young) (VIII-14.) If the betrothed bride or bridegroom died before marriage all cattle given away as kalim were returned (VIII-15).

If a Noyon gave a widow in marriage she was obliged to share her cattle equally between her husband and previous children, and the children set up separate establishments. If, however, the widow married without the consent of her Noyon she had to go to her husband "with a whip in her hands", *i.e.* without property (VIII-17). The groom's family paid the brides parents a ransom for her, in cattle (kalim) and the bride's parents provided a dowry (VIII). If a bridegroom, without making payment in cattle, entered his wife's family as a worker-son-in-law and then violated the agreement and left, he was obliged to pay 10 boda (large cattle) and 30 sheep. In such cases the sons of the union went with the father, while the daughters had to be ransomed at the rate of 2 boda for each girl (VIII-16).

The inner life of the family was of a strictly patriarchal character. The father was the head of the family and his rights were very great, so great that the Khalkha Djirum found it necessary to state that they do not extend to taking the life of his son (XV-final art.) From this it may be seen that children were subjected to their father who had the right to undertake corrective measures. Evidently, as with the Western Mongols, children could leave the household during the lifetime of their parents and set up their own economy (XIII). After the death of the father, the mother became the manager and administrator of the common property of the family. (VIII-17,20).

Inheritance.—Generally, inheritance was supposed to be evenly divided among the children (sons) "with the exception of generally known just and notoriously unjust sons". This meant that if such sons existed the former could receive more and the latter less than their legal share. The orders of Noyons as to the transfer of their property (by inheritance) had to be submitted to the Gegen and Khan and confirmed with the seal of the governing prince (Jassak). If the true mother of all the children was living she administered the estate (VIII-20).

Thus it is clear that, as a general rule, inheritance was evenly divided among the sons, but a mother or father had the right to increase the share of an especially good son and decrease that of a bad one. The father's orders in such cases, however, had to be drawn up in written form and submitted to the Gegen and Khan, who evidently verified the correctness and justice of the division with respect to the facts of the case and customary procedure. The seal of the Jassak validated the last will of the head of the family.

From this we may see that we are here dealing with not only the order and division of inheritance but also with the embryo of the Will—the distribution of property among heirs according to customary law, placed under the control of the temporal and spiritual authorities.

Criminal Law.

System of Punishments.—The punitive norms of the Khalkha Djirum were close to those of the Mongol-Oirat Regulations of 1640, and, in general, were not remarkable for severity. The death penalty was invoked very seldom (in two cases of criminal attack on monasteries and robbery, only the second case having actual application). Also rare were punishment by mutilation and deprivation of freedom, but enslavement was practised. As in the earlier Code (1640) the basic punishment was the property fine, reckoned customarily in nines of cattle. But here we meet more often the heavier property fines—in hundreds of head of cattle (300,150).

The Khalkha Djirum recognised and applied the following main punishments:

1. The death penalty (VI, VIII).

2. Breaking of an arm (IX).

3. Enslavement (IV-8), compulsory labour with family and without family (IV-8, final art; VIII, XIII), giving of wives and children in payment of fines (VI, VII).

4. Confinement in a pit or well (gaol) (V, VIII).

5. Confinement in stocks (IX).

6. Chaining together of the hands (IV-6).

7. Confiscation of all property (I-1, 10, VII, VIII-3, XIII), confiscation of movable and real property (VII), confiscation of the cattle (I-2, IV-1).

8. Confiscation of half the property (XIII), confiscation of half the cattle (I-6, VIII).

9. Deprivation of serfs, giving away of people (IX, VII).

10. Flogging with the whip or knout (I-4, IV-1,5, VIII-4, XIV).

11. Fines in human beings (IX, VII).

12. Property fines (commonly of cattle such as *andzo, boda, hal, aldang,* etc.) reckoned in hundreds of head, tens, units, and even parts of the carcass (haunch, rear parts), but commonly in nines of head (I-2,3,10 etc); and sometimes of things (IV, 3,27).

13. Forced labour: husbandry service, collection of firewood, argal (XI-2, V-1, IX, XIII).

14. Obeisances and circumambulations (around the kuren) (IV-1,5, XI-1).

15. Supply of tea to the monastery fraternity (IX).

The Khalkha Djirum distinguished between the chief criminal, the accessory and the concealer of a crime (IV-28,34), and between the first, second and third degrees of theft and robbery (IV-5,6.) The Khalkha Djirum also recognised the responsibility of the offender's family, and in some cases of his Noyon and Daruga (IV-6). In treating of the complete confiscation of property, the Code dictated that a share be left to the condemned (V-1). It permitted the substitution for a man sentenced to compulsory labour, of the payment of 5 *boda* (large cattle), for a man, 3 for a woman, and 1 for a child, (IV-6). Besides punishment, the Khalkha Djirum usually provided for the making good of any damages resulting from the crime. A nine of cattle, for purposes of fine, consisted of 2 horses, 2 bulls, 2 cows, 2 sheeps, and one calf. Let us consider the most characteristic crimes of which the Code treats.

Crimes against religion and its representatives.—The most important of these have been treated above.

Crimes of functionaries.—A Noyon or Sait showing partiality in giving a judicial decision was fined 5 boda (including one camel). A Sait wrongly deciding a case while in a state of intoxication was fined a stallion. An Elchi who did not carry out the decisions of the Court within 10 days and not producing the fine cattle was fined 1 boda and deprived of his maintenance (IV). If he failed to collect a fine as a result of pre-arrangement he was fined half andzo (*ibid.*) If the acting Sait beat or swore at anyone with just cause there was no punishment (XIII).

Offences against morals.—For adultery between a Noyon and a princess the fine was three families of serfs and 300 head of cattle. If a commoner committed adultery with a princess all his property was confiscated and both the culprits were enslaved. Adultery between commoners was punished with a fine of 300 head of cattle and 30 rare things (VIII-7, 8). The abduction of another's wife or daughter was considered equivalent to adultery (*ibid.*) Anyone pulling at the end of a blanket was fined 3 nines of cattle (*ibid.*) "If a woman crawls in to a man the fine will be 3 nines." (*ibid.*)

Offences against persons.—Homicide. For homicide for revenge or out of mischief the penalty was a fine of 30 *barkė* (things difficult to obtain) and 300 head of cattle andzo and compensation for the victim: if an official—of one man and one camel; and for a non-official, a man. In all these case the killer was further punished with 100 strokes of the whip and was given over as a slave of a slave to the Hoshun. If the killer was unable to pay the andzo he himself was handed over to the wife and children of his victim (XIII). If a Noyon killed a subject he paid andzo for the killing, and was further obliged to compensate for the victim with a man, or, if he did not have one, a camel and a stallion (*ibid.*) A thief killing a man during a robbery was confined in stocks for life (IX). Accidental homicide was punished with a fine of half andzo (XIII). The killer of a madman was fined 9 nines, unless he was first attacked by the madman, in which case he did not answer for the killing (XIII).

Wounding and Mutilation. Causing the lose of both eyes was punished in the same way as homicide. The knocking out of one eye was punished by 100 strokes of the knout and 100 andzo of cattle. For each tooth knocked out the fine was a nine of cattle plus compensation of 1 boda. For the breaking of an arm or leg, if the victim was thereafter unable to work, the andzo was the same as for an eye. If the injury was not permanent the fine was 3 nines of cattle. For permanent injury to the thumb or index finger the fine was 3 nines of cattle, for non-permanent injury one nine; for other fingers, one nine and five head of cattle respectively (XIII.) If anyone accidentally caused the crippling of any limb of a Noyon half his property was confiscated, and for a finger similarly crippled the fine was 7 nines of cattle. (*ibid.*)

Insult by words and actions. For insulting the Khan or Khanna by words all the offender's property was confiscated and he and his family were enslaved. The same punishment was applied to insult of a Noyon by word or action (XIII). If a Noyon drew weapon against another he was fined 5 nines including a camel; if both drew weapons they were fined one camel and 4 stallions each, the fine being appropriated by the authorities; and the same punishment applied if they were surrounded and disarmed by others (*ibid.*) If Noyons quarelled and began to fight and if the elder of them was at fault, the fine was one nine and five head of cattle; if the younger was at fault the fine was three nines of cattle. If they raised their voices and shouted at each other the fine was a nine and five head (*ibid.*) If anyone struck a commoner with a weapon the fine was 3 nines, with a stick or stone—one nine, and with the fist or a whip—five head (*ibid.*) If a commoner insulted another by word he was fined one stallion (*ibid.*) Severe fines were imposed for insults to the clergy, parents and teachers (up to 9 nines).

Libel (Slander). If a commoner slandered a Noyon with "big words, dangerous to life" the penalty was the same as for insulting a Noyon by words. For slandering a Taiji or Tabunan the penalty was the same as for drawing a weapon on a Taiji or Tabunan. For slandering a man of the slanderer's own rank the punishment was the same as that for striking with a weapon. Libel with "small words" was punished by 50 strokes of the knout, or a fine in the case of a Noyon of one five-year-old stallion (XIII). If a man slandered another to the governing Noyon the punishment was half that for slander before the Khan (*ibid.*) For slander to the Gegen a Noyon was fined 7 nines of cattle, a Taiji five nines, and a commoner 3 nines (XI.)

Opening of Tombs. For opening the tomb of a distinguished personage the fine was one nine of cattle; for that of an undistinguished persons, five head, and for that of a commoner—a haunch. (XV-2).

Crimes against property.—Robbery. According to the Great Statute of 1709 anyone committing a robbery was punished by 80 strokes of the knout and handcuffing of both hands in an iron bracelet for one year for the first offence, two years for the second, and for life after the third offence (IV-6). The Statute of 1728 provides for severer punishments: robbers were liable to confinement in a well (gaol) for one year and the wife, children, cattle and yurt of a ringleader were confiscated and given to the owner of the stolen cattle. Less important thieves were fined 3 boda each, given 100 strokes of the knout upon their release from gaol, and forced to collect firewood for three years (V). In the Regulations of 1746, in accordance with the Mongol Statute of the Emperor Kang Hsi, the punishment for ringleaders in robberies was further raised to the death penalty, while their followers were fined 3 nines of cattle and given 100 strokes with the knout (VI). If they did not have sufficient property to pay the fines imposed upon them their wives and children and the robbers themselves were enslaved in lieu of payment (V. VI).

Theft. A thief stealing from the treasury or herds of a princess, dowager Khanna, Khan or Beile (Prince) was punished as one stealing from the treasury or the herds of the Urga Gegen (see above). An ordinary thief was fined 20 *boda,* given 80 strokes of the knout, and compelled to make 100 circumambulations around a monastery and 1,000 obeisances. A second offence necessitated 200 circumambulations and 2,000 obeisances, and a third 1,000 circumambulations and 10,000 obeisances.

Besides this the Khalkha Djirum contains a detailed list of articles in common use among the Mongols prescribing a fine for the theft of each. Thus, for the theft of armour, a cuirass, gun, helmet, shield, etc., the fine was 7 nines of cattle; for a quiver and bow, more than five arrows, sword, cutlass, more than five loads of powder and shot—3 nines each; a knife, file, less than five arrows, less than five loads of powder and shot—one nine; for gold, silver, the fur of a sable or lynx, and silk cloth in excess of one piece—3 nines; for drinking the blood of a horse by opening a vein, cutting off a horse's tail or ear, cutting a tassel off a woman's head-dress, stealing a bridle or saddle, etc.—one nine; for the felt cover of a yurt, a door, the framework of a yurt—2 nines each; for mare's milk with yeast, wine in a vessel, counting beads, tea, tobacco, a chisel, a plane, an eagle, etc.—five head of cattle; for dung fuel and firewood gathered by the subjects of a prince, badger or marmot skins, the milking of other people's cattle, the theft of a winter sheepskin, a large needle, fire-tongs, shoes, trousers, hose, grain, etc.—1 horse; for writing paper, dung-fuel and firewood belonging to private persons, a dog-one sheep, and many others. For all these things, also, there was a fixed compensation. (IV-20,21,22.).

More severe punishments were provided for armed robbery (IX). The liberation of thieves from pit gaols and chains, concealment of thieves and fugitives, and refusal to pursue thieves and robbers, were also punished.

"Pal" (The Steppe Fire). Anyone inadvertently causing a pal was liable for all the damage it caused and paid a fine of one horse. All the population was obliged to aid in putting out a pal in a settled area, anyone refusing being fined one horse and one sheep. If a man perished in a pal, the causer of the fire paid half the andzo for homicide, plus adequate compensation. Anyone not putting out his fire before striking camp was fined one horse (XV).

Judicial System and Procedure.

The Khalkha Djirum does not contain sufficiently clear regulations concerning the organisation of Courts among the Northern Mongols. From several of its provisions, however, we gather that the judges were the Saits and Noyons, that appeals were, in at least some cases, possible, i.e. some sort of second instance existed, and that trials could be held before one or several judges. More detailed particulars of Court organisation among the Northern Mongols are not, however, available in the Khalkha Djirum. Procedure, however, is more fully treated in the Khlakha Djirum.

Thus, the Khalkha Djirum provided for measures to limit abuses and disregard of the law by magistrates, and strove to establish the principles of government. "A caught thief must not be killed; if he is killed he will not be fined" (IV-24). In other words, the Khalkha Djirum, under the threat of material loss (deprivation of andzo, fines, etc.) made it unprofitable to take the law into one's own hands, although it did not punish the killer. The Code was more definite on the subject of disregard of the law in the sphere of Private Law. "If anyone collect a debt by force during daylight, the debt will be cancelled. If he take it by force at night it will be considered as robbery." (XV-13).

In cases of litigation, application had to be made to the Noyon who fixed the day of the Court hearing, and, in case of non-appearance of either of the parties, sent an Elchi (messenger) for them. If he did not appear even after the summons, the case went to the other party by default; but if the litigant who did not appear was in the right, the Noyon was obliged to wait five days after which the case was dismissed. If the parties to the litigation were subject to different Noyons the day of the hearing was settled by agreement between their two Noyon. The oath (usually on the axe) and the calling of witnesses were accepted as proofs. Theft was investigated by means of tracking, and in case of necessity searches were effected. If the opinions of the Sait-judges differed the case was decided by lot, drawn before the Burkhan. Immediately after judgment was passed on a criminal, the Elchi executed the sentence, both in cases of punishment or fines and of recovery of claims. (IV-5, XV). "Generally, if there is a fine, it must not be seized by the beneficiary himself, without authorisation but he must take the Elchi and go with him to his (the thief's) Noyon for the collection of andzo," The parents and relatives, fellow travellers, messengers and carters, neighbours, lodgers, boarders, and generally-known friends of litigants were not admitted as witnesses (XV). The Elchi received maintenance at the expense of those sentenced, and witnesses were rewarded (XIII, IV).

The Regulations (Code) of 1789.[21]

PRIVATE LAW.

Property and Obligations. The Regulations contained only a few provisions on this subject. With regard to the utilisation of land, the Mongols were bound to camp on the sites assigned to them and not to migrate into the lands of their neighbours. If princes of the first or second grade overstepped their boundaries and entered the territory of others, they were fined 10 horses; Beiles, Beisses and Guns were fined 7 horses; Taidjis and Tabunangs, 5 horses, and commoners one ox for each family. If trespassers on the territory of others remained there for a long time such of their princes, Taidjis and Tabunangs as received no salaries were fined 50 horses; while in the case of commoners, both the trespassers and persons knowing of trespassing by others but not reporting it had all their cattle confiscated and handed over to the owner of the violated land (V-1,2). Trade was allowed only if permitted by the ruling princes and generals, and was placed under the control of a special official. If there were more than ten merchants, each ten were obliged to form a separate company (V, 3).

Family Law. The price given for a bride at betrothal (the ransom or Kalim) was fixed by the Regulations at 2 horses, 2 head of horned cattle, and 20 sheep in the case of commoners, and if more was given it was confiscated by the State Treasury. If the bridegroom died before the wedding, all the cattle (comprising the Kalim) were returned; but if the bride died, only a half was returned. If the prospective bridegroom refused to marry his fiancée, he lost his cattle.

If the betrothed bride reached the age of 20 and the bridegroom had not yet married her, her parents were permitted to give her in

21 For a more detailed account of the Codes (Regulations) of 1789 and 1815 *v.* the writer's, "Customary Law of the Mongol Tribes", ppg. 99-130.

marriage to another (II, 13).[22] If a prince had a betrothed and another prince married her both the latter (the husband) and the person giving her in marriage (the father) were fined, the amount of such fines being fixed at ten families (of serfs) for princes of the first and second grades, seven families for other princes, five families for Taidjis and Tabunangs, besides which the bride was taken from the husband and returned to her first betrothed. If a commoner took away the betrothed of another, he, as well as the person giving him the woman in marriage, was fined three nines of cattle if possessing rank and one nine if neither was a person of rank. Besides this, the bride was taken from her husband and given to her first betrothed (II, 15, 16).[23] Husbands were free to divorce their wives. Divorced wives did not have the right to demand the return of gifts made by them to their husbands, but could take away their personal property (the dowry) (II, 14). Persons having no children or heirs could adopt members of the same clan, or, in the absence of these, strangers. Anyone wishing to do this had first to communicate such desire to the Banner Prince and Hoshun Ch'anguin (general commanding a division) who drew up an official act authorising the petitioner to take the adopted child into his house and bring him up as his own son, at the same time entering the child's name in the banner register as the son of his adopted father. If anyone adopted a child without the permission of the prince and general, as well as the formalities detailed above, the child was taken from him and returned to his own family (II, 11).

Law of Inheritance. The heirs to the property of a deceased person were first of all his sons and descendants in the direct male line. If these did not exist, formally adopted sons of the same clan had the next claim and if there were no such sons, the inheritance went to the kinsmen or remote relations of the deceased. If, in the absence of sons or kinsmen, a child was adopted from another clan, he could inherit the property, but if there were living kinsmen of the deceased bearing the same family name, they were given preference. If a child born of a concubine was brought up as a son, his mother could neither be sold nor given in marriage, as otherwise her child was not recognized as a son. In the absence both of near relations and of adopted sons from another clan, the property was considered an escheat and reverted to the ruling prince or Taidji (II, 12).

---

22 *Cf.* arts. 35 and 37 of the Regulations of 1640.

23 *Cf.* art. 39 of the Regulations of 1640.

CRIMINAL LAW.

System of Punishments. Chinese criminal law had great influence on the system of punishments in the Regulations of 1789, penalties were numerous and cruel and sometimes provided for the holding up of the criminal to derision. Generally, they were not always in harmony with the simple mode of life of the Mongols and the peculiarities of their nomadic economy.

Of the punishments inflicted by the Regulations, the following must be noted.

1. Capital punishment with confiscation of property and enslavement of the criminal's family (IV, 10; VI, 1; X, 11).

2. Capital punishment by cutting to pieces (VII, 7; X, 16).

3. Capital punishment by decapitation (IX, 6; X, 11, 16).

4. Capital punishment by decapitation, usually followed by public exposure of the head in a cage (VI, 1).

5. Enslavement of the criminal and his family (VI, 1; X, 1).

6. Enslavement of the criminal (alone). (II, 2; IV, 10; V, 16).

7. Deportation (to the provinces of Fukien and Kwang Chen Fu) with enslavement (IX, 19).

8. Deportation to the remote provinces of Honan and Shantung for hard labour at the post-houses (IV, 6, X, 17 etc).

9. Deportation to the provinces of Yunnan, Kweichow, Kwangtung and Kwangsi to unhealthy places (VI, 6).

10. Flogging with the knout, rods or whips (IX, 20; X, 11).

11. Confiscation of property (IV, 10).

12. Fines in cattle calculated in nines, and in wages, meaning the forfeiture of a year's, six months' or three months' salary (X-11, 14).

13. Dismissal from service (V-15, 17).

14. Imprisonment pending definite decisions by the Court (VI, 1, etc.)

15. Confinement in the Cangue (portable pillory).

The Regulations provided for the responsibility of families for crimes committed by their individual members (IV, 10; VI, 1, 2; X, 11, 16; XII, 22).

A Mongol committing a criminal offence could redeem himself by giving nine times nine horses (XIII, 23).

Children who had not yet reached the age of ten were not tried (for theft). (XIII, 18).

If the criminal did not possess sufficient cattle to pay a fine, the penalty was changed to corporal punishment at the rate of 25 strokes of the knout for each animal, but it was provided that the number of strokes should in no case exceed a hundred (XII, 9).

A nine of cattle consisted of two horses, two oxen, two cows, two three-year-old oxen and one two-year-old (XII, 1).

Crimes. The Regulations dealt with crimes against religion, religious vows and discipline, crimes against the State and the administration, against public security and morals, crimes committed by officials, crimes against persons and personal freedom (homicide, wounding and crippling, insults by words and deeds) and crimes against property (brigandage and robbery, theft, etc.)

We shall not here deal in detail with the provisions of the Regulations on this matter[24] but shall discuss only the most characteristic of them.

Thus it was forbidden after the death of a man to kill horses, stick poles with pennants into the ground, obstruct mountain passes and hang out Khodaks (silk handkerchiefs). For the violation of this provision, a fine was imposed of five head of cattle which were given to the person reporting the offence (X, 11). This prohibition related to the ancient (heathen, shaman) Mongol custom of killing horses, etc. on the graves of deceased tribesmen (cf. the Inscription of Abakansk, para. 4 and the Tsadzu of the Hori Buriats 1759).

Fugitives to another country were liable to the death penalty (IX, 1), while deserters from one banner to another were to be rejected and returned to their own banners, being also punished with 100 strokes of the whip (II, 10). It was forbidden for monasteries to receive Lamas and novices above the number allowed them (II, 7, 8, 9.)

For adultery between commoners, the man was fined 5 nines of cattle in favour of the husband, while the woman was given to her husband "that he might kill her"; if he did not kill her the cattle fine went to the prince. Anyone "making up" to another man's wife was fined 3 nines of cattle (X-14). For adultery with the wife of a commoner, princes of the first and second degree were fined 9 nines of cattle and other princes 7 nines, Taidjis and Tabunangs, 5 nines, in favour of the husband; for adultery with a princess a commoner was cut to pieces, while the head of the princess was cut off and the adulterer's family was delivered into slavery (X, 15, 16).

For the premeditated murder of a man from another banner princes, Taidjis and Tabunangs had to pay man for man to the banner,

24 For further details *v.* the writer's "Customary Law of the Mongol Tribes", Part I, ppg. 105-113.

as well as a fine for the benefit of the victim's family (50 to 100 horses depending upon rank), while a commoner was imprisoned and decapitated (VII, 1). For the premeditated murder in hot blood or while drunk of a subject or slave, princes of the first and second degree were fined 40 horses; princes of other degrees—30 horses; Taidjis and Tabunangs —3 nines of cattle; and commoners—one nine, in favour of the brothers of the victim, while the victim's family acquired the right to leave the banner and go where it wished. In case of unpremeditated homicide a fine of nine months' salary was imposed upon the killer, and the victim's family remained in the banner (VII, 1). Homicide during a fight or the death (within 50 days) of a person severely wounded in a fight was punished by the strangling of the killer, while unpremeditated homicide under the same circumstances brought in its train a fine of 3 nines of cattle (VII, 3). For the premeditated murder of a wife the murderer was strangled; for unpremeditated murder in a fight or quarrel he was fined 3 nines of cattle for the benefit of his mother-in-law. The same fine was paid if the wife provided a pretext by her conduct, and the husband deliberately killed her (VII, 6).

If a Mongol inveigled another, male or female, and sold him or her into slavery, he was punished with 100 strokes of the whip and fined 3 nines of cattle while the person inveigled was given 100 strokes of the whip (X, 13).

For poking out the eye of another the offender was fined 3 nines of cattle; for breaking an arm or leg—nine head of cattle (VII, 5). Anyone knocking a child out of the hands of a woman was fined nine head of cattle; for knocking out a tooth without good cause in a fight the offender was fined 9 head, and for striking with the fist, tearing the queue, or pulling the tassel from the hat of another, the fine was 5 head of cattle (VII, 10).

The instigator and accomplices in the robbing and murder of a man were punished by decapitation with public exposure of their heads after execution, while if the victim was only wounded, the offenders were decapitated and their families and property were placed at the disposal of the victim (VI, 1).

The punishment for theft depended upon the quantity and value of the things stolen. For instance for the theft of more than 30 horses the instigator and accomplices were imprisoned and strangled; for the theft of 20-30 horses the punishment was mitigated; for the theft of 2 horses the instigator was exiled and the accomplices punished with 90-100 strokes of the whip. (VI, 1). In the calculation of fines 4 sheep were considered as equal to a head of horned cattle, a horse or a camel. For the theft of less than 4 sheep the punishment was 80-100 strokes of the whip (VI, 6). Anyone stealing a pig or dog was fined 5 head of cattle, and for the theft of a goose, duck or chicken the fine was a two-year-old ox besides full compensation for the thing stolen (VI, 35). If a Taidji committed theft, he was deprived of his dignity and degraded to the rank of a common soldier, his cattle were given to the victim and his serfs to his nearest relatives (VI, 11, 12).

Judicial System and Procedure.

The judiciary was not separated from the administration but closely connected with it. The first tribunal was the Djassak-prince or Taidji (administrator of a Hoshun or division). Appeals against the decisions of these could be lodged with the President of the Seim, and appeals against the decision of the latter with the Chinese Board of Foreign Relations. The Board, after having examined the case, either instructed the President of the Seim to re-try it or, if the case was important, petitioned the Emperor to send a high official to try the case. Appeals to the Board, before cases were heard by the Djassak and President of the Seim, were strictly forbidden under threat of punishment (VII, 5).

Mongols who committed crimes while in China were tried in accordance with Chinese law, and Chinese who commited crimes in Mongolia—in accordance with Mongol law (XII, 19).

Accused Mongols had to plead their case personally and outsiders were forbidden to intercede for them (VIII, 1). Pleas for reconsideration of cases tried by princes could not be lodged. Cases being heard in court could not be settled by private arrangement, parties to such settlement being fined 3 nines of cattle if princes, and nine head if commoners. Reconciliation of the parties to a dispute was permitted if publicly effected through mediators representing the banners of the plaintiff and defendant (XII, 13).

In case of doubt, statements made under oath were accepted as proof, e.g. persons suspected of committing a crime but against whom there was no direct evidence could be put upon oath (VI, 2; VII, 5; XII, 16). Tracking was resorted to trace the perpetrators of a crime (VI, 27). Search was permitted only in the presence of eyewitnesses (VI, 30).

The cattle fines were divided as follows: the prince received one head out of each nine (XII, 3); the denouncer—half the fine; the messengers of the Djassak to which the culprit belonged—a three-year-old ox, and those of the Djassak of the victim, one head of cattle out of each ten but not more than three head in all (XII, 2). Those who collected the fine received a three-year-old ox from the culprit (XII, 1).

The Regulations (Code) of 1815.

PRIVATE LAW.

Property and Obligations. The provisions of the Code on this subject were aimed towards the safeguarding of cattle-breeding, the chief occupation of the Mongols. Chinese were forbidden to cross the frontier and to cultivate the land of the Mongols while the latter were forbidden to lease their pastures for agricultural purposes on pain of severe penalties (vol. I, 165, 167). The cultivation of fields belonging to Mongols and leased by Chinese was, however, permitted in the territory under the jurisdiction of the Governor-General of Jehol, with the sanction and under the strict control of the latter (I, 170). Such cultivation was also allowed in the principalities of Korchin Korlos and Aohan (I, 171, 172, 173). The leasing of land was only permitted if effected by contracts sanctioned by the district chiefs and magistrates which were to be made public and entered into the register after which the prince in charge of the pasture-lands delivered a certificate to the lessee authorising the lease (I, 174). Part of the rent, collected in advance, was called earnest-money. If the rent was not paid the land was taken back (I, 175). The mortgaging and holding in pledge of land as security for debts was forbidden (I, 274). If such transactions had been concluded previous to the promulgation of the Code persons who had taken over land and had tilled it for three years were permitted to continue for another four years or at most for five year on the condition that the debt was paid out of the rent and the land returned to its owner (I, 176). All Chinese engaged in agriculture in Mongolia were ordered to pay rent (I, 179). The provisions of the earlier Regulations forbidding wandering beyond the bounds of one's own pastures were repeated.

Commercial transactions. No Mongol was permitted to leave his pasture-grounds without the permission of the authorities or, in the case of those belonging to a division, of the divisional commander. Anyone wishing to travel for purpose of trade had first to petition his divisional commander who appointed a special official to accompany and control each company of ten or more men (II, 76). Chinese merchants could come to Mongolia only with the permission of the Board of Foreign Relations.

Chinese were forbidden to make loans with interest (usury) of silver to Mongols. When this rule was violated only the principal of the debt was returned to the lender and he himself was deported to his native place (II, 86).

Family and Inheritance Law. Marriage. Chinese living in Mongolia were forbidden to marry Mongol maids or widows and if they did so the marriage was dissolved and the wife returned to her parents, besides which both the husband and wife were punished, being confined in the cangue and each given 100 strokes with the knout, the Chinese being afterwards deported to his native place and the authorities (Taidjis, commanders of regiments) involved punished for slackness of control (1,483). Marriages between Mongols of the same generation[25] were forbidden (1,481). The kalim paid by a Mongol prince for his betrothed varied in accordance with the rank of the bride's father: if he was a prince of the first degree he received, at the conclusion of the marriage contract, 1 camel, 4 horses and 4 sheep, and just before the marriage itself 6 oxen, 6 horses and 60 sheep and the wherewithal for a wedding feast of 36 tables. If the bride's father was of lower rank the kalim decreased accordingly so that princes of the 5th and 6th degrees received 2 horses and 7 sheep following the conclusion of the contract and 2 horses, 2 oxen and 20 sheep at the time of the marriage (1,471). The kalim paid by other officials and by commoners consisted of 2 horses, 2 oxen and 20 sheep (1,481). If the bridegroom-to-be died between the betrothal and marriage the kalim was returned in full and if the prospective bride died half the kalim was given back (1,481). The daughters of Manchu and Mongol princes were given dowries as follows: For the daughter of a prince of the first degree—her nurse with the nurse's husband, 3 maidens and 5 families of serfs, etc. and down through the various grades until the daughter of a prince of the 6th degree received her nurse with the nurse's husband, 3 maids and 2 families; and the daughter of a Manchu prince of the 7th degree or a Mongol Taidji or Tabunang, 3 families of serfs (1,478). For the abduction of the betrothed bride of another, princes of the first and second degrees were obliged to compensate the wronged bridegroom with 10 families of serfs, and other princes with 7 families besides the return of the bride. A commoner guilty of a similar offence gave nine head of cattle and returned the bride (1,482). If a Mongol divorced his wife he was obliged to return her dowry, but if the latter had been spent or consumed nothing was returned (1,484).

Adoption. Taidjis and Tabunangs possessing hereditary titles, and the sons of princes, (if they had no direct heirs) had the right to chose a worthy person from their clan and adopt him, whereupon the adopted person received the title of Taidji and the right to the inheritance. The widow of a deceased Taidji was permitted to adopt an heir after her husband's death. If there was no suitable individual within the clan a member of another clan could be adopted with the permission of the divisional commander, but such an adopted heir inherited only

---

25 *i.e.* between relatives from the same aimak (or otok).

the property and not the title of his adopted father (I, 61, 63). Legitimate wives were forbidden to sell the concubines of their husbands after the death of the latter (I, 64). Sons of concubines were considered equal to those of legitimate wives (I, 64).

Inheritance. The heirs of a man were first his sons and direct descendants, then the brothers and last of all the clan. Escheats were placed at the disposal of the divional commander for public needs. Wills were admitted in the absence of direct heirs but no heir could be appointed outside the dead man's own clan, and the sanction of the authorities was required for the execution of all testaments. The wills of persons having no direct descendants and designating an heir from the same clan had to be confirmed by the commander and other princes of the division (I, 63). Foundlings, adopted strays, and the children of slaves were in no case recognized as heirs (I, 63).

CRIMINAL LAW.

System of Punishments. The principal punishments imposed by the Code were as follows:[26]

1. Capital punishment with enslavement of the offender's family (II, 1).

2. Capital punishment by cutting to pieces (III, 76).

3. Capital punishment by decapitation (III, 16, 73). Beheading was usually followed by public exposure of the head.

4. Capital punishment by strangulation (III, 9, 73). The death penalty was inflicted, either immediately or following confinement, or execution was delayed until a definite decision was reached in the autumn.

5. Deportation to localities with an unhealthy climate, with hard labour (III, 74).

6. Deportation to the provinces of Yunnan, Kweichow, Kwangtung and Kwangsi (III, 18).

7. Deportation to the provinces of Kiangnan, Chekiang, Kiangsi, Hunan and Fukien (III, 36-41).

8. Deportation to the provinces of Shantung and Honan with hard labour at the post-houses (III, 73, 74).

9. Deportation with family to the provinces of Shantung and Honan (III, 19).

10. Confinement in the Cangue (III, 78).

---

26 The figures given in brackets indicate the sections and articles of the Regulations in which the punishments were defined, but are given only as examples and not exhaustively. (the same applies to the references on pg. 128).

11. Flogging with the knout accompanied by a fine (III, 107).

12. Beating with sticks (III, 107).

13. Whipping (II, 4; III, 105).

14. Flogging with rods (III, 105).

15. Imprisonment (III, 77).

16. Loss of dignities for members of the clergy (IV, 71, 85). Deprivation of other persons of their ranks or offices (IV, 81); of dignities or titles (II, 3, 12).

17. Confiscation of all the offender's property (III, 16, 183).

18. Confiscation of immovable property (II, 1).

19. Confiscation of subjects (serfs) (II, 1; III, 75).

20. Fines in cattle (III, 180; IV, 69); in salary (III, 12; IV, 81).

21. Ransom (II, 73).

For those unable to pay them the fines were commuted to strokes of the knout at the rate of 20 strokes for one animal, 50 strokes for 2 animals, 75 strokes for three animals and 100 strokes for 4 or more animals, more than 100 strokes being in no case given (III, 113).

A fine of nine head of cattle consisted of two horses, two oxen, two cows, two three-year-old and one one-year-old bullocks.

Crimes. The Code of 1815 dealt with crimes against religion, religious vows and discipline, against the State and official duties, against the person (offences against personal liberty, homicide, wounding or crippling, insults in word and deed), and against property (brigandage, robbery, theft, arson, damage to property). Let us consider the most characteristic of these.[27]

The violation of graves was treated in detail and the punishment for breaking into the graves of princes and Taidjis was death; of commoners—flogging and fines in cattle (III, 73).

It was forbidden for a monastery to have more than the prescribed number of Lamas and more novices than appeared on the list, the punishment for violation of this provision being loss of dignity and a fine for the responsible authorities (IV, 1, 8, 76, 82). It was forbidden to take slaves as Bandis and soldiers as novices on pain of the same punishment (IV, 80). For running away from a monastery Lamas and Bandis were deprived of their dignities and given 100 strokes of the whip (IV, 87).

Fugitives to another State were liable to the death penalty; but if they did no damage at the time of their flight and returned of their own free will the punishment was 100 strokes of the whip (III, 142).

27 For further details see the writer's "Customary Law of the Mongol Tribes", pps. 119-127.

Princes and nobles (Taidjis, Tabunangs) who did not appear when summoned for a campaign lost their rank and titles and were forced to join the campaign; those holding troops subject to them back from the campaign were put to death; those appearing late were fined (II, 3). If any member of a ten committed theft the Chief of Ten was fined a horse for slackness in supervision, but if the Chief himself discovered the crime and detained the criminal he was not held responsible (III, 71).

It was prescribed that malevolent persons and persons intolerant in social life be exiled to Shantung and Honan for hard labour at the post-house (III, 183).

Anyone denying a newcomer a night's lodging, especially if the time was winter and the stranger froze, was fined nine head of cattle; if the stranger did not freeze, a two-year-old bullock (III, 488). For adultery with the wives of commoners, princes and nobles were fined in favour of the husband (from 5 to 9 nines of cattle depending upon rank); for adultery by mutual consent between a commoner and a princess the former was to be cut to pieces and the latter beheaded; in case of adultery between a slave and the wife of a Taidji both were put to death while if the adultress was a concubine the punishment for both was 100 strokes of the whip; for adultery with a woman of equal rank a commoner was punished with a month's confinement in the cangue and 100 strokes of the whip and the woman with 100 strokes and payment of ransom; if, however, the commoner also persuaded the woman to elope with him he was confined in the Cangue for two months and exiled to Shantung or Honan (III, 75, 76, 77, 78).

For the deception and inveigling of free Mongols and selling them into slavery, or marriage, or concubinage, or for adoption as children or grandchildren, the offender was punished by 100 strokes of the whip and a fine of 3 nines of cattle, the Mongol sold being also punished if the sale took place with his consent (III, 79). It was forbidden to sell subjects (serfs) whose names were entered on the military registers, and those whose names were not so entered could not be sold outside their own divisions (III, 81; *cf.* Reg. of 1789, II, 23).

For the premeditated murder of a man from another division princes, Taidjis and Tabunangs commanding divisions were fined 9 nines of cattle of which 6 nines were given to the victim's family and 3 to his Noyon, irrespective of the motive of the killing. For the same crime Taidjis and Tabunangs not commanding divisions were fined 5 nines of cattle while commoners were liable to the death penalty in accordance with the general State Code (III, 1). If a prince, Taidji or Tabunang killed his subject or slave, irrespective of whether the deed was done in rage, hot blood, or while drunk, the offender paid 40 horses if a prince of the first or second class; 30 horses if a prince of another class; and 3 nines of cattle if a Taidji or Tabunang, the fines going for the benefit of the victim's family which at the same time acquired the right to leave its regiment for another (II,2). For the killing of slaves, Djassaks were fined 3 nines, squadron commanders and lieutenants, 2 nines; and commoners one nine. Officials and commoners guilty of homicide were strangled and the same punishment was inflicted on a husband so maltreating his wife that she died (III, 5). For the unpremeditated killing of a wife the husband was fined nine head of cattle in favour of her father (III, 8). For the unpremeditated killing of a subject or his own slave the offender paid a fine (of from 5 head to 3 nines of cattle). For accidental homicide officials and commoners were fined 2 nines of cattle (III, 6, 7, 8).

For mortal wounds, if death followed within 50 days, the offender was punished by strangling following confinement in prison (III, 9).

For inflicting a wound that was not dangerous the offender was fined 6 months' salary and if he did not receive a salary, nine head of cattle, or five head for a commoner. Officials or commoners accidentally depriving others of sight or breaking their arms or legs were fined 2 nines of cattle which were given to the victim, and in cases where the wounds were not dangerous the fine was one horse (III, 14). For crippling injuries in course of a fight the fine was 3 nines of cattle and nine head if the injury was not dangerous (III, 15). For knocking out a tooth or tearing off a queue the offender was fined 9 head of cattle; for tearing a tassel from the hat of another—3 head (III, 15).

The Code distinguished between the theft of public (horses, cattle, timber, etc.) and private property, the former being punished more severely than the latter. The theft of private property was punished in accordance with the quantity and quality of the articles stolen; for the theft of more than 30 head of cattle the chief thief and his physical accomplices were strangled and mental accomplices (instigators, etc.) exiled, etc. As for smaller cattle, 4 sheep, 4 young bullocks and a colt or young camel were considered equal to one ox, horse or camel, and if less than 4 head of smaller cattle were stolen the punishment was from 80 to 100 strokes of the whip. For stealing articles of silver from 1 to 10 lan in value the chief thief was given 90 and the accomplices 70 or 80 strokes of the whip; if the value of the stolen article was from 10 to 40 lan the respective punishments were 100,90 and 80 strokes; if from 40 to 70 lan—the chief criminal was exiled; and if the value was 120 lan or more the chief criminal was strangled and his accomplices exiled (III, 45, 50).

For arson of a dwelling place, out of rage or revenge, which caused the death of anyone the penalty was death, the offender's property being given to the victim; if no one perished the criminal, if an official, was deprived of his rank and if a commoner received 100 strokes of the whip, the offender's property (in both cases) going to the victim (III, 183).

Judicial System and Procedure.

The judiciary and administration were closely connected. The first tribunal was the Djassak (Divisional Commander) with whom the complaint or suit was to be lodged. In case of dissatisfaction with his verdict the case could be submitted to the Corps Commander (President of the Seim) who constituted the second instance; and against his decision an appeal, to which copies of the documents of the Djassak and Corps Commander relating to the case had to be attached, could be filed with the Chinese Board of Foreign Relations. The Board then examined the case and, if it considered it necessary, instructed the Djassak or Corps Commander to review it in accordance with its directions; important cases were submitted to the Emperor in order that a special Amban might be sent to examine the case (III, 82). For taking a suit direct to the Board over the head of the Djassak and Corps Comander, Taidjis and officials were fined 3 nines of cattle and commoners were punished with 100 strokes of the knout. But even in these cases the Board was bound to examine the case submitted to it and, if it found it to be an ordinary one, to transmit it to the respective Djassak or Corps Commander to whom it referred; in extraordinary cases the Board could ask for the despatch of a special Amban (III, 83). The Board of Foreign Relations had the right not only to examine appeals against the decisions of the Djassaks and Corps Commanders but also to retry the cases if it discovered evidences of partiality in these decisions (III, 84).

Mongols were bound to appear in Court personally and outsiders were forbidden to intercede for them, the penalty for doing so being a fine of one horse (III, 91). When, after an appeal had been made against the decision of a chief, it was proved groundless upon examination, the appellants were fined 9 head of cattle if the appeal referred to a decision by a prince of the first or second degress; 5 head if against decisions of lower princes; and a horse for appeals against the decisions of other military officials (III,86).

Thefts were investigated by means of tracking (I, 93; III, 122, 123) and if the track led to a spot within bowshot of some camp the owner of the camp was sworn and the matter settled by his testimony under oath, but if the track passed at a distance of more than a bowshot from a camp no suspicion attached and the owner of the camp was not given the oath (III, 123). The homes of suspects could be searched, but only in the presence of witnesses, and anyone refusing to allow search to be made was considered guilty of the theft (III, 65). Great importance was attached by the Code to the evidence of witnesses. In some cases, especially if there was no direct proof, settlement was made on the basis of statements under oath, and suspects could take the oath to assert their inocence. If they thus swore their innocence they were acquitted but if they hesitated or refused to take the oath they were declared to be guilty (III, 116, 117). Princes, Taidjis and Tabunangs could not be put to oath except in particularly important cases (III, 124).

The Law of Autonomous Mongolia.[28]

As we have had occasion to state above, in Autonomous Mongolia customary law was effective in the sphere of private legal relations while Criminal law was under the influence of Chinese law, exercised through the Codes of 1789 and 1815, with the addition of some Mongol provisions.

PRIVATE LAW.

The Law of Property. The right of individual ownership of land was not recognized. The land was in use by a Hoshun of Mongols and was at the disposal of the Hoshun Djassak whose authority, in Autonomous Mongolia, did not at first decrease. The Mongols could use the land for the nomadic pastoral economy which was their chief occupation. Agriculture was at a very low level of development. Steps were taken for its promotion by the Urga Gegen who, in 1917, even issued an order providing for the compulsory sowing of grain. This order did not, however, have any great effect.

The renting of land was permitted but practised only with respect to foreigners predominantly Chinese and to a smaller extent Russians, who rented land chiefly for cultivation. The renting of land by Chinese for purposes of cultivation attained large proportions at the beginning of the XX-th century but showed a sharp decrease (by more than half) under the Autonomous regime.

Law of Obligations. The following transactions existed: Purchase and sale, exchange, gifts, personal hire, loans, guarantees, rent of land to foreigners, and a few others. The mortgaging of property and renting of land by Mongols to Mongols were unknown to Mongolian

28 Maisky, "Modern Mongolia", 1921; Minutes of the Great Huruldan, 1924; Replies to special questions by the writer, etc.

customary law as was the promissory note. Transactions were, as a general rule, concluded orally. The allowable rate of interest was 36 per cent per annum, a circumstance reflecting the influence of Chinese law which permitted the same maximum rate.[29] The detention of persons for debt was not practised. In case of the insolvency of the debtor his nearest relatives were held responsible as well as his Bak (community).

Family Law. With respect to marriage Mongol customary law allowed polygamy, one of the wives (the first) being considered the chief and enjoying greater rights than the others. Marriages were arranged by parents and by elder relatives generally. The customary earliest marriageable age for men was 17-18 years and for women 15-16 years. The bride's parents received a ransom for her and the bride brought a dowry to her bridegroom, the amounts of both being fixed by mutual agreement before the marriage took place. The amount of the ransom and dowry depended upon the prosperity of the parties.[30] The ransom (Kalim) was usually given before the marriage but if it was not delivered or its delivery was held up the marriage was not considered fully valid until it had been fully paid and even the children were considered as belonging only to the mother (in the same way as illegitimate children). The dowry, however, was paid in the course of a year or even after a year had elapsed from the time of the marriage. Besides this the bridgroom's father, at the time of marriage, gave the young couple a yurt while the bride's father contributed the inner fittings of the yurt. The marriage ceremony was performed with the participation of a Lama, but ordinary cohabitation was often met with. Generally the Mongols are remarkable for the liberty of sexual relations among them, both before and after marriage. As a result of the expenses involved in the usual form of marriage, elopements by mutual consent were not uncommon. Mongol law did not impose any limitation on the number of times a man could marry.

The husband was the head of the family. The mother participated in decisions affecting the affairs of the family and in the upbringing of the children. Parents could apply measures of domestic correction with respect to their children. The property of married couples was considered common.

Divorce was extremely simple being accomplished not only by mutual consent but also by unilateral expression of the desire to be divorced upon a pretext sanctioned by custom, the participation of a

---

29 *v.* Ta Ch'ing Liu Li, section 149, Boulais, "Manuel du droit Chinois, I, No. 729, etc.

30 "Princes gave to their daughters as dowry (engi dagasche) not only cattle and other property but also people. This practice continued during the period of Autonomous Mongolia. The quantity of the dowry depended entirely upon the property status of the Noyon" (Information given by a Councillor of the Mongolian Ministry of Justice).

Lama not being obligatory. The husband, for instance, was by custom given the right to send back to her parents a wife who was childless or had thrice deserted him, while in the same way a woman had the right to divorce a man who had thrice driven her from his house. Occasionally divorce was formal, but in the majority of cases it was accomplished by simple separation of the parties. At divorce the wife received back her dowry alone and was not entitled to any share of the common property of the couple.

Adoption of the children of others was permitted with the consent of their parents and the Hoshun administration. Children so adopted had the same rights as the proper children of the adopted father.

The institution of guardianship over minors under the supervision of the Hoshun administration also existed.

Law of Inheritance.—Inheritance by will and by law (custom) were both allowed. The will, which was oral, was executed in the presence of a Lama confessor and witnesses (although the presence of the latter was not obligatory). The contents of the will, evidently, could not run counter to custom.[31]

In inheritance according to custom the widow and orphans were first of all called, and if there were no children the widow received only her dowry. In the absence of direct descendants the inheritance went to collateral relatives, including the most distant. Escheats were entrusted to the Hoshun administration and included in the assets of the Treasury (or monastery).

An interesting circumstance with respect to inheritance by direct descendants was that (when they did not live with their brothers) daughters, as well as sons, were admitted to the division of the inheritance although their shares were smaller (an allotment being made to them, evidently, in lieu of dowry). Illegitimate children also received a smaller share of the inheritance. On the other hand the son who inherited the father's household and paid taxes and levies (Alba) on the latter received a larger share than the others.

The customs (provision) relating to inheritance varied somewhat in different localities.

The problem of the responsibility of heirs for the debts of the deceased was not clarified. Children who inherited the household of their father were evidently responsible for his debts without limitation by virtue of the strength of family relations.

---

31 *Cf.* the provisions of the Code of 1815.

Criminal Law.

As has been stated above, Chinese law exercised great influence upon the criminal law of Mongolia (through the Mongol Regulations (Codes) of 1789 and 1815). In general outline the provisions of Criminal law which were applied by the judiciary of Autonomous Mongolia were as follows:

System of Punishments. In Autonomous Mongolia the following punishments were applied:

1. The death penalty in various forms, by shooting, decapitation, and strangling; and qualified execution with torture, cutting to pieces and starving to death.

2. Severing of the extremities (the arms, the legs) and putting out of the eyes.

3. Imprisonment for various periods (up to 10 years, a heavy punishment for nomads).

4. Corporal punishment—flogging with whips (up to 200 strokes) or sticks (up to 100 strokes), and sometimes with canes.

5. Detention, ordinary and with confinement in neck (the cangue) or leg stocks or chains.

6. Public confinement in stocks.

7. Exile from the Hoshun or Aimak.

8. Fines, heavy: from 9 to 9 times 9 (i.e. 81) lan[32]; and light, from 3 to 3 times 5 (15) lan; also cattle fines.

9. Reprimand.

10. Warning.

Princes and Taidjis, as before, were exempted from corporal punishment and the payment of levies and taxes.

Crimes and Offences. Crimes and offences against religion and the clergy: Blasphemy and mockery were punished by imprisonment and the imposition of tribute for the benefit of the church; the chopping-down of holy forests, by whipping, imprisonment, tribute to the church and confiscation of the chopped lumber. Insults to the clergy were also severely punished.

Crimes and offences against the administrative order and official duties: The unauthorised or fraudulent assumption of a title was punished by flogging and imprisonment, and in serious cases even by

32 A lan was equal to 1.40 in Silver (Mexican) dollars.

death. Persons dodging military service were punished by imprisonment, flogging and death; insults to the head of the State and high officials, by flogging, imprisonment and even death, and insults to other civil officials by corporal punishment. For corruption officials were deprived of their rank and sometimes imprisoned; the embezzlement of State or Church property was punished by imprisonment.

Crimes against the person and morals: Homicide was punished with death (head for head) while the murderers of their parents were cut to pieces. The inflicting of wounds and crippling injuries was punished by corporal punishment, imprisonment with a chain around the neck, and payment of medical expenses. Mutilation brought corporal punishment and imprisonment upon the offender. Beating, insults in words and deeds, false witness, violations of tranquillity and order, brawls and fights were all penalised by corporal punishment. Adultery was looked upon as a slight misdemeanour for which the offender paid a saddled horse to the injured party; rape was punished by a fine and, in case of complications, by short terms of imprisonment and payment of medical expenses.

Crimes against property: Robbery was punished by whipping and imprisonment and in the more serious cases by death. Theft (most frequently the theft of cattle) was classified as follows: the first theft was punished by 20-30 strokes of the whip and payment of damages; second theft—by 40-45 strokes, 1 to 2 months imprisonment and double payment of damages; third theft—by 50-100 strokes of the whip, 1 to 2 months' imprisonment and 40 to 50 days of public confinement in stocks, etc. Incorrigible thieves had their hands or legs severed, and were sometimes even deprived of their eyes or castrated. Forgery and swindling were punished in the same way as theft. The trampling of crops was punished by fines in cattle. Embezzlement of private property brought capital punishment in its train.

Brigandage and arson were not mentioned. Mitigating circumstances (poverty, ignorance and some others) were taken into consideration. Minors were not punished but were committed to the supervision of their parents. Members of the nobility were exempt from corporal punishment.

Organization of the Courts.

In the sphere of judicial organization few changes were made under the Autonomous regime. For less important cases of a general character the first instance was the Hoshun administration. The second instance was the President of the Seim and his administration. The

President of the Seim also represented the first instance for more important cases. The third instance was the Ministry of Justice in Urga which, besides this, was the second instance for more important cases and the first instance for cases involving princes which were removed from the jurisdiction not only of the Hoshun administration but also of the Seim. Gegens, Hutukhtus and Shabinars were not subject to these common courts, being judged in the Shabi Yamen.

The competence of the Hoshun court was limited to small cases as, for example, in the Tsetsen-Khan aimak where it could deal with cases involving not more than 2 head of horned cattle, 8 head of smaller cattle, or 39 lan, and impose punishments not above 100 strokes of the whip, 3 months' confinement in the cangue and fines of not more than 9 head of small cattle or one horse. More important cases came under the jurisdiction of the President of the Seim as the court of first instance.

No distinction existed between the procedure in civil and criminal cases.

In the investigation of criminal cases some tortures were applied, but the cruellest of these were abandoned under the influence of European and chiefly of Russian culture. Under the Autonomous regime, however, the following tortures were still applied: 1) Beating on the cheeks with a strap; 2) Beating with sticks on the buttocks (up to 100 strokes); and 3) Standing the accused upon sharp stones. Besides this various tests and oaths were applied such as the kissing by the accused of the muzzle of a loaded gun pointed at him, oaths by the names of the children of the accused, etc. Towards the end of the Automous period tortures and corporal punishment were abolished.

Appeals to the next instance were permitted in both civil and criminal cases but no term was set for such appeals.

It may be seen from the above that in Autonomous Mongolia the spheres of criminal law and Procedure were governed chiefly by the provisions of Chinese legislation for Mongolia, only partially supplemented by some institutions of purely Mongolian law (e.g. fines in cattle, whipping, the mild punishment for adultery and the violation of tombs and some others). In the sphere of Civil law, the customary law of the Mongols continued effective.

CHAPTER III.

SOURCES OF MONGOL LAW.

No system of law has ever been unitary throughout its entire history. Every such system has different sources of origin and is subjected to different influences. Besides one or another basic source there usually exist supplementary sources from which the given positive law draws some of its features.

The writer supposes that the basic source of Mongol Law may be found in the customary law of the Mongol tribes, and that Mongol Law is pre-eminently customary, although it has other supplementary sources.

A. Custom (Customary Law).

The *communis opinio* of legal historians on this question is that the original codes of various peoples represented, in the main, a crystallization of their customary laws. In these codes (where private or official codification existed) there were also provisions of a mandatory character (laws) and reflections of foreign influence, but basically these codes remain collections of customary law. This applies to the original legislation of Greece and Rome (e.g. the Law of the XII Tables), the barbarian laws of the European peoples, the first Russian Code, "Russkaya Pravda" and others. Such also was the ancient Mongol Law. The writer's acquaintance with the contents of the basic Mongol Codes—The Great Yassa, the Regulations of 1640, and the Khalkha Djirum, as well as extensive legal and ethnographic material relating to the Mongol tribes, has brought him to the conclusion that the ancient Mongolian Codes are collections mainly of customary law, i.e. that they contain customary law with the addition of a certain number of provisions of a mandatory character (laws) and some reflections of other legal systems (Chinese Law and Lamaist Canonical Law). Of the same customary character in their essentials, are Buriat and Kalmuck law, which also reflect the influence of Russian Law and, to some extent, of Lamaist Canonical Law.[1]

The opinion stated above may be confirmed by analysis of the contents of the basic records of Mongol Law and the investigation of the sources of the origin of this law.

1 For an opposing opinion see the article by G. K. Guins, "The Mongol State Organisation and Law" in "Vestnik Kitaiskogo Prava" 1931, No. 3. (in Russ). For the writer's answer see the sketch "Is Mongol Law Customary Law?", 1932 (in Russ).

The Great Yassa.—The writer supposes that the Yassa of Jenghiz Khan is mainly a collection of provisions of customary law supplemented by certain mandatory provisions (influenced to a certain extent by Chinese Law, of which more will be said below).[2]

In order to prove this assertion, we shall compare such fragments of the Yassa of Jenghiz Khan as have come down to us with the customs, way of life and morals of the Mongol tribes.

The first fragment of the Great Yassa speaks of the death penalty for adulterers.

Similar provisions (concerning the punishment for adultery) may be found in all ancient legislations (Manu, Hammurabi, Moses, The XII Tables, etc.) and their origins are common. They are all designed to protect the family, the individual character of which was just then taking shape. When from group or unordered marriage the individual (polygamous or monogamous) family began to emerge, new social conditions gave rise first to customs and then to laws, providing measures for the defence of such indivualized families; and the idea of adultery and the punishment for it arose. Thus the origin of the provisions for the punishment of adultery lies in customary law. This was probably how it originated among the Mongols.[3] But the form in which it is set out in the Yassa of Jenghiz Khan (its severe sanction) causes us to suppose that Chinese Law might have exersised some influence upon its contents.

The process of the individualization of the family did not develop among the Mongols to the same extent as among some other ancient peoples and the death penalty for adultery stood in contradiction to the views of the Mongols on adultery and to their customs. In particular, the severity of the provision in the first fragment of the Yassa contradicts the views of Jenghiz Khan himself as expressed in his maxims Nos. 19, 22 and 29, which express the sensual ideal of earthly happiness.

Such a severe attitude towards adultery was out of harmony with Mongol life and law. Almost all investigators have remarked on the

---

2 "The very meaning of the word Yassak, or its abbreviation Yassa is law or orderliness, which shows that the original Yassa was a collection of provisions based on popular customs "Yusun" (cf. the "Adat" of the mountain people of the Caucasus)" Berezin—"Outline of the Inner Organization of the Ooloos of Jushi" Works of the Oriental Section R. Arch. S., VIII, 1863, 405.

3 Rubruquis informs us that: "They punish homicide with the death sentence which is also a penalty for living with a woman not one's own" (op. sit. pg. 79). By "one's own woman" Rubruquis explains should be understood a wife or servant.

well-known freedom of sexual relations among the Mongols.[4] The ancient Tsaadjin-Bichik provided a fine of one horse for ordinary adultery, while adultery with women living with priests went unpunished (Art. 3 and 1). By the terms of the Regulations of 1640, adultery was punished by a moderate fine; and adultery with a maid was not punished at all (Art. 70) According to the customary law of Autonomous Mongolia, adultery was punished only in cases of *flagrant delit,* only the adulterer being punished by a fine of one horse. In China, on the other hand, adultery was rather severely prosecuted and the purity of family relations zealously guarded. The ancient punishment of castration, one of the five basic executions of China, was prescribed precisely for such violation of continence. By the law of the Ta Ch'ing dynasty the penalty for adultery was from a hundred strokes of the rod to death, and in cases of *flagrant delit,* the husband could kill his wife and her lover.[5] It is characteristic that the death penalty for adultery (undoubtedly the result of the influence of Chinese law) appeared again in the Codes issued by China for Mongolia in 1789 and 1815. Besides this, it may be noted that in the Yassa of Jenghiz Khan it was specially emphasized that all adulterers should be punished, regardless of whether they were married or not, while Mongol Customary Law did not punish a maid for adultery. All this has given us reason to suppose that the severity of the punishment for adultery in the Yassa of Jenghiz Khan may be explained by the desire of the legislator, under the influence of Chinese Law, to more energetically combat this practice.[6] We may therefore consider Frag. I as a legislative provision.[7]

Fragment 2 deals with the death penalty for persons guilty of sodomy. Sexual relations with animals are a crime common to pastoral peoples and are met with among peoples other than the Mongols, e.g. among the Jews (Exodus, Chap. XII).

Fragment 3 provides for the death penalty for deliberate liars, soothsayers, persons spying on the behavior of others, and persons interfering between participants in a brawl.

The last mentioned provision arises from the customs of the steppe. Steppe-dwellers have always been fond of unusual sights and contests. When, in the steppes, two men wrestled or fought, a ring of

---

4 Of the modern authors, v. Maisky, "Modern Mongolia", 1921, pg. 41; Geleta, "The New Mongolia," 1936, pg. 242.

5 *v.* next paragraph.

6 For further particulars see the next paragraph.

7 Unfortunately contemporary sources shed no light on this question. Plano-Carpini writes: ". . . further they have a law or custom to kill a man or a woman whom they discover in flagrant adultery" (Op. cit. 15.) And the words of Rubruquis, given above, are placed in Chap. X which may contain both customary and mandatory laws.

onlookers was formed around them but it was not permitted to interfere in the battle. The contestants were first permitted to conclude their trial of strengh and only then was it decided who was in the right. Rubruquis wrote of this as follows: "Of their administration of justice know this, that when two fight on one dares interfere, even a father may not help his son; but he who proves to be the weaker must appeal to the court of the King, and if after this appeal the other touch him he is killed. But he had to go there at once, the one who suffered the insult leading the other as a prisoner."[8] It is evidently this custom that is treated in Fragment 3 of the Yassa. Article 71 of the Mongol-Oirat Code contains a similar provision.

Here too, in Fragment 3 of the Yassa, we meet the death penalty for soothsaying. On this subject Rubruquis writes: "...... in the same way they put to death witches, of whom, however, I shall tell you later, as they consider such women to be poisoners."[9] And indeed, Rubruquis devotes the whole of a succeeding chapter (Chap. XLVII) to clairvoyants and magicians, demonstrating that the Mongols believed in the evil influence of magic charms and put witches to death. We thus see that Art. 3 of the Yassa simply formulates the popular customs and superstitions of the Mongols.

Framents 4,15,8 and 32.

Fragment 4 formulates another custom based on the beliefs and superstitions of the Mongols. "He that urinates into water or ashes shall be put to death."

Banzarov writes: "Esteeming fire as the source and symbol of purity, the Mongols held it in great honour and strove to preserve it in cleanliness; they did not throw into it things giving rise to a bad odour or which weakened its intensity or brightness; and considered it a sin to pour water on it, spit upon it, etc. Sacrifices delivered to the fire had to be such as would increase the flame: wine, butter or fat. Besides this, fire was treated with the same honour as the effigies of the gods; it was forbidden to step over it or to threaten it with sharp weapons."[10]

Another such custom is contained in Fragment 15. "He forbade them to wash their clothes while they wore them and until they were completely worn out."[11]

---

8 Op. cit. Chap. X, pg. 79.

9 *Ibid.*

10 "The Black Faith, or Shamanism, Among the Mongols", 1891, pg. 23-24. *v.* Lama Gomboev, "On the Ancient Mongol Customs and Superstitions Described by Plano-Carpini", Works of the O.S. R. Arch. So., vol. IV, 238-240. Cf. also Petri on the Buriats—"Elements of Tribal Relationships Among the Northern Buriats", ppg. 9-10. The offering by newly married women of sacrifices to the family fire formed part of the Buriat marriage ceremonies (*v.* "Cus. Law of Mong. Tribes," ppg. 230-232, note).

11 *Cf.* Gomboev—Op. Cit., ppg. 255-256.

Still another custom is formulated in Fragment 8, which prescribes the method of slaughtering animals ("the legs should be tied, the belly slit open, and the heart squeezed in the hand") and not according to the Moslem practice. Hara-Davan has pointed out that this custom is still preserved among the Kalmucks.[12]

Finally, Fragment 32 contains the following resolution, based on the superstitions of the Mongols: "A man choking on his food shall be dragged under a tent and immediately killed; and a man who steps with his foot on the threshold of the chief's tent shall also be put to death."

In elucidation we shall permit ourselves to quote the following from Plano-Carpini's history of the Mongols (Para, 11, "On That Which They Consider Sinful."[13]).

"Although they have no law on just actions or preservation from sin, they nevertheless have some conception of that which they consider sinful, conceived either by themselves or by their ancestors. One of these is that it is evil to plunge a knife into a flame or in any other way to touch fire with a knife, or to use a knife to take meat out of the pot, or to chop with an axe in the neighbourhood of a fire, as they believe that in this way the head is taken off the flame; also to lean on the whip with which they drive their horses (since they wear no spurs); also to touch arrows with a whip; also to catch or kill young birds; to strike a horse with a bridle; to break a bone against another bone; to pour milk or any other food or drink on the ground; to urinate in a tent. If anyone does these things voluntarily he is put to death; if otherwise, he must pay much money to the sorcerer to cleanse him and make his tent too and all that is in it to go through two fires, and before it is so purified no one dares enter it or take anything out of it. In the same way, if anyone put a piece into the mouth of another and he cannot swallow it and throws it out of his mouth, they make a hole under his tent and drag him out through this hole and kill him without any mercy; and in the same way, should anyone step on the threshold of the tent of a chief he is put to death in exactly the same way. And they have many other things like these of which it would take too long to tell."[14]

Lama Halsan Gomboev writes of this evidence given by Plano-Carpini: "The enumerated actions which the Mongols considered sinful are almost all considered as such to this day."[15]

---

12 "Jenghiz-Khan", pg. 154, ftn. 4.

13 *Op. cit.* ppg. 9-10. Cf. Rashid-Eddin—"History of the Mongols, Introduction, Proceedings of the O.S.R.A.S. *v.* XIV, 142.

14 *Cf.* "The Travels of Sir John Mandeville", 1900, Ch. XXVI, pg. 163, evidently from Plano-Carpini.

15 Op. cit. 248-9.

Further on the same author (Plano-Carpini) writes: "They consider it a great sin if any food or drink be allowed to go to waste, and in this connection do not permit the throwing of bones to dogs before the marrow had been sucked out of them. Their clothes they likewise do not wash, or allow to wash, and especially at such times as it begins to thunder and until such time as the thunder ceases."[16]

Rubruquis informs us that: "...... they never wash their clothes, as they say that God will be angry and there will be thunder if these are hung out to dry. Moreover, they beat those washing their clothes and take their clothes away."[17]

In the Hsi Yu Tze we find: "Your subjects, in Summer, do not bathe in the rivers, neither do they wash their clothes or make felt, and it is forbidden to gather mushrooms in the fields: because they fear the wrath of heaven."[18]

From the extracts quoted, without any commentaries, it is clear that the Fragments of the Yassa with which we have dealt gave expression to the customs and superstitions of the Mongols.

Fragment 5 provides for the death penalty for threefold bankruptcy and represents a provision of mandatory law.

Fragments 6,7 and 9.

Fragment 6 deals with the putting to death of persons giving food or clothing to captives without the consent of their captors, Frag. 7, with the execution of persons hiding fugitive slaves or captives, Frag 9, with the execution of persons refusing to take part in a battle. All these bear the imprint of Mongol custom.

Many sources note in particular the wide application among the ancient Mongols of the general principle of mutual aid.[19] This may be explained by the strength of the clan order. It is easy to understand the place of mutual aid during campaigns and battles—all the more since the Mongols took part in campaigns and battles in clans and tribes under the command of their clan and tribal chiefs (heads of ten, a hundred, a thousand, and ten thousand). This mutual aid, not only in battle but also in ordinary life (it arose in the communal hunts) was especially emphasised in the Mongol-Oirat Regulations of 1640. Because of this it is difficult to see in the principles of mutual aid in battle set forth in Fragment 9 an innovation introduced by Jenghiz Khan.

---

16 Op. cit. ppg. 14, Rashid Ed-din—"History of the Mongols", Introduction, Proceedings of the O.S.R.A.S. XIV, 142.

17 Op. cit. pg. 78.

18 Works of the Members of the Russian Orthodox Mission, IV, pg. 157.

19 Cf. e.g. Plano-Carpini, 13, Hsi Yu Tze, 138, etc.

Similar traces of Mongol custom are present in Fragments 6 and 7 (in which captives are treated as slaves and both are regarded as the absolute property of their masters, to be jealously guarded as such.)

Fragment 10—on the exemption from taxes and tribute of representatives of science and religion, was a mandatory provision.

Fragments 11 and 16.

Fragment 11: "He resolved to respect all faiths, giving preference to none; all this he prescribed as a means of pleasing God." This item bears the mark of a moral rule and relates rather to the Maxims of Jenghiz Khan, as do undoubtedly Fragment 33 of the Yassa and, in part, Fragments 30 and 31 (see further).

The absence of penal sanctions in this provision, and the religious sanction with which it concludes, go to support this supposition. But we cannot state this with sufficient assurance due to the low level of the juridical technique of the times. It is possible that Jenghiz Khan, in his Yassa, wished to give expression to the principle of religious toleration without prescribing penalties for its violation.

Of the same character is Fragment 16, forbidding the distinction between the pure and impure.

Fragments 12,13 and 14 are undoubted expressions of the customs of the steppes.

Fragment 12 forbids "the eating of anything in the presence of another without inviting him to partake of it." This is an expression of the Mongol custom of hospitality. Plano-Carpini writes of the Mongols: "Though they have little food they gladly divide it among themselves."[20] And Rubruquis states: "With the meat of one sheep they feed to 50 or 100 persons, they cut it into small pieces on a tray, together with salt and water and extend to every man of those around one or two pieces, depending upon the number of eaters."[21] "This habit of hospitality remains in full force at the present time", states Lama Halsan Gomboev.[22] Investigators of Buriat life, (Shchapov, Hangalov, Petri) state that each time a Buriat roasted food the whole settlement came to him and partook of his fare. This practice existed also among the Kalmucks.

Another prohibition contained in Article 12 forbids anyone "to eat from the hands of another until the offerer himself has bitten a piece out of the offered food."

---

20 Op. cit. pg. 12

21 Op. cit. pg. 73.

22 Op cit. pg. 259.

This is an expression of ancient Oriental caution, here fear of poisoning (*cf*. the death of Jenghiz Khan's father).

The third prohibition contained in Frament 12 is also of customary origin. It forbids "stepping over the festal fire and over dishes from which food is eaten" (this is analogous to the prohibition contained in Fr. 4, forbidding urination into water or ashes). Among the steppe Mongols (and Shamanists) water and fire are sacred. Sacred too are food and drink. "They consider it a great sin if any food or drink is in any way wasted", writes Plano-Carpini.[23] From this we see that Fragment 12 too contains expressions of Mongol custom.

Fragment 13 undoubtedly contains provisions of customary law relating to the hospitality of the steppes. It states that anyone passing persons engaged in eating may dismount from his horse and join the meal without asking permission. The Hsi Yu Tze corroborates this: "Coming upon a dinner they (the Mongols) unceremoniously seat themselves together with the hosts."[24] Hara-Davan records the preservation of this customs among the Kalmucks.[25]

Not only Fr. 13, but also Fr. 14, is closely related to Fr. 12. Fr. 14 states: "He forbade them to dip their hands in water and ordered them to use some vessel to bail water." The Yassa forbade the dipping of hands into water—for what purpose? The answer emerges from the end of the Fragment. For the purpose of drinking. The Yassa forbade cupping water in the hands for drinking and prescribed the use of vessels for this purpose. Why is this prohibition made? Because some of the precious fluid, if taken up in the hands, is spilled on the ground and lost. We have given above the testimony of a contemporary, Plano-Carpini, to the effect that the Mongols considered it a great sin if any food or drink were wasted. And in another place the same author states that the Mongols considered it sinful to "spill on the ground milk or any other drink" (Op. cit. pg. 9). It is evident that Fr. 14 of the Yassa gave expression to the Mongol custom, reinforced by religious sanction, of conserving the liquid so precious in the steppes.

Fragments 17 and 24.

Fr. 17. The Great Yassa contains Jenghiz Khan's prohibition forbidding anyone "to pronounce words emphatically, employ titles of honour, or in addressing a sultan, or each other, to use anything but simply his name." This provision is also a crystallisation of ancient customs. The customs of the Mongols were simple, but, after the con-

23 Op. cit. pg. 14, cf. Rashid Ed-din., op. cit, Proc. of the Arch. Soc., XIV, 137.

24 Works of the Russ. Orth. Mission, IV, 1910, pg. 138.

25 Jenghiz-Khan, pg. 15, ftn. 2.

quest by Jenghiz of various cultured peoples such as the Uigurs, the Turcoman Moslems and especially the Chinese, the more complex customs and pompous ceremonies of these peoples began to spread among the Mongols. Men Hun, a contemporary of Jenghiz, testifies to the simplicity of the life and morality of the Mongols and of Jenghiz Khan himself, and points out that under the influence of Chinese (Chin) officials the Mongols began to lose this simplicity in their relations.[26] This foreign influence was combatted by Jenghiz Khan in Fr. 17 (and 24) of his Yassa by means of reinforcing the old Mongol customs.

The same purpose, evidently, is pursued by Fr. 24, which forbids Emirs (on pain of death) to appeal to anyone except the sovereign. This provision supports the personal contact between Emirs (commanders of thousands, hundreds and tens) and the sovereign. No court barriers were to hinder this. This simple relation to the sovereign was not created by Jenghiz. It existed among the Mongols before him and he only strove to reinforce and preserve it.

Fr. 18, containing instructions to the successors of Jenghiz Khan to personally inspect their troops and arms before battle, is a mandatory provision.

Fr. 19 reads: "He prescribed that women accompanying the troops carry out the work and duties of the men when these go to battle." This provision has customary significance.

Plano-Carpini says of the Mongols: "The men do nothing at all, except making arrows and taking partial charge of the herds: but they hunt and practise archery. Maids and women ride on horseback and gallop as well as the men. We also saw that they carried quivers and bows. Like the men, the women can ride long and persistently. Their wives make everything: jackets, dresses, shoes and boots, and everything is sewn out of leather; they also drive carts and mend them, lead camels, and in all their affairs are very swift and able. All the women wear trousers and shoot just like the men."[27]

M. N. Bogdanov, writing of the communal hunts of the ancient Buriats (approximately of the epoch of Jenghiz Khan) states: "Women took part in the hunt just as did the men and competed with them, often excelling them in horsemanship, archery, ability in wielding the sword and spear, etc."[28]

---

26 *v.* Groom-Grzimailo—"Western Mongolia and the Urianhai Region", II, pg. 434, ftn. 4. *v.* also Hsi Yu Tze, or Description of Travels to the West, Works of the Russian Orthodox Mission, 1910, pg. 138 *in fine*.

27 Op. cit., ppg. 15, 15.

28 "Outline of the History of the Buriat-Mongol People", pg. 14.

Thus, in times of peace, the Mongol women did a large part of the work of the men, participated in the communal hunts of wild beasts and often accompanied their husbands to batle, helping them and taking their places wherever they could do so.

Fragment 20—on the introduction of taxes is a mandatory provision.

Fr. 20 contains the order that all men "present their daughters to the Sultan at the beginning of each year, that he may chose from among them for himself and his sons." This prescription is of a purely customary character and certainly not a legislative innovation introduced by Jenghiz Khan. However great the authority of Jenghiz, it is difficult, if not impossible to believe that he could introduce such a practice by decree. But as an expression of an already existing custom, the presence of this provision in the Yassa is both understandable and appropriate. We may here recall that a similar custom existed among the Russians. In Muscovite Russia, before the marriage of a young Czar, brides were likewise summoned from all the cities of the country and the Czar inspected them and chose a wife from among them. In Muscovite Russia monogamy was the rule, and therefore such summons and inspections were rare. In the Mongolia of the time of Jenghiz, however, widespread polygamy was practiced and the custom consequently took on a systematic character.

The evidence of contemporaries also supports the supposition of the customary nature of this phenomenon. Plano-Carpini writes of the Mongols of his time (1246 A.D.) that: "each of them has as many wives as he can support; some a hundred, some fifty, some ten, some more and some less." In another place, when describing the power of the Mongol Emperor, Plano-Carpini writes: "...... in the same way, if he asks for a maid or anyone's sister she is given to him without any resistance. More than this, every year or every few years he collects maidens from all the Tartar territories and if he wishes, keeps any for himself or gives them to his people as he sees fit."[29] Marco Polo points out that such presentation of daughters to the Khan bore the character of an inspection at which the fittest were selected, so that the fathers "looked upon it as a mercy and an honour done to them."[30]

Fragment 22 of the Yassa (on the division of troops into tens, hundreds and thousands) was also evidently not a novelty, being an expression of Mongol custom. A contemporary of Jenghiz Khan, the historian Men Hun, tells us that Yesukai, the father of Jenghiz, was a chief

---

29 Plano-Carpini, "History of the Mongols", 1911, ppg. 5, 23.

30 "The Travels of Marco Polo", by M. Komroff 1928, ppg. 125, 127.

of ten men.[31] The Secret Chronicle reports the existence of chiefs of a hundred men, and chiefs of ten thousand before the proclamation by Jenghiz Khan of the system of organization of his troops.[32] From this we may infer that the decimal system of organization of troops existed among the Mongols before Jenghiz Khan. Academician Vladimirtsov, describing the organization of his armed forces by Jenghiz remarks that "...... in accordance with the old custom, dating back to ancient times, he divided them (the troops) into thousands, hundreds, and tens."[33] Similar testimony is offered by Academician Barthold: "As among all nomadic peoples, chiefs of ten, a hundred, a thousand, and ten thousand headed the troops, long before the time of Jenghiz Khan."[34] The Russians, at the time of their conquest of the Northern Buriats, found still extant among them the decimal system of division of the Buriat tribes, the origin of which M. N. Bogdanov traces to the epoch of Zegete Aba or community hunts which preceded the epoch of Jenghiz Khan.[35]

Fragment 23 commands even the highest Emir to deliver himself into the hands of even the lowest servant sent by the Khan to punish or even execute him. Fragment 24 prescribes the death penalty for non-fulfilment of the commands of the Khan. Khan Guyuk defined the duties of a Mongol as follows: "To carry out my will; to appear wherever I shall call him; to go where I command; and to put to death anyone I sentence."

This absolute rule of the Khan was not created by the Yassa, neither was it an innovation introduced by Jenghiz Khan. Rather it expressed the power of the tribal elder and chief as it was formed during the struggle of the Mongol tribes for existence. Plano-Carpini has the following to say in this connection: "The Emperor of these Tartars has a wonderful power over all. No one dares to stay in a country where the Emperor has not commanded him to go. He himself orders the great chiefs where to live, the great chiefs fix the domicile of the chiefs of a thousand, the chiefs of a thousand that of the chiefs of a hundred, the chiefs of a hundred those of the chiefs of ten. Besides this, all his orders at any time and at any place, concerning war or life or death, are obeyed by them without any contradiction."[36] "The same power is possessed by

31 Groom-Grzimailo, Op. cit., pg. 406, ftn. 2.

32 Yuan Ch'ao Mi Shih (The Secret Chronicle), was a Mongol chronicle dated 1240 A.D. It was translated by Palladius. (Works of the R. Orth. M. IV, 1910, ppg. 29, 47 etc. cf. 49).

33 Jenghiz Khan, 1929, pg. 65.

34 Barthold—"Turkestan in the Epoch of the Mongol Invasion", p. II, 1900, pg. 415.

35 "Outline of the History of the Buriat-Mongol People", 1926, pg. 15. "Such organization could have arisen", he stated, "in the hoary epoch of the formation of the military-nomadic empire of the Mongols which was later to be united under the rule of Jenghiz Khan."

36 "History of the Mongols", 1911, pg. 23.

the chiefs over their people, i.e. Tartars and others who are apportioned among the chiefs. . . . In short, the Emperor and his chiefs take from their property whatever they may want. With their persons too, they deal in whatever way they see fit."[37]

The Yassa speaks of the absolute power of the Khan, and Plano-Carpini points out that the same power (within the limits of their competence) was exercised by the chiefs. It is evident that we are here dealing with the power of the tribal chiefs of the Mongols, and of the highest chief over them, and that this power was created not by the Yassa but by life itself. The Yassa only fixes and applies on the scale of the entire Empire that which was formed on a tribal scale by the Mongol tribes in their battle for existence.

That this is precisely the viewpoint from which this question must be considered is made evident by data relating to a sphere far removed from the Yassa of Jenghiz Khan, the customary law of the Northern Buriats. Hangalov and Clementz,[38] the investigators of the life and law of the Northern Buriats, maintain that in ancient times and before the Russian conquest, the power of the Noyon heading the tribe, which developed in the struggles with other tribes bore an absolute character and included the right of full control over the persons and property of their subjects, and the power of life and death. Even the Taishas who replaced the Noyons after the Russian conquest, had, in spite of the softening Russian influence, exceptional powers over their tribes. "In the past", writes Hangalov, "the power of the tribal chief, i.e. the head Taisha, was extremely great; and the Buriats literally trembled before him and obeyed unconditionally all his orders and instructions. The head Taisha was once the only chief of his jurisdiction; his assistant, the Zaisan-Noyon, the tribal Shulengas, Ooloos elders and other Buriats were in all respects subject to his will. The decisions of the chief Taisha were considered final and if anyone dared to appeal against his decisions to the Russian government, this was considered a great crime and generally a most unusual event."[39] In the light of these customs it is clear that neither Fragment 23 nor many of the others represent any novelty introduced by Jenghiz Khan. On the contrary, they stem from the tribal life and customs of the Mongols.

---

37 Ibid. pg. 24.

38 *v.* the following articles. Hangalov & Clementz: "Communal Hunts Among the Northern Buriats", Materials on the ethnography of Russia, vol. I; Khangalov: "Juridical Customs of the Buriats", Etnographicheskoe Obozrenie, 1894, No. 2; Khangalov: "Zegete—Hunts." Proceedings of the N. E. Sect. of the Russ Geogr. Soc., 1888, XIX, No. 3 (all in Russ.).

39 To the above we may add that the same features characterized the power of the Kalmuck khans (Khoo Urluk, Shu-kur-Daichin, Puntzuk and Ayuk) although the Code by which the Kalmucks were ruled (the Mongol-Oirat Code of 1640) contains no resolutions analogous to Fr. 23 of the Yassa.

Fr. 25 provides for the establishment of permanent post offices. It is a mandatory measure.

Fr. 26 entrusts to Jagatai, the son of Jenghiz, the task of seeing that the provisions of the Yassa were carried out. This is a provision of a technical character. It shows how great an importance was attached to the Yassa by Jenghiz, who entrusted the supervision of its application to his second son, the stern Jagatai.[40]

Fr. 27, which contains provisions for the severe punishment of negligent soldiers and hunters letting a beast escape during a hunt, bears evident marks of its origin in the customs and life of the Mongol tribes. The prescriptions of this fragment may be considered as measures for the strengthening of the discipline in the army. They did not, however, represent innovations introduced by Jeghiz Khan. The punishment of soldiers for negligence undoubtedly existed before Jenghiz Khan, and independently of the Yassa. The interesting feature of this provision is the identity of the status of soldiers and huntsmen. In the epoch we are considering, communal hunts of wild animals served not as recreation and amusement, but as a very necessary and important source of securing the means of existence of the tribes engaged in them.[41] This put them on a level with cattle-breeding (and war). Among certain tribes just beginning to enter the stage of pastoral economy, (e.g. the Buriats) the hunts served as the main means of existence.[42] As we know the Great Khans of the Mongols, Jenghiz Khan, Ogodai, Guyuk, Munké and Kublai, personally led such hunts. The same regulations as governed the hunts were applied in military campaigns. It is therefore not surprising that the negligence of a participant in a tribal hunt was considered by the Yassa as equivalent to negligence on the part of a warrior, and therefore worthy of severe punishment. The provision simply expresses the exigencies of the social life of the period, which had their origin before the time of Jenghiz Khan.

Fr. 28 introduces ransom from punishment for homicide. It is possible that we are here dealing with a Mongol custom which replaced

---

40 *v.* "Secret Chronicle of Jenghiz-Khan", Works, IV. pg. 69. Juchi said to Jagatai: "Besides your wrathful character what other talents have you?" Jagatai never smiled and inspired terror in his subordinates (Barthold, Turkestan, 1900, II, 497).

41 *v.* Rubruquis—"Travels to Eastern Lands", 1911, pg. 76: "And so by hunting they procure for themselves a large part of their nourishment." cf. the description of a hunt, in the same work.

42 Investigators of the life of the ancient Buriats (Hangalov, Clementz, Bogdanov) even suppose that the entire social system of the Buriats (and partly of the Mongols) arose from the tribal hunts.

the concept of the blood feud.[43] Marco Polo reports the existence of the substitution of fines for the death penalty and also for punishment for theft.[44]

Fr. 29, which prescribes a ninefold fine or death for the theft of a horse, is a customary-legal provision.

Theft, generally, was severely punished among the Mongols. This was true in particular with regard to the theft of cattle, which was their basic form of property and means of existence. Punishment for the theft of cattle by a ninefold fine (in cattle) or in units of nine head, was an ancient Mongol custom which found expression as well in the Mongol Oirat Code of 1640, Khalkha Djirum and in the law of the Kalmucks. The system of punishments in the Mongol-Oirat Code of 1640 and Khalkha Djirum was chiefly based on property fines calculated in nines of cattle. The customary significance of the number nine among the Mongols may be seen, for instance, from the Yuan Ch'ao Mi Shih: nine genuflections, to deliver from nine punishments, a gathering of people of nine dialects, etc.[45]

Fragments 30 and 31 are not original provisions of the Yassa but a condensed account of the contents of the Yassa by the Armenian writers Vartan and Mahakia.

Analysing the contents of Fragments 30 and 31 of the Yassa we notice two types of provisions. In the first place both fragments contain brief summaries of the articles of the Yassa on the prohibition of lying, theft and adultery, the exemption of the clergy from taxation (cf. Fr. 1, 3, 10, and 21 of the Yassa), and secondly some moral rules representing the Maxims of Jenghiz Khen (to love one's neighbours, to forget insults, to spare temples from destruction, etc.) An analogous example is found in Fr. 33 of the Yassa ("If it is impossible to stop drinking, it is permitted to get drunk thrice a month." . . . .). Fr. 33 also contains a moral injunction. Some historians consider this fragment to have been part of the Yassa, while Rashid Ed-din and others ascribe it to the Maxims of Jenghiz Khan (cf. Maxim 20.) It is undoubted that Fragment 33 contains sayings of Jenghiz Khan. This is also evidently true of Fragments 30 and 31 (which, besides provisions of the Yassa, also contain similar sayings and moral rules referring not to a time of war but to a state of peace.) Such a conclusion is supported

---

43 The existence of the blood-feud among the Mongols may be seen from Yuan Shih. Thus Jenghiz Khan took vengeance for the death of his father, justifying his invasion of North China by the fact that the Chins killed his ancestor. Krause, "Cingis-Han", 1922, pg. 28, Secret Chronicle, ftn. 536, *v.* also Maxim 21.

44 Pg. 91, see above.

45 Pg. 25 and ftn. 144, ppg. 59, 65, etc. Cf. also Rashid-ed-din.

by the reasons which follow. If the rule to love others as one's self, not to offer insult, etc. was a provision of the Yassa whose violation was punishable by death, then the first person deserving the death penalty would have been Jenghiz Khan himself, who utterly wiped out such towns as Gazna, Balkh and others and put all their inhabitants to the sword. We know well the saying of Batu: "Anyone who violates the Yassa shall lose his head." Yet we Russians are well aware that Batu himself often violated Fragments 30 and 31 of the Yassa, the sacking of Kiev, Vladimir, and other towns, the slaying of their inhabitants and destruction of their churches being sufficient proof of this. Consequently Batu too was deserving of death, both by virtue of Fragment 31 of the Yassa and of his own promise. It is evident that a ruler as wise as Jenghiz would never introduce a measure and prescribe a penalty for its violation if he knew that that measure was absolutely impossible of fulfilment for himself and his commanders and successors. Attaching great importance to the Yassa and charging his son with the supervision of strict adherence to its provisions he might then have put himself and his successors in the anomalous position of being the first violators of the Code. It is clear that we are here dealing with the Maxims (wishes) of Jenghiz Khan.

Fragments 30 and 31 (as well as 33) of the Yassa must therefore be excluded from the scope of our review (recapitulation of laws and customs), since their moral rules belong neither to the body of customary nor to that of mandatory law. Their legislative provisions also have no independent significance, being merely repetitions of provisions (customs or laws) recorded in other fragments of the Yassa and thus already noted in these pages.

Fragment 33 is not an article of the Yassa but one of his maxims. This may be seen both from its contents and from the fact that Rashid Ed-din considered it to belong to the maxims (cf. maxim 20) and it was one of the other writers who included it in the list of fragments of the Yassa.

Fragments 34, 35 and 36, contain provisions of private law which are undoubtedly of customary origin.

Thus we meet here the institutions of polygamy and concubinage, both institutions of customary law natural to pastoral life. The division of inheritance among sons with the exclusion of daughters from the heritage, the privileges of eldest sons[46] and the legacy of the father's house to the youngest son are all based on Mongol customs (they are met also among the Kalmucks). Also based on Mongol custom is the right of the son to dispose of his father's wives, etc.

46 "Ten to the elder, four to the younger," said an old Mongol proverb (Rashid Ed-din).

Having considered all the 36 fragments of the Yassa which have come down to us, we may come to the following conclusion:

Four of the fragments (26, 30, 31, and 33) must be excluded from the scope of our study for reasons already given above. The contents of the other 32 fragments may be summarised as follows:

Twenty fragments contain provisions of customary law or are based on such provisions (2-4, 8, 12-15, 17, 19, 21-24, 27, 29, 32, 34-36); four fragments (6, 7, 9, 28) contain traces of customary law; the nature of three is uncertain being variously interpreted as belonging to the body of customary law, mandatory law, or the Maxims (1, 11, 16) and five fragments are purely mandatory (5, 10, 18, 20, and 25.)

To the above we may add that the fragments of the Yassa often contain not one but several provisions. This applies especially to the fragments containing customary provisions (e.g. Frs. 12, 17, 35 etc.) Because of this the inequality in the number of customary and mandatory provisions contained in the Yassa respectively is actually greater than the inequality in the number of the respective fragments.

It may therefore be supposed that the foregoing analysis of the contents of the Great Yassa justifies us in regarding the Yassa as a record of predominantly customary law supplemented by several mandatory provisions.[47]

The Ancient Tsaadjin-Bichik.—The provisions of the ancient Tsaadjin-Bichik are customary in character.

Thus, we consider that the provisions concerning adultery, contained in articles 1-4 of the Tsaadjin-Bichik are of customary origin. This view is convincingly supported by the lightness of the punishment provided by the Tsaadjin-Bichik for adultery which is characteristic of Mongol customary law (cf. the Mongol-Oirat Code, art. 69, and the customary law of Autonomous Mongolia) which expressed the customs and morals of the Mongols in this respect and their toleration of a certain degree of sexual liberty. The punishment of adultery by the fine of one horse, as decreed by the Tsaadjin-Bichik, was also found in the customary law of Autonomous Mongolia[48] (while, at the same time, the written Code provided extremely severe penalties, including that of death, for the offence[49]). The exemption from punishment of those having relations with women cohabiting with priests may be explained as follows. The article deals with adultery with the priest's concubines

47 This conclusion is not contradicted by the testimony of Rashid Ed-din that the Yassa was composed of innovations and ancient rules. It is indeed undoubtely true that the Yassa contains both innovations and ancient regulations, with a significant predominance of the latter.

48 And in the Code of the Hori Buriats, 1781 and the Steppe Code of 1808 (art. 61).

49 *v.* the Code of 1815, III, 75-78.

or paramours, not with his wife, while the next article speaks of adultery with the wife of a prince. Evidently priests did not have wives and were bound to celibacy; and, since they could have concubines only illegally, adultery with these women was not punished. Thus the toleration of adultery with their paramours (while adultery with the slave of other persons was punished, *v.* Art. 4) was, as it were, a punishment imposed upon the priests for the violation of their vows of celibacy. The fact that the penalty for adultery with the wife of a prince (Art. 2) was lighter than that for ordinary adultery (Art. 3) can be explained as follows. By ordinary adultery was meant adultery between Mongol commoners (analogous expressions being found in Mongol documents). Article 2 treats not of such ordinary adultery but of adultery between persons of princely rank (relatives). Although the terms of the article bear a general character and may also cover adultery between a princess and a commoner, the expression "in sign of penitence" instead of the ordinary punitive sanction points to the privileged position of the criminal. It is necessary at the same time to bear in mind that the Mongol commoner committing a crime against a prince was subject to more than ordinarily severe penalties, while adultery with the relatives of one's husband was more lightly punished (cf. Steppe Code of 1808 art. 61). Thus we may take it that the first four articles of the Tsaadjin-Bichik dealing with adultery contain provisions of customary law.

The next article (5) of the Tsaadjin-Bichik contains the following resolution: "As soon as a youth is grown and can work for himself he is no longer subject to his father and may demand, if he wishes, the allotment to him of a part of the herds, and may separate himself completely and become the direct subject of the prince."

This article deals with the institution of the division of families or the separation of sons. The right of sons to such separation and allotments arises from the concept of property as something belonging to the entire family. This concept and the rights of sons arising from it are both of a customary legal character. There was no need for the intervention of the prince in such separations and allotments and all this could be and was accomplished within the family without the prince's participation: a special yurt was set up for the grown son, the fire was brought over from the yurt of the father and the basis of a new household laid. Among the contemporary Mongols and Buriats such allotments are still accomplished in accordance with customary forms, with or even without that participation of the family council.[50] It is possible and even probable that the new household was immediately considered

50 *v.* the writer's "Mongol Law", pg. 277 (in Russian); cf. Maisky, "Modern Mongolia", pg. 24; Petri, "Internal Tribal Relations Among the Northern Buriats", 1925; ppg. 37-39.

as a new taxable unit, a new subject of the prince, but these were secondary and supplementary considerations. In its essence the institution was customary in character. Moreover, the rights of sons described above are indicative of the weakening of family ties and the disintegration of common property with its accompanying individualisation of property.

The three succeeding articles were expressions of the customs and life of the Kalmucks (Oirats). The first dealt with fights between Kalmucks, in which it was permitted to pull one another by the hair hanging from the crown of the head but not by the queues, the signs of citizenship (6); the second with the position of women as housewives: a woman sitting in her usual place at the hearth at the foot of the master's bed could not be touched by anyone, whereas she herself could curse any other person or throw a piece of wood or anything else at him; but if she left her place or went out of the yurt she lost these rights and was subject to the usual penalty for insult (7). The third treated the position of women generally: if a woman appealed to a prince for the exemption of her relatives from fine, the prince, out of respect to her sex, usually annulled small fines and reduced larger ones by half.[51] Generally, among the Kalmucks women were protected and insults to women were more severely punished than those to men (8). All three of these provisions were expressions of Mongol custom and were of a customary character. This is confirmed, among others, by Academician Pallas, who reports that all these provisions were applied, in his time, by the Russian Kalmucks, i.e. that they were Kalmuck customs (since we have no knowledge of the application of the old Tsaadjin-Bichik among the Kalmucks). Thus we see that the majority of the provisions of the Tsaadjin-Bichik Code of the XV-th century which have survived to our day were customary in character.

The Mongol-Oiral Regulations (*Code*) *of 1640*.—In the writer's opinion, the basic and most important sources of the Code of 1640 was the customary law of the Mongol tribes. But it cannot be denied that there were other sources, such as the old Tsaadjin-Bichik and the canonical law of the Lamaists. Moreover, the Code contains provisions of intertribal mandatory law. In other words, the writer regards the Mongol Oirat Code of 1640 like the Yassa of Jenghiz Khan, as a collection of predominantly customary law. This conclusion is confirmed by an analysis of its contents.

The provisions of the Code dealing with tribal life are undoubtedly customary in character: the combination of yurts into hotons,

---

51 Cf. art. 65 of the M.O. Regulations of 1640—if a woman bringing wine and sheep took anything, she was not bound to return it; but if she took much, she had to return half.

aimaks, otoks and tribes (15, 23, 22 etc.); compulsory marriages to preserve the clan; the obligation of tens to aid in the marriage of their individual members (37); the obligation to produce tents at designated places (132); the recognition of relationship only through the male line (118)—all these were customary institutions.

The provisions relating to cattle-breeding and hunting were also customary in origin (66, 120, 57, 80, 68, 81, 113, 55 etc.)

Private Law.—The Code contained a score of articles devoted to questions of private law. All of them can be considered as provisions of customary law.

The right of property in real estate did not exist. Each generation and each tribe was obliged to camp in definite locations and the land was subject to the common use of the entire tribe. Common family property in movables (chiefly cattle) and the beginning of the emergence of private movable property created by the labour and industry of its owners (132, 79, 50, 27, 30 etc.) were, however, provided for. All these were institutions of customary law. In the sphere of obligatory law we witness a feeble development of the law of contracts, gratuitous agreements prevailing—gifts, loans etc. (119). The payment of damages was subject to custom (15). Family law was based on the strong patriarchal power of the head of the house (the father and husband) and upon exogamous marriage, with the institutions of ransom for brides and polygamy (33-37, 40, etc.). Heritages were divided according to regulation, i.e. to custom (34). All these were customary institutions.

Criminal Law.—In this sphere the Code provides not only for punishments but also for rewards. This rare phenomenon of encouraging rewards (on a par with penalties) had, among the Mongols, a customary origin. It existed both among the Mongols proper (in the Mongol-Oirat Code and the Khalkha Djirum) and among the Buriats[52] and Kalmucks.[53] This may be explained by 1) the clan and tribal solidarity which regarded mutual aid in misfortune as a good deed deserving reward, and refusal to render such aid as an evil worthy of punishment; and 2) the community hunts (Zegete-aba) so widespread among the Mongols, which provided a splendid school for their social usages.

"The Zegete-aba were one of the varieties of community hunts which represented one of the most ancient institutions of Mongol cus-

52 Anyone saving an animal which subsequently died had the right to claim the carcass (Steppe Code, 67); a reward of a horse was given for saving a man from fire or water; while negligence in this respect was punished by flogging (St. Code 85 etc).

53 For the saving of animals from "wolves, storms and hurricanes, or of those drowning in mud or a well, a reward should be given equal to the saved cattle" (Kalmuck Code—168).

tomary law", writes M. N. Bogdanov. "The Zegete-aba was not only a co-operative group of hunters but also a military detachment. The power of the leaders and chiefs of the hunters' group coincided with the authority of the military chieftain."[54] As has been stated above, the Great Khans of the Mongols themselves led such hunts. Groups of hunters sallied forth under the command of one leader and his assistants and were divided into smaller groups in conformity with the number of hunters. The booty was divided among the participants, those who had distinguished themselves naturally receiving the best part, while the negligent were punished.

The community hunts were not only an important source of nourishment for the nomadic Mongols but also a school of war. The rules which were developed to govern the hunts also held good in military campaigns. It is therefore understandable why Fragment 27 of the Yassa provides penalties for negligent soldiers equivalent to those imposed on hunters letting their quarry escape. It is understandable also why Jenghiz Khan, in his maxims, often compared the hunts with war (v. maxims 10, 11, 16.) The Mongol-Oirat Regulations of 1640 also regulate the organization of hunts (113).[55] The distribution of booty after a hunt may be gathered from the vestiges of it in Buriat customary law. According to the custom of the Horins, if anyone wounded a wolf or fox and set out to pursue the wounded beast, but the beast was finally killed by another hunter—the first hunter received the carcass and the killer its four paws (Steppe Code, 104). By the custom of the Selenguins it anyone witnessed how a hunter killed a sable, fox or wolf, he (the witness) received the two front paws; while if the quarry was a large beast, he received the meat of the rump (Customs of the Selenga Buriats, 142). This was a vestige of the old co-operative hunts in which the witness of a killing was also a participant. Thus the one who worked most also received most. An analogy may be found in another article of the Code which states that a warrior killing an enemy in battle received his cuirass as a reward, while other participants in the struggle received his armour, helmet and other equipment (Art. 50).[56] But the rules of tribal and social solidarity developed during the community

54 "Outline of the History of the Buriat-Mongol People", ppg. 10, 14. The development of community hunts and the social order based upon them were dated by M. N. Bogdanov as belonging to the period preceding the rise of Jenghiz Khan, but the hunts themselves existed much longer. Thus Pallas tells of having seen such a hunt in the year 1772.

55 Art. 130-133 of Leontovich's edition.

56 Or, for instance, the Yuan Ch'ao Mi Shih (Secret Chronicle, translated by Palladius; Works of the Russian Spiritual Mission, IV, 1910, 27) reports the following episode from the life of Jenghiz Khan: "Those 300 people who came to Burkhan mountain and rode around it thrice were exterminated to the last man; those of their wives who were fit to be wives were made wives, while those fit to be slaves were made slaves." Cf. the following provision of the M.O. Reg.: "Who kills a husband in battle receives his wife as a reward" (50).

hunts and the demands made for its observance and punishment for neglect naturally affected other phases of the life of the Mongol tribes before they appeared in legislation.[57] Because of this we find in the Mongol-Oirat Regulations provisions for rewards for the saving of perishing human beings, the curing of the sick, for the recovery of stolen cattle, for saving cattle from wild beasts, drowning and fire (57, 80, 82, 83, 134).[58] All these were provisions of customary law.

Let us now pass on to the penalties. The punishments provided for by the Mongol-Oirat Regulations were predominantly customary in character. Many of its punitive provisions were characteristic of the life and psychology of a nomadic people.

We shall first consider the system of punishments in the Mongol-Oirat Regulations. The basic penalty of this Code is the property fine, calculated chiefly in units of nine head of cattle (an ancient Mongol customary institution). Flogging with the whip and knout (not with rods) was also often practised. The death penalty was rare (being present in only three articles) and still more rare was punishment by deprivation of liberty, a penalty foreign to the nomadic peoples of the steppes (only in one article we meet the penalty of "putting in irons" —123). Also met with in the Code were penalties involving disgrace which were characteristic of the life of the Mongols. For running from the enemy, for instance, the offender, besides being fined, was forced to wear a sleeveless woman's gown (11); for freedom with a maiden—a flick in a shameful place (73); the delivery of the offender's person to the plaintiff in case of poverty or inability to pay the imposed fine (86); ruin of the offender (complete confiscation of property—1, 20, 30); family and generally collective responsibility (exile of offspring—13, responsibility of brothers—15, responsibility of a ten for not communicating the news of a theft-(123, etc.) Persons of higher social position and the heads of clans and families enjoyed special protection, the murder of, and personal insults to, such persons being more severely punished (20, 28, 72). All these institutions were of customary origin.

Many of the crimes described reflected features of the life of the Mongols. For instance, the beating of a person by an official in pursuance of carrying out the instructions, laws and commands of the sovereign was not considered a crime even if the victim died of his injuries, and the maximum penalty in such cases was a fine (21).

57 The Hsi Yu Tze reports the readiness of Mongols of the time of Jenghiz to come to each other's aid in cases of calamity: "In cases of calamity they run one faster than the other". pg. 138. Plano-Carpini says of the Mongols: "One sufficiently respects the other and all are sufficiently friendly among themselves; and though they have little food they willingly share it among themselves" pg. 13.

58 *cf.* Khalkha-Djirum, XIV-3.

Interruption of supplies to a prince was punished by a fine (26). Neglect in providing for the care of the poor was punished (122). Adultery between a man and a maid was punished by a fine, the maid going unpunished (69). Sodomy was punished by a fine (69). Refusal to provide a change of horses and refusal of a night's shelter and of Koumiss (mare's milk) were likewise fined (24, 87). A person pushing wood into a hearth where a fire was burning was fined 9 nines of cattle for a princely hearth and one nine if the hearth belonged to a commoner (90). It was emphasised in the Code that there was nothing criminal in the killing of a person choking on his food in the house of another, although a fine of 5 nines of cattle was provided for such homicide (49). There was no punishment for the killing of a man who ran amok (went violently mad). The responsibility for deaths caused by cattle and domestic animals was borne by their owner irrespective of whether anyone was minding the cattle at the time (46, 48) and the same applied to the bites of mad dogs (44). Anyone tearing the apparel worn by another was fined a colt; for tearing a man's queue or the tassel on his cap the fine was 5 head of cattle; for pulling out a beard—a horse and a sheep, etc. In articles 72 and 73 there is a detailed recapitulation of various personal insults, characteristic of the life of the Mongols, the punishment for insulting persons of high rank being more severe than that for insults to commoners. Theft, which was severely punished by the Code, was likewise treated in detail. Especially severe was the punishment for the theft of the Mongol's basic property and source of nourishment—his cattle. Thus, the theft of a camel was punished by a fine of 15 nines of cattle; the theft of a gelding by 10 nines; of a mare by 8 nines; a cow—6 nines; etc. The Code likewise provides casuistically and in detail for the theft of military equipment and articles of domestic use (armour, cuirasses, etc., the theft of fur coats, rugs, skins, fire-making apparatus, knives, saws, rope, reins, lassoes, needless, buttons, etc.) characterising the life of the time. Irregular delivery of supplies to a prince, fraudulently pretending to the title of an emissary and fraudulent use of cartage were all punished with fines of cattle. This list of crimes and punishments illustrating the life and customs of the Mongols could be further extended.

The only mandatory provisions were the few, mentioned below, dealing with the defence of religion and the interrelations of allied tribes.

We can thus say with confidence that the criminal law of the Mongol-Oirat Regulations, the code of rewards, the system of punishment and the code of penalties[59] were expressions primarily of the customary law of the Mongol tribes.

---

59 Comprising in general about half the total number of articles in the Regulations.

The provisions forbidding loitering in aimaks and hoshuns other than one's own and the forming from them of new aimaks, the prohibitions forbidding a change of camp-sites (125, 132, 133) confirm the customary-legal common use of the steppes, but here administrative influence is possible.

Three articles indicate the influence of the Lamaist clergy and are mandatory in character; Art. 111, containing a penalty for inviting a shaman; Art. 9, containing the prescription that "of ten persons the clergy has the right (for the service of God) to take one" (with the right of ransom); and Art. 18, prescribing a heavy fine for renunciation of priestly rank. To these may be added a fourth, Art. 112, prescribing a fine for the slaughter, in pursuance of Shamanist rites, of a widgeon, sparrow, and dog.

Moreover, the provisions regulating intertribal relations may be regarded as contractual provisions, the legislative creation of the authors of the Code. Of such provisions there were six (1-3, 6, 8, 99). As regards provisions dealing with attack and defence, those of them which were aimed at regulating the mutual warfare and defence of the Oirat tribes can also be included in this group, as for instance Art. 4, prescribing mutual resistance to the enemy (and also, perhaps, Art. 13). Similar provisions regarding attack and defence, but bearing an intratribal character, were part of the body of customary law. The following are examples: when the alarm was given everyone was obliged to appear before his prince (19); flight from the enemy was punished by a fine and the dressing of the offender in a sleeveless woman's gown (11) (cf. 15 and others.)

There were only four articles dealing with the organization of Courts (62, 63, 106, 109). In them we find such ancient institutions as tracking, false accusation, the rewarding of witness for their aid in the administration of justice; and at the same time a certain strengthening of the concept of government.

Thus there were about 20 articles in the Code containing clearly defined mandatory provisions; and the remaining dominating majority of the articles were primarily customary in content. To this must be added the fact that the larger part of the mandatory provisions dealt with the organization and defence of the Oirat League. This League existed for some forty years, then fell apart and the abovementioned articles of the Code lost their effectiveness and significance. But the Code itself remained in effect for a much longer period (in Djungaria approximately until the end of the XVIIIth century). Moreover, after almost 200 years, the Zinzili conference of 1822 attested to its strength and effectiveness in the Kalmuck steppes. It was effective there in the second part of the XIX-th century and did not lose all its significance until the revolution of 1917. What then was the source of its influence and power? Certainly not its mandatory provisions, the majority of which lost their significance with the dissolution of the Oirat League. Rather it was in its customary provisions, in the fact that the Code was predominantly a collection of customary law. Customs change slowly, and with extensions and amendments, the Mongol-Oirat Code of 1640 existed for more than two and a half centuries.

The Khalkha Djirum.—The Khalkha Djirum, by the character of its provisions, is closely reminiscent of the Mongol Oirat Regulations of 1640. This resemblance is based on the similarity of the cultures of the Northern and Western Mongols.

It is indisputable that the provisions of the Khalkha Djirum dealing with tribal life were customary in character. The wanderings of the Northern Mongols in hotons, ooloos and otoks subject to tribal chiefs (chiefs of ten, shulengas, demchis and darugas-IV, XVI, XVII) was also of customary origin. The obligation to occupy definite campsites, the ancient division into tens, the recognition of relationship only through the male line and the patriarchal system of relations (V, XIII, XVI)—all these were institutions of customary law.

The provisions governing mutual relations were permeated with the general principles of the Mongol customary law of solidarity, mutual help and support. Thus both Khans and commoners were forbidden, on pain of punishment, to refuse a night's lodging to a stranger, to abandon sick comrades in uninhabited spots, while the saving of perishing cattle and other property was rewarded (IV, VII, XIII, XV.)

The provisions dealing with cattle-breeding were essentially of a customary character, regulating the distribution of the natural increase in herds, treatment of strayed cattle, cattle dying of disease, etc. (VII, XIII).

The provisions of private law were also predominantly customary in nature.

The right of private property was not recognized. The land, for purposes of pastoral economy, was given over to the use of the tribal units—hotons, ooloos and otoks. Separate treatment was given to private property in movables, especially those acquired by the labour or exploit of the owner (XV, XIII). In the sphere of obligatory relations we find a certain development of contract relations and a series of separate cases where compensation for damages was provided, these provisions being rooted in the social relations of the time (XV, XVI, XVII). Here we meet also some mandatory provisions regulating trade and protecting the Mongols from undue exploitation at the hands of traders (XVIII, XIX). The Family Law was based on the strong patriarchal power of the husband and father, on exogamous marriage with ransom for brides, and polygamy (VIII, XV). All these are institutions of customary law. In the law of inheritance, inheritance in accordance with custom still predominated (VIII).

In the sphere of Criminal Law we meet in the Khalkha Djirum, just as in the Mongol-Oirat Regulations of 1640, not only punishments but also rewards, based on the principle of tribal and communal solidarity. Besides rare concrete cases there even exists a general statement on this practice: "If anyone, during a theft or robbery, commit a particularly good deed, let the Noyon reward him." (IV-23). These encouraging rewards were of a customary character.

The system of punishments was also based on property fines calculated in nines of cattle and on flogging with the knout. The death penalty and deprivation of liberty occurred rarely. Persons of high rank enjoyed a great degree of protection. All these are institutions of customary law.

Many of the crimes enumerated reflected peculiar features of Mongol life. Thus, for instance, beating or insults by a ruling Sait "with cause" went unpunished while the same actions done "for sport" were punished (XIII). Refusal to provide a night's lodging and refusal to give a horse water was punished by a fine (XV). Cutting off the tassel on the cap of a woman was punished by a fine of a nine of cattle; drinking the blood of a horse by opening the vein, cutting off the tail of a horse, by one nine, etc. Theft of military equipment and articles of household use was treated casuistically and in detail, reflecting the life of the Mongols. The theft of cattle was punished with especial severity.

The provisions dealing with juridical procedure also contained many elements of customary law, although here at the same time we witness the strengthening of the state-principle. For instance, the killing of a thief caught in *flagrant delit* was not yet punished, entailing only the cessation of proceedings against the victim.

It is necessary to note that the influence of canonical law was stronger in the Khalkha Djirum than in the Mongol-Oirat Regulations of 1640. Moreover, mandatory provisions (provisions of a legislative character) were here more strongly marked, including the regulation of trade, the protection of the Mongols from abuses by traders, struggle against epidemics among human beings and cattle, and also some administrative prescriptions. But all this did not change the essential character of the Khalkha Djirum which was customary-legal in nature.

Buriat Law—As is known the central Russian authorities did not meddle with the material law of the Buriats and gave them the right to be governed and judged according to their own customs. These customs were set down in special codes, statutes and instructions for the needs of the Buriats themselves and for presentation to the Russian officials. The attempt of Count Speransky to codify the customary law of the Siberian natives was not brought to a conclusion and the collections compiled by him did not receive legislative confirmation. The project he drew up received practical application as a collection of customs, since it reflected the custom of the people.[60]

The customs of hospitality, the principles of mutuality and reciprocal aid, the clan system and co-operation between tribes were characteristic of the life of the Buriats. The patriarchal clan order lay at the base of their social relations. The principles of solidarity and mutual aid were well developed. The administration and judiciary were built up on clan and tribal lines. Relationship was recognized only through the father. The family was patriarchal in character and was based on exogramic marriage, polygamy being permitted, on the ransom of brides and the strong power of the husband and father of the family. The use of the land was partly tribal, partly family in character, but the beginnings of individual property in land were also present. Crimes were not complex, the chief of them being personal insult and the theft of cattle. The system of punishments was based on property fines and flogging. Responsibility often spread to the entire family. The entire social organization outlined here stemmed from customary origins.

The customs met with among the Buriats had different origins. Some of them represented customs common to all or most nomadic tribes of clan-patriarchal culture. Such, for instance, were the customs of clan organization, the absence of the right of immovable property and the utilisation of the latter by clan unions for purposes of cattle-breeding and hunting, exogamy, polygamy, ransom for brides (Kalim), the reckoning of relationship in the male line, property fines (in cattle), etc. Another group of customs, was common to the Mongol tribes as a whole and stemmed from a common Mongol source, such as the existence of rewards for altruistic actions, the right of sons to an allotment of property, the inheriting by the younger son of the household of the father, property fines in nines of cattle (a survival of which existed in the Buriat "Yal"), the mild attitude towards adultery, flogging with the knout,

60 Generally speaking the Russian authorities undertook the organization of courts among the Siberian natives and made, though they did not complete, an attempt to codify their customary law, but they did not directly interfere with this law.

etc. Some customs respresented phenomena peculiar to the life of the Buriats. Among these were customs connected with the irrigation of haymows (and ploughlands), the renting of land by Buriats to Buriats, exchange marriages (in which the son of one family married the daughter of another, while the daughter of the first family married the son of the second), flogging with rods, etc. Furthermore, among the Buriats themselves we perceive differences of legal customs, a kind of legal particularism. Thus, the legal customs of the Northern Buriats (Bulahats and Echirites) were different from those of the Southern Buriats (Horins and Seleguins), this difference being expressed in some provisions concerning compensation for damages and losses caused, the allowed rates of interest, some provisions concerning marriage, etc. Finally, among the Southern Buriats we meet a certain particularism of legal provisions, e.g. between the Horins and Selenguins, and the same phenomenon is evident among the Northern Buriats (e.g. among the Buriats of Balagansk and Verkholensk).

For these phenomena there is a satisfactory explanation. Although the Buriats entered into the empire of Jenghiz Khan, and possibly into the Mongol-Oirat Federation of 44 tribes, and maintained contact with the Mongols (this being especially true in the case of the Southern Buriats), they had broken off at an early period (even before the XIII-th century) from the common Mongol root and lived on the frontier of the Mongol State, in an environment somewhat different from that which surrounded the Mongols proper. Here the influence of local peculiarities was more marked. Besides this, there were also internal peculiarities—noticeable first of all among the Northern and Southern Buriats. The former were distinct from the latter in anthropological type, and in their dialect, written language (the Northern Buriats did not know the Mongol script, which was used by the Southern Buriats), religion (the Northern Buriats were Shamanists and Christians, the Southern—Buddhists), etc. The Northern Buriats knew agriculture from olden times, the Southern Buriats knew almost nothing of it; the Northern Buriats were more under the influence of Russia, the Southerners under that of Northern Mongolia, etc. All this could not but be reflected by differences in some of their respective legal customs. Finally, it is easy to understand the differences between the legal customs of the ancient inhabitants of the Transbaikai region—the Hori Buriats—and the Selenga Buriats who were comparatively recent migrants from Northern Mongolia (in the end of the XVII-th century), etc. All these common and local customs of the Buriats found their expression in local tribal codes, regulations, and statutes, the chief contents of which they comprised.

Thus Buriat law was customary in origin. Its development took place chiefly by internal means, i.e. by means of the development of customary-legal provisions, and only afterwards under the direct influence of Russian administration and culture. But this influence did not bring about any fundamental changes in Buriat law which, in its essence (civil and criminal law) remained customary in character until very recently.

Kalmuck Law.—The chief legal source of the law of the Kalmucks were the Mongol-Oirat Regulations of 1640. As has been shown above, this Code was a record primarily of customary law. The extensions added to the Mongol-Oirat Regulations in the reign of Khan Donduk Dashi (1742-1761 A.D.) contained not only customary provisions (tribal life and mutual relations, some punitive and procedural provisions) but also mandatory ones (relating to religion and the clergy, and a series dealing with penalties and procedure). The draft of the Kalmuck Code (1822-27), which did not receive legislative confirmation, was based on the Mongol-Oirat Regulations, some obsolete provisions of which were removed and to which were added additional provisions of the customary law of the Kalmuck tribes and some mandatory provisions reflecting the influence of Russian culture and law. It is interesting to note that even the Government Commission which examined the most important part of the Kalmuck Code, the Zinzili resolutions, from the point of view of their correspondence to the Government laws, left in force about half of the provisions of the Mongol-Oirat Code, recognising them as effective and applicable among the Kalmucks. In actual fact the number of such articles of the Mongol-Oirat Regulations which preserved their force and effectiveness among the Kalmucks was considerably greater, as the Commission eliminated from the Regulations all such laws as they considered to be in conflict with the laws of the Government, although these provisions also lived on in the customary law of the Kalmucks. Thus it must be recognized that after almost 200 years the greater part of the Mongol-Oirat Regulations of 1640 remained the effective law among the Kalmucks and remained in force for a long time after this. The strength and effectiveness of the Mongol-Oirat Regulations in the Kalmuck steppes derived from the fact that the Regulations gave expression to the slowly changing customary law of the Mongol tribes.

Thus, on the basis of our analysis of the records of Mongol law, we may say that its chief sources were customary, and that Mongol law is predominantly customary law.

B. Chinese Law.

Throughout almost all its history, Mongolia has had relations with China, for a century as a conqueror and for two and a half centuries as a dependency. The higher culture of China could not but have its influence on Mongolia, and this applied in particular to the relations between the detailed, more highly developed law of China and the simpler law of the Mongols. The traces of Chinese influence are found already in the Yassa of Jenghiz Khan. The M.O. Regulations of 1640, being a collection of Mongol customary law, escaped this influence, and the Khalkha Djirum was but slightly affected by it. But the influence of Chinese law was strongly renewed from the time of the subjection of Mongolia to China and found its expression both in the Mongol Codes of 1696, 1789 and 1815 and in the legal customs which have been formed under the influence, of these codes. In this connection it is necessary to note that the influence of Chinese law on that of the Mongols found its application (besides the administrative sphere) chiefly in criminal law and judicial procedure. Civil law and the inner structure of the private-legal relations of the Mongols were not directly affected by Chinese law, the influence of which in these sphere was in any case negligible. This circumstance may chiefly be explained by the difference between the cultures of the Chinese and Mongols. An agricultural people, such as the Chinese have been from time immemorial, could not exercise any great influence on the customary law of a pastoral people such as the Mongols have remained until the most recent times. And as we have seen the Chinese legislators of the past two centures did not attempt to exercise such influence on Mongol private law. They confined themselves to the spheres of administrative and criminal law, leaving the regulation of private legal relations in the competence of local customary law. This last found its application in the effectiveness of the code of customary law, Khalkha Djirum, which, in the Shabi department, remained in force until very recently, and also in unwritten customs of private law. It is necessary to make the reservation that in the sphere of criminal law Chinese legislation did not and could not destroy a series of purely Mongol institutions and moreover that it did have some, though not great, influence also on the private law of the Mongols.

From these general observations we may pass to a consideration of the influence of Chinese law on that of the Mongols in its concrete manifestations, beginning with the Yassa of Jenghis Khan.

To speak with assurance of the influence of Chinese law on the Yassa of Jenghiz Khan is, of course, very difficult. The Yassa has reached us only in fragments and not in the original but through the evidence of ancient writers who were, moreover, foreigners. These circumstances aggravate the difficulty of satisfactorily solving this problem. In view of this we can make only hypothetical statements, and the author's opinion on the subject of the influence of Chinese law on the Yassa of Jenghiz Khan is only a hypothesis, possessed (it seems to him) on a certain degree of probability.

The China and Chinese culture with which Jenghiz Khan had to deal from the beginning of his reign, exerted great influence on the organization of the Mongol state. We know what influence was wielded in this state by Yeh-Liu-Ch'u-Ts'ai, a former Chinese official and the right hand of Jenghiz and Ogodai in their organizing reforming activity. We have given above the evidence of a contemporary the Chinese historian, Men Hun, to the effect that Jenghiz Khan promulgated edicts (chang), orders (ch'i) and other documents; a thing he was taught to do by the Chin officials who had gone over to him.[61] The Hsin Yuan Shih testifies that a surrendered Chinese military leader, Kuo, advised Jenghiz Khan to publish a Code of Laws. As we have already indicated above, one of the old Mongol records contained the statement that Jenghiz Khan considered "the laws and regulations of the Chinese to be strong, subtle and unchangeable" and invited from China "a great teacher of letters with eighteen of his clever pupils" whom he commissioned to compile his laws, and in particular "a book of laws (Huli Yosonu Bichik) for the protection of his rule." After the laws had been compiled, Jenghiz Khan looked over them, found them to be in accord with his ideas and rewarded the compilers. All this gives us reason to believe that Chinese participated in the compilation of the Great Yassa. In any case, and in whichever way it was exercised, in what did the influence of Chinese law on the Yassa of Jenghiz Khan consist?[62] For the solution of this problem it is necessary first of all to consider Chinese legislation and, by means of comparison, determine possible traces of its influence.

Chinese legislation has its roots in the most ancient times. Its origin is ascribed to the time of the Five Legendary Emperors, Fu, Shen Nung, Huang Ti, Yao, and Shun (in the third millenium B.C.)[63]

---

61 Proceedings of the Siberian Section of the Russ. Geog. Soc., vol. V, pg. 89; Bagaley, "Russian History", I, 374.

62 Acad. Krimsky even states that "the state mechanism and social order prescribed by the Yassa was borrowed from Chinese models." (Brockhaus-Efron Encycl. Dict. 82, pg. 840). Generally speaking this is an exaggeration, but a certain degree of influence of Chinese law on the Great Yassa was, evidently, present.

63 On this subject *v.* Father Hyacinth—"China in its Civil and Moral State", Part II, 1912, (Russ.) Introduction; Alabaster, "Notes and Commentaries on Chinese Criminal Law", 1903 (Russ. ed.). Introduction and ppg. 46, 47; Dareste, "Etudes d'Histoire du droit", II, 1926, pg. 284 et sqq., Escarra, "Code penal de Chine", traduit par J. Escarra, 1930, Introduction.

In any case, the one of the most ancient of the sacred books of China, the Shih Ching (Book of History), we find the following testimony as to the (criminal) legislation of Shun (2255-2205 B.C.)

"He inspired the people with fear, showing it the example (and threat) of severe corporal punishments provided for by law. In the interests of mitigation (of punishment) he permitted the substitution of exile for the five chief penalties. In his time the knout (whip) was used in the residences of officials, and rods in schools. Offences committed through neglect or by accident were pardoned. Offences committed with premeditation or repeated several times were punished by death or other penalties in accordance with their seriousness. How worthy of respect were such decisions! In them severity was tempered with mercy."[64]

The commentaries pertaining to this article indicate that the five chief penalties here mentioned were: branding of the face, cutting off of the nose, chopping off of the legs, castration, and death.

"Shun banished the Minister of Public Works to an island or the province of Yu, exiled Huang Tou to Chou mountain, exiled and imprisoned in the land of San Wei the Prince San Miao, exiled K'un and kept him in chains on the mountain of Yu. He applied against them these four penalties and the whole Empire was inspired with faith in his justice."

The commentaries explain that the four penalties indicated: banishment, exile to a distant place, imprisonment in the place of exile, and chaining and supervision in the place of exile.[65]

In the same book of Shih Ching are quoted the criminal laws of the time of the Emperor Mu Wang (1001-960 B.C.), representing amendments and clarifications of the legislation of Shun, which was considered as a model and remained the basic source.

"The Emperor said:

"When both sides have appeared and when (witnesses, judicial documents) all is in readiness, the judges must hear all that concerns the crimes, punishable by the five forms of execution. Then, having certainly separated the truth from falsehood, it is necessary to ascertain whether the crime is punishable by one of the five executions. If it does not require the application of one of the five executions, the judges must determine whether the crime belongs to those five for which is fixed ransom in money. If there is no assurance that the crime is sufficiently serious to be placed in the category of the five subject to ransom, it must be regarded as one of the five unintentional offences (for which there is no punishment) . . ."

---

64 Chou-King, texte chinois avec traduction par Fr. Couvreur, 1916, Part I, Chap. II, Para. 11.
65 Ibid. Para. 12 and note pertaining thereto.

"When, in case of doubt (as to the seriousness of the crime) the culprit is released from punishment by branding, instead of this 600 ounces (of copper) are demanded, but it is necessary for his guilt to have been firmly established. When in case of doubt the culprit is released from punishment by cutting off the nose and instead of this a double quantity of copper (1200 oz.) is demanded, guilt must have been exactly established. When in cases of doubt the culprit is released from punishment by chopping off the legs, instead of this 2½ times the amount of copper (1500 oz.) is demanded, but guilt must have been well proved. When in case of doubt a culprit is released from punishment by castration, 3600 oz. of copper is demanded on the condition that guilt was well established. When, in case of doubt, the death penalty is mitigated, a fine (ransom) of 6000 ounces of copper is required, guilt having previosly been well established. Punishment by branding may be replaced by ransom in 1000 cases, punishment by cutting off the nose also in 1000 cases, severance of the legs in 500 cases, castration in 300 cases, the death penalty in 200 cases. Altogether 3000 kinds of crimes must be punished by one of the five executions (punishments). . . ."[66]

We thus see that even in the most ancient times China had well developed (criminal) legislation. According to the Shih Ching the five chief executions (death, castration, severance of the legs, of the nose, branding) were established even before Shun, who, in the interests of mercy, allowed judges to diminish the five capital punishments and to replace them by exile and established four kinds of exile (banishment, exile to a certain point, exile with imprisonment at the place of exile, and exile with chains). Besides, he introduced punishment by whipping and flogging and allowed these to be substituted for by ransom. There are some indications that torture was already used in that epoch.[67] One thousand two hundred and fifty years later this system was still used in a more detailed form. From some of the corresponding articles in Shih Ching we can see that in some crimes the five capital punishments were used without being substituted by fines (ransom), while such substitution was allowed in respect of some other crimes. Fines (ransoms) were strictly defined in a definite amount of copper: 600, 1200, 3000, and 6000 ozs. Whipping and tortures were used. Classification of crimes was extremely detailed. The Shih Ching finds some 3000 crimes subject to the five principal punishments. Exact evidence against the accused was required and circumstances either mitigating or aggravating the crime were taken into consideration and punishments meted out accordingly.

---

66 *v.* Chou-King, part IV, Chap. XXVII, Para. 15-19.

67 Id. §3 (the five kinds of tortures)

This carefully worked out system, was used without any great change until the period of the Chin dynasty (255-220 B.C.), which, struggling against the centrifugal tendency of the states composing the Empire and trying to maintain the unity of power, had to increase the severity of punishment. The Han dynasty which followed next (202 B.C.-226 A.D.) diminished these punishments and created the principles of the code (9 chapters of the Han dynasty, circa 200 B.C.) The Sui dynasty (581-618 A.D.) formally established the changes in the five principal punishments, which had previously taken place in usage, and introduced definite forms of punishment—the small and large cane, temporary or lifelong exile, and death; castration, cutting off the legs or nose, and flogging were abolished. The small cane punishment was divided into five grades from 10 to 50 blows, the large cane punishment being also of five grades from 60 to 100 blows; lifelong exile had three subdivisions, from one to three thousand li from the place of residence; capital punishment, two divisions, strangling and decapitation. Money ransom, decrease of punishments, and amnesty were allowed.

The system of punishments adopted by the Sui dynasty became the foundation of all the succeeding Chinese codes until the code of the last dynasty (Ta Ch'ing Liu Li). The dynasties after the T'angs (617-917 A.D.) made but very slight changes in this system. Every dynasty found it necessary to issue its own code,[68] which contained not only criminal norms, but also norms, relating to other social and even some private relations, which were, however, treated from the point of view of criminal law and of the punishments which violation of these provisions involved. The peculiarity of these codes was that they were continuous in their principal rules. In accordance with the general course of Chinese civilization from the time of Confucius, which was conservative in its essence and directed towards the preservation of family principles, and out of pious devotion to the past each code repeated the fundamental rules of the previous ones supplementing and changing them only in some particulars. Consequently each succeeding code was derived from the previous one and has its origin in ancient times.

According to available evidence the first attempt at the codification of Chinese legislation was made under the famous unifying Emperor of China, Ch'in Shih Huang-ti (died 210 B.C.). In the epoch of the Han dynasty (202 B.C.-9 A.D. and 25-226 A.D.) a small Code was already issued which has come down to us.

The basic Code of China, however, which influenced future Chinese legislation, was the Code of the T'ang dynasty 唐律疏義 T'ang Liu Shu I, comprising the laws of the T'ang dynasty with com-

68 The code of T'ang dynasty (about 654 A.D.) served as an example.

mentaries. This Code contained 30 books and 500 articles. It was divided into the following 12 sections:

1) General Principles (of the application of laws); 2) Guarding of the Imperial Palace; 3) System of Administration; 4) Civil Affairs; 5) The Treasury and Horsebreeding; 6) Disregard of the Law; 7) Theft and Robbery; 8) Fights and Quarrels; 9) Swindling and Extortion; 10) Various crimes; 11) Detection of Criminals; 12) Judicial Decisions.[69]

The Code (General Principles) opens with the scale of five punishments: 1) The lesser Bamboo Rod (on the palm); 2) The Greater Bamboo Rod (on the buttocks); 3) Hard Labour (instead of imprisonment or near exile)[70]; 4) Exile; and 5) Death.

Further are enumerated the 10 major crimes: Rebellion; Sabotage against the Emperor and the Imperial Family; Coup d'Etat; Murder of Elder Relatives; Murder of Three Persons and Cutting to Pieces; Disrespect to the Emperor; Disobedience to Parents; Unfriendly Attitude to Elder Relatives; Immoral Acts (with respect to wives, teachers, friends etc.), and Adultery with Elder Relatives.

The eight applications of punishment (i.e.mitigations of punishment) were indicated in the following cases: for relatives of the Emperor, for old persons, for wise persons, for able persons, for persons rendering great services, for old officials, for persons who have rendered long and faithful service, and for honourable persons.

The Code provided for the mitigation and intensification of pnnishments, and for a scale of degrees. Furthermore, besides the 10 major crimes listed above, the Code dealt, in its five parts, with numerous crimes including not only those mentioned in the headings of the parts but also many others such as various forms of homicide, robbery, theft, wounding, assault and battery, adultery, disregard of the law, perjury, swindling, forgery, extortion, arson, falsification of weights and measures, surrender of a fortress, retreat before the enemy, the counterfeiting of coinage, violations of building regulations, gambling etc. Besides this the other sections of the Code also contained a series of crimes. Thus we have here a highly developed Criminal Law with a detailed system of crimes and punishments pertaining to them.

We will not stop here to deal with Private Law, for which see further.

69 If we keep in mind that Section 6 deals mainly with military affairs and Sections 7-12 deal with criminal affairs, the contents of the Code of the T'ang dynasty can be divided into the following 7 Sections: 1) General Principles; 2) Guarding of the Imperial Court; 3) System of Administration, 4) Civil Affairs; 5) Treasury and Horse Breeding; 6) Military Affairs, and 7) Criminal Cases.

70 Corresponding to the temporary exile of the Sui dynasty, which was always accompanied by hard labour.

Generally the T'ang Code became the basis of the codes of succeeding dynasties and thus received its further development.

Thus, the legislation of the succeeding (after the 50 year period of the Five Dynasties) dynasty of the Southern Sungs (920-1280 A.D.) recapitulated the fundamental principles of the T'ang Code, as did also the legislation of the Northern Chin dynasty (1126-1234 A.D.) Later the T'ang Code in its essential parts, entered into the composition of the codes of the Yuan (1271-1368 A.D.), Ming (1368-1644 A.D.) and Ta Ch'ing (1644-1911 A.D.) dynasties. In these Codes it remained as the common basis, supplemented and developed (chiefly by means of detailisation and changes of separate items).

The same applies to the code of the last (Ta Ch'ing) dynasty (1644-1911), the Ta Ch'ing Liu Li, or Fundamental Laws of the Great Ta Ch'ing dynasty, and some supplementary rules. While *liu* were the fundamental laws taken from the code of the Ming dynasty (1368-1644)[71], which represent in themselves the invariable foundation of the code and have their origin in ancient times; *li* were only supplementary rules issued in the epoch of the Ch'ing dynasty.[72]

The code of the Ch'ing dynasty consisted of seven books (general legislation, public duties, revenue regulations, rites, military, criminal and the laws of public works). Criminal law proper was contained in book six. As has been mentioned before, other norms were also considered from the point of view of criminal law.

The whole code is preceded by four tables: 1. Punishments, 2. Ill-gotten property, 3. Ransom for crimes instead of punishments, 4. Mourning. The first three tables, referring to criminal law and stating the system of punishments, will be first taken into consideration.

The first rule of table one says: "There are five punishments—the small cane, the large cane, temporary exile, exile for life, and death." Here we can see that the fundamental rule of Sui dynasty formulated about 581 A. D. is repeated again.

Each of these principal punishments is subdivided into several grades. Thus the small cane is of five grades—from 10 to 50 blows; the large cane is also of the same number of grades—from 60 to 100 blows. Temporary exile is also graded into five divisions—from one to three years, and followed by 60 or 100 cane blows, and with the wearing of

71 That is shown directly in the manifesto concerning the enforcement of The Ta Ch'ing Liu Li (1647).

72 Ta-Ch'ing-Liu-Li is translated into English by Staunton "Ta-Ts'ing-leu-lee," 1810 (chiefly the fundamental laws), and into French by Father Boulais—"Manuel du Code Chinois", 2v., 1923 and 1924 (the complete translation). There is an old translation into Russian by Leontieff, 2v., 1778 and 1789. Here we use translation by Boulais.

special yoke (cangue) during 20-40 days. Li (the supplementary law) established still another four years exile, 100 cane blows and 45 days of wearing the cangue; and five years exile according to decree, 100 cane blows and 50 days of wearing the cangue. The exile was to perform hard labour. Exile for life was of three grades; from 2000 to 3000 li distance, from 50 to 60 days of the cangue and 100 cane blows. Still more severe forms of exile existed, for soldiers, and these were divided into five grades; from 2000 to 4000 li distance, from 70 to 90 days of the cangue, and 100 cane blows each time. This exile was generally followed by branding. Besides, there existed a degree of exile under which the condemned was sent to the far borders of China (e.g. to Ili or the banks of the Amur) for hard labor and slavery. Capital punishment was of two grades: strangulation and beheading, while the revision of the case by the high court was made immediately—followed by an immediate execution—or postponed until autumn with a view to mitigation of punishment or possible amnesty by the emperor. If the crime was mean or disgraceful, the head of the executed was placed in a cage for public exhibition. In some cases the condemned was cut to pieces.[73]

Tools of punishment and execution were: bamboo-canes, the cangue or a heavy square wooden board with an opening for the head, to be put round the neck on the shoulders of the condemned (this cangue did not allow one to lie down), handcuffs, iron chains, fetters (for some great crimes), racks for the feet and hands, weights to pull the arms and legs, chain with rings for torture.[74]

Thus we can arrange the following grades of punishments legalized and used in the time of the Ch'ing dynasty.[75] Capital punishment: cutting of the body into small pieces (slow death), followed by the destruction of the family (or to be more exact the male descendants of the executed); by simply cutting the body into pieces; by beheading, followed by display of the head in public places; by simple beheading; strangulation; exile; exile for life for soldiers (of four grades); ordinary exile for life (of three grades); and temporary exile (of five grades); exile to the farthest provinces with hard labour (slavery, of three kinds and five grades); the cangue as a separate punishment or additional to some other, lifelong or temporary; wearing of iron fetters or a piece of iron (for life or temporarily); branding (ordinarily in cases of recidivists); imprisonment (temporary); fines; confiscation of property (in favour of the government or private persons).

---

73 In some cases (and frequently) the execution was carried out in public.

74 See Boulais, Manuel, I, 1923, pp. 2-6.

75 See Alabaster's Notes and Commentaries. p. 17 and the next (Russian edition).

Alabaster says that in practice there were punishments which were not legalized, such as slow death through strangulation (incorrigible murderers) and castration (male descendants of persons convicted of high treason).[76]

Special rates were established as ransom for various crimes, while except for some extraordinary cases, this privilege was given in extenuating circumstances, and if granted by an emperor. This privilege was not given in cases exempt from ordinary amnesty.[77]

In inflicting punishments some circumstances diminishing the punishments were taken into consideration, such as: illness, extreme youth, confession, and others as well as some privileges; and some aggravating circumstances for example such as, kinship of the accused with the plaintiff and some other social relations (between pupil and his teacher, master and man). Amnesty was recognized but the gravest crimes were excluded from amnesty.

The crimes dealt with by Chinese criminal law were listed in six sections (that is in the first five parts of the sixth book of the Code): first part—robbers and thieves, second part—murder, third part—quarrels, abuses, and blows; fourth part—complaints and accusations, bribery, cheating, and other similar crimes, sixth part—imprisonment, prisons, courts.

Also in all other parts of the Code there were introduced certain actions subject to punishment.

Father Hyacinth found 2852 various kinds of crimes included in the Code of the Ch'ing dynasty, 644 of which were subject to capital punishment.[79]

Of these crimes ten were considered the gravest: 1. Rebellion, 2. Plotting against the dynasty, 3. High treason, 4. Patricide, 5. Inhuman murder, 6. Crimes of *laese majestatis* (five cases), 7. Disobedience to parents and senior relatives (five cases), 8. Family discord (murder and sale of relations, etc.), 9. Great injustice (murder of a senior, teacher, etc.—five cases). 10. Incest (adultery with near relatives).

The above mentioned crimes were excluded from amnesty.[80]

Here I refrain from the detailed consideration and analysis of all the crimes included in Chinese Code, as this would take us too far from the aim originally intended. Here I have to remark that the detailization

---

76 Op. cit. p. 60-61.

77 Boulais Manuel, I, pp. 11-16, See specially par. 6.

79 China, II. pp. 18-19 (in Russian).

80 Father Hyacinth—China, II, 5-6.; Alabaster—Notes and Commentaries p. 129. The latter gives about 70 subdivisions of crimes excluded from amnesty.

and casuistry of the crimes were extremely extensive and that the punishments were too severe and cruel; ransom and amnesty were not applicable to all cases of crimes, and tortures were widely used.

Now, after a short review of Chinese criminal law, I shall try to show the influence of Chinese law upon the Mongol.

Mongol law did not reach such a point of development as the Chinese. Mongol law was simpler, more primitive, because the social level of development of Mongolia was lower. On the whole, it is impossible to compare the developed Chinese law of the epoch of the Sung dynasty contemporary with the formation of the Mongol kingdom, with the first experiment of Mongol law codification—the Yassa of Jenghiz-Khan, because the difference of their social life in its origins and development was great. But a more developed law, in favourable circumstances, can and must exercise influence upon one less developed. And here I will try to show what influence was exerted by Chinese law upon the great Yassa, and also upon the succeeding development of Mongolian law.

The five chief punishments of the Sui dynasty, which remained unchanged under the rule of all the dynasties that followed (until the introduction of the provisional criminal code, 1911): capital punishment, lifelong and temporary exile, large and small cane, were logically reduced to three; capital punishment, exile and canes. In fragments of the Yassa that have reached us we find the two principal punishments: death and canes, but the third kind of punishment—exile, also was used (see the 23rd maxim of Jenghiz-Khan).[81] Thus the systems of punishment of both Chinese and Mongol law can be paralelled. And this parallellism can not be taken as accidental, if we consider that the great Yassa did not pay great attention (mentioning it only once) to the principal punishment of the Mongols: fine in cattle reckoned in nines or ninefold (see 29th frag. of Yassa).

Further, one of the two (or three) principal punishments of the Yassa was canes. This was often mentioned in the Yassa and was an ordinary punishment in the epoch of Jenghizids,[82] having relegated the principal Mongolian punishment, whips, to a minor position. This punishment (canes) disappeared at the time of Mongol-Oirat Regulations (1640), and Khalkha Djirum (1709), and reappeared in Mongolia in the epoch of Chinese rule (in the codes of 1789 and 1815). This circumstance can be quite satisfactorily explained in the following manner: Punishment by canes (bamboo) was an ordinary punishment among the

81 And in general Mongolian law often used exile, banishment from the clan-aimak.
82 See Marco-Polo—Voyage p. 91.

Chinese. From the time of the Sui dynasty (practically even earlier) it became one of the fundamental punishments in the Chinese system and remained such till the time of the Republic, and even now it is used in China as an administrative measure. Nomadic peoples ordinarily use whips but not canes as means of punishment. The same applies to the Mongols (see Mongol-Oirat Reg. 1640 and Khalkha Djirum). The place of flogging with canes as the principal penalty in the Yassa of Jenghiz-Khan, its disappearance in the Mongols-Oirat Regulations of 1649 and Khalkha Djirum and its appearance again in Mongolian codes of 1789and 1815 and in the customs of Autonomous Mongolia (1911-1924) can be explained by the influence of Chinese law upon the system of punishments of the Great Yassa and the Mongol law and customs of the last 150 years.

One can see the influence of Chinese law upon the very contents of the provisions of the Yassa; fragments 1, 5 and 25 of Yassa draw our attention to this matter.

Fragment one of the Yassa prescribes death for adultery. Such an attitude to adultery does not correspond with Mongol law and custom. Those who have investigated the matter unanimously declare that there was a certain freedom in sexual relations among the Mongolian tribes before and after marriage. And they find certain traces of hospitable prostitution (haetarism).[83] Mongol customary law was very condescending to adultery, imposing only very slight punishment (fines) or no punishment at all. Thus the ancient Tsaadjin-Bichik imposes fines at the rate of one horse for adultery (art. 3), and adultery with the concubines of priests was exempt from punishment (art. 1) According to the Mongol-Oirat Regulations of 1640, adultery was only fined very moderately (with 4-5 head of cattle) and the adultery of maidens went unpunished (art. 70). And in the customary law of Autonomous Mongolia adultery was punishable only in case of *flagrant delit* and the abuser had to pay one horse as a fine. This circumstance can not be explained by the ordinary mitigation of punishment under the influence of Buddhism, because the ancient Tsaadjin-Bichik appeared earlier than Buddhism in Mongolia. Evidently such an attitude to adultery was an ordinary phenomenon of Mongolian usage, being one of the ancient customs.

Adultery was prosecuted severely in China, and the purity of family relations was carefully guarded. The old punishment by castration, belonging to the number of the principal penalties of China, was

83 See Leontovich, Ivanovsky, Petri.

applied especially for the abuse of chastity.[84] According to the laws of the Ch'ing dynasty punishment for adultery became less severe (from 100 cane-strokes to capital punishment).[85] However, a husband could kill his wife with her lover, if caught on the spot, according to Alabaster.[86] And it is well worth mentioning that punishment by death for adultery (under the immediate influence of Chinese law) again appears in the Mongolian codes of 1789 and 1815. Thus, in the former, adultery between commoners involved a fine of five nines of cattle on behalf of the husband and the woman was given over to her husband "to be killed" in default of which the cattle received as a fine was presented to the prince. In case of adultery between a princess and common Mongol, the latter was cut to pieces and the princess beheaded, while the family of the adulterer was given into slavery.[87] According to the second code, adultery with a woman of equal standing among the common people was punished by the wearing of the cangue during one month for a man, one hundred blows were added, and the same number of blows plus a fine (ransom) for a woman. In the latter case death was substituted by fine (ransom). For adultery between a princess and a common Mongol the latter was cut into pieces and the princess beheaded.[88] But while the written law was so severe in cases of adultery, the customary law of Mongolia found it sufficient in cases of flagrant delit to fine only the adulterer, who paid one saddled horse.[89]

The above statement leads us to believe that such a severe punishment for adultery in the Great Yassa can be explained by the tendency of the legislator to be influenced by Chinese law to take drastic measures against adultery.[90]

The fifth article of the Great Yassa, prescribing the death penalty for the third bankruptcy is evidently a result of more developed business transactions than those existing among the Mongols. The Mongols did not then or even later engage in trade. Trade in Mongolia was carried on by the Chinese, Persians, and some others; and in still later times by Chinese and partly by Russians. This provision was in all probability created specially for foreign merchants and according to their customs [91] And finally article 25 of the Great Yassa dealt with the establishment of

---

84 See Chou-King, p. I, chap. II par. 11 rem., p. IV, XXVII, par. 18 rem. (imprisonment for women).
85 Boulais—Manuel, II, N 1590.
86 See Alabaster, op. c., p. 115.
87 See Mongolian code of 1789, X, 14-16.
88 III, 75-78.
89 See above, pg. 143.
90 *v.* also the preceding paragraph, pg. 146-147.
91 In particular, in Chinese Law the insolvency of a merchant was punished more severely than that of a private person.

regular postal communications. As testified by some historians this institution was organized after the Chinese manner (Groom-Grzimailo, Bagaley).

We may further note the struggle of the Yassa against Chinese influence. Fragments 17 and 24 guard the simplicity of Mongol manners generally and in particular the simplicity of their relations with the Great Khan, in contradistinction to the pomp and ceremony of Chinese relations which were beginning to invade Mongol life. For this we have the testimony of Men Hun.

These are the facts and considerations leading us to belief in the possible influence of Chinese law upon the Great Yassa.

The Mongol-Oirat Regulations of 1640 were a collection of Mongol Law (predominantly customary). Essentially the same may be said of the Khalkha Djirum. But it is nevertheless necessary to perceive in the latter a certain degree of influence of Chinese law, chiefly through the Mongol Statute of the Emperor K'ang Hsi (1696), which, although it was not effective in Northern Mongolia, had a certain amount of influence on its law.

Thus, in the continuation of the Statute of 1728 (included in the Khalkha Djirum) it was directly stated that if a Taidji comitted theft, he was to be deprived of the status of Taidji after the first offence in accordance with the Statute of His Majesty (i.e. the Emperor K'ang Hsi) (VI) (cf. Mongol Statute of 1789, VI-10, 11, 12).[92]

The influence of Chinese law can also be seen in the provisions defining the punishment for robbery and theft. Thus, in accordance with the basic Statute of 1709, robbery was to be punished by 80 strokes of the knout and the fettering together of the hands for one year, while in the Statute of 1728 the penalty was considerably increased, the robber being confined in a pit (well) for one year, and the wife, children and cattle of the chief criminal were confiscated and turned over to the owner of the stolen cattle.

Here we meet for the first time deprivation of liberty by means of confinement in a pit (well). Mongol law rarely deprived culprits of their liberty, this penalty being foreign to the customs and spirit of the steppe-dwelling Mongols.[93] Punishment by deprivation of liberty by means of confinement in a pit occurred in Chinese law and was evidently borrowed from it. Thus, in the chronicle of the Northern Chin dynasty, (Chin Shih), in the chapter on "Criminal Legislation" it is stated that: "The prison consists of a hole which is dug several fathoms

---

92 *v.* The Author's "Customary Law of the Mongol Tribes, p. 112, above, p. 131.
93 Thus, in the M.O. Regulations of 1640 we meet only once (Art. 123) a reference to confinement in iron fetters.

deep, into which the criminal is lowered."[94] As is well known (see Chap. V), the Chin legislation was applied in China in the epoch of the Yuan dynasty. It may be supposed that this punishment came from Chinese law to that of the Mongols possibly by way of the Statute of the Emperor K'ang Hsi (1696). Furthermore, the cruel punishment falling on the family and property of the offender is closely reminiscent of the penalties contained in the Chinese statutes for Mongolia, created under the influence of Chinese law (cf. Mongol Statute of 1789, VI-1).[95]

Later, in the Regulations of 1746, the punishment for the chief robber was further raised to the death penalty, direct reference being made to the Statute of the Emperor K'ang Hsi: "any man who has committed robbery must be executed, and his yurt, cattle, wife and children must all be given to the owner of the cattle in accordance with the Statute of His Majesty." (VI).

An analogous reference to the Statute of 1696 is here also made with reference to the question of the substitution of whipping for the cattle fine in cases where the offender did not posses enough cattle to pay it, fixed at 25 blows for each head of cattle but not more than 100 in all (VI) (cf. Mongol Statute of 1789, XII-9).[96] Similar substitution, though without reference to the Kang Hsi Statute, was provided for in the articles on marriage which composed the continuation of the Statute of 1709. (VIII).

The influence of Chinese law is also noticeable with regard to the question of adultery. The great severity of the punishment for this offence in the Khalkha Djirum, although it does not reach the death penalty[97] as in Chinese law, and the Chinese codes for Mongolia, closely approximates it (in providing for the confiscation of all the offender's property and his delivery into slavery in cases of adultery between a commoner and a princess). The contradictions between these penalties and the provisions of the ancient Tsaadjin-Bichik and the Mongol-Oirat Regulations of 1640 as well as the customary law of Autonomous Mongolia and the customs and views of the Mongols generally, are convincing evidence of the presence of Chinese influence upon the Khalkha Djirum in this question.[98]

94 The Russian translation of this chapter is contained in Appendix I of the author's work: "The Great Yassa of Jenghiz Khan" (in Russian), pg. 64. An analogous indication is given by Acad. Vassiliev, *op. cit.*, 207.

95 Cf. The author's "Customary Law of the Mongol Tribes" pg. 111., also above pg. 130.

96 Ibid., pg. 104-105, also above pg. 129.

97 The Khalkha-Djirum, under the influence of Buddhist canonical law, avoided the death penalty altogether.

98 The Mongol Statute of the Emperor K'ang Hsi (1696) was recently discovered in Mongolia. We may hope that it will soon be published as it will then be possible to determine more exactly the extent of its influence on the Khalkha-Djirum as well as the influence upon it of Chinese legislation.

As for the Mongolian codes of 1789 and 1815 (and possibly the code of 1696 as well) there is no doubt about their being edited specially for Mongolia by Chinese legislators and reflecting the great influence of Chinese law.

So the system of punishments in both is in accordance with Chinese principles. The punishments are too severe and sometimes are quite contrary to Mongol custom; crimes are considered in detail and during investigation tortures are used, etc. Death, exile, and corporal punishment were the principal penalties. Death by cutting into pieces, beheading, and strangulation (with or without exhibition of the head in public places) were as in Chinese law; hard labour, exile to far-off provinces of China, lengthy imprisonment, cangues, canes, ransom—all these are certainly institutions of Chinese criminal law unknown in most cases to pure Mongol law. From this comparison only of these two systems of punishments it is evident that the influence of Chinese law upon the Mongolian was great. It is of importance however to remark that in the Mongolian codes there are some purely Mongol customs taken into consideration. Thus, imposing fines on property in general and cattle by nines in particular, whipping and flogging for tributaries (serfs) are to be found there.

As for the crimes and punishments connected with them, some of them have the characteristic of being influenced by Chinese law, for instance the abovementioned attitude towards adultery or the violation of graves, for robbery which was severely punished, and on which special minute regulations existed.[99] Moreover, it was Chinese law which particularly sacred the cult of ancestors and their graves;[100] while the Mongols do not necessarily bury their dead, but often leave the corpses in the open and impose very slight punishment for sacrilege (compare Khalkha Djirum, XIV-2). These codes also deal with in detail and severely punish the setting on fire of dwelling places,[101] a crime almost unknown to the Mongols, because wooden buildings were seldom found in Mongolia, and some other crimes.

It seems to me that there is no point in seeking other facts proving the application of Chinese norms to the Mongolian codes of 1789 and 1815 and the influence of these upon the latter. This is quite evident from what has already been given. And such application is easily understandable. It represented the policy of the ruling nation trying to spread her culture and influence among the subdued.

---

99 See the Mongolian code of 1815, 111-73.

100 Boulais-Manuel 11, 1911-1915, also Alabaster, o.c., pp. 294-296.

101 See the Mongolian code of 1815, 111-183.

The following question is of special interest to us: how great was the influence of Chinese law upon Mongol life and customary law when Mongolia was under Chinese rule for some two and a quarter centuries? There is reason to answer that such influence in the sphere of criminal law and procedure was strongly expressed. Chinese criminal law and procedure exerted great influence upon Mongolian customary law in this field (chiefly through the Mongolian codes of 1789 and 1815 as well as through judicial practice of the high court in Peking and partly through administrative practice).

On the other hand, if we make a clear investigation of the matter, we shall see what Mongolian criminal law represented after the Chinese withdrawal from Mongolia (the so called Autonomous Mongolia, 1911-1924), and we shall be obliged to agree with the above.

On the whole it was nothing else but a combination of Chinese written norms and Mongolian customary law, with the preëminence of the first. So in the system of punishments we see the death sentence (in various forms), ransom, exile, long imprisonment, the cangue and chains, canes, exile to the provinces of China, fine by nines, whipping, banishments from hoshuns and aimaks, and others. Some of these correspond to Chinese punishments such as various kinds of capital punishment and especially qualified capital punishment, ransom, exile to the provinces of China, long imprisonment, the cangue and wearing it in public, and chains; as well as Mongol punishments such as whipping, fine, banishment from the hoshun or aimak. The general severity of the punishments is foreign to the Tsaadjin-Bichik and Khalkha Djirum, the use of maihem in the practice of Autonomous Mongolia (such as cutting in pieces in cases of patricide, and castration) being the result of Chinese influence.[102]

Of course it is well to remark that the influence of Chinese law even during the two centuries' rule of China over Mongolia did not absorb all the institutions of Mongolian law. Thus it could not turn adultery into one of the important crimes, nor the opening of graves into sacrilege, these conceptions not existing in Mongolian customary law. Also it did not destroy a series of purely Mongolian punishments-whipping, fines in cattle, and some others. But on the other hand it moved some Chinese institutions into foremost positions putting its customary traits upon Mongolian judicial practice in the sphere of criminal law and procedure and making them nearer to Chinese law than Mongolian.

So it was in the sphere of criminal law and procedure. But it was otherwise in the sphere of civil law. The Chinese influence in

102 *v.* above, pg. 142-143.

Mongolia was not deep, not extending so far as to penetrate into her private inner life. This was hindered by the difference in cultures: the one being agricultural, while the other was nomadic. Mongolia was left untouched in her inner life, guided by her own local customs. However, the two centuries' rule and business relations between these two countries did leave their mark also in the sphere of private law. We shall not here make any general review of Chinese private law[103] and compare it with the Mongolian. This is superfluous, because the influence of the first upon the second was very slight. Some traces of this influence can be seen in rural as well as in business relations.

Lack of land in China forced Chinese farmers to emigrate to Mongolia and to lease land there. Lease of land was not known in Mongolia until the Chinese farmers came. It had its origin under Chinese influence and in Outer Mongolia was practised with regard to foreigners only, chiefly Chinese and partly Russians. The Mongols themselves did not lease land. The use of leased land for farming purposes did, however, become an example for the development of native farming in Mongolia, though to a small degree.

In the sphere of business relations except for some trade customs brought into Mongolia by Chinese tradesmen we see an immediate influence of Chinese written law upon the rate of allowed interest. The extent of the allowed interest in Mongolia was 36% per annum—a norm evidently borrowed from Chinese law through the Chinese merchants.[104]

The right of a Taidji's widow to adopt her dead husband's son as an heir (according to the code of 1815) also bears the traces of Chinese influence.[105]

Such are the most striking examples of the influence of Chinese private law upon the Mongolian.[106]

C. Other Sources of Mongol Law.

The Canonical Law of the Lamaists.—The prevailing religion in Mongolia is Buddhism, in its Lamaist form, which was brought from Tibet in the XVI-th century and found favourable soil for its growth.

103 This observation can be found in the writer's works: The Fundamental Institutions of Chinese Civil Law, 1926; The Modern Civil Law of China, p. I-1927, p. II-1928.

104 See Boulais, I, 729.

105 See Riasanovsky—The Modern Civil Law of China, I, p. 179.

106 It is well to add that this influence of Chinese law upon the Mongolian represents the influence of old Chinese law upon the ancient law of Mongolia. In China and in Mongolia many social changes are taking place, bringing new laws with them. Because of this the investigation of the old law, which is being superseded by the new, is particularly timely now, while its traces are still fresh.

The spiritual centre of this faith is Tibet and its pontiffs the Dalai Lama and the Panchen Erdeni. The Mongols have always been a very religious people. Each family considered it a duty to give at least one of its members to the Lama priesthood. Until very recently all Mongolia was covered with a net of monasteries. The Lamaists have three degrees of spiritual rank, those of the Gelung, Getsul and Bandi. The peculiar feature of the Lamaist faith is its belief in the reincarnation of Buddhas and Bodhisatvts (future Buddhas) on Earth and the worship of the incarnate Buddhas and Bodhisatvas, the Hubilgans. Of such Hubilgans there were several hundred in Mongolia, and the most prominent of them bore the titles of Gegen and Hutukhtu. The most revered of the Hubilgans was the Urga Hubilgan of the Bodhisatva Djebtsun Damba, the Urga Bogdo Gegen Hutukhtu, High Priest and spiritual head of Mongolia. From 1911 to 1924 he was also the temporal ruler, being the last to bear the title of Edzen Khan (sovereign). Of the remaining Hubilgans the most revered were the next eight, the Changchia, Sheret, Mindol, Samsa, Achzia, Donhur, Tzain and Tongun Hutukhtus.

Beginning with the XVI-th century Lamaism gradually permeated the entire life of the Mongols. The Lama became the spiritual father, physician, and teacher in the life of every Mongol. None of the serious household problems of the Mongols were decided without the advice of the Lama. The number of these grew exceedingly and according to the census of 1918 comprised about 45% of the entire male population of Mongolia. The number of monasteries and their tributaries (Shabi) increased correspondingly. Thus the number of the Shabinars of the Urga Gegen alone reached about 90,000 souls. Numerous other Gegens, Hutukhtus and monasteries also had their Shabinars. It is natural that the extent of Lamaist influence, as well as the influential position of the Lamaist clergy could not but have its effect on Mongol Law.

Special expressions of piety before the religion and its representatives were usually contained in the introductions (and sometimes conclusions) to Mongol codes which sometimes remind one of religious hymns. Such introductions precede the M. O. Regulations of 1640, the Khalkha Djirum (a general foreword before the Code of 1709 and a special introduction to the Codes of 1728 and 1746), before the additional articles of Khan Donduk Dashi and some other instruments. In these introductions the legislative provisions of the codes are placed under the protection of religion. Among the participants in the compilation of such codes were always found representatives of the higher Lamaist clergy, and the contents of the Mongol codes reflected the influence of Lamaism.

The extent of such influence on the Mongol-Oirat Regulations of 1640 was comparatively moderate. But, unlike the Great Yassa, this code already considered Buddhism as the one true faith and persecuted Shamanism. Thus it was prescribed that Ongons be confiscated and that Mongols inviting male or female Shamans be fined. Shamans were fined for making charms and the killing of widgeons, sparrows and dogs for ritual purposes was also punished by a fine (Arts. 111, 112). Severe punishments were provided for insults to the clergy (5, 17). At the same time the code also contained the following general rule: "Out of ten men the clergy have the right to receive one"; i.e. out of every ten men one had to be dedicated to God, although a ransom was fixed by which he could buy himself out (9).

But the provision described, which was contained in the Regulations of 1640, was greatly exceeded by life itself. Within 70-100 years, in the Khalkha Djirum, we find the influence of religion and the clergy to have substantially increased. In the Khalkha Djirum we find a special "Regulation on the Relations between the Clergy and the Laity", dated 1746; "Statute on the Theft of Monastery Property", 1676 or 1736 outlining the privileges of the clergy, and a series of other provisions of similar character.

From the Khalkha Djirum we see the special position of the Urga Gegen, "The High", who was placed above crime and punishment, above the Khans and Princes, as a person who was regarded with especial reverence and whose will had to be done by everyone. Moreover his monastery enjoyed the right of sanctuary and his property was specially protected etc. We meet here the special privileges of the clergy and the monasteries which were released from the payment of taxes and tribute and whose property was specially protected from attack, robbery, theft etc. by augmented penalties. The persons of the clergy were also specially protected from libel, insult and assault. Entrance into the clergy was made easier and simpler, etc.

The moral commandments of Buddhism forbidding the killing of living creatures found their expression in the Khalkha Djirum in the form of the command of the Gegen: "Do not kill any living creatures nor leave them hungry for the night" (1-3). This basic doctrine of Buddhism had, it is to be supposed, some influence on the rarity of the death penalty in the Khalkha Djirum. The death penalty was here provided for in only two cases; according to the Code of 1746 (VI) for robbery, in accordance with the Mongol statute of the Emperor K'ang Hsi, i.e. under the influence of Chinese law; and for attacking a monastery (VII). But the last mentioned provision, although of Mongol origin, evidently arose in 1676, i.e. before the compilation of the

Khalkha Djirum. Further in the Khalkha Djirum we find a prohibition forbidding the slaughter of certain animals (horses, geese, snakes, frogs, widegons and skylarks) which arose under the same influence, and also a prohibition against slaughter on certain days of the month (the 8th, 13th, 15th, 25th and 30th) (XI-final art.).

The influence of Lamaism was also reflected in the system of punishments of the Khalkha Djirum. Here we meet punishments of religious penance—obeisances and circumambulations of monasteries (IV-1,5, XI-1); punishments for offences against spiritual discipline; the preparation of tea for the brethren of a monastery and, finally, the special additional penalty for violation of the right of sanctuary in the monastery of the Urga Gegen: the prohibition against ever again worshipping the Gegen (XI-3).

Thus not only the position of the Lamaist church in Mongolia, but also the influence of Lamaist canonical law, were reflected in some provisions of the Mongol-Oirat Regulations of 1640 and in particular in the provisions of the Khalkha Djirum. But this influence was not even here a basic source of legislation but only a supplementary one.

It is necessary to note that the laws of the Southern Buriats and of the Kalmucks[107] were also subject to the influence of Lamaism. Here we find the wide distribution of monasteries and Lamaist clergy and the privileged position of the latter (cf. Tsaadza 1759, Customs of the Selenga Buriats, 95; Zinzili Resolutions-1,2,4); the battle against Shamanism (Customs of the Selenga Buriats-95; Steppe Code-105); special punitive penance (obeisances, repentance, sacrifices, preparation of tea for monasteries, fines for the benefit of temples—Customs of the Hori Buriats-II, 1; XII, 26, Customs of the Selenga Buriats-80; Donduk-Dashi-73,4; Zenzili Resolutions-185,199) etc. But it is necessary to note that the influence of Lamaism on the life and law of the Southern Buriats and Kalmucks, although significant, did not compare in extent with the same influence in Northern Mongolia, being-moderated by the influence of Russian government and culture.

Russian Law.—Two large Mongol tribes, the Buriats and Kalmucks, have long lived in Russia (now the R.S.F.S.R.) under the administration of the Russian government and the rule of its laws. The culture and law of Russia, therefore, could not but influence the culture and law of the Buriats and Kalmucks.

Thus the Russian influence in the sphere of criminal Law expressed itself among the Buriats through the consideration by the common judicial institutions of important "criminal" cases involving Buriats

107 The Southern Buriats— The Horins and Selengas—were Lamaists, and those of the North—the Echirites and Bulahats—Shamanists and Christians. The Kalmucks were Lamaists.

and also through the consideration by the district courts of cases coming to them as appeals against the decisions of the tribal courts and police.

Russian private law exercised its influence chiefly in the sphere of property and obligatory relations. Thus it found application in the domain of agriculture. The transition of the Buriats, especially those of the North, to agricultural ways of life which took place under Russian influence, was to a substantial extent accompanied by the growth of rent relations which were formerly unknown among the Buriats (Customs of the Buriats of Verkholensk 38,50) and in separate cases led to the establishment of private ownership in land (Customs of the Selenga Buriats, 163; Customs of the Verkholensk Buriats-38,40). This transition was connected with the further evolution of Buriat Law: the enclosure of fields (C. of S.B. 154,155,163; C. of H.B. X-8, XII-26; Steppe Code—74,78), compensation for trampling of crops by cattle (C. of V.B.-41,44), There were references to the development of rent, etc. The general development of money-economy gave rise to the appearance of percentage loans with a maximum allowed rate of 6 or 12 per cent (C. of H.B.-VII, 5; of Sel. B.-103), as it existed in old Russian law and generally such credit transactions as existed among the Russians, and also the Russian institution of the ten years prescription.[108]

The influence of Russian law upon the law of the Buriats became much stronger in the 50 years preceding the Russian Revolution, in connection with the general cultural development of the Buriats. At this time an important channel through which Russian law exercised its influence was the "Code of Steppe Laws of the Nomadic Peoples of Siberia" which was effective among the Buriats and in which, on a par with the codification of native law, the gaps of the former were filled by provisions of Russian law.[109]

It is therefore not surprising that when in 1918, after the Russian Revolution, the Buriats convened their national Buriat court, this court was permitted to use Russian material law insofar as it did not contradict the sense of justice of the Buriat people (*v.* Art. 4, of the Novel No. 3, on the Buriat National Court and 366 of the statute on

108 The influence of Russian custom was noticeable also in other cases. Thus, together with the borrowing of agriculture from the Russians there were also borrowed Russian customs connected with this occupation, e.g. in Art. 74 of the Steppe Code of 1808 of the Buriat Horins (Lamaists) there is mention of punishment for the grazing of cattle on grain fields after the feast of the Intercession of the Holy Virgin (a festival of the Russian Orthodox Church taking place on 1/14 October). Or, as e.g. in a decision of the Horins (Dec. 18, 1817) it was prescribed that all community archives were to be kept in Russian houses and not Buriat Yourts.

109 Let us consider one or two examples. Although in the Buriat regulations the subject of prescription was passed over in silence, the Buriat courts (as well as Buriat business practice) applied the Russian ten year prescription specified in the Steppe Code. The same position obtained with regard to the maximum term of personal service (5 years) and in other cases.

Judicial Procedure in the Hoshun and Aimak Courts). This circumstance is sufficient proof of the fact that Russian law had a marked effect on the legal consciousness of the Buriats.

Kalmuck Law was also subjected to the influence of Russian law through the channels of the Russian administration and courts. The more serious criminal cases were removed from the competence of the Kalmuck courts (Zargo) and made subject to the ordinary government courts. Furthermore, in the less important criminal cases and also civil suits, the Russian courts represented the higher judicial instance, the sentences and decisions of which had its influence on the practice of the lower instances (the Kalmuck Zargo). Generally speaking, the higher culture and state organization of the Russians could not fail to influence the culture of the Kalmucks and their administrative and juridical practice. The additional laws of Khan Donduk Dashi owed their existence to the new conditions of life among the Kalmucks of the Russian steppes. Changes prompted by the demands of Russian government and law also had their place in the Zinzili Resolutions of 1822-27.

Provisions of a Legislative Character (*Mandatory Provisions*).—We must not ignore the fact that all provisions of this description in Mongol Law were not the product of the influence of other systems of law, and that there existed also legislative (mandatory) provisions of purely internal origin. The Great Yassa of Jenghiz Khan included a number of such provisions which arose from the reforming activity of the great conqueror, from his attempt to create a world empire. The Mongol-Oirat Regulations of 1640 also comprised a series of such provisions dealing with the regulation of intertribal relations, questions of common defence and attack, etc. The additional edicts of Galdan Khan contained a considerable number of new provisions designed to regulate the discharge of justice. In the code of the Northern Mongols, "Khalkha Djirum", we find not only a number of provisions outlining the privileges of the clergy but also some regulating trade, protecting the Mongols from exploitation, providing for measures against the spread of contagious diseases and epidemics, and a number of other administrative measures. The same applies to Buriat and Kalmuck law. Generally it is possible to note the following natural circumstance: the nearer we approach our time the greater the part of legislation in the legal life of the Mongols. In the Mongol-Oirat Regulations it is greater than in the Yassa of Jenghiz Khan; in the Khalkha Djirum than in the Mongol-Oirat Regulations. However, this constantly increasing legislative activity did not do away with the application of provisions of customary law which retained their fundamental character, the mandatory provisions only supplementing these, replacing those of them which had become obsolete, and defining their relation to the demands of the State. Legal customs, both those which had been codified and those which had not, were slow to change. This slow rate of change of customary law, which was connected with the slow changes in the general structure of the life of the nomadic steppe-dwellers, was the basis for the long period of effectiveness of the M. O. Regulations of 1640 among the Volga Kalmucks and of the Khalkha Djirum among the Northern Mongols, as well as of the Buriat Codes. The majority of the mandatory provisions incorporated in these codes have long ago either lost their force or been replaced by new ones. Some provisions of customary law have also lost their significance, but the greater part of them, giving expression to the legal customs of nomadic steppe economy and the patriarchal structure of society, retained their force and effectiveness until the XX-th century which brought with it the fundamental reform of this economy, and of the whole way of life of the Mongols, Buriats and Kalmucks which took place after the Russian Revolution of 1917.

Thus, it is clear from the above that the legal customs of the Mongol tribes were the main source of their law. The supplementary sources were Chinese law in the case of the Mongols, Russian law in the case of the Buriats and Kalmucks, the canonical law of the Lamaists in relation to the Mongols, Southern (but not Northern) Buriats and Kalmucks, and mandatory provisions in all three cases. The law of the Mongol tribes was codified in the chief Mongol records—the Great Yassa of Jenghiz Khan, the Mongol-Oirat Regulations of 1640 and the Khalkha Djirum, the Buriat statutes and regulations, the Zinzili Resolutions of the Kalmucks, etc.

It is, however, necessary to note that among the records of Mongol law described above (in Chapter I) there are also some in which the mandatory provisions form the majority: the Codes (Regulations) of 1789 and 1815. In these, the mandatory norms predominate in the spheres of administrative and criminal (but not private) law. But these codes were not national records of Mongol law but represented Chinese legislation for Mongolia, expressing Chinese rather than Mongol law.

To the question: "Up to what time did the effectiveness of legal customs predominate in Mongol law?", it is possible, in relation to Mongol law proper, to give the formal answer that it predominated until the end of the XVIII-th century, i.e. until the promulgation of the Code of 1789. However, such an answer would not be accurate. The fact is that even during the effectiveness of the Codes of 1789 and 1815 private law was regulated by custom. Moreover, the old national code "Khalkha Djirum" continued effective (until about 1925) among the Shabinar tributaries of the Bogdo Gegen, as well as of other Hubilgans and monasteries which were subject to the Great Shabi Yamen and the Bogdo Gegen.[110] It is thus necessary to recognize that the predominance of the effectiveness of customary law in Outer Mongolia lasted until 1789, and it retained a considerable measure of force until the most recent times, up to the promulgation of the Criminal and Civil Codes of the Mongolian People's Republic. In Buriat and Kalmuck law, customary law predominated until the promulgation of the new Soviet legislation.[111]

---

110 Besides the Bogdo Gegen, four Hubilgans who had their own territory also had their Yamens which, were subject to the final authority of the Bogdo Gegen.

111 Of course, even after the promulgation of the Mongolian People's Republic and the Buriat and Kalmuck Soviet Republics, customary law was not entirely destroyed (especially in the sphere of private law), but this question carries us beyond the scope of the present work.

CHAPTER IV.
FUNDAMENTAL INSTITUTIONS OF MONGOL LAW.

Many of the features and characteristic institutions of Mongol law present a picture of legal life at a stage which, with a few exceptions, was long (over 1,000 years) ago superseded among the modern European and American peoples, but which is of considerable interest from the point of view of sociological science and comparative jurisprudence. In Mongol law many features of the distant past, which give a key to the understanding of some aspects of present day life, were preserved in a sufficiently clear form. These survivals also offer evidence in support or contradiction of some of the theories of social organization and comparative jurisprudence that have been advanced by science.

For greater clarity we shall first give a condensed systematic survey of Mongol law. Further, we shall consider in greater detail the fundamental institutions of this law with reference to the spheres both of public and of private law, indicating, so far as in possible, the tendencies of their development.

(a) A Short Historical Survey of Mongol Law.

The historical process is uninterrupted and all divisions must therefore be of an artificial character. They are, however, necessary for convenience in presentation and to facilitate the study of the material. It seem to us more correct to divide the history of Mongol law, in accordance with the character of that law, into the following periods: 1. *General Mongol Law* of the epoch of Jenghiz Khan and his successors; 2 *Local National Law* of Mongolia; 3. General Law of *Chinese origin*; 4. Law of *Autonomous* Outer *Mongolia.* Chronologically the first period falls roughly into the XIII-th and XIV-th centuries; the second into the XVth, XVI-th, XVII-th and part of the XVIII-th (until the Regulations of 1789); the third from 1789 to 1911; and the fourth from 1911 onwards.

First Period (XIII-th and XIV-th cent.) Territory: The territory of the Great Mongol Empire founded by Jenghiz Khan was enormous, occupying approximately half of the then known world. The Empire reached its greatest extent in the reign of Khan Mangu (Munké) when it included the greater part of Asia (with the exception of the far North, Japan, Korea, Tibet, India and Arabia) and Eastern and part of Southern Europe. After the death of Mangu (Munké), Kublai, a grandson of Jenghiz, was proclaimed Great Khan in 1260 A.D., the proclamation being made at Kaifeng (China) by the chiefs subject to him, without the convocation of the Great Kurultai. This circumstance resulted in the secession of the Western appanages and the disintegration of the Great Empire into the gradually more and more independent Mongol kingdoms of Persia, Jagatai, and the Kipchak. Although Kublai Khan conquered Korea, Southern China, Tibet and part of India, he remained, as a result of the non-recognition of his power by the Western Oolooses, only the nominal ruler of the great Mongol dominions. His power, and the power of his successors until the fall of the Mongol Yuan dynasty he founded in China, which took place in the year 1368, extended over China, Mongolia, and a few adjacent countries.[1]

Population: The Mongols were never a numerous people, and they comprised only a small proportion of the population of the Great Mongol Empire. Their numbers at the present time may be put at approximately 2½-3 millions and it is doubtful whether they exceeded this figure in the epoch of the Great Empire (Maisky estimates 2½ millions). At the same time, the numbers of the peoples subject to the Mongols during the reign of Munké Khan exceeded 100,000,000 souls.

Even in the army the Mongols were in the minority. The greater part of the Mongol armies consisted of detachments formed from the conquered peoples, but officered by Mongol chiefs. Thus, in Batu's campaign against Russia and Europe, the Mongols comprised only from a quarter to a third of his entire forces.[2]

Socially the Mongols of the Great Empire were divided into two classes; the White Bone, or nobility (Princes of the Blood, Ooloos princes, Beks and Murzas); and the Black Bone, or commoners (merchants, artisans, cultivators, warriors, and slaves). They secured the means of their existence by war, hunting and cattle breeding. In religion, the Mongols of the time were Shamanists, worshipping the forces of nature and their outward manifestations.

State Power: The social organization of the Mongol Empire was based on the clan principle. At the head of the State stood an autocratic ruler, the Great Khan, and the clan of the Great Khan (the "Golden clan of Jenghiz Khan") was in possession of the government. The Khan's closest clansmen ruled over the chief Oolooses and the conquered peoples. Jenghiz Khan himself divided his empire into appan-

1 At times, some Western Khans (Jenghizids) were prompted by political considerations to recognise the Great Khan (e.g. the Khan of the Golden Horde, Urus) while others, at the same time refused (e.g. Gazan, Khan of Persia); but this did not re-establish the unity of the Empire.

2 Plano Carpini, for instance, estimated the total force under Batu at 600,000 men, of whom 160,000 were Mongols.

ages among his sons, and at the head of these appanages stood the Great Khan elected by the Kurultai. The power of the Great Khan was limited only by custom. The appanage Khans had the same power over their dominions as the Great Khan had over the whole empire, except that their power was to a certain extent limited by that of the Great Khan, this limitation falling away after the disintegration of the Empire.[3]

In accordance with custom, however, all questions of prime importance were solved at the Kurultai, the Seim (conference) of ruling princes. This conference, although it had only consultative powers, was of considerable customary significance. It showed that the Great Mongol Empire was not considered as the personal affair of the Great Khan, but as the common heritage of his entire clan, and the most important decisions were reached through common consultation.

Records of Law: The chief legislative instrument of the epoch was the Great Yassa of Jenhiz Khan (supplemented by the decrees, or edicts, of the Khans). The Great Yassa was published in about the year 1218. During the XIIIth and XIVth centuries it had force and effectiveness throughout the Great Mongol Empire and in the separate States into which it fell apart, but it was applied only to Mongols and other nomadic peoples and not to the settled agricultural populations of these countries (e.g. China, Persia, Russia).

Administration: Men Hun (or Chao Hun), a contemporary of Jenghiz Khan, wrote: "The Tartars (i.e. Mongols), in imitation of the Chin bandits (i.e. the Northern Chinese dynasty of Chin), also introduced among themselves the title of Min Lu Shan Chu (Minister), Lin Tsao Yu Tsiang (Chief administrator), the Right and Left Pin Chang (director), and other offices. They also appointed Viziers (T'ai Shih), Commanders-in-Chief (Yuan Shuai) and others who carry on their persons (as a mark of distinction) P'ai Tze made of gold."[4] Furthermore, we know from other sources that during the reigns of the Khans Ogodai and Munké regulations of official service were established, secretariats were formed, and decrees issued dealing with separate departments of the administration.

Private Law: The ancient Mongols did not know individual property in land or generally any transactions in immovable property. They were likewise not acquainted with agriculture. The land was held for the common use of the tribe and served the purposes of hunting and nomadic cattle-breeding. Civil legal life (civil transactions) had

---

3 *v.* Plano Carpini, *Op. cit.*, ppg. 23-24.

4 Vasiliev, "History and Antiquities of the Eastern Part of Central Asia", Works of the Or. Sec., R. Arch. Soc., 1859, IV, pg. 229.

reached a certain degree of development (*v.* Fr. 5 of the Yassa). The Mongols lived under a clan-patriarchal order with exogamy, widespread polygamy, and the strong power of the husband and father in the family, but there also existed among them some vestiges of the matriarchate. One of the wives was considered the eldest or superior. Marriage was by ransom of the bride from her clansmen, this giving the transaction the form of purchase. In spite of the high power of the husband, the position of the woman in the family was not too bad. In the absence of her husband, and after his death, the wife-mother ruled the house and family economy and occupied an honourable position (Yassa, Fr. 19; Maxim 14). The Mongol's heirs were his sons, including sons by concubines, the eldest son receiving more than the others and the youngest inheriting his father's household and wives, becoming full master over the fates of the latter (with the exception of his own mother) with the right of marrying them himself or giving them in marriage to others (Yassa, Frs. 21, 34-35; Plano Carpini, Rubruquis and Marco Polo).

Criminal Law: The system of punishments of the Great Yassa was simple, the penalties being: death, flogging with rods, and exile.

The punitive law of this epoch was distinguished for its severity. The chief and commonest punishment was death. The death penalty was used in the Yassa to uphold the power of the Khan and a number of military regulations, and death was the punishment for a number of crimes, e.g. murder, sodomy, and large thefts, as well as for some minor offences such as premeditated lies and urinating into water or ashes, etc. The Yassa, however, permitted the substitution of ransom for the death penalty; and maihem (crippling) punishments were unknown.

Organization of the Courts: The organization of courts was at an embryonic stage. Jenghiz Khan instituted the office of Chief Judge, and one of his successors decreed that litigations and disputes were to be brought for decision to the Court of the Khan. This procedure, however, bore an administrative rather than a judicial character. A definite court organization and rules of judicial procedure did not exist. More important cases were brought up before the Chief Judge, and the accuser himself could be the judge. Less important cases were solved by administrative decision. In many cases *en flagrant delit* Mongols were allowed to take the law into their own hands and do justice in accordance with the cruel and superstitious customs of the times.

Second Period, (XV, XVI, XVII and part of the XVIIIth century). Territory: During this period the territory of the Mongols shrank considerably and consisted of Mongolia proper and the territories of related and conquered tribes (e.g. the Bargu-Buriats, Altai Kalmucks, Uriankhais, etc.). Even this limited territory did not represent a unit but was split up into three separate parts: Southern, or Inner Mongolia; Northern (Eastern) Mongolia or Khalkha; and Western Mongolia, or Djungaria.

Population: The great majority of the population was composed of the Mongol tribes: Chahars, Tumets, etc., in Southern Mongolia; Khalkhas and Durbets in Northern Mongolia; and Choros, Torguts, Khoshots and Khoits in Western Mongolia. Among these several non-Mongol tribes were also met with, such as Kirghiz, Sarts and Chinese. The number of the last named increased considerably towards the end of this period.

The chief occupation was cattle-breeding. The religion of the Mongols changed, in the latter half of the XVI-th century, to Buddhism in the form of Lamaism which became particularly widespread.

The Mongols of this period were split up into three main classes; the nobility, commonalty and clergy. There existed, however, a middle layer: Tarkhans, the lower clan chiefs, and some military ranks.

State Power: Originally the Great Khan at Karakorum was the ruler of all Mongolia. Defeats in the armed struggle with China, however, considerably reduced the power of the Great Khan. In the year 1402, the Great Khan Goltzi changed the name of the Yuan dynasty back to its old designation of Tatan, and by this act renounced all claim to China and to the imperial status. The appanage system then gradually developed in Mongolia. At times great personalities, such as Essen (d. 1453), or Dayan Khan (d. 1544), succeeded in uniting all Mongolia, but such union was not long-lived and Dayan was the last Khan of all Mongolia. After his death the appanage system finally triumphed in Mongolia which ceased to have an actual, or even a nominal, supreme ruler. In Northern Mongolia the appanage Hoshun princes were grouped into three Aimaks ruled by three Khans (Tushetu Khan, Tsetsen Khan, and Jassaktu Khan). These Aimaks sometimes united in the common interest, chiefly for purposes of attack or defence against a common foe. The Western Mongols, or Oirats (the Four Oirats—Derben Oirat) also sometimes united into federations, e.g. in the XVth and XVIIth centures. More rarely there appeared in Mongolia even wider alliances, such as the alliance of the "Forty and Four" Mongol tribes, i.e. the Eastern and Western Mongols, in 1640. But such unions were temporary and ceased to exist after the achievement of the common object for which they had been created, or as a result of internal dissension; and even within the unions the respective princes enjoyed the widest freedom of action.

The descendants of Jenghiz Khan bore the titles of Khan, Djinong (crown-prince, heir), Khun-Taidji (Khan of several Oolooses), and Taidji (prince). These titles were also adopted by the Western Mongols, whose tribal princes were not descendants of Jenghiz.

During the first half of the XVII-th century Southern Mongolia was subjugated by China, to be followed in 1691 by Northern Mongolia and 1757 by Western Mongolia. After the last named date the Chinese Emperor became the Great Khan of all Mongolia.

Records of Law: The basic records of the law of this period were the Ancient Tsaadjin Bichik, the Mongol-Oirat Regulations of 1640, the Great Code of the Seven Hoshuns, and the Khalkha Djirum.[5] Of these, the Regulations of 1640 were of most importance, being, for a time, the effective code in both Eastern and Western Mongolia. After the disintegration of the alliance of "Forty and Four", this code remained effective in Djungaria, where it retained its force until the promulgation of the Regulations (Code) of 1789. In Eastern (Northern) Mongolia, the Regulations were replaced by the Great Code of the Seven Hoshuns, and later by the Khalkha Djirum, which also retained its effectiveness until 1789. Besides this, the provisions of the M. O. Regulations of 1640 continued to have effect among the Russian Kalmucks (until 1917). The Khalkha Djirum also continued to function after 1789 among the Shabinars of the Urga Gegen, until superseded in 1925.

Administration: During the period under consideration the administration was centred in the Headquarters of the appanage or Ooloos (Hoshun) prince, where there were special officials concerned with the conduct of military affairs, administrative and judicial function: the Yassaoul (administrator); Daruga (commander); Demchi (tax collector); Elchi (court messenger), and others. Chiefs who governed parts of appanages, Otoks, etc., bore the titles of Taishas, Chinsans, Zaisans, Darugas, etc.

During the epoch of the subjection of Mongolia to China, the administration was reorganized. In 1719 the Mongol princes were deprived of the right of foreign relations; in 1725 there was created in Khalkha the fourth Aimak of Sain-Noyon Khan; and in 1727 the administration of Khalkha was handed over to the four Seims (Leagues) headed by their elected representatives. This reform destroyed the political importance of the four Khans of Khalkha. The number of Hoshuns was considerably increased. The Uliassutai Chiang Chun (Commander-in-Chief of the Chinese troops) represented the super-

5 Sanang Setsen stated that Tumet Khan (1558-1592) promulgated laws, but all trace of these has been lost.

visory organ over the Hoshun and Seim (League) administrations, and the Ambans at Urga and Kobdo were named as his assistants.

Private Law: The right of property in immovables did not exist. The land was held for common use by the clan units, the Hotons, Aimaks, Otoks, etc., for the purposes of pastoral economy (arts. 15, 122 of the M. O. Regulations; Khalkha Djirum, IV-IX; etc.) The right of private property in movables was, however, defined. Economy was, for the most part, natural, and civil legal life was little developed, although the Khalkha Djirum was more advanced in this respect than the Regulations of 1640. Relationship was recognized only in the male line. The family structure was patriarchal in character. The power of the husband and father was great, but not to despotism. Marriage was exogamous and based on the payment of ransom for the bride; and polygamy existed. Vestiges of the matriarchate were, however, evident. Elder sons could separate themselves from the paternal household (Anc. Tsaadjin Bichik, 5). Inheritance was determined by custom and divided among the sons, the custom of the handing over of the household to the younger son being followed (according to the Khalkha Djirum, the sons received equal shares in the inheritance—VIII, 20). The widow-mother managed the inherited property.

Criminal Law: Crimes and offences were primarily customary in character, as were many of the penalties applied. The penal systems of the Regulations of 1640 and the Khalkha Djirum were more complex (since more than ten varieties of punishment were provided for in each) than that of the Great Yassa, but also considerably milder. The death penalty was rare and the commonest punishments were the property fine in cattle and flogging. The punishments for personal insults were determined by the social position of the insulted person (as well as the person offering the insult). A peculiarity of the Regulations of 1640 and the Khalkha Djirum was the provision, alongside of the system of punishments, of a system of rewards for certain (altruistic) actions, such as the saving of human lives, cattle and property.

Organization of the Court: The courts were organized as State institutions. Among the Western Mongols there were two judicial instances, the Hoton court and the High Court. Two instances also evidently existed among the Northern Mongols, but among them the courts were more closely tied up with the administration. Definite, although not detailed, rules of procedure existed. The number of cases in which Mongols were permitted to take the law into their own hands was considerably diminished.

Third Period (1789-1911). Territory: The territory of Mongolia as a State coincided with the geographical conception of Mongolia, i.e. it comprised Southern, Northern (Eastern) and Western Mongolia. It was otherwise divided into Inner (Southern) Mongolia and Outer (Western and Northern) Mongolia. Inner Mongolia fell earlier under Chinese sovereignty and was more closely connected with China. It was divided into six Seims (Leagues) and 49 Hoshuns, while Outer Mongolia comprised the four Seims (Leagues) (Aimaks) of Khalkha and two Aimaks of Djungaria, containing 111 Hoshuns and the Department of the Urga Gegen. Besides this, one Aimak (corps) of Altai Mongols, was included in Outer Mongolia.

Population: The main part of the population was composed of the Mongol tribes, but the Chinese were especially numerous in Inner Mongolia, where they engaged in agriculture and trade; and there was a small number of Russians in Outer Mongolia, as well as some Kirghiz, Uriankhais, etc. The total number of the population during the period was from 2,500,000 to 3,000,000 (closer 2,500,000). The chief occupation was nomadic cattle-breeding. This period witnessed a progressive weakening of clan ties among the Northern Mongols, although they retained their force to a greater extent among the Mongols of the West.

State Power: The supreme power was now vested in the Emperor of China. The Mongol princes were divided into six degrees: Chin Wang, Chun Wang, Beile, Beisse, Tushetu-gun and Tusalakchi-gun. The Taidji (nobility) were divided into four degrees. Besides this, the princes were divided in Djassaks (ruling a Hoshun) and Noyons (non-ruling princes).

Records of Law: The chief juridical records of this period were the Chinese Codes for Mongolia, promulgated in 1789 and 1815 (the Code of 1696 was effective in Inner Mongolia).

Administration: The highest organ of the internal administration of the Aimak was the Seim (League, conference). Seims were called once every three years for the decision of judicial cases, apportioning of levies in kind, and the taking of a census of the population. The president of the Seim was the League elder (Chigulganu-Daruga) who was elected from amongst the princes of the Aimak and confirmed in his post by the Emperor. This official had an assistant or substitute, and an administrative office (Yamen). The President of the Seim (League) was entrusted with the duty of supervising the condition of the Aimak and the activities of the Hoshun princes, and had the right of appeal to the Li Fan Yuan (the Chinese Board of Foreign Relations) against any order of the Manchu authorities. At the head of each Hoshun (division) was a Djassak, a prince ruling over a Hoshun. The office of Djassak was hereditary, but subject to confirmation by the

Emperor. Each Djassak had one or two assistants (Tusalakchis) who had charge of civil affairs. These Tusalakchis were usually appointed from among the Noyons and Taidjis of the Hoshun, and were the actual administrators of the Hoshun attached to the hereditary princes. The military affairs of the Hoshun were in the hands of a special Commander (the Zahirakchi), whose staff contained one assistant—a Tzalan (regimental commander), or two assistants (a Tzalan and a Meiren). Two Tusalakchis, a Zahirakchi, a Tsalan and a Meiren composed the Administrative Council (Tamga).

The supervisory organ was composed of the Uliassutai Chiang Chun (Commander-in-Chief) and the Ambans at Uliassutai, Urga and Kobdo (two at each point, one Manchu and one Mongol).

The Shabinars of the Urga Gegen were governed by the Shabi Yamen.

Private Law: Private law was represented almost entirely by custom. The Regulations (Codes) of 1789 and 1815 contained only a few provisions of private law. In the Shabi department the provisions of the Khalkha Djirum were still applied. In general, the character of private-legal relations remained the same as during the preceding period.

Criminal Law: The criminal law of both codes, as well as the administrative law, was strongly influenced by the law of China. The penal system was extremely complex and contained qualified capital punishment as well as various forms of maihem and torture. In place of the comparatively mild provisions of the Regulations of 1640 and the Khalkha Djirum, we meet here a criminal law of great severity with various forms of the death penalty (including qualified capital punishment), hard labour, imprisonment for long periods, beating with rods, etc., as well as punishments of a local character. The severe penalties for some crimes were glaringly out of keeping with the spirit of Mongol law, e.g. the punishment for arson (there were no houses in Mongolia), for violation of graves (the Mongols rarely buried their dead), and for some others.

Organization of Courts: The courts were identified with the administration. The first judicial instance was the Hoshun prince and his administration (Tamga); the second instance—the President of the Seim (League) and the Seim administration; and the third instance, the Li Fan Yuan, or Board of Foreign Relations, in Peiping. The rules of court procedure were not sufficiently defined. Torture was commonly applied in investigation. Tracking, search, the testimony of witnesses, and the oath were allowed. The personal attendance of the litigants at court was required.

Fourth Period (from 1911). Territory: The territory of the Mongol State was considerably diminished in comparison with the previous period. In 1911 Mongolia declared her autonomy and, in accordance with the terms of the treaty of 1915, Outer (i.e. Northern and Western) Mongolia was declared to be an autonomous State under the sovereignty of China and the protectorate of Russia. Since that time (with the exception of a short interlude of about 15 months from November 1920 till February 1921) Outer Mongolia has remained practically autonomous. Inner Mongolia, on the other hand, remained under the direct rule of China, being organized into the three territories (later provinces) of Jehol, Chahar and Suiyuan. Outer (Autonomous) Mongolia is divided into the four Aimaks of Khalkha and two Oirat Aimaks.

Population: The population of Outer (Autonomous) Mongolia was composed chiefly of the Mongol tribes (about 550,000 souls), Chinese (about 100,000), Russians (5,000), some Kirghiz, Uriankhais, etc. The chief occupation remains, as before, nomadic cattle-breeding. In Autonomous Mongolia, according to the census of 1918, 5.7% of the population belonged to the nobility; 22.3% (44.6% of the male population) clergy; and 72% to the commonalty (including serfs); towns (the chief of which is Urga, now Ulan Bator) were not populous and their permanent population was composed more of foreigners than of natives.

State Power: The head of the State was the Urga Bogdo-Gegen-Hutukhtu. During the first period of autonomy (1911-19) he was an autocratic monarch. He had a Council of Ministers with five members, and when problems of especial gravity came up for settlement, a conference of Hoshun princes was called. However, the decisions of both the Council of Ministers and the conference of princes were consultative in character, and were subject to the sanction of the Bogdo-Gegen. During the second period of autonomy (1921-1924), the Bogdo-Gegen was a constitutional monarch having only a limited power of veto[6], and the country was governed by the Mongol Provisional People's Government.

After the death of the Bogdo-Gegen, in June 1924. Outer Mongolia was declared the Mongolian People's Republic, the supreme power in which was vested in the Great Hural (congress of people's representatives) and the government elected by it.

Records of Law: During the period of the socalled Autonomous Mongolia (1911-24), no general codes were issued. A Code of Laws was, however, prepared (34 books being printed) and draft Civil and Criminal Codes were compiled. During the second period of the existence of

6 By the Agreement of Nov. 21, 1921.

Autonomous Mongolia (1921-24) a series of important separate laws was issued, e.g. laws abolishing serfdom, separating the Church from the State, abolishing corporal punishment, etc. This second period represented the stage of transition from Autonomous Mongolia to the Mongolian People's Republic and its legislation.

Administration: Administrative power was vested in the Hoshun authorities—the Tamga; and in the Aimak administration or Yamen. The Tamga rendered decisions in the administrative affairs of the Hoshun, dispensed justice, collected levies, attended to the upkeep of the roads, managed State property located within the territory of the Hoshun, kept a register of the male population, mobilised and trained troops, etc. In military affairs the Tamga was subordinated to the special Aimak Chiang Chun (Commander-in-Chief); in civil affairs to the Aimak administration or Yamen. The President of the Seim (Aimak, League) and his administration supervised the proper rendering of tax-funds, the proper discharge of the duty of Urton (compulsory cartage), examined administrative questions which exceeded the competence of the Hoshun Tamga, confirmed the appointment of Hoshun officials and represented a judicial instance (court of appeal).

The supervisory organ over the Hoshun and League (Aimak) administrations was the Ministry of the Interior at Urga.

Private Law: The right of private property in land was not recognized in Autonomous Mongolia, and the purchase and sale, and mortgage of land was not allowed. The renting of land was allowed only with regard to foreigners. Civil legal life was more developed than previously. The family remained patriarchal. Polygamy was permitted, and divorce was easy. The power of the husband and father prevailed in the family, but the mother also participated in decisions with regard to family affairs, and in the rearing of the children. Inheritance belonged first of all to the widow and her children (sons), and if there were no children the widow received her dowry while the rest of the inheritance passed to collateral relatives. The youngest son inherited the household of the father in accordance with ancient Mongol custom. The making of wills (usually verbal) was permitted if the provisions of the will were not in violation of custom.

Criminal Law: The influence of Chinese law (through the Code of 1815) was strong in the criminal legislation of Autonomous Mongolia, with its complex penal system and severe punishments. Qualified capital punishment, imprisonment for long terms, the cangue, rods, and some other purely Chinese punishments which had long been applied among the Mongols, were also practised in Autonomous Mongolia, along with the cattle fine, whipping, and some other Mongol punishments.

At the same time, although the written law prescribed severe punishments for adultery, the violation of graves, etc., the courts acted in accordance with custom and imposed light penalties. Thus, in the criminal law of Autonomous Mongolia we find a mixture of Chinese institutions and Mongol customs, the former being in considerable predominance.

Organization of the Courts: During this period the courts were still identified with the administration. In Autonomous Mongolia, the first instance in minor cases was still the administration of the Hoshun prince; and the second instance (in minor cases) was the Seim (League) administration (Yamen). The latter also represented the first instance in more important cases. The Ministry of Justice in Urga serving as the third instance in minor, and the second in major cases or in cases in which the Seim administration served as the first instance. Finally, the Ministry of Justice was the first instance in cases involving princes, which were removed from the competence of both the Hoshun and League authorities. The final instance in such cases was the Bogdo Gegen.

Gegens, Hutukhtus and Shabinars were judged by the Shabi Yamen.

As has been stated above, we shall not limit ourselves to this short summary of Mongol law but shall pass on below to a more detailed consideration of the fundamental institutions of the public and private organization of the Mongol tribes.

(b) Fundamental Institutions of Public Law.

Social (clan) Organization. In its essential manifestations, among the Mongols, Buriats and Kalmucks, Mongol law presents a picture of a definitely developed type of clan relations. Clan organization, according to L. Morgan, is one of the most ancient institutions of mankind and one of those which have had the most widespread significance. It was the almost universal form of organization of the ancient Asiatic, European, African, American and Australian societies and the means by which society was organized and preserved.[7]

Clan organization expressed itself in two basic kinds, the Matriarchate and Patriarchate in their various forms. Among the Mongols it bore a patriarchal character in harmony with the nomadic, patriarchal clan culture of that people. Of course, the Mongol tribes

7 Morgan—"Primitive Society", (Russian Ed.), pg. 61.

were not the only representatives of this culture. But it may be said that among them it expressed itself very vividly and was fairly completely preserved.

The patriarchal clan mode of life, with its accompanying military organization of the people, already found clear expression in the surviving fragments of the Great Yassa of Jenghiz Khan (*cf*. Frs. 18, 22,43) and of the Maxims (19,23,24), as well as in the descriptions of contemporaries; and still more in the provisions of the Mongol-Oirat Regulations of 1640 and other records.

Maxim 23, for instance, stated:

"If anyone of *our clan* act in violation of the approved Yassak, let hm be admonished verbally; if he do it again, let him be persuaded by eloquence; if he do it a third time, let him be sent to the remote place Baljuin-Khuljur. When he returns thence, he will be attentive. But if he be not brought to his senses, let him be put in irons and imprisoned. If he come out of imprisonment good-humoured and reasonable, well and good. If not, let his *relations* assemble and deliberate as to what is to be done with him.

Maxim 19:

"After us the descendants of *our clan* will wear gold embroidered garments, eat rich and sweet food, ride fine horses and embrace beautiful women, but they will not say that they owe all this to their fathers and elder brohers, and they will forget us and those great times."[8]

The Secret Chronicle gives the following description of the battle between, Jenghiz Khan and Wang Khan (of the Kereits)[9]. "Jurchedei[10] said: 'My Uruut and Mankhut[11] will fight before the king, in the van.' With these words he drew up both clans before Jenghiz. No sooner had he thus arrayed them than from the side of Wang Khan, the vanguard of the latter, Djirgin[12] advanced to the attack. Uruut and Mankhut went out against them and defeated them, but while engaged in the pursuit they were attacked by one of Wang Khan's auxiliary detachments, under the chieftainship of Achikh-Shi-Runya, of the Tumen-Tubegan clan, who stabbed our Khuildar[13] and threw him from his horse. The Mankhut detachment them turned back and established itself in the place where Khuildar had fallen. Jurchedei, at the head of the Uruuts, fell upon the auxiliary detachment and smashed it, and while pursuing, he met Oman

8 *v*. also the "Autobiography of Timur and the Heroic Chronicles of Jenghiz Khan and Aksak-Timur", 1934, pg. 263 (in Russ.).

9 *v*. Works of the Members of the Russian Orthodox Mission, vol. IV, 1910, pg. 42; also Acad. Vladimirtzov, "Social Organization of the Mongols", pg. 92.

10 Chieftain of the Uruut clan.

11 Two Mongol clans.

12 One of the Kereit clans.

13 A Mankhut chieftain.

and Dunkhait[14] and also defeated them; then Shilemin-Taidzi with 1,000 bodyguards attacked him, but these also were beaten by Jurchedei."

From this extract it is clear that the Mongols and Kereits went to battle in clans, each clan forming a separate detachment under the command of the clan chief. Of all the military units only the bodyguards were chosen from different clans. This form of clan organization was adapted by Jenghiz Khan (*v.* Great Yassa, Fr. 22) who preserved the ancient division of the warriors into tens (scores and forties), hundreds, thousands and tumens (a tumen was 10,000 men). A tribe comprised an Ooloos-Tumen, while large clans were represented by thousands and smaller ones by hundreds, etc.[15]

In the ancient Mongol clans relationship was traced through the male line from a common male ancestor, and the clan was therefore agnate and patriarchal. Genealogies were jealously guarded. The Mongol clan was also exogamous: it was forbidden to marry within the clan and wives were taken only from other clans. For this reason it was sometimes necessary to travel far for wives and even to abduct them.[16]

As may be seen from the Mongol-Oirat Regulations, the Kibitkas (Yurts) of the Mongols were grouped into Aouls or Hoshuns (arts. 15-125), the Aouls into Aimaks (art. 23), the Aimaks into Otoks (generations, Oolooses—art. 122), the Otoks into tribes, and the tribes into Leagues (*cf.* the fourhold federation, the Derben-Oirat of the four western tribes and the general union of the 44 Mongol tribes, 1640). The Hoshun or Aoul (camp) represented one large family, while the neighbouring Aouls, which formed part of the same Aimaks, were inhabited by close kinsmen (clansmen). The Otok united several Aimaks, and formed part of the tribe[17]. A tribe usually formed a separate principality.

To preserve the clan the Regulations prescribed compulsory marriage: out of every forty Kibitkas four were annually obliged to marry off their sons. In view of the fact that the Kalim for the bride was quite great and often beyond the means of the bridegroom, it was prescribed that ten households were obliged to help one man at marriage (37). Separate Mongols, and also entire Aimaks, were forbidden to change their camping grounds; and fugitives were to be returned to their Aimaks (132, 133).

---

14 Two Kereit clans.

15 In some cases, however, the composition of the thousands was more complex, and consisted of representatives of different clans; and tumens—of different tribes (*v.* Rashid Ed-din, op. cit, XV, pg. 33, 147, etc., also Secret Chronicle, pgs. 49, 56-58, 60). Of course these figures were only approximate.

16 *Cf.* Acad. Vladimirtzov, *Op. cit.*, 46-48.

17 An Otok was a military-administrative unit connected with clan organization (*Cf.* Leontovich, "Kalmuck Law", 1880, ppg. 208-212).

Clan mutual aid and social solidarity, developed by the clan mode of life, wars and community hunts, were general among the Mongols (see further).

The family life of the Mongols was strictly patriarchal. The head of the family, the lord of the household, father and husband, enjoyed great power. Anyone killing a husband in battle had the right to take his wife as a reward (50). A husband could desert or even kill his wife, and in the latter case he was fined only as for the killing of a slave (32,33). The severity of penalties was increased in the case of crimes and offences against elder relâtives (17-3). The Regulations also provided, in some cases, for the collective responsibility of kinsmen (13,15,11). Relationship was recognized only in the male line. Property belonged to the entire family, but a grown son could demand an allotment and found his own family (*v.* art. 5 of the Ancient Tsaadjin Bichik; arts. 34,118 of the Regulations) and individual property was recognised with respect to some movables. There existed also family gods and a family hearth from which sons, about to set up a new household, took the fires for their new yurts.

As may be seen from the contents of the Khalkha Djirum, the Northern Mongols also lived under such a clan patriarchal order, under the rule of their clan chiefs. Thus the Khalkha Djirum speaks of units of clan organization among the Northern Mongols: Hotons, Oolooses, and Otoks; and of clan chieftains such as Shulengas, Demchis and Darugas (XVI, XV, VIII),as well as of the division of the Northern Mongols into tens (XV). It was specially pointed out that a father had no power over the life of his son (XIV). Relationship was recognized in the male line; and provision was made for rewards to persons giving succour in times of misfortune, etc. The Regulations of 1789 and 1815 also mention the clan (v. II-11,12 of 1789 and I-61,63 of 1815).[18]

The well known Russian investigator of Mongolia, Prof. A. M. Posdneev, wrote as follows: "The original form of the Mongol clan society was undoubtedly the family, composed of persons descended one from another, and mutually connected by three or four degrees of blood relationship (from grandfather to great grandchildren inclusive). The head, who was the eldest member of such a family, enjoyed general respect and had power over each separate member of the family group, and all family property; all being bound to obey him. He married off his sons and, when doing so, put up for each a new kibitka, arranging such kibitkas in line to the right or western side of his yurt. For his grown daughters he likewise set up new yurts; but this time on the

---

18 Academician Vladimirtzov was therefore not right when he indicated that the Eastern Mongols had already abandoned clan organization in the epoch of the Khalkha Djirum (*Op. cit.* pg. 171).

left or eastern side of his own where the yurts of his distant relatives were also located. Thus there developed entire groups of yurts, "Hotons", the centre of which was the yurt of the head of the family which was called the "chief" yurt or "Orgo". In this yurt were the family hearth and the essential articles of the family economy, while the other yurts did not contain independent hearths and were called 'Hochi'. Grown and married sons could separate themselves from their parents and brothers, set up their own hearths, and give rise to their own Hotons of which they were the heads and in which they had the power over junior members of their families who composed a dependent and subordinate retinue. Thus there appeared among the Mongols entire generations united among themselves by more or less close ties of relationship."[19]

It is necessary, however, to note that as time passed, the clan order among the Northern Mongols underwent a significant degeneration and became much weaker than among the Western Mongols. In the XX-th century only vestiges of it remained. For instance, the Hoshuns of Outer Mongolia were divided into Baks (communities) or Otoks, and the Baks and Otoks into scores (Horin), or tens. These were evident survivals of the former military clan organization.

The Buriats were divided into three main tribes, the Bulahats, Echirites and Horins, and into separate "generations". The tribes, in their turn, were divided into clans (about 200 in all) which had from the most ancient times been governed by their clan chiefs—the Shulengas and Zaisans. At the head of each tribe stood a Taisha. The Buriat clans, for the most part, drew their names from the names of the localities and rivers in which they camped. Thus, in the province of Irkutsk, there were 1. the Tunkinsk Buriats—14 clans; 2. Kitoisk—3 clans; 3. Kubinsk—16 clans; 4. Kapsalsk—4 clans; 5. Alarsk—11 clans; 6. Balagansk—24 clans; 7. Idinsk—29 clans; 8. Verkholensk—7 clans; 9. Lenski—7 clans; 10. Olkhonsk—9 clans; 11. Nijneudinsk—2 communities. In the Trans-Baikal region there were the Buriats of 1. Barguzinsk—5 clans; 2. Kudarinsk—4 clans; 3. Selenga—38 clans; 4. Hori—14 clans (11 old and 3 new); 5. Aginsk—10 clans. Besides this, there existed a number of separate generations. These tribal units served as a basis for the former Russian organization of the Buriats: a camp (Kochevie) of 15 families comprised an Ooloos, with a clan administration composed of an Elder (Zasaoul, Shulenga) and one or two assistants. Several Oolooses, comprising a clan, were subject to the Clan

---

19 A. M. Posdneev, "Mongolia and the Mongols", vol. III, chap. on "The Khalkha Mongols". The MS. of this work was kindly made available to the present writer by Prof. G. V. Podstavin, a pupil of Professor Posdneev.

Office Executive Bureau (headed by Zaisans and Shulengas), and several mutually connected clans had a Steppe Council, composed of the chief clansman—a Taisha, and several elected members—Taishas, Zaisans and Shulengas.[20] The administration and judiciary, in the lower instances, were represented by the clan chiefs, whose authority, according to Hangalov, who wrote concerning the end of the XIX-th century, was very great.[21] Each tribe, and each clan within the tribe, was obliged to camp on the territory allotted to it. The Buriats paid a Yassak (levy, formerly consisting of furs) by clans and through their clan chieftains. Common family property existed (individual property in movables also being permitted), and even common family responsibility. Relationship was recognised in the male line. For insults to parents and senior clansmen increased penalities were imposed.

The following is an extract from Schapov's description of a Buriat settlement as he saw it in 1874.

"Each Ooloos ordinarily consists of several low stake enclosures, usually in the form of a circle or ellipse. Within each enclosure are one, two, three or more yurts with their auxiliary buildings such as outhouses, storehouses, stalls, barns or sheds, bread-bakeries, etc. In one of these yurts lives the senior Buriat of the family, an old man with his wife and, occasionally, a few orphaned relatives. In another yurt, standing beside it, is the son of this old man, with his wife and children. If the old man has any other married sons, they live in separate yurts, but still within the same enclosure on either side of the yurt of the father. Within this clan-family circle, connected by blood relationship, everything is common—ploughlands, hay-mows, pastures (Outougs), cattle—everything. All the inhabitants of the enclosure work together. Sometimes they even all eat together and generally, whenever there is a "roast" or any collection of guests, they function as one family. Furthermore, close beside them in another similar enclosure live the nearest relatives of the head of the first group of yurts; for instance his brothers with their families and blood-clan—and here again the yurt of the senior relative stands in the centre of the enclosure with the yurts of his sons beside it. Further, in more distant enclosures, live the more distant relatives, these being called 'neighbours'.[22] Thus the Ooloos clan community, as the original clan line, increased and branched out, stemmed off more and more into separate enclosures or groups of

---

20 The Buriats also preserved a vestige of the old military organization, the division into Horins (scores). *v.* Bogdanov, "Outlines", pg. 101.

21 *v.* Hangalov, "Juridical Customs of the Buriats", *Ethnographic Review* (Russ.), No. 2, 1894.

22 Here, in analogous relations, we must seek the roots of the right of neighbours to escheats, which is known among European peoples—*jus vicinorum,* Nachbarshaftrecht (*Cf.* Heussier—Institution des deutschen Privatrechts, II, para. 191; Schroeder, "Lehrbuch der deutschen Rechtsgeschichte", 5th Ed., 347).

yurts. Finally the most distant kinsmen organized an Ooloos of their own in which the same organization of the Ooloos clan community was repeated. And the entire group of similar and neighbouring Oolooses still represented a single clan, a single clan community, divided into genealogical branches in the shape of Ooloos communities, just as the Ooloos communities themselves were divided into smaller family communities."[23]

The same investigator testifies to the existence, as late as the 70's of the last century, of the community hunt or Aba which, even though it had lost its previous significance to the tribe, nevertheless preserved within certain clans the essential characteristics of the ancient hunts—the collective chase and common division of the game under the direction of elected chieftains.

A contemporary investigator of the life of the Buriats, B. E. Petri, has written: "The Buriat clan represents a strictly exclusive community made one by the presence of a hereditary clan elder, common territory, one Ooloos, common camp sites, common local deities, common rites and sacrifices (*Talaiga*) and many other elements which shall be discussed further. Such a community lived as one large patriarchal family, closely bound together not only by common descent and blood relationship but also by a community of material interest."[24]

The elements of clan relations among the Northern Buriats, according to the same author, were common descent and blood relationship, the presence of a Clan Elder, clan lands, clan irrigation system, clan deities and clan sacrifices (Talaiga), a clan Shaman, clan sacred fire, clan Kurunga (sour milk), clan honour, and clan courts.

In the life of the Kalmucks two basic features may be discerned, the clan mode of life and vestiges of the old military organization.

The basis of the nomadic social organization of the Kalmucks was the Kibitka-Khosh. A group of related kibitkas (Khosh) formed a Hoton at the head of which stood a clan elder; group of Hotons, Aimaks, were administered by a Zaisan; several Aimaks formed an Angi (Otok); several Angi an Ooloos; and several Oolooses a tribe. At the head of each tribe stood the tribal Taisha who himself administered the principal Ooloos, while other Oolooses were headed by his closest relatives such as his sons and brothers. The Kalmucks were divided into three tribes—the Torguts, Durbots, and Hoshouts; there were also separate generations of emigrants from Djungaria (comprising 8 Oolooses, 37 Aimaks and 180 Hotons of the Astrakhan Kalmucks, 3 Oolooses of Don

23 Schapov, "The Buriat Ooloos Clan Community", Journal of the Siberian Section, Russ. Geog. Soc., vol. V, 3-4, pg. 129.

24 "Elements of Clan Relations Among the Northern Buriats", 1924, ppg. 2 *sqq.*

Kalmucks and some others). At one time a Khan ruled over all the Kalmuck tribes. Besides this the Otoks and Aimaks preserved the old nomadic military division into tens, forties and hundreds.

The Kalmucks were organized on the clan principle and their life was patriarchal. The clan chieftains, the Noyons, were also administrative rulers and their power over the person and property of the commoners was very great. The Kalmucks camped on the steppe in Hotons, Aimaks and Oolooses.

"The composition of the kibitkas and their organization into Hotons is determined by the ancient customs of the clans", wrote Professor Leontovich in 1880. "Among the contemporary Kalmucks, the kibitkas of the sons and other members of the Hoton are commonly situated near the paternal kibitka in accordance with the customary form observable among all Asiatic nomads. According to Kalmuck custom the kibitkas are arranged in such a way that they form a more or less regular circle. The centre of the Hoton is occupied by the kibitka of the father and from it the kibitkas of the rest of the family stem out to form a semicircle. The arrangement of the kibitkas is determined by seniority of birth and kinship, since the distant and impoverished Kalmuck kinsmen do not split off from the clan Hoton. In short the arrangement of the kibitkas is strictly in accordance with the clan order, from which no departure is on any account made."[25]

Single kibitkas were forbidden to camp away from their Aimaks, while Aimaks and clans were obliged to stay within their Ooloos. The Kalmucks were obliged to subordinate themselves to the clan Zaisans, etc. The provisions of the Mongol-Oirat Regulations concerning the preservation of the clan were confirmed; and each forty kibitkas were obliged to marry two (instead of four) couples annually and collectively cover the expenses of the marriages. Relationship was recognized only in the male line. Until the most recent times there existed among the Kalmucks the institution of common family property with separation of individual movable property and clan responsibility (Zinzili Resolutions, arts. 119-121, 154, 196).

Socially speaking, the Mongols did not represent a homogeneous mass but were divided into classes or separate social groups.

On the basis of the Yassa of Jenghiz Khan we may distinguish two main classes: the White Bone or nobility (princes, Beks, Murzas) and the Black Bone—merchants, craftsmen, commoners and the slaves who occupied the lowest rung of the social ladder. The Mongol-Oirat Regulations of 1640 also indicate the existence of these same two

---

25 Leontovich, "Kalmuck Law", 1880, pg. 190.

classes, the White Bone or nobility (princes, Tabunangs, and clan chiefs) and the commanalty, as well as the slaves. Here, however, there was a middle layer (social group) composed of the Tarkhans (persons who as a reward for services rendered were exempted from taxation), banner-bearers and some other military ranks. The Regulations also indicated the appearance as a separate group of the clergy which, 70 years later in the Khalkha Djirum, was already significantly developed and finally attained an altogether exceptional importance in Mongolia. The Khalkha Djirum distinguishes between the following social groups: 1. Nobility; 2. Tarkhans and warriors; 3. Semi-dependent persons, slaves and serfs; and 4. The clergy, who were extremely numerous. In Autonomous Mongolia, according to figures compiled in 1918, 5.7% of whole population belonged to the nobility, 22.3-to the clergy and 72% to the common people.

Among the Buriats, during the period under consideration, it is necessary to distinguish between the upper class—the higher clan chiefs (Chief Taishas, Taishas, Zaisans), and the lower—the commoners. An intermediate position was occupied by the lower clan chiefs and honourable clansmen. Besides this a clerical group existed among the Southern Buriats.

The Kalmucks also had the same two main classes as the Western Mongols: the White Bone or nobility—Khans, Lieutenants, Noyons and Zaisans; and a lower class composed of free commoners and serfs. The Tarkhans and lower clan chiefs formed an intermediate group. The clergy occupied a separate group.

State Structure.—It is necessary to note that, in view of the strength of their clan organisation, the state institutions of the Mongols were not of a high order.

This was true of the greatest and relatively most stable of the Mongol unions—the empire of Jenghiz-Khan.

The organisation of the State under Jenghiz-Khan assigned a purely military character to the scattered Mongol tribes which were made parts of a permanent organized army. Each nomad with his kibitka (household) belonged to a certain Ten, the Tens formed part of Hundreds, the Hundreds of Thousands, and the Thousands—of Tens of Thousands or Tümens (armies), each of these units having its own special chief (cf. Fragment 22 of the Great Yassa of Jenghiz Khan and the third of his Maxims). This military organization was closely bound up with that of the clans, hundreds being made up out of small clans and thousands out of more numerous ones. An army (10,000 kibitkas) constituted a province, or Ooloos.

Each nomad cattle-breeder was at the same time a warrior, coming under both the civil and military organization of the Mongol State. Under this system the entire people was an army, and the army was the entire people. The social organization of the Empire of Jenghiz Khan and his successors was based on aristocratic principles, and was aristocratic in spirit. Jenghiz Khan himself was by birth a member of the nobility, and the nobility was the ruling class in the Mongol State which was permeated throughout with the spirit of clan organization, militarism and autocracy.

At the time of Jenghiz Khan and his immediate successors, the military art attained high development among the Mongols, and could serve as a model to other races and States. The same could not be said, however, of their civil administration.

Jenghiz Khan was not only a great warrior and conqueror, but also an able administrator. His ambition was to create a stable and powerful State for ages to come. Well understanding that the Mongols of his time were not prepared to undertake such a task, he was compelled to attract to his aid in this attempt to organize an empire, many Uigurs, Chinese and other foreigners (Tashatung, Chin-Gai, Yeh-Liu-Ch'u-Ts'ai). Jenghiz Khan brought into existence the first beginnings of religious toleration, appointed special officials to administer certain branches of State Affairs, and in particular established the offices of Chief Bek and Judge-in-Chief. He also organized special means of communication for the urgent needs of the State, established offices for the keeping of records and archives, and gave orders that Mongol youths should learn the Uigur written language. A code of laws was created, known as the Great Yassa. Under Jenghiz Khan's successor, the Great Khan Ogodai, the limits of power of the Mongol rulers over the conquered countries were laid down, the rules of State Service were fixed, and a measure of order was introduced into the system of taxation. Evidently at this time also, the dispensation of justice was established at the Court of the Great Khan.

But the Mongols remained a nation of predatory nomads who had not grown out of primitive conditions of clan life; and not only suffered from scarcity of education, but did not even possess a written language of their own. Such a nation could not provide the necessary material for the creation of a stable and cultured State, notwithstanding all the talents and ability of Jenghiz Khan, his assistants and his successors.

The empire of Jenghiz Khan had already virtually disintegrated during the lives of his grandsons into independent appanages, governed by the descendants of the four sons of the conqueror. These appanages were, in their turn, split up into smaller units in which the power of the Jenghizids was not long lived. This applies to the eastern dominion in China, as well as to those of the West-in Persia, Transoxiania, Russia, etc.

Subsequent attempts to achieve a stable State in Mongolia failed for similar reasons. The result was the same under Daiyan Khan in the North, Lingdan Khan in the South, and Essen and Galdan Khan in the West. Finally Mongolia became a dependency of China.

The various related tribes of the Mongols were often not connected among themselves in any definite way.

The Buriats, for instance, were divided into three tribes (the Bulahats, Echirites and Horins) and failed to create any lasting union or common administration, the Northern and Southern Buriats fighting separately against the conquest of their territory by the Russians.[26]

As we know, there existed among the Western Mongols or Djungars the Oirat Federation of tribes which was now consolidated, now fell apart, the chief stimulus to its formation being the presence of common danger. This union was not stable and did not represent permanent State unity.

The Northern Mongols of Khalkha, notwithstanding their common composition, were split up into a multitude of principalities (appanages) and did not (until the XX-th century) create any common power or common State. Concerning them, Professor A. M. Posdneev wrote as follows:

"In their internal life these principalities were completely independent and unconnected with each other. They had no common laws and all their relations were based upon the ideas belonging to the clan mode of life, in which all the natives of Khalkha were instructed. There was, however, no external alliance or agreement which might have fused the principalities of Khalkha into one whole and formed of them an impressive tribal union. Each prince was the lord of his own actions, independently governed his subjects, judged and punished them in accordance with his personal decision, being guided in this only by custom and his own whim; and at his own wish concluded alliances with or was hostile towards any one of his princely relatives. In private questions

26 M. N. Bogdanov had the following to say concerning the organization of the Buriats before the coming of the Russians. "There is evidence of the fact that, under the power of one or another chief, unity was sometimes attained within a tribe; and occasionally among two tribes or at any rate the greater part of two tribes living on the same territory. But we have as yet no indication of the duration of such unity. It is probable that, as with the appanage territories of the Mongols, separate Oolooses, clans and tribes sometimes united for the achievement of some definite object, the union being effective only within the limits of this common purpose."—"Outlines", pg. 41.

or separate cases having common social significance, the princes of Khalkha met in common Seims and concluded alliances, but the resolutions of these Seims were not binding for those who disagreed with them and each participant of an alliance could secede from it if it seemed to him that it was acting against his wishes or interests."[27]

A certain unity prevailed among the Mongol tribes at times of military danger, prompted by the necessity of common defence against external aggression; as for instance among the Oirats and their Kalmuck kinsmen who settled among hostile peoples. Unity was also at times attained by simple military force, as during the reigns of Jenghiz Khan or Galdan Khan. But as soon as the common danger passed or the leader-conqueror and unifier left the historical scene, the alliances of Mongol tribes feel apart into their constituent parts.

This is easy to understand. Where the clan is strong and has economic, religious and political functions, there the State principle is usually weak. Between the State and the individual stands the clan (or the tribe—a collection of clans) whose interests predominate over the interests of the State, and whose protection makes the State less necessary. It is evident that under these circumstances governments are not strong and the State power is unstable.

It is necessary to note that during the past two and a half centuries, under the Chinese domination which promoted the weakness and isolation of the Mongol appanages, the social life of Mongolia fell to a large extent under clerical influence and became permeated with the spirit of theocracy. The religiousness of the Mongols, the great number of monasteries and Lamaist clergy, their privileged position and economic significance, and the great influence of the clergy upon all aspects of Mongol life could not but put a clerical-theocratic stamp on the social and even the administrative organization of the country. These circumstances gave rise to the worship of the Urga Gegen, the spiritual head of Mongolia who was at the same time the temporal lord of a tremendous number of Shabinars (comprising 8 Hoshuns),[28] and stood above the Khans and Princes, enjoying almost divine status during his lifetime. At the same time there was a weakening of the significance of the former Khans and princely lines (the Jenghizids) and generally of the principles of clan organization. These twin processes led finally to the unification of the temporal and spiritual power in Mongolia in the hands of the Pontiff. In 1911, thanks to favourable external circum-

27 Erdeniin Erikhe, pg. 141.

28 These were under a special administration or Yamen at the head of which stood the Shanzotba Lama. At the same time (1727) the Khans were reduced to mere rulers of their own Hoshuns.

stances, a shortlived semi-theocratic State, the socalled Autonomous Mongolia, was set up under the rule of the Urga Gegen.

Thus in place of the feudal-like power of the Chinese Emperors of the Ta Ch'ing dynasty, the year 1911 saw the appearance on the scene of Mongol history of another still more anachronistic form of government—of a semi-theocratic, semi-feudal character—the absolute power of the spiritual head of Mongolia, the Bogdo Gegen Hutukhtu, incarnation of the Bodhisatva Djebtsun Damba, who took the title of Edzen Khan. The Bogdo Gegen based his power on his high authority in spiritual matters in the eyes of the population, on the importance of the Buddhist church and the ruling section of the Mongol nobility, which included not only temporal princes but also spiritual rulers, princes of the church.

The spiritual authority of the Bogdo Gegen in Mongolia was extremely great. As the reincarnation of the Bodhisatva he stood above sin. The Lamaist church knowns no councils, and against the decisions of the Bodgo Gegen in matters of religion and the church in Mongolia there was no appeal. The Pontiff appointed or confirmed in their positions all the higher dignitaries of the church and personally solved questions of faith and the church for the entire country. Theoretically, his spiritual authority was exceeded by that of the Dalai and Panchen Lamas of Tibet but in practice his power was supreme in Mongolia. Under him was the Great Shabi Department which carried on the affairs of the Lamaist church in Mongolia and ruled the Shabinars (tributaries) of the Bogdo Gegen.

As has been stated above, the Bogdo Gegen, aside from his spiritual authority, was also a powerful temporal ruler. He had 8 Hoshuns of Shabinars (divided into 179 Otoks) who wandered through the other Hoshuns of Khalkha, as well as his own territory near Lake Kosogol, where lived 15,000 to 20,000 of his Shabinars. Altogether the Bodgo Gegen had almost 90,000 Shabinars (of a total population in Outer Mongolia of 542-550,000 according to the census of 1918).

Besides this, there were in Outer Mongolia 13 spiritual principalities, 4 of them with their own territory, and 30,000 Shabinars. There were about 150 monasteries in the country, more than 100 Hubilgans and 115,000 clergy, comprising 22.3% of the entire population of Outer Mongolia or 44.6% of the male population. It is necessary to add that the greater part of the clergy lived not in monasteries but among the lay population, engaging in economic pursuits and appearing in the monasteries only on feasts and holidays. According to the calculation of Maisky, the annual income of the Mongol church for religious services and from contributions amounted to from 1,000,000 to 1,500,000 roubles (the unit being the gold rouble of 1913).[29] Moreover, it had a large income from the sale and hiring out of cattle, monetary loans, etc. Altogether the church owned about 23% of the entire national wealth of the country.

The juridical position of the Bogdo Gegen was always exceptionally high as has already been indicated above, but with his assumption of temporal power it rose still higher. He became not only a spiritual but also a temporal autocrat. The Council of Ministers did not have decisive powers, all its resolutions being subject to the approval of the Bogdo Gegen. In the same way, the congresses of princes of Outer Mongolia, summoned for discussion of the most important affairs, had only a consultative character.

The Bogdo Gegen was the first and final court of appeal in matters pertaining to the princes and combined in his own person the supreme spiritual and temporal power in Outer Mongolia, being thus in a position similar to that of the Dalai Lama in Tibet.[30]

The princely estate in Autonomous Outer Mongolia consisted of more than 100 princely houses[31] containing approximately 400 men and women of princely rank. Considerably more numerous was the nobility (Taidjis) numbering about 27,000 persons or 5.6% of the population. The Khans, princes and Taidjis possessed tributaries (Hamjigla). They were exempt from torture, corporal punishments, taxes and levies. Princes governed Hoshuns and Aimaks while the Taidjis composed the higher officialdom in the Hoshun and Aimak administrations. Princes and Taidjis had the right to the labour of their tributaries, while the ruling princes of Hoshuns also had the right to impose a number of levies in kind upon their subject populations. Moreover, they had an almost unlimited right of levying "Alba" (taxes and levies) upon the Hoshun population and raising loans, participation in which was compulsory for all their subjects.

The subject population (both freemen and tributaries) comprised approximately 72% of the entire population of the country and owned 77% of the total number of cattle. They paid all the taxes and levies. Their chief occupation was cattle-breeding with hunting as a supplementary occupation.

---

29 Maisky—Modern Mongolia, 1921, p. 307.

30 After the end of 1921 the Bogdo Gegen became a constitutional monarch. In 1924 he died, and with him died the form of government outlined above and even the social system it represented.

31 In 1920 there were 91 Hoshuns in Khalkha, 20 in Kobdo, and 13 Shabi Hoshuns (of which 4 had their own territory), besides the special Department of the Urga Gegen.—Maisky, "Modern Mongolia", 1921, ppg. 27, 271, 278.

Some investigators regard the social organization of the Mongols as feudal in type.[32] The writer cannot entirely agree with such an opinion but must make the following reservation. Some features characteristic of feudal relations may indeed be remarked in the social organization of the Mongols. It is necessary, however, to keep in mind the fact that at some stages of social development in many States there arose analogous forms of social life, reminiscent of feudal relations, e.g. weakness of State power and its division among a number of rulers in hierarchic subordination one to another, a mixture of functions pertaining to private and public law exercised by such wielders of power, the connection between power and landed property, etc. (*cf.* the benefice and feud in Western Europe, the Moslem *Iktach,* the Byzantine *Pronia* and Russian *Votchina.*) Yet not all, but only one of these institutions is designated by science as the feud (feudal estate).

One of the Russian historians (Miliukov) calls the first named institutions, in view of their general character, the generic features of feudalism, while he characterises the latter as the species forms. The writer does not consider these terms to be sufficiently definitive, but they correctly express the thought that in many given social forms there are features common also to feudalism, as well as special distinctions. It is evident that a wider and more general classification is possible, which would comprise the idea of the West European feud, the Russian *votchina,* the Mongol *hoshun* and other similar institutions with reference to their common features (mediaeval or feudal-like forms of social relations). But such a classification has not yet been proposed or attained widespread scientific use. Only in this general sense (of some feudal-like state of social relations) may we speak of feudalism among the Mongols.

Because of this, the idea that the Great Khan at Karakorum was the suzerain and the Khans of Persia, the Golden Horde, and some others were his vassals, the Kiev and Moscow princes being sub-vassals, etc., or that the Emperor of China was the suzerain of the Mongol Hoshun princes who were his vassals, the Mongol Arats being the sub-vassals, seems to the Author to be permissible only from the point of view outlined above. However, it must be taken into consideration that this feudalism of the steppes had its peculiarities which it is not here possible to treat in detail.

System of Punishments and Rewards. The Penal System of the Great Yassa was severe but simple: death, flogging or bastinado, and exile. The death penalty was imposed often, but the Great Yassa per-

32 *v.* especially, Acad. Vladimirtzov "Social Organisation of the Mongols", 1934 (Russ).

mitted the alternative payment of ransom for murder, for theft and porbably for many other less important crimes and offences. The Yassa did not provide for punishment by mutilation, and capital punishment was not qualified.

The basic penalty of the system was death; flogging and exile were supplementary punishments.

The penal system of the Regulations of 1640 was more complex. Here we find more than ten varieties of punishment.[33] But the punitive provisions of the Regulations were considerably milder than those of the Great Yassa. Capital punishment was imposed seldom, as were maihem punishments and deprivation of liberty. More commonly met with was confiscation of property (total or partial). But the basic penalty was the property fine, usually reckoned in nines of cattle, and next to it—flogging with whips (the knout).

The same may be said of the Khalkha Djirum. Here death and maihem were met with even more rarely than in the Regulation.[34]

A comparison of the contents of the main (national) records of Mongol law shows us that the punitive provisions contained in them tended to be come progressively milder. The penalties imposed by the Regulations of 1640 were lighter than those of the Yassa, and the punishments prescribed by the Khalkha Djirum were milder than those in the Regulations. The same process may be observed in the case of Buriat and Kalmuck law, if one compares the ancient punishments of the Buriats with those practised in the XVIII-th and XIX-th centuries,[35] and the punitive provisions of Khan Donduk Dashi with those of the Kalmuck Code.[36]

This change is in accordance with the scientifically recognised tendency of penalties to become milder, as those applying them pass over from the mediaeval to the modern phase of life.

It is necessary to remark the existence in Mongol law of an interesting phenomenon having some connection with its punitive provisions, viz. the existence, on a par with the system of punishments, of a system of rewards.

We have already referred to this feature above[37], pointing out that its origin may be explained by the principle of clan solidarity, under which social help in misfortune was regarded as a good deed meriting reward; and refusal to render such aid as an evil deserving punishment;

---

33 *v.* above, pg. 103.
34 *v.* above, pg. 121.
35 *v.* Riasanovsky, "Customary Law of the Mongol Tribes", ppg. 203-204.
36 *v.* *Ibid.*, ppg. 268, 279.
37 *v.* above, pg. 163-165.

and that the strengthening of this principle among the Mongols was the result of their frequent military campaigns (*v.* Frag. 9 of the Great Yassa) and communal hunts (Zegete Aba) which served as excellent schools for the development of these social habits.[38]

The rules of social solidarityy, with their rewards and punishments, arose from the clan mode of life and were developed in the campaigns and communal hunts; and it was natural that they spread to other sides of the life of the Mongol tribes.

The Hsi Yu Tze (Journey to the West) notes the readiness of the Mongols of the time of Jenghiz Khan to come to each other's aid in all misfortunes: "In times of calamity they run (to help) one faster than another."[39] Plano Carpini, writing of the epoch of the successors of Jenghiz, wrote of the Mongols as follows: "One respects the other and they are all sufficiently friendly among themselves, and although they have little food they willingly share it between them."[40]

According to the Mongol-Oirat Regulations of 1640, a Mongol killing an enemy in battle received his armour (art. 67 in Leontovich's edition), and for delivering princes and officials from danger in battle the status of Tarkhan (which exempted its possessor from all taxation) was awarded. For abandoning such persons in danger during a battle the culprit was, on the other hand, punished by death and ruin (*Ibid.*, art. 14). For saving a man in flight from the enemy the reward was a suit of armour and two horses (68), and for delivering a man from the noose, and aid to a mother giving birth, a reward of a horse was given (109); for the healing of a sickness—one horse (110); rewards were also given for bringing a man back from war or the hunt on one's own horse (111); for saving cattle from savage beasts, and "from drowning in mud" (108); for recovering cattle from thieves, if by fighting, one of every five cattle so recovered, and if without fighting—one out of each ten (69); for helping a child who had fallen under a horse (*Ibid.*, 144). For refusing a night's lodging or a drink of koumiss to a thirsty man punishments and fines were established (arts.24,87).

According to the Khalkha Djirum, travellers leaving a sick companion in an unhabited place were fined; but if anyone remained with the sick man and gave him aid he was rewarded (XII). Persons giving chase to thieves and recovering stolen cattle were rewarded and refusal to give chase was punished (VII, X). For saving perishing or stampeding cattle a reward was fixed (XV-3); for refusing a night's lodging to a stranger—a punishment (XV,3). The Khalkha Djirum even contained a

38 Prof. Leontovich sees here the humane influence of Buddhism (*v.* Kalmuck Law, ppg. 383,384). But in fact these practices arose before the Mongols adopted Buddhism.

39 *Op. cit.*, pg. 138 (Works of the Members of the Russ. Orth. Mission, IV, 1910).

40 *Op. cit.*, pg. 13.

provision of a general character which read as follows: "If anyone, during a robbery or a theft, commit a particularly good deed, let the Noyon reward him." (IV,23).

Buriat law likewise prescribed a reward (one horse) for saving a man from fire or water, while a punishment (flogging) was inflicted for reluctance or neglect in aiding such a victim. Art. II of the ancient Code of the Horins, 1781, stated: He who did not give aid to a perishing man was subjected to corporal punishment; while he who saved a man received a horse in reward." An analogous rule was contained in art. 85 of the Steppe Code. "Seeing a man who has fallen victim to fire or water, do not abandon him without pulling him out and giving him your attention. Anyone seeing such a thing must give aid and pull him out. As a reward for saving the victim, a horse shall be given. . . And if anyone pays' no attention, let him be scourged" (Steppe Code, at 85).

The Digest of Kalmuck Laws also contained a provision prescribing rewards for the deliverance of cattle from wolves, storms, snowstorms, rain, or drowning in a bog or well "in accordance with the number of cattle saved". (art. 168). "Anyone saving another's cattle from fire shall receive a reward corresponding to the number of cattle saved (221)."

The provisions quoted show that in the days of hoary antiquity, when social relations were first formed, a system of rewards for brave and good deeds existed alongside of the system of punishments for crimes and offences. The sense of justice of those times demanded punishment of crimes and offences against the interests of the clan (and its members), tribe and nation, and rewards for brave and good deeds committed in the interests of the clan, tribe or nation. In modern society this conception has disappeared from the field of law and retreated to the province of morality. But the preservation in Mongol law of the vestiges of the system of rewards shows us that some of our moral values had their origin in the principles of clan solidarity; and were at one time cultivated by means of rewards for certain (altruistic) actions, and punishment of neglect in this regard.[41]

Judiciary System.—The records do not mention any kind of judiciary system as having existed among the Mongols before the time of Jenghiz Khan. The Mongol clans avenged upon other clans any offences and injuries committed against them or their members (the blood feud). Personal discretion, sanctioned by custom and usage, was the agent of justice in the internal affairs of any one clan.[42]

---

41 The same phenomenon was also present among the Tunguses (*v.* art. 41 of the Customs of the Nerchinsk Tunguses, Samokvasov's "Collection", pg. 34.)

42 *v.* Yuan Ch'ao Mi Shih, trans. Palladius, *v.* pg. 32; Rashid Ed-din, *op. cit.*, XIV, 56; also the 21st Maxim of Jenghiz Khan.

Jenghiz Khan did not create any definite system of courts in his State, but he instituted the office of Chief Judge, which we meet also in the reigns of his successors. Furthermore, during the lifetimes of his immediate successors, claims and complaints were brought to the Court of the Khan, where they were considered evidently by some special official. But this institution did not bear so much the character of a court as of administrative (executive) decisions. Furthermore, the field in which the victim could take the law into his own hands was still extremely wide (especially in cases of *flagrant delit*).

In this connection, Plano Carpini made the following observation: "The abovementioned Emperor has a director (of his chancery), first secretaries and scribes, and in affairs public and private he has different officers, except attorneys because among them everything is performed *without the noise of a legal proceeding according to the will of the Emperor*. And the other Tartar princes act in the same way with respect to affairs that concern them."[43]

Rubruquis wrote: "As regards their judicial customs, understand that when two men fight, no one has the right to interfere and even a father dare not help his son; but the one who proves weaker may lodge a complain with the Court of the Sovereign. And if the other man touches him after he lodges such a complaint, the attacker is put to death. But the plaintiff must go thither immediately, without delay, and the injured must lead his injurer as a captive. They do not condemn anyone to death unless he is convicted of a crime or has confessed. But if many people give him a bad character he is subjected to painful torture to make him confess."[44]

A considerable proportion of cases was solved by the discretion of the parties on the basis of the prevailing customs which were often cruel and superstitions. For instance persons taken in *flagrant delit* in adultery, robbery and evident theft were put to death on the spot, as were persons stepping on the threshold of the tent of a chief, urinating in a tent, spitting out food, or acting in violation of some other superstition.[45]

The Mongols considered the confession of the accused to be a necessary preliminary to conviction; and to secure this confession, they applied the rack and other instruments of torture.

43 "History of the Mongols", (Russ.), pg. 59.

44 "A Journey to Oriental Countries", pg. 79 (Russ.); *cf.* Minaev, "Travels of Marco Polo" 1902, pg. 91, (Russ.)

45 Plano Carpini, *Op. cit.*, ppg. 9-10. The famous Yeh Liu Ch'u Ts'ai described the condition of the judiciary in the Mongol Empire to the wife of Khan Ogodai in the following words: "The high officials of the Empire sell offices and justice, and the Mongol prisons are now filled with people guilty only of acts of opposition to the violence of their oppressors." (Groom-Grzimailo, *Op. cit.*, pg. 440).

The organization of the judiciary was further developed in the legislation of the Oirats. Here the court took its place as a permanent institution of the State connected with the clan organization (the Hotons) and having two instances, the Hoton courts and the Chief Court (Zargo). These had definite rules governing their organization and activity, including material provisions and provisions governing procedure and providing for State compulsion. In the organization and activity of the Oirat courts, however, there still remained vestiges of the epoch of private reprisals. Thus, any suit (including criminal cases) was begun by the plaintiff (accuser) directly summoning the defendant (accused) to court and informing the court of such summons. The presence of both parties was considered indispensable, witnesses received rewards for their co-operation in the dischance of justice, etc. Besides this, there remained a certain, although, it is true, limited, number of cases in which the parties were permitted to take the law into their own hands, as for instance in the case of the seizure of a debt by the creditor after payment had thrice been demanded from the debtor in the presence of witnesses and due notice had been made to the Shulenga (art. 63). Successful tracking of a thief, concluded in the presence of honourable witnesses, led to the immediate application of the law concerning theft (without resort to court) (art. 62). It is evident that such taking of the law into one's own hands was permitted in undisputed cases: in the first case if the debt was not disputed by the debtor and in the second when the clarity and indisputability of the guilt was established by the presence of honourable witnesses. The further development of State principles in procedure may be observed in the legislation of the Northern Mongols and to a still greater extent among the Kalmucks.

Thus the Khalkha Djirum forbade the killing of a thief (in *flagrant delit*), but when such killing took place it was not punished, the killer being merely forbidden to recover the stolen property and fine from the dead thief's property (IV, 24). This Code also forbade seizure of a debt by creditors and if such seizure took place during the day, the debt was declared annulled, while if it took place at night the culprit was punished as for theft (XIV, 13). It was prescribed that in such cases a petition for an award be made to the Noyon, and the execution of the recoveryy was entrusted to the Elchi (XIV, 26,29) while in these cases also the witnesses were rewarded (XIV).

The system of courts of the Oirat Federation was carried over by the Kalmucks in their migration to the South Russian steppes. The Kalmucks also had two judical instances, the local court and the higher court or Zargo. The personnel of the courts included Yargatchis (court constables) and Elchis (messengers). The rules of procedure were generally analogous to those of the Oirats but the State principle was more highly developed.[46]

Among the Kalmucks, according to the laws of Donduk Dashi, suits were instituted by the direct summons of the defendant-accused by the plaintiff-accuser. The presence of both parties at the proceedings was obligatory and witnesses were rewarded for their aid to the processes of justice. But if the defendant did not appear in court after being summoned by the plaintiff-accuser, the latter was bound to apply to the Yargatchi and summon his opponent (the other party) through an Elchi. If the defendant thrice failed to appear after being summoned by the Elchi, the case went to the plaintiff by default. Creditors were obliged to demand payment of a debt in the presence of witnesses; but if the debtor refused to pay, the creditor was bound to apply to the Yargatchi, whereupon the debt would be recovered through the Elchi (if this procedure was not complied with, the debt was annulled and a fine imposed, 68, 1).[47] Thus personal forcible recovery of a debt by the creditor himself was already abolished among the Kalmucks in the epoch of Donduk Dashi; and non-payment after a demand had been made was followed by an application for recovery through regular judicial channels. In the same way, the practice of personal punishment of a culprit on the spot of the crime when detected became obsolete. In the Kalmuck Code of 1822 we meet, in general, the same state of affairs except that here the State principle plays a still greater part, this being exemplified for instance in the prohibition against reconciliation (personal settlement) with a thief (art. 18), the provision that a defendant was to be summoned to court only once (75,61) and that even if a thief was tracked down he was to be prosecuted through the courts (106), and witnesses (in theft cases) were no longer rewarded (111 Comm.[48]).

Thus we see the gradual transition of Mongol law from a system of clan-revenge and the taking the law into one's own hands to a permanent organization of the judiciary of the public-legal type.

(c) Fundamental Institutions of Private Law.

The Family.—The basic features of a patriarchal society and a partriarchal clan order are: 1. The reckoning of relationship in the male line; 2. Permanence of marriage (the marriage of a definite man to one

46 Among the Buriats the organization of the courts was connected with the clan order, the court being composed of the clan chiefs assisted by honourable clansmen, but until the Russian Statute of 1822 there was no unified judiciary. *v.* Riasanovsky, "Customary Law of the Mongol Tribes," ppg. 217, 233.

47 *v.* Riasanovsky, "Customary Law of the Mongol Tribes", ppg. 270-272.

48 However, the killing of a robber who had entered a house or was pursued, was not considered a guilty act (107), being regarded as self-defence.

or several definite women); and 3. The lordship of the father over the family, *patria potestas*.[49] These features were observable among the Mongols, though with certain vestiges of a still more ancient order, the matriarchate.

According to the Mongol-Oirat Regulations of 1640 and the Khalkha Djirum, relationship was recognized only in the male line. The same is true of the customs of the Buriats, among whom relationship in the male line served as an obstacle to marriage while relationship on the mother's side was previously not taken into acount at all. In Kalmuck law likewise, kinship was recognised only on the male side and relationship on the mother's side was not considered and could not serve as a bar to marriage.[50] Thus we have here the most vivid manifestations of the patriarchal-clan order and apparent extinction of its antithesis—the matriarchate. On the other hand, however, in spite of such definite clan-patriarchal features in Mongol life, the matriarchate also left its traces on the customary law of the Mongol tribes, which offers full confirmation of the theory of the supplanting of the matriarchate by the patriarchate and of the patriarchate by the mutual equal (individual) family. Under the first order the typical form of marriage was the group marriage, under the second—polygamy, under the third—monogamy.[51]

---

49 Prof. Jenks, "The Origin of Supreme Power", 1907, pg. 17. (Russ. Ed.).

50 *v.* Hyacinth, "Notes on Mongolia", 1828, II, 182; Prjevalsky, "Mongolia and the Land of the Tangauts", vol. I, pg. 49; Hangalov, "Juridical Customs of the Buriats", Ethnographic Review, 2, 1894, pg. 141; Nefediev, "Detailed Information Concerning the Volga Kalmucks", pg. 199, etc., etc. More lately the ignoring of the maternal line among some Mongol tribes was modified somewhat and close relationship in the maternal line began to be considered a bar to marriage.

51 We have noted here only the essential features without going into particulars which are extremely interesting but would lead us astray from the basic purpose of the present work. Thus, Spencer distinguished the following forms of the family disorderly sexual cohabitation, polyandry, polygamy, monogamy ("Principles of Sociology", II, 1877, part III, chaps. V-VIII); Morgan: the blood related family, the syndiasmic, patriarchal and monogamous family ("Primitive Society", 1900, chap. VI); Muller-Lier: disorderly sexual cohabitation, group marriage, polyandry, polygyny and monogamy ("Formen der Ehe, der Familie und der Verwandtschaft," chap. III). It is, however, necessary to note that the theory concerning disorderly sexual cohabitation from which these authors begin the history of the family, has been the subject of considerable scientific opposition (*v.* especially, Westermarck, "The History of Human Marriage", I, 1921, chaps. III-IX, also M. M. Kovalevsky, "Outline of the Origin and Development of the Family and Property", esp. ppg. 17-18, also other works by the same author; Crawley, "The Mystic Rose", II, 1927, chap. XVII, etc.) and is not recognised at the present time. Such institutions as polyandry and the syndiasmic family were only particular aspects of the general process.

The theory of the succession of the matriarchate, the patriarchate and the individual family is also not unopposed. Although it is supported by the majority of investigators (among them Bachofen, "Das Mutterrecht"; MacLennan, "Primitive Marriage"; L. Morgan, "Primitive Society"; Kovalevsky, *Op. cit.;* Engels, "Origin of the Family, Private Property, and the State", 1906; Kohler, "Zur Uhrgeschichte der Ehe", 1897, esp. Chap. II, para. 7) it has found opposition among others (*v.* Westermarck, *Op. cit.*, I, VIII; Rivers, "Social Organization", 1924, V; Leontovich, "On the Origin of the Family", Jour. of the Min of Just., 1900, VII).

Let us now consider the organization of the family and forms of marriage of the Mongols.

Exogamy, the prohibition of marriages within any one group of comon descent, is one of the most ancient institutions of the human community. Exogamy was originally closely connected with the matriarchate but was preserved in the patriarchal society. Different theories of its origin are held by various scientists (*cf.* MacLennan, Morgan, Westermarck, Kohler, Kovalevsky, and some others.)

M. M. Kovalevsky wrote concerning this question (referring to Fison) as follows:

"The simplest and probably most ancient of the known forms of family organization. . . . permitted the existence within each tribe of only two groups, the men and women of each of which bore a common family name. Under this organization relationship was recognized only on the mother's side and members of one group were forbidden to enter into sexual relations with each other. Let us take an example. The Kamilaroi tribe, of Mount Gambier, South Australia, was divided into only two groups reminiscent of the clan or the Roman *gens,* the Kumit group and the Kroki group. Each of these consisted of both men and women who were strictly forbidden to marry among themselves. Thus, these groups were exogamous. At the same time each male member of the Kumit group was considered the legitimate husband of every female of the Kroki group; and each Kroki male of every Kumit female. A child born to some Kroki woman by some Kumit male was included in the Kroki group, while the offspring of cohabitation between a Kroki man and a Kumit woman belonged to the Kumits. Every child was named after its mother and became a member of her group. Neither of the groups had its own separate territory. Both lived in the same settlements, scattered over a distance of several thousand miles. Because of this, the possibility always existed of occasional connections between a passing Kroki and a Kumit woman who never quitted the village of her birth, since each Kroki had all the rights of a husband over each Kumit woman and each Kumit—over each Kroki woman. Hence the origin of the custom of offering women for the pleasure of passing guests, known under the name of hospitable haetarism. . . .

"Both in Australia and among the redskins of North America, more complicated forms of social organization were more often met with. Here the two original groups were subdivided into different numbers of clans. The descent of this more complicated form from the organization described above may be proved by the fact that indiscriminate marriages between members of these clans were forbidden, members of the clans of one group having the right to marry only members of clans belonging to the opposite group. . . ."[52]

Exogamy also existed among the Mongols, who preserved its essential features until the most recent times. Marriage between relatives and persons having common distant relatives were not permitted among the ancient Mongols. For instance we know from the "Secret Chronicle" and the "Altan Tobchi" that the father on Jenghiz Khan went a long distance to a strange clan to seek a wife for his son.

According to article 116 of the Mongol-Oirat Regulations an abandoned wife could be bought (ransomed) back by her brothers and Aimak brothers (clansmen). This provision indicates that a woman married at least out of her Aimak. The Mongol Regulations of 1815, forbade marriages between Mongols of the same generation (I, 481).[53] Among the Buriats and Kalmucks marriage also bore an exogamous character and relationship in the male line served as a bar to marriage. This is confirmed by the modern investigator of Buriat life, E. B. Petri. "The Buriat clan," he writes,[54] "is completely exogamous and no marriage can take place within the clan. In relation to any given clan all other clans fall into two groups, the 'Halu' or 'Halun' (warm, own) and 'Hari' (foreign). Marriages with the 'Halu' are forbidden. This group includes clans related teritorially, and also clans bound to the given group by common descent which had not yet performed the ceremony of 'separation of the bones'. The 'Hari' group included all other clans and marriages with their members were permitted."

Although, as we have seen above, Mongol law was strongly influenced by patriarchal principles, especially in the system of relationship, the customary law of the Mongol tribes nevertheless retained certain traces of the matriarchate. Thus the Secret Chronicle, Altan Tobchi and the Chronicle of Jenghiz Khan name a woman, Alan-Goa,[55] at the head of the list of Jenghiz Khan's ancestors.

We know what an important position, under the matriarchate, was occupied by the maternal uncle (*avunculus*) who replaced the absent father and was the patron and protector of his sister and her children. Quite often he, and not necessarily the mother, stood at the head of the family. Under the matriarchate (and sometimes even in later epochs)

---

52 M. M. Kovalevsky, "Outline of the Development of the Family and Property", Lectures given at Stockholm University, Trans. from French, ppg. 19-21, 1895; *cf.* L. Morgan, "Primitive Society", 1900, pg. 49 *sqq.*, 351 *sqq.* (Russ. ed.).

53 In Mongol terminology a "generation" was equivalent to an Otok (*v.* M. O. Regulation, arts. 122 and others).

54 "Marriage Provisions of the Northern Buriats", Collection of Works of the Government University of Irkutsk, VIII, 1924 pg. 5.

55 "Secret Chronicle", 25-30; "Chronicle of J. Kh.", 254-5; "Altan Tobchi", Works of the O.S., Russ. Arch. Soc., VI, pg. 121.

he occupied the first place in the system of kinship. As a result of this not the sons ,but the wife's nephews (sons of her brother) were the heirs of the dead husband. This state of the family relation is designated the avunculate. Many writers consider the period of the avunculate as being transitional between the gynocracy and the patriarchate.[56]

The Yuan Ch'ao Mi Shih relates: " . . . when Temuchin was nine years old, his father, Yesugai, took him to his maternal uncles in the Olkhun clan, to ask for a maiden to be Temuchin's wife. . . ."[57]

From this item we may see that the mother's clan was then considered a foreign one from which it was permissible to take a wife, but maternal uncles still preserved a certain significance in relation to marriage and were treated with respect.

A vestige of the matriarchate may also be perceived in the custom of giving sons as sons-in-law into the house of the wife or betrothed bride; Jenghiz Khan being so given into the house of Dai-Setsen.[58]

Concerning marriage among the Mongols of his time, Plano-Carpini reported that the Mongols had many wives, a hundred, or fifty, or ten, and that "they can enter into marriage generally with all their relatives with the exception of their mothers, daughters, and sisters from the same mother; but sisters only from the same father they could marry, and their father's wives after his death also."[59]

From this and previous testimony it is evident that though in the epoch of the Mongol Oirat Regulations, i.e. the beginning of the XVII-th century, the patriarchal-clan organization assumed fully legal form among the Mongols, some four centuries previously the presence of the patriarchate with polygamy was still accompanied by significant survivals from the matriarchate. In particular, the prohibition against marrying sisters by the same mother, even though marriage to sisters by the same father was permitted, shows that in spite of the fact that in the XIII-th century it was permitted to take a wife from the clan of the mother (as a foreign clan), maternal relationship was still recognised in the closer degrees (the mother, and sisters by the same mother); and in relation to marriage kinship in the maternal line was chiefly considered. Nevertheless, the prohibition against a father's marrying his daughter shows that here too the closest relationship in the paternal

56 Other writers, however, consider the avunculate to have been a usual feature of the matriarchate. For a discussion of these problems in the Russian language, *v.* Kovalevsky's conclusions in "Scientific Results", v. X, pg. 31 *sqq.* Incidentally, Schrader traces the word *avunculus* itself not from *avus* (paternal grandfather) but from the ancient form *avi* (Lat. *avia*, grandmother), *v.* "The Indo-Europeans", 1913, ppg. 143-144.

57 Pg. 35, *cf.* Altan Tobchi, Works of the O.S. Russ. Arch. Soc., VI, 1858, pg. 124.

58 "Secret Chronicle", pg. 17.

59 "History of the Mongols", pg. 5 (Russ.).

line was recognised. The right of succession, recognised by art. 34 of the Yassa as belonging to the sons (and not to maternal nephews, etc.) again confirmed the rights of the paternal line and recognition of descent from (and relationship through) the father.

It is thus undoubted that in the XIIIth century the patriarchal order was already dominant among the Mongols but had not yet reached its culmination and full development. Although descent was recognised in the male line, the system of relationships still preserved vestiges of the matriarchate. Such vestiges, however, were preserved in Mongol customary law in later periods also.

The Mongol-Oirat Regulations of 1640, in spite of the recognition of relationship only in the male line, prescribed that there could be no debt accounts between maternal nephews and uncles; and theft from maternal relatives was not considered a crime but led only to the restitution of the loss by payment or gift (art. 118). The Khalkha Djirum likewise forbade the collection of Yal (fine) between relatives in the maternal line, (the grandfather and, in case of his death, uncles and maternal grandsons (nephews) (VIII). Among the Buriats the mother's clan was called the Nakhsanut, i.e. the clan of the maternal uncle (Nakhsa—maternal uncle). The Buriat himself, in relation to this clan, was called Ze-hu-bun, i.e. nephew through the sister. The entire Nakhsanut clan patronised its Ze-hu-bun and treated him with gentleness and concern, being obliged to help him in difficult times and care for him in misfortune. The Ze-hu-bun, in his turn, manifested respect for all members of the maternal clan as his seniors, even though the younger members of this clan might be young enough to be his grandchildren. He commonly addressed all of them as "Nakhsa" and treated them with respect and courtesy. Marriages with the Nakhsanut clan were considered particularly auspicious. The Buriat was obliged to show a special respect likewise towards the clan of his wife. He was obliged to address all its members, even the youngest, as "Akhe" (senior) and tolerate indifferent treatment from them. A son-in-law was bound to bear everything in silence and could not reply even to reprimands and scoldings administered by his wife's relatives. To scold the father or brothers of one's wife was considered a great sin.[60] In Kalmuck law nephews and other relatives through the mother had the right to drive away the cattle of their uncles and other relatives after asking the latter for a gift of such cattle which they, in violation of custom, refused to grant (arts. 54, 47, Digest of Kalmuck Laws).

All this undoubtedly represented survivals of the matriarchate and the family and hereditary law of the matriarchal epoch.

60 *v.* Petri-"Marriage Provisions", ppg. 27-29.

We do not meet with group-marriage among the Mongols but only marriage between a definite man and definite women, i.e. permanent marriage in its polygamous form. Nevertheless some vestiges of the previous epoch (of group marriage) may be noted. For instance the Mongol tribes evidently practised hospitable haetarism.

Thus, article 24 of the Mongol-Oirat Regulations forbade a childless woman to refuse night's lodging to a traveler and punished failure to provide such hospitality with a fine, even demanding that the woman be put to the oath in case she remonstrated. Professor Leontovich regarded this as evidence of hospitable prostitution. A. A. Ivanovsky pointed out that the custom of hospitable haetarism was preserved among the Torguts of Tarbagatai.[61] The evidence offered by Professor Leontovich and Ivanovsky concerning the existence of hospitable haetarism among the Mongols was to some extent confirmed by the practices of the Buriats. Concerning these, E. B. Petri reported that he was told of distant places inhabited by Northern Buriats where the custom of hospitable haetarism was still supposed to exist. In one such place the inhabitants denied this but told of other localities where they alleged the practice to exist, sometimes naming places already visited by the investigator. This circumstance leads one to the supposition that a similar custom existed in recent times but had become obsolete at the time of the investigation. Petri also notes, however, that in the Kudinsk steppe there existed another custom having some connection with the one considered above, viz. if an unmarried friend from another clan came to visit his friend, the latter was to persuade his concubine (Tala) to give herself to the visitor (Gargaje Ugo—to lead out and give).[62]

There existed among the Mongols yet another survival from the group marriage, the levirate. Under the levirate a widow became the wife of the younger, or one of the other brothers of her deceased husband. This institution is a survival from the community of wives among close relatives—brothers.[63] It outlived the epoch of the matriarchate and was met with among peoples which had attained a higher level of development, e.g. the Jews, Greeks and Hindus. Their survival may be explained by the necessity of carrying on the (deceased husband's) line and also by economic considerations (the retention of the widow, with her dowry, in the family; the conception of the wife as the property of the family for whom a purchase price or ransom had been paid, etc.). Plano-Carpini wrote as follows concerning the existence of the levirate among the Mongols: "His next youngest brother, or

61 "Anthropological Sketch of the Torguts of the Tarbagatai Region of the Chinese Empire."
62 *Op. cit.*, pg. 25.
63 Some sociologists (Bachofen, MacLennan, Kautsky) see in the levirate a survival from the practice of polyandry (the group marriage of brothers with one wife.)

another of the younger brothers, is even obliged to marry the widow of the deceased."[64] The same custom could be observed among the Northern Buriats. In the Customs of the Verkholensk Buriats we may read the following: "A wife taken in exchange, or in default of this for Kalim, has no right whatever to separate herself from her husband, all the more if there are children living with her (art. 20); in the event of the husband's death she has no right whatever to separate herself from his relatives, since in payment for her the husband's sister or other close kinswoman was given, or Kalim; and in this case she is bound to become the wife of her husband's brother, or his other close relative, or even of her father in law." (art. 21, *cf.* art. 90 of the Steppe Code.)

But in Buriat law the custom of the levirate was modified and lost its strongly obligatory character. A widow could refuse to marry a brother-in-law or other relative of her husband, in which case a property settlement was made, the parents of the husband being obliged to marry off the widow to another and appropriate the Kalim, which was paid to the husband's heirs. On the other hand, if none of the relatives of the deceased husband wished to take his widow to wife, she was considered free except that, if she married, the Kalim given for her was to go to the heirs of her first spouse (arts. 21, 22).

The roots of both polyandry and polygamy must evidently be sought in the group marriage, the first-named institution being predominantly connected with the epoch of the matriarchate (gynocracy), the second with the patriarchate. Under the patriarchate polygamy was supported by social and especially economic factors (the wife being a valuable worker in the household economy), the necessity of maintaining friendly relations with neighbouring clans and tribes, etc. But even under the patriarchate, polygamy began slowly to yield ground to monogamy, the transitional phase being characterised by the separation of one wife who was given the status of chief wife (having the right to participate in the worship of ancestors and the duty of guarding the hearth, etc.) and the demotion of the others to the position of second or subordinate wives or concubines, the taking of a second wife sometimes being permitted only in cases where there was good cause (childlessness, consent of the first wife, etc.)[65]

Mongol law recognized polygamy as a customary institution of family law. Mention of it was made in the Great Yassa of Jenghiz Khan (21,34,35), the Mongol-Oirat Regulations of 1640 (33), the Mongol Regulations (Code) of 1789 (11,12), the Mongol Regulations (Code) of 1815

---

64 Plano Carpini, "History of the Mongols", Mahlein's translation, 1911, pg. 5; *v.* G. Gomboev, *Op. cit.*, pg. 246.

65 *cf.* Muller Lyer, "Formen der Ehe", pg. 48.

(1,164), and in Buriat law in the Customs of the Southern Buriats (Customs of the Selenga Buriats, 59,60), and of the Northern Buriats (C. of Verkholensk B., supp. to art. 17; Hangalov, 6) etc. Polygamy was also known to the Kalmucks.

According to Plano-Carpini (*v.* above) polygamy was highly developed among the Mongols of his time.

At the same time the Great Yassa already considered one of the wives as the elder or chief wife (34).[66] The Ancient Tsaadjin-Bichik stressed the importance of the wife as the guardian of the hearth (7), the cult of which was also known among the Mongols.[67]

Among the Buriats the worship of the hearth fire and the feeding of her new clan fire by the bride with oil or fat was a part of the marriage ceremony, as in the marriage customs of the Buriat Shamanists of the Irkutsk district (the Saigut separate clan of the Bardinsk region) and the Balangansk district (*v.* "On Marriages Among the Buriats", *Siberian Archives,* 7,1912; also Potanin, "Outlines", IV,31). The bride's dowry once included a kettle for the hearth, the guardian of which she became in the husand's new yurt.

The Khalkha Djirum contained certain restrictions on polygamy in the cases of princesses who were forbidden to become the second wives of Tabunangs, while Tabunangs were forbidden to take additional wives if the first wives were princesses (VIII, 1,2,3,4). The Mongol Regulations (Code) of 1815 distinguished between the legal and subordinate wives (I, 164). According to Maisky, polygamy is rare in modern Mongolia.[68]

Among the Buriats, as was already pointed out by Georgi in the XVIII-th century, some had four or five wives, many had two, and some only one. "They can take to themselves as many wives as they can buy. Some have four or five, many only two, and the others, whether from poverty, modesty or love, have only one."

Among the modern Buriats polygamy exists but is now not widespread. Thus, according to the customs of the Selenguins, if a couple was childless or especially had no sons, the husband could, with the consent of the first wife, marry another, and if there were still no sons, he could take a third wife with the consent of the first two. It was prohibited to have more than three wives (59). However, even if a

---

66 *v.* also Plano Carpini, *Op. cit.*, 15.

67 The Khalkha Djirum also mentions the untouchability of the hearth, *v.* IV 19: "if at the time of the oath the kettle on the hearth (or the hearth itself) is touched, there is nothing bad in this; but if the kettle (or hearth) is overturned compensation is required."

Buriat had a son, but needed a second wife, he could marry again with the consent of the Lamas and chief Elders, these giving permission if they found that he had good cause to desire another spouse. Marriage without such permission was punished (60). In the Code of Steppe Laws of 1841 this rule was promulgated for the Buriats of Hori, Selenga and Barguzinsk. The Northern Buriats, according to Hangalov, seldom had two or three wives. The cases where they did were commonly the outcome of the barrenness of the first wife and the failure of the second to bear sons, in which case they were obliged to take a third (Hang., 6). The first wife of a Buriat was considered superior in the household and supervised the domestic economy, the second and third wives being obliged to obey her and being considered as her younger sisters. No Buriat commonly had more than three wives. Most of the Buriats had only one wife, the chief cause for this being the economic position of the majority and the absence of sufficient reasons for a second marriage. Besides this, the spread of Christianity among the Northern Buriats played a large part in this process. Thus it is possible to say that the modern Buriats are close to monogamy.

As regards the forms of marriage it is undoubted that one of the most ancient of these is marriage by seizure or abduction of the bride. This mode of obtaining a wife was evidently often demanded by exogamy. It is possible that the abduction of brides served as the basis for individual (instead of group) possession in marriage. A modified form of the primitive abduction of brides was abduction with the consent of the bride, by collusion with her.

Vestiges of this form of marriage are met with in Mongol law. Article 41 of the Mongol-Oirat Regulations of 1640 imposes a fine on anyone persuading an unbetrothed maid to elope with him. The Mongol Regulations (code) of 1815 prescribed return of the bride and payment of a large fine for abduction of the affianced wife of another (1,382,484). Abduction of wives and daughters was also mentioned in the Khalkha Djirum, abductors who sought sanctuary with the Gegen being fined the equivalent of a normal Kalim. Articles 12 and 39 of the Code of Steppe Laws (1841) dealt with abduction and kidnapping of maidens for the purpose of marrying them and obliged the culprit to pay a moderate Kalim (daughters involved in such cases being punished by flogging on the complaint of the parents). Abduction of brides with their consent is still practised in modern Mongolia.[69] Among the Northern Buriats even at the present time, abduction with the consent of the bride is practised in cases where the bridgroom is unable to pay the Kalim and the bride's

69 Maisky, "Modern Mongolia", pg. 52.

parents refuse to give her up. The abduction is carried out with the participation of all the young men of the husband's clan (Petri).

A representation of abduction forms part of the marriage ceremony among the Mongols.

Rubruquis wrote: "Thus, when anyone concludes with another an agreement for the taking of his daughter, the maid's father gives a banquet and the maid runs to her nearest relatives to hide among them. Then the father says: 'Now my daughter is yours, take her where you can find her.' Then the other searches for her with his friends until he finds her, and he must take her by force and as if forcibly bring her to his house."[70] A similar custom exists among the modern Buriats. The relatives who take the bride to her bridegroom pull her to themselves, while those relatives who remain at home pull her to their side; and only when the former have pulled her over may they take her to her man.[71] Symbolic abduction also enters into the marriage ceremony among the Kalmucks.[72]

As is known, disputes between tribes and clans resulting from the abduction of brides were in time replaced by payment of a ransom or purchase price by the abductors. A vestige of this practice is payment for brides (the Veno, Kalim, etc.), which gives to marriage an appearance of purchase.

This latter form of marriage was the one recognized by Mongol law as customary and widespread.

Writing of the ancient Mongols, Rubruquis said: "Of their marriages know that no one of them has a wife if he does not purchase her."[73] And Plano-Carpini testified: "All other women they take to wife without any discrimination, and they buy them from their parents very expensively."[74] The Mongol-Oirat Regulations indicated that at the time of the giving of a maid in marriage, her parents or guardians received for her a ransom or purchase price (payment being made chiefly in cattle) while they gave the bride a dowry the amount of which depended upon the social position of the marrying couple (arts. 35,40). The same provision appears in the Khalkha Djirum (XIII), the Mongol Regulations (Code) of 1789 (11,13) in which the ransom is called the "Gift for the bride", and the Mongol Regulations (Code) of 1815

70 V. de Rubruquis, "A Journey to Eastern Countries", 1911, pg. 79; (Russ.) *v.* also Hyacinth, "Notes on Mongolia", II, 184.

71 Among the Alar Buriats the men try to pull over the bride while the women do not let her go (*v.* Potanin, "Outlines of Northwestern Mongolia", IV, pg. 31.)

72 *v.* for instance, Lubbock, "The Beginning of Civilisation and Primitive State of Man", 2nd. Ed., pg. 83.

73 Rubruquis, *Ibid.*, 1911, pg. 78.

74 *Op. cit.*, pg. 78.

(1,471,481). Buriat law calls such ransom by the name of Kalim (Steppe Code, 12,13; C. of Hor. B., VI, 1,2, etc.; C. of Verk. B., 17,19; C. of Bal. and other B., VI, Hangalov's "Juridical Customs" 3, etc.), such Kalim having once been paid in cattle but more recently in money.

Mongol law has preserved yet another ancient form of marriage—by working for the bride, a form that takes us back to Biblical times and is reminiscent of Jacob's labour for Laban, first seven years for Leah, then seven years for Rachel. In this connection we find the following provision in the Khalkha Djirum: "If anyone take to himself a wife without paying cattle (Kalim), and having entered (the household of the bride's parents) as a working son in law later himself betrays and leaves, let him give 10 Boda and 30 sheep." In Hangalov's "Juridical Customs" the following more detailed provision is quoted. If anyone, in consequence of poverty, was unable to pay a Kalim and marry, he was hired as a worker on the condition that he work a certain number of years for which his master would pay his Kalim and thus enable him to marry and, after the expiration of the term fixed for his labour, let him go, giving him a horse with harness, plough, harrow, a sledge, a cow with a calf, a mare with a colt, a sheep with a lamb, and goat with a kid. Sometimes the master built him a house or a yurt and gave him a dessiatine of ploughland and a dessiatine of sown land, for which the worker was obliged to labour for from 6 to 8 years (Hang., "Jur. Cust." 7.). Such a master was usually one of the bride's relatives or even the future father in law. In arts. 347-349 of the Code of Steppe Laws, mention is likewise made of working for a bride's parents to pay for the bride. B. E. Petri wrote concerning this: "The custom of working for a bride has its origin in hoary antiquity. Young people, having no possibility of paying the Kalim, went to the clans of their affianced brides and lived there as ordinary labourers for a stipulated number of years. . . . Working for the bride is still practised at the present time, with the difference that half the Kalim is now supposed to be paid in money while the other half may be worked for."[75]

Buriat law also takes cognizance of matchmaking and mutual marriage or "Anda" as it is called among the Southern Buriats, or marriage "by exchange" among the Northern Buriats, when two pairs of children of two fathers marry among themselves; for instance the son of the first marries the daughter of the second and *vice versa* (St. C., 14; C. of Hor. B., VI, 1,2, etc.; C. of Verkh. B., 17, 19; C. of Bal. and other B., VI; Code of Steppe Laws, 343, 304). In such cases the Kalim was mutually cancelled this arrangement forming the economic bases for this variety of marriage.

75 *Op. cit.*, pg. 19.

It is natural that the necessity of paying for a wife made the Mongols treat her with more consideration. In the customs of the Balagansk and other Northern Buriats we find the native statement that "a wife taken by a Buriat in marriage is deemed as one bought but not a serf, being his equal helper in their mutual life." (VI, introd.).

In addition to what has already been said concerning the kinds and forms of marriage among the Mongols, it is necessary to note that marriage was not regarded by them as the private business of the marrying couple but as an affair of concern to the entire clan. The sole remnant of this at the present time is the necessity of securing the consent of parents, or failing these of elder relatives, before marriage; and the payment of Kalim by and to these.

Thus the Mongol-Oirat Regulations contained a provision to the effect that for the preservation of the clan out of every 40 kibitkas (households) four had annually to marry off their sons, the parents (and guardians) giving and receiving ransom and dowry (arts. 37,35,40). With minor alterations this provision was repeated in Kalmuck law (Digest of Kalmuck Laws art. 154). But Kalmuck law already contained prohibitions against parents giving their daughters in marriage without their consent (*Ibid.*, 161). According to Buriat law, betrothal was carried out by the parents of the bride and groom, or, failing these, by their nearest relatives in the presence of honourable clansmen acting as witnesses, such betrothal often concerning minors (*v.* Decisions of the Horins, 1763 and 1788; C, of Hor. B., VI, I; St. C., 12; C, of Sel. B., 42; C. of Verkh. B. 17,19; C. of Bal. and other B., VI), and sometimes children not yet born. Refusal on the part of the bride and groom to consummate a betrothal concluded by their parents did, however, occur, as well as independent marriage without the knowledge or consent of the parents. Both of these acts were considered as offences and punished by property fines or payment of Kalim (C. of Sel. B. 43, 45; C. of Verkh. B., 24. 28.).

That marriage was regarded as an affair of concern to the entire clan is evident from the mode of property settlement incidental to it. Thus, according to the Mongol-Oirat Regulations, ten men were obliged to help one to marry, and under Kalmuck law the expenses of (compulsory) marriage were borne by the community. Concerning the Buriats, B. E. Petri had the following to say: "The Kalim is paid by the bridegroom's family, but the whole clan participates in its payment and in the covering of the expenses of the wedding feast by lending money to the bridegroom's father (without interest) for the payment of Kalim and giving him money (not subject to repayment) for the wedding expenses. Besides this each clansman brought his Tarasun (wine) to the wedding and considered it his duty to participate in treating the guests. This alone makes it evident that the marriage is considered the affair not of one family but of the whole clan. In former times, when cattle was the property of the entire clan, the Kalim was paid from the common clan funds into the treasury of the other clan as compensation for the loss of one of its members."[76] Among the Kalmucks, also, the clan took part in the payment of Kalim for the bride.[77]

Divorce was simple in Mongol law. From the Mongol-Oirat Regulations of 1640 we know that a husband could desert his wife and her relatives could buy her back (art. 100, *cf.* art. 116). For the husband divorce was free, and according to the Chinese codes for Mongolia the divorced wife was entitled to receive back her dowry (1789-11,14; 1815-1,[4]84). According to the customs of Autonomous Mongolia divorce was easily accomplished, both by mutual consent and by unilateral appeal on a pretext sanctioned by custom. Sometimes divorce was formally carried out, e.g. through a Lama, but more usually it was accomplished by simple separation of the parties. A husband had the right to send back to her parents a childless wife and a wife who had run away from him thrice. A wife thus thrice driven out by her husband had the right to a divorce. At divorce, she received back her dowry (v. Maisky).

In Buriat law too, divorce did not present any great difficulties. Divorce was allowed in cases of mutual consent, of the unilateral desire of the husband, and the persistent reluctance of the wife to live with her husband (with different property consequences).

Divorce by mutual consent was perfectly free, the dowry being returned to the wife (C. of Hor. B., VI, 7; C. of Bal. & other B., VI, 2). Divorce by the unilateral desire of the husband (e.g. in the case of a childless wife) was also allowed (C. of Hor. B., VI, 7), and even as a result of the husband's simple reluctance to live with his wife (C. of Sel. B., 49; C. of Verk. B., 26), but in such cases the Kalim was not returned. Finally, divorce was also permitted at the expressed desire of the wife, e.g. in the case of insistent reluctance (C. of Sel. B., 51,52; C. of Verkh. B., 26, 27,-Petri) but in this case Kalim was returned.

The simplicity of divorce among the Mongols corresponded to their general views on marriage and sexual relations. Nevertheless, in the sphere of divorce a considerable evolution took plac. In ancient Mongol law divorce was free only for the husband (M. O. Regulations of 1640, Codes of 1789 and 1815). Gradually, however, the wife too began

76 *Op. cit.*, pg. 19.
77 Leontovich, "Kalmuck Law", pg. 218.

to obtain the right to divorce, this being evident especially in the customary law of Autonomous Mongolia and Buriat law. At the same time, divorce was attended by material consequence—the retention or return of Kalim, depending upon the nature of the causes for the divorce.

Concerning the internal family relations of the Mongols, it is necessary to say that their family life was based on strongly patriarchal principles and the head of the family, the husband and father, had great power over his wife and children, a power extending in ancient times, to the *jus vitae ac necis*. Thus the Khalkha Djirum found it necessary to specify that a father was not lord over the lives of his sons (XV), from which it may be inferred that this right previously belonged to him. In the period under consideration, however, this power must not be regarded as having been wholly despotic, nor must the position of the junior members of the family be imagined to have been that of slaves without rights.

A fairly high ransom was paid for wives and this alone forced their husbands to appreciate them, besides which the economic role of the wife in the family tended to exalt her position.

Already in the Great Yassa of Jenghiz Khan we meet the prescription that "women accompanying the troops do the work and perform the duties of the men while the latter are absent fighting." (Fr. 19). Maxim 14 said concerning the role of women. "A man is not like the sun and therefore cannot appear everywhere before people; when the master is away hunting or at war, the wife must keep the household in good condition and order. . . ."

The mother-wife ruled the house and domestic economy in the absence (or after the death) of her husband, occupying an honourable position. Under the clan-patriarchal conception of the State she also ruled the kingdom after the death of her Khan husband, as Turakina did after Ogodai, and Ugul-Gamish after Guyuk. The wives of Noyons also discharged the functions of their husbands when the latter were ill or after their deaths.

One may see from the ancient Tsaadjin-Bichik that the women of the time were treated with respect and honour, and insults to them were punished more severly, while as mistresses of the household they were untouchable to others (arts. 7, 8).

The Mongol-Oirat Regulations, while permitting measures of domestic correction, provided that if a mother-in-law "without cause" beat her daughter in law she was fined: for serious beating—nine head of cattle, for a less severe beating—5 head, and for a mild beating—a horse. If a father-in-law delivered the beating under the same circumstances he was fined 2 nines of cattle, one nine, and a horse respectively (art. 29). From the Khalkha Djirum it may be seen that the widow-mother became, after her husband's death, the manager of the common family property and in certain cases was allowed to dispose of it at her discretion (VIII-17, 20).

Among the Buriats the paternal power was shared by both parents, although in the lifetime of the father his authority was predominant. No wonder that in the Customs of the Balangansk, Idinsk and other Northern Buriats it was provided that: "a wife taken by a Buriat in marriage is esteemed as one bought but not a serf, being his equal helper in their mutual life". (VI, introd.)

After the death of her husband, the Buriat widow could go on living with her children, in which case she remained the full mistress of the house and could dispose of all the property at her absolute discretion. She brought up her children, married off her sons, paid Kalim for their wives, etc. But a widow could also take her dowry and go back to her parents or relatives, and could marry again if she wished (Hangalov, "Jur. Cust.", 7; C. of Hor. B., 6, 11, 16; C. of Sel. B., 61, 62, 65).

Although the parental power was great, the children were not defenceless. The Ancient Tsaadjin Bichik gave grown sons the right to separate themselves from the paternal household (5). The Mongol-Oirat Regulations punished the killing of a son by confiscation of all the offender's property (31) and fines were imposed for beatings "without cause": for serious beatings—nine head of cattle; for moderate beatings —5 head; and for a minor beating a horse (29).[78]

Under Buriat law, parents were obliged to provide for their children, bring them up, give them dowries, and endow them with property at separation (Horin Code of 1781; C. of Hor. B., XII, 6; C. of Sel. B., 130; Hang. "Jur. Cust.", 1, 2.) Buriat law thus provided not only for the rights of parents with respect to their children; but also for their duties with respect to the latter.

Kalmuck law forbade parents to marry off their daughters without their consent (Digest of Kalmuck Law, 161).

Modern investigators of the life of the Mongols and Buriats (such as Maisky and Petri) confirm the fact that although the authority of the husband and father in the family is quite strong, it is not despotic in character; and family relations are permeated with mutual tolerance, the concern of parents for their children, etc.

78 Compare with this the fact that according to the Customs of the Kirghiz, parents were not liable to punishment for the murder of their children (C. of Kirgh., art. 87).

We are thus here witnessing the general evolution of family relations: from absolute power in the interests of the father, the latter's authority changes into general parental authority; and gradually from this into the power of a guardian exercised in the interests of his wards (although this latter process has not yet reached its culmination). Besides the rights of parents over their children, there arise the duties of the former and rights of the latter, and the patriarchal family gradually becomes permeated with the elements of the mutually-equal (individual) family.

Mongol law also provides some material for the study of another important question of contemporary sociology, the question of the origin and development of private property.

Private Property.—There are many theories of the origin of private property, and to consider them here is not our problem. Mongol customary law provides evidence in support of the theory which sees the basis of the origin of private property in labour, in the application of individual labour to the production of goods in connection with the division of labour within the confines of one social group (Engels, Kovalevsky, etc.).

The right of individual property in movables developed a considerable time before property in immovables, which for long afterwards remained the common right of the tribe, the clan, and finally the family.

Engels wrote as follows concerning the origin of private property in movables: "All the implements contrived by the man for his pursuits composed his property; the implements made by the woman for her occupations were her property; arms, hunting and fishing gear, belonged to the man, and the household utensils to the woman. . . . All that was produced and consumed in common was common property; the house, the vegetable plot and the boat."[79]

M. M. Kovalevsky indicated that property had its origin in "the application to production of the personal power of the individual. The flint axe which belonged to the savage was hewn with his own hands. Hunting together with his companions, he delivered the death-blow to an animal and therefore kept the animal's skin for himself. The customs of savages are very precise on this point. . . . If two hunters struck a cornered animal, the skin went to the one whose arrow penetrated nearer the heart. . . . The man who plants a fruit tree becomes its owner, this being true not only of the modern savages but also of the ancient Germans. Anyone discovering a beehive by that act acquired the right of ownership over it. Such was the ancient Swedish law. . . .

79 Engels, "The Origin of the Family, Private Property and the State", 1906, page. 107 (Russ).

Later one warrior owned everything acquired by him while at war; and in the same way the presents given to a priest did not become common family property but the property of the individual." But "once the separate individual is helped by his relatives and family property is employed, once the product ceases to be the result of individual exertions, the right to its use belonged to the entire family in common."[80]

Vinogradov names three forms of primary acquisition of property: acquisition (occupation), labour, and domination.[81]

We have indicated above that during the period of effectiveness of the Mongol-Oirat Regulations, the right to property in immovables did not yet exist among the Mongols; and the land was the object of common use by the whole clan. But individual property in movables existed. Thus a beast killed by an automatic crossbow was the property of the crossbow's owner (art. 79), anyone killing a man dressed in armour was entitled to the armour (50), and anyone giving a helmet to another was entitled to receive for it 5 head of cattle (38). The Regulations provided rewards for military prowess (50,51), and the separate property of sons (27, 30, 34). All this indicates that in the epoch under consideration, individual property existed in the form of things obtained by the owner's own labour.

In the Khalkha Djirum, likewise, the increase of cattle was the property of the owner of the cattle (XII); found cattle was returned to the owner (XIV, 6); anyone appropriating wandering cattle was obliged to pay compensation and a fine to the owner (XII); a fox cornered in a hunt was the property of the person first reaching it (XII); insults by word to parents (or a teacher) with whom the offender had common property were punished more severely than similar insults in the absence of common property (XII).

The same phenomena may be observed in Buriat law.

A hunter killing a beast acquired the right of ownership over its carcass and skin; and anyone catching a fish or animal in a net or trap had the right of ownership over the living animal and the caught fish. If the hunt or fishing expedition bore a common character, there arose the right of common ownership which was followed by equal division of the game. According to the customs of the Horins, if anyone wounded a fox or wolf and gave chase to the wounded beast, and if the beast was slain by another hunter, the beast belonged to the first hunter and

80 Kovalevsky, "Outline of the Origin and Development of the Family", 1895, pg. 49. In another subsequent work Kovalevsky adopted the view that labour was one of the factors in the origin of private property but not the only one, being accompanied by a psychological factor, v. "Results of Science", vol. X, 1914, ppg. 108 etc.

81 "Custom and Right", 1925, pg. 70.

its four paws to the second. But if the first wounded a she-goat and the second killed it, the entire beast went to the second (St. C., 104). It was presumed that for a small beast the first shot was fatal, while for large game the fatal shot was the second. The customs of the Selenguins differed somewhat from those of the Horins. Among them the first hunter who wounded the beast and the second who killed him divided the game evenly. If anyone was a witness of how a hunter killed a sable, fox or wolf, he was entitled to the forepaws, while if a large beast was killed, such as a wild goat, boar etc., the witness received the hindquarters (Code of 1775, 129; C. of Sel. B. 142). During the formerly customary community hunts (Aba) only participants in the hunt were recognised as such witnesses, i.e. hunters, beaters and so forth. From this circumstance the custom described above becomes comprehensible as a survival from the common hunt when the game was shared among the participants.

The increase of cattle belonged to the owner of the parent cattle. The increase from stray cattle joining a Buriat's herds belonged to the owner of the herd if he had previously given notice of the fact that a stray had joined it (St. C., 131). The carcasses of cattle killed by wild beasts or drowned belonged to the owner of the cattle (St. C., 65,66).

As regards immovables, Mongol law recognised no right of real property. This right was still at that stage of development when all the land of the nation or tribe was considered the property of the Khan or prince, being more nominally than actually at the disposal of the latter, and belonged to no one in the sense of individual property. At a certain stage of development, this view was common to many peoples. Only recently one could meet it in Chinese and Moslem law. "All the land under the wide sky is the ruler's and all the inhabitants of the earth are his servants", states the Chinese classic, Shih Ching. This conception, however, did not interfere with the development of the right of private property in China.[82] The same may be said of Moslem law. Here, too, the land was considered the property of the Imam, but this did not prevent the Turks and Tartars from buying, selling, giving and mortgaging it. The majority of other peoples long ago abandoned this conception. As distinct from them, Mongol law has preserved to this day the negation of the right of private property in immovables. This circumstance is connected with the preservation among the Mongols of a nomadic pastoral culture.

Some embryos of the right of private property in immovables may generally be noted in Buriat law. The Buriats are now going through

82 *cf.* Riasanovsky, "Modern Civil Law of China", Part II, pg. 8 *sqq.*

the transition from a nomadic to a settled mode of life. They have huts for the winter but move into yurts in the summer, with which they wander over the steppes; and some even remain in yurts in the vicinity of the winter camp (village). Their chief occupation is cattle-herding, but they have partly passed over to agricultural pursuits. The clan community had common pastures. Besides this, the clansmen had individual plots which were cultivated for hay (Ootougs) and also ploughlands. Good lands for haymows and ploughland were divided equally among the members of the clan. If, however, anyone fenced in a plot near his camp, cultivated it and irrigated it, such a plot did not come up for redivision but remained in his possession (C. of Sel. 8., 163).

The above provision demonstrates the labour character of the acquisition of individual plots. This is shown still more clearly by the following provision: "If anyone cultivates a plot of land for ploughing, or a haymow, and then does not use it and the fence falls into ruin and some one else wishes to use the fenced-in plot, then, if the first owner brings suit against him, he is to be given three years to cultivate the plot; if he fails to cultivate the land during this time, it becomes the property of the other who manifested his desire to make use of it; he has the right to fence it in but must, if possible, compensate the first owner for clearing the land (C. of Sel. B., 160, *cf.* C. of Verkh. B., 34,40).

We thus see that personal labour in the cultivation of land (and more particularly in irrigation which in the waterless steppe was a matter of especial difficulty) served as the basis for individual possession under Buriat law, but this possession was not yet fixed; and stoppage of cultivation could lead to the transfer of the plot to the possession of another for the same purpose. At the same time, it is evident that the origin of private property in immovables was connected with the transition to a more intensive economy, to the cultivation of land for haymows and ploughlands and to agriculture generally.

Other Institutions of Private Law.—The study of a number of other essential institutions of Mongol private law (e.g. the origin of responsibility for damages, the development of contracts, inheritance in accordance with law (custom), Wills, etc.) opens before us the same picture of regular development in accordance with general laws established by the science of comparative jurisprudence.

Thus in the question of responsibility for damages, primitive law did not distinguish between civil and criminal violations, and connected responsibility with the causing of damage independently of the subjective fault (*culpa*) of the author of it. Whether the person causing the damage acted with or without premeditation and evil intent, (*dolus*), consciously or unconsciously, the very fact of the damage having been caused served as a ground for responsibility, for which reason responsibility was attached to minors, madmen and even animals. With the development of social relations, criminal offences were separated from civil violations of law and at the same time the grounds of responsibility underwent a gradual change: from the outward objective criterion of damage, law (both criminal and civil) passed to an inward subjective view based on considerations of justice—the fault of the author in the causing of the damage. Acts which could not be proved to involve the fault (*culpa*) of their author, and were not the result of his evil intent (*dolus*) or at any rate negligence (*culpa*) came to be regarded as accidental and not involving responsibility on the part of anyone. Roman law already firmly established responsibility for damages on the principle of fault. From Roman law this principle passed over into Pandecten law and contemporary doctrine (*cf.* paragraphs 1382 and and 1148 of the French Civil Code, paras. 823 and 276 of the German Civil Code, para. 41 of the Swiss Law of Contracts, etc.)[83]

In this question Mongol law presents a picture of transition from primitive responsibility for damages on the principle of causing (cause) to the fixing of responsibility on the principle of fault (*culpa*).

Thus the Mongol-Oirat Regulations attached responsibility for homicide to a madman, punishing him with confiscation of half his property (44). For accidental homicide during a hunt half of the usual fine was imposed (55).

The Khalkha Djirum attached responsibility for homicide, wounding, and damage to property to madmen, owners of mad dogs who had no knowledge of their animals' state, and hunters putting up automatic crossbows in uninhabited spots (XII) as well as to persons setting up such crossbows as a practical joke in populated areas, etc.

Buriat law passed over to the fixing of responsibility (not only in criminal, but also in civil cases) on the principle of fault. Thus, according to the customs of the Southern Buriate, if cattle fell into a cutting in the ice made for them, no responsibility attached if the cutting was of proper width (2 chetvert = ½ yard), but if the cutting was greater

83 It is essential to note that of late the above quoted view has not represented the *communis opinio* but has met objections among a number of civilists who advance as the basis of responsibility not fault but the very fact of the causing of the damage (Gierke, Tohn, Adler, Kosak, Saleil, etc.) This represents, in its way, a return to the old point of view of primitive law. This viewpoint is not, however, shared by the majority of scientists and modern legislation, in which the principle of the causing of the damage is applied chiefly in the idea of professional risk. We cannot here go into this interesting problem of modern civilistics, for more details of which *v.* Riasanovsky, "Lectures on Civil Law", IV, pps. 29.44 (in Russ.).

than the established width, the person making it was answerable for the damage done (St. C., 99). If anyone, while catching a horse, collided with the horse of another and killed or crippled it, he was bound to make good the damage (St. C., 72). If anyone opened the gate of a fence and neglected to close it, he was held responsible for the damage (St. C., 129; C. of Sel. B., 166, etc.). Children (under eight years old) were not answerable for damage caused by them (St. C., 70). If anyone accidentally ran against a fence, the owner of the latter was not responsible for the damage (St. C. 94). If a labourer hired out for money died of disease or was crippled through his own carelessness, the master was not responsible (C. of Sel. B., 119) etc.

According to the customs of the Northern Verkholensk Buriats in cases of the trampling of fields by cattle, the owner of the cattle was liable for damages if the offence occurred through his negligence; but if the fence around the field was in bad condition, the owner of the fence was held responsible and the owner of the cattle was not considered responsible (C. of Verkh. B., 41,44).

However, besides these provisions fixing responsibility, on the principle of fault (*culpa*), we meet with a series of provisions of private law in which the other (old) point of view (the causing) was applied but with diminution of responsibility.

Thus if anyone accidentally caused damage and loss to another, the damages were borne equally by both parties (C. of Hor. B., 11, 10). If anyone commissioned another to make a hilt for a knife, or a handle for an axe, and the other during his work accidentally cut himself or even died, the man who commissioned him was liable for two thirds of the expenses (St. C. 24, 25; C. of Hor. B., 11, 11) etc. If, during a hunt, an arrow struck another hunter, the man who shot it was obliged to make good the damage (St. C., 126).

It is thus evident that Mongol law originally fixed responsibility for all causing of damage, that is, according to the principle of cause. With time this viewpoint was modified, and in cases of unintended causing of damage, the responsibility was mitigated to two thirds or a half of the damage done. Finally, in later practice, we see responsibility attached to the author of the damage for his guilty activity, some survivals of the old viewpoint being at the same time retained (in a milder form).

Of contracts the most widespread among the Mongol tribes were contracts without remuneration: gifts, borrowing, loadings, loans without interest (loans with interest being condemned), etc; and transactions with remuneration developed only gradually, especially among the

Buriats, but here too, loans from clansmen for wedding expenses did not carry interest, and in the use of a clansman's property, or in renting land, fellow clansmen enjoyed certain privileges etc. (*v.* arts. 47,83,108, 132 etc., St. C.)

Deserving of attention are the provisions concerning inheritance, which throw light on the origin of Mongol law.

Art. 34 of the Yassa of Yenghiz Khan contains the following provision: "The distribution of property is to be carried out on the basis of the senior son receiving more than the junior, the younger son inheriting the household of the father." Where did such a provision of customary law come from? And more particularly, why should it have been the younger son who inherited the household of the father?

Mongol law provided for the separation of sons in the lifetime of their parents, not only if the parents so desired, but also at the desire of the sons themselves. Thus art. 5 of the ancient-Tsaadjin-Bichik provided: "As soon as an adolescent son is grown and can work for himself, he leaves the power of his father and may, if he wishes, demand that a part of the herd be given to him, and leave his father in order to become an independent subject of the legitimate prince."[84]

In this connection the question naturally arises of whether the posthumous division of property was a repetition of the customary practice during the lifetime of the father. If the father separated all his elder sons from his housheld, only the youngest remained with him.[85] It was this son who inherited the household of his father when the latter died. Even if the sons lived with the father without separating from him until his death, the posthumous division of property naturally took place along the lines of the customary division during the father's lifetime. A confirmation of this may be found in the Mongol-Oirat Regulations of 1640.

Article 34 of the M.O. Regulations stated: "The father must divide the inheritance among his children in accordance with the established rule[86] and if the father becomes impoverished he can take (retain) one animal out of very five."[87]

From this it may be seen that by the terms of the Regulations inheritance was determined by the established rule or custom. However,

84 This right of sons originated in the conception of property as belonging to the entire family in common.

85 Hangalov confirms that according to the customs of the Northern Buriats, the elder sons separated from their parents while the youngest remained with them (Hang., "Jur. Cust.", 1, 2.).

86 *v.* also art. 161 of the Digest of Kalmuck Laws, of which art. 163 provided that the eldest son should receive the largest share.

87 Kalmuck law also considered such an allotment sufficient for a poor father from the herds of a son who was not supporting him (*v.* Digest, art. 53).

art. 34 had in view not only inheritance after the father's death (division of property in the direct sense) but also division during his lifetime, this being evident from the end of the article. The latter provided for the case of a father who had divided his property among his sons and had become impoverished and lacking in means of livelihood, in which case he was entitled to take back from his sons one head of cattle out of every five which he had given them. We see here that inheritance and division of property during the father's lifetime were governed by the same customary norms and that such division during life was regarded as equivalent to the division of the inheritance (the anticipated inheritance of Russian Law, vol. X, part I).[88]

Here we have confirmation of the theory that inheritance by custom, i.e. the posthumous division of property, had for its basis the customary procedure of division during the lifetime of the father.

Thus inheritance in accordance with law (of Mongol law) originated in family law, from the division of common family property in the lifetime of the father, this remaining the basis for similar division after his death.

In the question of Wills, the materials of Mongol law confirm the supposition that inheritance by law (custom) was the original form of inheritance, and that the Will appeared later and did not here attain its full development.

In Mongol law the Will is first met with at quite a late period. By the provisions of the Khalkha Djirum the father could, by written instructions (sealed and marked by the Djassak), increase the share of a son "commonly known as just" or decrease the share of a son "commonly known as unjust", but the application of this provision was under the control of the Khan and the Gegen. In the Mongol Regulations (Code) of 1815 the Will was met with, with considerable limitations, only in the absence of direct descendants, and the heir named in the Will had to be a clansman of the deceased, his right to the inheritance being subject to confirmation by the authorities (1,63). Thus property did not leave the clan and the right of the testator was reduced to that of appointing a distant instead of a near relative as his heir; and even then only with the consent of the authorities who controlled the justice of his disposition.

---

88 Even if, basing ourselves on its conclusion we regard art. 34 as referring to the division of property among the children during the lifetime of the father, it is nevertheless clear from its contents that such division was considered equivalent to inheritance. The provision of the Khalkha-Djirum concerning the division of the inheritance was likewise applicable both to posthumous division, and division of property during the father's lifetime (*cf.* VIII, 20).

In Buriat law the Will is met with as a supplement to inheritance by custom. Thus, according to the Customs of the Selenga Buriats: "If anyone have no wife or children nor brothers or relatives, but shall yet have a good superfluity, he must during his lifetime nominate a man who may use his property after his death. . . . and he must confirm this by a Will certified by the clan elders and leaders of the community." (C. of Sel. B., 133). According to the customs of the Horins and Selenguins Wills were permitted which named adopted children and wards as heirs (Steppe Code, 311; C. of Sel. B., 132) but according to the customs of the Selenguins these could in any case, and without a Will, inherit property on equal terms with the deceased's own children (C. of Sel. B., 131,136).

Here we have the circumstance, usual in undeveloped law, of the predominance of inheritance by law (custom) over inheritance by Will, the Will appearing much later and then only in the absence of the chief, or even of any customary heirs, or in the form of regulation of the division (allotment) among the legal heirs. Considering the strength of clan and family organization, it would be difficult to expect anything else. The principle of freedom of the individual from clan and family ties, the expression of which is freedom of disposition of property in the Will, was here still absent.

(d) Some Parallels and Notes on Comparative Jurisprudence.

The public and private organization of the Mongol tribes described above represented a well-preserved expression of a mode of legal life which has long ago been left behind by the modern European peoples (with the exception of some miner tribes). But all the European peoples passed in ancient times through forms of social life analogous to those of the Mongols. For this we have the evidence of ancient authors and also some survivals from those times.

Thus clan organization once existed among the ancient Greeks: "The warriors, O Atrides, divide into their tribes and generations", says the Iliad, Book II, Verse 362. We know of the following divisions of the ancient Greeks: the *phila* (district), *fratria* (tribe) and *genos* (clan). The last named traced their descent from one common ancestor, bore a common name had clan deities and common religious ceremonies, a common clan cemetery, and common clan property. The right of inheritance and guardianship belonged to clansmen and the power of the father, the lord of the household, was extremely great.

From the works of Roman legal writers, such as Paulus, Julianus Gaius and others, the individualist Romans also once knew the clan-union, the paternal clan or *gens* with its connections and the rights and duties it involved. The clan members (*gentiles*) here bore a common name and there existed a while series of clan institutions. *e.g.* the *dii gentiles, sacra gentilitia, ager gentilitium, tutela legitima,* and *successio legitima* in favour of clansmen. Marriage among the Romans was permanent in character. The power of the father, the lord of the household (*patria potestas* and *manus mariti*) was extremely great and extended, as in Greece, to the power of life and death.

The ancient Germans and the ancient Slavonic tribes lived under the same kind of patriarchal clan order. Thus, Caesar wrote of *"gentes et cognitiones hominum qui una coierunt"* among the ancient Germans and of the fact that the ancient Germans *"suas copias. . . generatimque constituerunt."* (De bello gallico, 1,51). Here the clansmen bore a common clan name, avenged insults offered to fellow clansmen, paid and received Wehrgeld (ransom), appeared to swear for clansmen in the courts, etc. The power of the husband and father (Munt) was very great, he could at his discretion kill a newly born child or let him live, etc.[89]

The ancient Russian chronicler also said of the Polyans: "They lived each with his clan in his place which is owned by his clan." (Ancient Russian Chronicle, Laurentian MS., 1,4). The same order is described by the Serbian and Czech historians. Among the ancient Slavonians, also, we find a common clan name, common clan property, a common cult, the blood feud, mutual responsibility, and the strong power of the head of the household.[90]

Without going into further particulars it may be stated that the patriarchal clan organization of European peoples in its developed form represented not only a union of persons of common descent but also a religious, political and economic union. The same may be side of the Mongols, among whom the clan organization was essentially analogous to the clan organization of European peoples but had also some distinguishing features.

---

89 Among the later Germans it was permitted to leave the clan union. Thus, according to the *Lex Salica*: "Anyone wishing to exclude himself from the clan union has to appear before the Assembly of one hundred and the chief of a hundred, and there break over his head three sticks, each an elbow in length, and, having thrown the pieces to the four corners of the Assembly, declare that he has renounced the right to swear for clansmen, inheritance and all other relations with his clansmen. If, after this, any one of his clansmen is killed or dies, he has no part either in the Wehrgeld or in the inheritance. All property that he himself leaves goes to the Royal treasury." (Art. LX).

90 For a summary of evidence concerning survivals of clan organization among the Aryans, *v.* M. Kovalevsky, "Clan Life", 1905, Part II.

Thus, the ancient Greeks, Romans and other European peoples were divided into clans which bore common clan names and traced their descent from common ancestors, and the same may be said of the Mongols among whom descent was a matter of great importance. The ancient Greeks and Romans had their clan deities (*dii gentiles*), clan sacrifices (*sacra gentilia*), ancestral cult (*lares et penates*), and worship of the family hearth, and the same things existed among the Mongols. The latter had their clan gods, clan sacrifices (*e.g.* the clan Talaiga of the Buriats), clan Shamans, clan fire, and ancestor worship (*e.g.* the cult of Jenghiz Khan). In the absence of strong State power, the clan and clan authorities took the place of that power among the ancient European peoples, defended (the blood feud) and protected their members, judged them and aided them in litigations, paid their fines and generally gave them all necessary help, and led them to battle. The same may be said of the Mongols. The blood-feud, as an institution for the defence of clansmen from persons outside the clan, existed among them in ancient times. The Mongols also had their clan courts, clan protection, and clan authorities. They went to battle and to the hunt in clans and under the command of their clan chiefs. The Mongol clan also represented an economic union with clan camp sites, clan property (cattle), clan irrigation, and clan mutual help (when departing for a campaign, in marriage, in epizooties) etc.

The power of the husband and father, the lord of the household, was also great among the ancient Mongols. If among the ancient Greeks, Romans and Germans this power extended to the *jus vitae ac necis*, vestiges of a similar position may be found in the records of Mongol law. In the Khalkha Djirum, for instance, a special reservation was made stating that a father was not the master of the lives of his sons, pointing to the conclusion that this right previously existed in Mongol law. In the events composing the national epic, the "Geseriad", we find a mother proposing that her husband kill their newborn son, the hero Geser, and the husband refusing to consent.[91]

Among the features peculiar to Mongol clan organization we may note 1) the existence of a well developed system of rewards beside the system of punishments; and 2) the position of the Mongol woman in the family and State.

The first of these features has already been sufficiently treated in the present work,[92] while on the subject of the second it may be said that in ancient Greece the women lived in *gynekeios* (in separate quarters) and spent their lives under the protection of their fathers, husbands and

91 "The Geseriad", Russ. trans. by Kazin, 1935, pg. 45.

92 *v.* above, pg. 208.

relatives. In ancient Rome likewise the wife was considered equal in status to the daughters (*filiae loco*) and regarded as one lacking in ability to act her herself, being placed under the power and protection of her husband and, after his death, of his or her nearest relatives. This position of the woman was reflected in later European legislation (French, German, English, etc.) which deprived or limited the right of women, and especially married, women to act for themselves. Among the Mongols, as we see from the 14th maxim of Jenghiz Khan, the wife replaced her husband in the home during his absence, and Fragment 19 of the Yassa shows that wives took the places of their husbands in the campaign. History tells us in this connection that the mother of Jenghiz Khan ruled the entire clan and its property after the death of her husband, and that the widows of the Great Khans ruled over the Great Mongol Empire until the election of a new Great Khan, and also that during the illness of absence of Noyons their duties were discharged by their wives.[93] In more recent times too the Mongol woman enjoyed considerable independence in the family and community.

But if among the European peoples (with the exception of a few small nationalities) the phase of clan organization has receded into past history, it retained its force and significance among many Asiatic peoples until the XX-th century. Not only the Mongol tribes, but also the Yakuts, Tunguses, Kirghiz, Golds, Altais and Teleuts, as well as several other Asiatic peoples, entered the XX-th century as representatives of clan organization.

Let us confirm the assertion made above.[94]

The social organization of the Yakuts, for instance, bore a clan character. Its basis was descent (Usa, or Aga-Usa—descent by the father). Until quite recently, states Seroshevsky, the Yakuts used the expression Yie Usa (descent by the mother). Altogether there were more than 70 clans of Yakuts. At the head of the clan stood the clan elder. Several clans comprised a Nasleg which was called by the name of the senior clan. This was headed by a prince. Of several Naslegs an Ooloos was formed, its chief or head being elected from the lines of princes and elders, preference being given to the senior line. There were meetings (conferences) of the clans, Naslegs and Oolooses. The

---

93 *v.* the account, by Men-Hun, of the daughter of Jenghiz Khan who, after the death of her husband, ruled the White Tartars; Vasiliev, "History and Antiquities of Eastern Asia", Works of the O.S., Russ. Arch. Soc., 1859, VI, 221; *cf.* also Palladius, "Secret Chronicle," note 501; Vladimirtzov, "Social Organization of the Mongols", 117.

94 Seroshevsky, "The Yakuts", vol. I; Haruzin, "On the Question of the Origin of the Kirghiz People" (*Ethnographic Review*, 1895, 3); Lopatin, "The Golds", 1921; Riasanovsky, "Some Features of the Customary Law of the Altais and Teleuts", (*Monitor of Chinese Law*, 1931, 3); Kovalevsky, "Clan Life", 1905, II; Samokvasov, "Collection of the Customary Law of the Siberian Natives", 1876.

meetings considered community business and litigations. Until recently marriages between members of the paternal clan were absoluetly forbidden, as complete exogamy existed. More recently this prohibition has been limited to eight degrees or generations. Clan festivals existed and vestiges of totemism were in evidence. In the sphere of land utilisation, the haymows were divided by clans.

The Tunguses were also divided into clans (over 70 in all). The clans usually bore the name of the senior clansman. At the head of each clan stood an elder or Daruga, at the head of each 2 or 3 clans a Zaisan. Several related clans formed a tribe headed by a Toyon or tribal prince. Families descended directly from the founder of the clan comprised a privileged class, the nobility; and from their midst were elected the Darugas and Zaisans, of whom one was promoted to the status of Noyon. Marriages between members of the same clan were forbidden among the Tunguses, i.e. full exogamy existed. Litigations and disputes were settled by the clan elders alone or with the participation of honourable clansmen.

The Golds, a hunting tribe, were divided into clans and lived under clan organization. Descent (Khala) was traced from the father and the clan was headed by an elder or Khalaida. There were clan deities and clan sacrifices and prayers. All clansmen bore the same family name. The courts were organized on the clan principle. Marriage was exogamous. Polygamy and the levirate were practised and there were survivals of totemism and primitive clan.

The Kirghiz are a people of mixed descent. They were divided into three main branches, the Greater, Middle, and Lesser Hordes (part of the last mentioned branch formed the Bukeiev Horde). Besides these there were the Kara-Kirghiz. Each Horde was divided into tribes, each tribe into several clans, and the clans into Bones (Suyeks). The Kirghiz were governed by clan chiefs (Aksakals and others) and each Horde was formerly headed by a Khan. Marriages within the clan were forbidden up to the sixth degree of relationship inclusively and full exogamy was observed within the Suyeks. Levirate was practised. Women were not permitted to inherit. The blood feud among members of different clans was preserved. Winter pastures were divided by clans.

The Altais (Altai Kalmucks) and Teleuts (White Kalmucks) are two neighbouring small peoples. They lived under clan organization and were divided into clan units (Suyeks). The Suyeks were headed by clan elders. Among the Altais, the Suyeks were united into Duchins, and the whole nation of Altais was headed by a Zaisan. The members of the Suyeks among both peoples used the land in common and practised clan mutual aid (in cases of the death of cattle and in the payment of Kalim). Relatives on the mother's side were not considered as relatives in the direct sense, since they belonged to another Suyek (and relationship with them was recognised only to the third degree). Among these peoples one could observe interesting vestiges of a very ancient type of social organization, such as the classificatory system of relationship, the avunculate, levirate, etc.

Clan ties were strong even in the largest and most highly cultured of the nations of Asia, in China. There we find property belonging to the entire clan or to its separate branches, such as clan cemeteries and ancestral temples. The cult of ancestor worship and respect for elder relatives kept the clan together. The performance of rites connected with the cult of ancestors and dead elder relatives fell upon the clansmen of the deceased depending upon the closeness of their relationship to him (mourning, worship in the ancestral temple, etc.) and especially upon his junior successors. Marriages between members of the same clan were forbidden. More than this, the law until recently adhered to the fiction that all persons having the same family name were descended from the same ancestor and were therefore kinsfolk, marriage between whom was forbidden (Ta Ch'ing Liu Li, 107). Inheritance was open to all members of the clan. In certain cases the elder clansmen formed a family council. The power of elder clansmen and heads of families was here still extremely great.[95]

We shall not here quote further examples since it should be abundantly clear from the short sketch given above that many Asiatic peoples are still living under forms of social life which among European peoples were essentially superseded thousands of years ago. We meet here, as among the Mongols, with clan-patriarchal life with an admixture of survivals from the matriarchate in the majority of cases, and certain special peculiarities in some.[96]

The well-known investigator of ancient institutions and law, Professor M. M. Kovalevsky, wrote as follows concerning this question: "In speaking of the organization of the Turki tribes of Siberia and Southeastern Russia, we more than once pointed out the similarity between their clan divisions and those of the Mongols. Our readers will therefore not be surprised by the statement that the first model of the entire clan organization of the groups of natives which we are now considering must be sought in Inner Asia, in Mongolia and Manchuria.

---

95 For further particulars *v.* Riasanovsky, "The Modern Civil Law of China", Part I, ppg. 45-56, 137-139, 177-179, etc.

96 For instance one of these peoples (the Kirghiz) preserved the blood feud until our days, others (the Altais and Teleuts) preserved the qualificatory system of relationship, a third people (the Yakuts, Golds) have retained considerable vestiges of totemism, etc.

Here this organization was quite ancient."[97] We may therefore suppose that the clan organization of the Mongols was one of the most ancient and fundamental in Asia, and as such it could not fail to influence the development of the related organizations.

The ancient division of the Mongols into hundreds, thousands, and tens of thousands, which was connected with this organization and attained its highest development in the military forces of Jenghiz Khan, was employed as late as the end of the XIV-th and beginning of the XV-th centuries in the army of Tamerlane.[98] Moreover, remnants of this divisions persisted until the most recent times (in the scores and forties) and were found not only among the Mongols but also among the Buriats, Kalmucks, Altais, Teleuts, and some other tribes.

Thus, Mongol law represents a species of law based on ancient clan organization and clan culture. In briefly summarising the basic features and tendencies of its development the following must be said:

In its main expressions (among the Mongols, Buriats and Kalmucks) Mongol law delineates before us a highly developed type of law based on nomadic clan-patriarchal culture with division into clans and their subdivisions and clan administration, but a weak development of the State principle. Among the Mongols relationship was recognised only in the male line. The family was patriarchal in character. It was based on exogamous marriage with the institution of ransom for the bride, and on polygamy, which was allowed, as well as on the authority and power of the head of the family and respect for elders. The right of property in immovables did not exist and immovable property was used in the common (clan and tribal) interests of pastoral economy.[99] Civil legal life was generally little developed (although the Buriats were somewhat in advance of the others in this respect). By the side of the system of penalties, the basis of which was the property fine and corporal punishment by flogging, there existed a sufficiently developed system of rewards.

The institutions of Mongol law showed a noticeable tendency to further evolution (disintegration of the clan, recognition of close relationship on the mother's side, weakening of exogamy, weakening of polygamy, evolution of the power of the father, the lord of the house-

97 "Clan Life", vol. II, pg. 263.

98 *v.* Hara-Davan, *op. cit.*, pg. 159.

99 Reference is made here to the process of the internal development of Mongol law, and for this reason the fact that the Kalmuck and Tungus (and in some cases Buriat) nobility sometimes owned estates on the basis of Russian legislation (*v.* St. C., 137) is not given consideration. So far as internal development is concerned we can note only early beginnings of the right of immovable property among the Buriasts.

hold, etc.). At the same time it is possible to discern the presence in Mongol law of survivals from the matriarchate (e.g. vestiges of the avunculate, haetarism, the levirate, the special respect shown to the clan of the mother and wife, and some other institutions) which were formerly stronger but gradually began to retreat before the advance of new forms of social relations.

It is thus necessary to admit that the original type of social organization among the Mongols was not the patriarchal clan order but the matriarchate, which was superseded by the patriarchal clan order which in turn showed tendencies towards further evolution.

From the records of Mongol law one may likewise draw the conviction that some of our moral rules concerning aid to neighbours in distress trace their origin from the clan mode of life, originating in clan soldiarity which was formerly promoted by a special system of rewards and punishments.

Among the Mongols, the State power had its origin in the power of the clan chief, and the Great Mongol Empire was organized on clan principles. But the State unification of the Mongols, built on clan principles, was not stable; and clan relations served as an obstacle to the creation of a strong State.

We may further see from the records of Mongol law how the organization of Mongol courts gradually developed from a system of clan vengeance and the taking of the law into the hands of the individual into a system of institutions of public law.

In the sphere of private law, the theory of the successive development of the patriarchal, the matriarchal, and the mutually equal family finds confirmation in the materials of Mongol law.

Individual property among the Mongol tribes was developed only in connection with movables. Individual property in movables slowly separated itself from clan and family property. In its original form it represented property acquired by the personal labour or exploit of its possessor, *e.g.* in war, in the hunt, etc.[100] As regards immovable property, there was no general recognition of the right of individual property in this connection in Mongol law. Only its beginnings were met with among the Buriats, being connected with the development among them of agriculture and the cultivation of haymows.

100 *Cf.* the origin of the private property of children in Roman law, *peculium castrense* and *quasi-castrense*.

Besides this, study of the basic institutions of Mongol private law (the family, property, responsibility for damages, the development of contracts, inheritance) leads to the conclusion that the origin and development of these institutions was subject to the general principles of evolution and proceeded in accordance with the general laws of this process as they have been established by the sciences of sociology and comparative jurisprudence.

CHAPTER V.

MONGOL LAW AND THE LAW OF THE CONQUERED PEOPLES.

Jenghiz Khan and his immediate successors conquered half the known world, and for a certain period of time the Mongols ruled over many conquered peoples. The question naturally arises of how their overlordship affected the law of the subject nations and what relations existed between the legal codes of the conqueror and conquered. Some authors have supposed that the Great Yassa of Jenghiz Khan ruled among all the subject peoples of the Mongol Empire.[1] This is far from being the truth. In this connection the following problems first of all deserve our attention: the relations between Mongol Law and the legal systems of the settled peoples (the Russians, Chinese, etc.) and further between Mongol Law and Law of the nomadic tribes of Asia and Eastern Europe (the Tunguses, Yakuts, Kirghiz etc).

A. Mongol Law and Russian Law.

Representatives of Russian historical science, both historians and jurists, have given much attention to the question of the influence exercised by Mongol culture and law on Russian culture and law. These investigations have yielded different results. Some authorities (to a certain extent Karamzin, but chiefly Kostomarov and Leontovich and also Zagoskin, Sergeevich, Engelman, etc.) have found that the Mongols greatly affected the development of the Muscovite Princedom which was built up under the influence of Mongol principles of government.[2] Others, who form the majority, (Soloviev, Kliuchevsky, Platonov, Shmurlo, Pokrovsky, Bagaley, Vladimirsky-Budanov, Diakonov, etc.) are of the opinion that the so-called "Tartar Yoke" did not deeply influence the course of our history or produce great social overturns in the life of the Russian nation. It accelerated some processes and held up others. But the processes themselves began without the influence of the Mongol-Tartar conquerors and continued independently of such influence. The Tartar invasion and its repercussions represented only one

1 Hara-Davan, "Jenghiz Khan as a Military Leader, and His Heritage", 1929, p. 60 etc. (in Russian); V. Vernadsky, "Essay on the History of Eurasia", 1934, p. 88 (in Russian); J. Barckhausen, "L'Empire jaune de Jenghis Khan", 1935, p. 88.

2 Karamzin, "History of the Russian State", vol. V; Kostomarov, Monographs, vol. XII; Leontovich, "The Mongol-Kalmuck or Oirat Regulations on Punishment", 1879; Sergeevich, "Antiquities of Russian Law", vol. II and other (all in Russ.).

of the factors in this historical development, a factor that was by no means fundamental or decisive.[3]

Lately there has appeared an entire trend of scientific-publicist thought, the so-called "Eurasianism", which assigns not only capital, but exclusive importance to the part played by the fact of the Mongol-Tartar invasion and its influence in the life of the Russian people. The adherents of this tendency regard the Russia of the principality or appanage period as a part of the great Mongol Empire, which later developed into an independent (the Muscovite) State under the direct influence of Mongol culture in general and Mongol principles of government in particular. This State in its later development (the St. Petersburg Empire and the present U.S.S.R.) represents, according to them, a geographic, ethnographic and cultural world unto itself, uniting the Aryan and Turanian peoples of the Eurasian steppes and being thus the natural successor of the great Empire of Jenghiz Khan.[4]

We find that in view of the objective data of the social development of the two peoples, and particularly the differences between their cultures, Mongol culture generally and Mongol legal culture specifically could not have exerted, and did not exert, any significant influence on Russian culture and law.

However, we shall not here consider the general question of the effect of Mongol culture on Russian culture,[5] but shall treat only the problem of the influence of Mongol Law on Russian Law.

The Yassa of Jenghiz Khan never obtained in Russia, and could never obtain there because it was written for a people with a different (nomadic) culture and thus could not satisfy the requirements of the Russian people. The institution of a special Code for Russia (like that later established by China for Mongolia) was also not undertaken by the Mongol-Tartars who were incapable of accomplishing such work because of their inferior culture. During the epoch of the Mongol invasion there was created in Northern Russia a Code surpassing not only the Yassa of Jenghiz Khan but also later Mongol Codes (the Tsaadjin-Bichik

---

3 *v.* relevant chapters of Soloviev, "History of Russia", vol. I; Kliuchevsky, "Course in Russian History", vol. II; Platonov, "Lectures on Russian History", 6th. Ed. 1909; Pokrovsky, "Russian History", vol. I, special supplement III; Bagaley, "Russian History", vol. I, 1914; Vladimirsky-Budanov," Outline of History of Russian Law", 1909; Diakonov, "Sketches of Social Order and Government in Ancient Russia", 1912; Shmurlo, "Russian History," 1922 (all in Russ.).

4 Trubetzkoy, "On the Problem of Russian Self-Knowledge", collected articles, 1927; and "Europe and Mankind" (undated); Savitzky, "Russian, a Separate Geographic World", 1927; Vernadsky, "Sketches in Russian History", 1927 (all in Russ.) and "A History of Russia",1929.

5 For details see the Author's works: "On the Question of Influence of Mongol Culture and Law on Russian Culture and Law, 1931 and "On the Study of Ancient Russian Painting", 1934 (in Russ.).

and Khalkha Djirum). We refer to the "Pskovskaya Sudnaya Gramota" (Judicial Charter of Pskov).

Thus, Mongol Law had no direct influence upon the Russian, either through the application of a Mongol code or the creation of any special code based upon it. Consequently it is possible to speak only of indirect influence, of the influence of administrative practice. It is necessary, however, to note that there were no definite channels for such influence, nor was there a State order sufficiently developed to exert it.

Let us examine in greater detail the question of the influence of Mongol Law on Russian Law—civil, criminal and State (including administrative).

Where Civil Law is concerned it is possible to say quite definitely that no traces of Mongol influence can be discovered. Neither the "Pskovskaya Sudnaya Gramota" nor "the Sudebniki" yield any material. Mongol Law had no effect on Russian Civil Law, this being impossible owing to a difference of cultures (nomadic pastoral and settled agricultural).

In the sphere of Criminal Law the intensification of the severity of punishments in the Sudebniki is pointed out as the result of Mongol influence. Into this category come the institution of the death penalty, flogging with the knout, and torture, none of which existed in the "Russkaya Pravda",[6] the latter two being also absent from the "Pskovskaya Sudnaya Gramota". These changes may be ascribed to the general crudening of moral standards resulting from the Mongol-Tartar invasion. Thus, they represent only an indirect effect, and the influence of Mongol Law itself is here also difficult to trace.

It is necessary to note that the "Sudebniki", as a legal code, represent a certain regression in comparison with the "Pskovskaya Sudnaya Gramota". This degeneration was the result of the general cultural deterioration caused by the Mongol invasion.

Finally, in the field of State and administrative law we meet with the assertion that the Mongol law of government and Mongol governmental principles had direct influence upon the development of the Muscovite State.

Was this really so? Let us consider what was represented by the Mongol system of government and what it could give to the Russian.

In Central Asia, during the fifteen centuries before the appearance of the Mongols on the historical scene, there existed a series of State structures whose influence spread far beyond the confines of Central

6 "The Russian Truth."

Asia. But these States were not long-lived and disintegrated quickly as a result of the absence of a common stable culture and internal unity among the tribes and nations composing them, and the internecine dissensions resulting from these defects, as well as external pressure. Among such States, which were not limited in their influence to Mongolia and often reached immense proportions covering not only Central Asia but sometimes all Asia and part of Europe, was that of the Hiung-nu (Huns), a people of Turkish origin (from the III-rd century B.C. to the beginning of our Era). After the Huns came the Sanbia (I-IVth centuries A.D.) and the Jujans (IV-VIth centuries), peoples of Tungus and Turko-Tungus origin, and after them the Tugu-Turks (VI-VIII-th centuries). The Tugu-Turkish State was destroyed by the Uigurs, another people of Turkish origin (from the middle of the VIII-th to the middle of the IX-th century) who were in turn supplanted by the Khagas, a nation of mixed origin (IXth—early Xth cent.). These were replaced by the Khitans, a Tungus people (Xth-XIth cent.) who were driven out in the beginning of the XII-th century by the Manchus, who were in their turn defeated by the Mongols.

The Mongols created another of these short-lived empires. While Temuchin (Jenghiz Khan) was still living, his nomad State grew and spead on the ashes of destroyed countries and the bones of their slain inhabitants. But the Empire did not long outlive Jenghiz Khan. In the time of his immediate successors it had already split up into its composite parts, in which the influence of the Jenghizids quickly waned. Thus, in the year 1260 A.D. Kublai built Khanbaluk (Peking), in 1280 he completed the conquest of South China, and in 1368 his descendant, Toghon Timur, was driven from the capital and country and the Mongol power in China came to an end. In 1256 A.D. Hulagu founded the Jenghizid dynasty in Persia, and in 1344 this dynasty ceased to exist. Hara Kulagu asserted his rule over Trans-oxiania (Bokhara) in 1242 A.D. but in 1370 the line of Jagatai fell apart in that country under the blows of Tamerlane. As for the Golden Horde, it passed its existence not in the centres of the cultured world but in the steppes of Southwest Europe where the opposition to the conquerors was much less. Even here, however, the conquest of Russia by Batu in 1240 A.D. was followed already in 1380 by the battle of Kulikovo Plain which dealt a death blow to the Golden Horde, whose power after this began to disappear.

The decline of the main branches of the line of Jenghiz Khan which has been described above was the result of the fact that the Mongols were not able to create a stable State organization. The clan principle was too strong among them, prevailing over the concept of the State, and the general culture level of the Mongol people was far too low.

Inspite of this some authors speak of the extraordinary stability of the State-sense of the descendants of Jenghiz, and of the monolithic strength of the Mongol system of government in contrast to the lack of governmental ideas of our regional Princes and the general governmental backwardness of the appanage period in Russia. This Mongol system of government is supposed to have served as a model for the creation of a stable system in Muscovite Russia and later the St. Petersburg Empire, the second coming as a consequence of the first. Actually this theory is not borne out by the facts of history.

Indeed, the Mongols went through an analogous and even more confused appanage period than that of Russia, with the one single difference that they were not able to cope with it.

It was Jenghiz Khan himself who divided his Empire into appanages (Oolooses) for his four sons: Juchi (Khoresm, the Caspian coast, and latter Greater Bulgaria and Russia); Jagatai (Maveranagr (Bokhara) or Transoxiania and other regions), Ogodai (Djungaria), and Tului (Mongolia); Persia being afterwards assigned as an appanage to his son, Hulagu, and China to his son Kublai. Jenghiz Khan did not provide for any fixed order of succession after his death and his Empire fell apart into appaganes which in their turn underwent further disintegration. As his direct successor, Jenghiz nominated not the eldest of his sons (Juchi) or the most talented (Tului), but the third, Ogodai, a fact which soon gave rise to great rebellions.

After the death of Jenghiz Khan (1227 A.D.) and the regency of Tului, the Kurultai of Princes in 1229 elected Ogodai the Great Khan of the Mongols. The authority of Jenghiz, who had himself named Ogodai as his successor, served to keep the reign of the latter apparently free from internal revolts. Ogodai died in 1241, of drunkenness and excesses.[7] His death was followed by an interregnum lasting almost five years, during which the kingdom was administered by his widow Turakina. The Kurultai of 1240 elected as Great Khan the ailing eldest son of Ogodai, Guyuk. The princes of the older line of Juchi, headed by Batu, did not recognize Guyuk. As a result the latter launched a campaign to force Batu into submission, in the beginning of which he died (1248). After the regency of his widow Ugul-Gamish, the Kurultai of 1251 nominated as his successor Mangu (Munké), son of the popular Tului. This may be ascribed to the influence of Batu. Thus the Great

7 Plano-Carpini, however, states that he was poisoned by Guyuk's aunt, she and many others being killed for this crime.

Khanate passed to the line of the youngest of the sons of Jenghiz, arousing the resentment of the older lines (Ogodai and Jagatai). The result of this was a conspiracy against Mangu by the grandsons of Ogodai, supported by the Jagatids, but this plot was discovered and Shiramun, Buri, the regent Ugul-Gamish and a whole series of Princes of the lines of Ogodai and Jagatai paid for their participation in it with their lives. Academician Barthold defines the events that accompanied the election of Mangu as the destruction of the appanages of Ogodai and Jagatai.[8]

Mangu made his brothers Kublai and Hulagu lords of China and Persia respectively. After his death in 1259, Kublai was proclaimed Great Khan in Kaifeng, China, by the princes subject to him without the formality of a legal Kurultai. This event was the cause of cruel internal strife and the practical disintegration of the Empire. Kublai's brother Arik-buga called a Kurultai in Karakorum and was there elected Great Khan, the ensuing war between the rival brothers lasting several years and ending with the victory of Kublai. The victor then had to face Khaidu, energetic grandson of Ogodai who in 1269 was recognised as Great Khan by the lines of Ogodai and Jagatai which enjoyed the support of the Juchids who were led in the Golden Horde by Mangu-Timur. Later one of their chief protagonists of Khaidu was the head of the Jagatids, Prince Duva. The latter created a powerful coalition which gave Kublai much anxiety (especially in the period 1286-89) which lasted until his death (1294). Even after Kublai's death, Khaidu and Duva continued to fight against his successor, Timur, and this war ended only with the death of Khaidu in 1301. This fundamental and cruel struggle between Khaidu and Kublai was contemporary with the no less cruel war between Khaidu and Hulagu (Persia) and Borak, of Bereke with Hulagu and Algui, of Hara-Hulagu and Mangu-Timur with Borak, etc. The entire empire of Jenghiz Khan heaved with internal strife and the Oolooses of Juchi, Jagatai and Ogodai practically separated from Kublai, whose dominions remained untouched only in the East.[9] After the death of Khaidu (1301) peace reigned for almost three years, but by 1305 the struggles began afresh. The death of Timur in 1307 marked the beginning of the decline of Mongol power in China which was swept away not long afterwards.

Timur's direct successor was Khuluk, who, after killing another pretender, Ananda, and his following, died in 1311 of drunkenness and dissipation. He was replaced on the throne by his brother Buiantu, who

8 S. Lane-Poole—"The Moslem Dynasties", 1899, in Russian, pg. 175, ftn. 3.

9 Thus, with the accession of Kublai and the separation of the Eastern Ooloos, came the cessation of the visits of Russian princes to the Great Khan and of the direct connection between the latter and Russia.

was a better ruler, but whose reign witnessed the bloody uprising of Essen-Buga Khan. After Buiantu, who died in 1320, came his son Shodi-Bala, killed in 1323, and the completely incompetent Yissun-Timur (died 1328). Yissun Timur's successor, Rodjiabek, was in the same year overthrown by a coalition of princes and killed, the next Khan being Kheshila, who reigned only 50 days. Then followed his nephew Tob-Timur (1329-33), Ilan-Die-Ban, who ruled only a few months, and Toghon-Timur (1333-70), whose reign was marked by internal unrest, control of the Empire by favourites, and natural calamities which ended in the overthrow of the Mongol dynasty in China in 1368 A.D.

In view of these circumstances the Western parts of the Empire achieved factual independence in the time of Kublai. Some of them renounced even nominal dependence upon the Great Khan after the death of Timur.[10] Also the Ooloos of the Juchids enjoyed real independence. Some Khans (e.g. Mangu-Timur) did not recognize the power of the Great Khan at all. Some others, like Khan Usbeg, recognized it nominally.

How was the Mongol Empire administered?

The system of government and administrative methods of the Mongols were aptly characterized by Yeh-Liu-Ch-u-ts'ai, who said that an Empire could be conquered on horseback but not ruled from the saddle. In fact, predatory rule from the saddle was characteristic of the Mongols.

Jenghiz Khan was a talented military leader and conqueror, but he was the child of his people and his epoch. His predatory-nomadic ideals may be clearly seen from his Maxims.

Maxim No. 30, for instance, states:

"It is delightful and felicitious for a man to subdue rebels and conquer and extirpate his enemies, to take all they possess, to make their servants howl, to make tears run down their faces and noses, to ride on their pleasant-paced fat geldings, to make the bellies and navels of their wives his bed and bedding, to admire their rosy cheeks, to kiss them and to suck their red lips."

Other maxims are equally characterist of the mentality of Jenghiz.

In maxim No. 19 we read:

"After us the descendants of our clan will wear gold embroidered garments, eat rich and sweet food, ride fine horses, embrace beautiful

10 The Khan of Persia Hassan (1295-1304), a Moslem, refused to recognize even the nominal sovereignty of the heathen Great Khan during the lifetime of Timur.

women, but they will not say that they owe all this to their fathers and elder brothers and they will forget us and those great times."

And another maxim, No. 22:

"My bowmen and warriors loom like thick forests: wives, sweethearts and maidens shine like red flames. My task and intention is to sweeten their mouths with gifts of sweet sugar, to decorate their breasts, backs and shoulders with garments of brocade, to seat them on good geldings, give them drink from pure and sweet rivers, provide their beasts with good and abundant pastures, and to order that the great roads and highways that serve as ways for the people be cleared of garbage, tree-stumps and all bad things; and not to allow dirt and thorns in the tents".

The same predatory-nomadic views are met with in the Yassa, which lavishly imposes the death penalty and values the lives of humans no more than those of cattle.

Thus Article 29 of the Yassa states:

"The man in whose possession a stolen horse is found must return it to its owner and add nine horses of the same kind; if he is unable to pay this fine, his children must be taken instead of the horses, and if he have no children he himself shall be slaughtered like a sheep."

In Article 8 we find: . . . " if anyone slaughters an animal after the Moslem manner he himself shall be slaughtered."[11]

Jenghiz Khan was wise and understood the inapplicability of the nomadic Mongol culture to the problems of administration in an extensive Empire which included a number of highly cultured countries. He enlisted Uigurs and Chinese to organize and administer his Empire. However, in spite of the talent of Tashatung, Chingai and Yeh-Liu-Ch'u-Ts'ai, and other Uigur and Chinese officials it became evident that to build a stable house from bad materials was impossible, that a predatory nomadic people could not be turned into efficient administrators of the most cultured States of the time. (e.g. China, Persia, etc.). That which is useful for a nation organized as an army, for a nation of conquerors while it is still conquering, is usually unsuitable for cultured administration of subject countries. The unlimited power of the military leader and tribal chief is distorted in peace into despotism and abuses, the power of the strong over the weak, and complete disregard of the law. Corruption, which is testified to by all sources, lack of enlightenment, the absence of a regular organization of justice and a

11 Let us remember that the "Russian Truth" (Russkaya Pravda) did not provide for the death penalty.

centralised system of financial administration—the existence of all these defects in the Mongol government is well known.

Yeh-Liu-Ch'u-Ts'ai has left us the following characterisation of the situation during the reign of Ogadai: "The higher officials of the Empire trade in appointments and justice,[12] and the Mongol prisons are now full of people whose sole fault was that they resisted the violence of the extortioners". This state of affairs led the monk Odoric, in the beginning of the XIV century, to come to the naive conculsion that the Mongols had a law which stated that no one was to appear before an official with empty hands. And from Plano-Carpini we have the following quotation: "In short, the Emperor and chiefs take of anyone's property whatever, and as much as they want. With the persons of their subjects, also, they deal as they see fit". There is an abundance of other evidence. Although some of it may be exaggerated, the general picture of unsatisfactory administration remains. Moreover, the results of these methods are known to history: the swift shipwreck of all the State institutions set up by the Mongols, in China in 1368, in Persia in 1344, in Turkestan in 1370, etc.

Let us now turn our attention to the Ooloos of Juchi. After the latter's death his appanage fell apart into a series of branches, the appanages of his sons: Ordu (the White Horde or the Eastern Kipchak), Batu (the Blue Horde—Western Kipchak), Sheibani (the Uzbek steppes), and Tevkal (the Khanate of Siberia). The Kipchak was still designated as the Golden Horde, composed of the White and Blue Hordes. The Golden Horde was also the object of attraction of the Uzbek steppes (Sheibandies) and Greater Bulgaria.[13]

The seniority in the Golden Horde belonged to the line of Ordu, but the real leadship was exercised by the stronger line of Batu (the Blue Horde).

The Golden Horde on the West was no less torn by internecine strife than the Great Khanate on the East.

The son and successor of Batu, Sartak, was murdered by his uncle, Bereke, who mounted the throne in 1256-7. This potentate waged fierce wars against the Persian Hulagu and the Jagatid Algui, Kublai's appointee. After Bereke's death in 1266 his children were unable to retain the throne (his descendants afterwards appeared in the role of pretenders) which passed again to the Batu branch in the person of the energetic Mangu-Timur (1266-1280). This ruler took part in the

12 *vide* the assertion of our historian that in the Golden Horde the Grand-Ducal throne itself was the object of auction with bidding and counter-bidding.

13 According to some sources Great Bulgaria formed the appanage of Juchi's son Tuka-Timur.

struggles against Kublai and the Persian descendants of Jenghiz. His successors also participated actively in the internal affairs of the other Mongol appanages. In the same way, the Juchid Ooloos was torn by internal dissension. After the death of Mangu-Timur, his relation Prince Nogai (of the younger line) acquired great influence in the affairs of the Golden Horde, occupying a semi-independent position with his nomads on the shores of the Black Sea and in the Balkans. It was he who deprived Khan Telabuga of his throne and killed him (*circa* 1290). This finanally led to a war between Khan Toktu and Prince Nogai which ended in the defeat and death of the latter (about 1296). After this his horde retired to the Urals and Embe, separating completely from the Golden Horde and becoming the Nogai Tartars. After the death in 1340 (or 1341) of Khan Uzbeg, the throne was occupied by his eldest son and appointed successor, Tinibeg, who was soon killed by his brother Janibeg, who also killed his younger brother Khadirbeg. Janibeg was murdered in 1357 by his son Berdibeg who at the same time slaughtered his twelve brothers. He himself perished in 1359. After this followed an intensification of revolts within the Golden Horde, and during the following 20 years nearly twenty Khans replaced each other on the throne, while several branches of the line of Juchi and several power-loving Murzas fought for overlordship by means of assassination, bribery and violence. At times several Khans reigned simultaneously. By 1380 the Murza Mamai was in control of the Horde, ruling in the name of now one, now another of the fictive Khans. Mamai was severely defeated by the Russians on Kulikovo Plain (1380), and then overthrown by a descendant of Ordu or Tuka-Temur, Toktamish (of the White Horde).[14] The latter subjected to his rule the White and Blue Hordes and united the entire Golden Horde (Moscow Campaign of 1381). But by 1391 he had already been defeated and deposed by Tamerlane and again in 1395, and in 1398 he returned to the Sarai but was driven out by Timur-Kutluck (of the Ordu Klan, grandson of Khan Urus). After this there was another great revolt, during which the tümen chief Edigei came into prominence (Moscow campaign of 1408) but also failed to establish order. Several lines of Juchids (descendants of Toktamish, Tuka-Timur, Sheibani, and others) fought for the throne and a number of Khans often ruled at one time, shaking the Golden Horde with bloody internal strife. Then began the disintegration of the Horde. The year 1430 marked the secession of the Khanate of Crimea, followed in 1436 by the Khanate of Kazan (from which in 1452 seceded the Kasimov Dukedom) and in 1466 by the Khanate of Astrakhan. 1480 A.D. is

14 Toktamish in his turn waged an internal struggle in the White Horde with Khan Urus (1361-75) and his sons Toktaka and Timur Melik. He dispossessed the latter of his throne and conquered power over the White Horde.

given as the date on which Russia proclaimed her independence, which in fact began much earlier.[15] In 1502 the Golden Horde fell under the blows of Russia's ally, Crimea.

We shall not here go further into the details of the history of the Golden Horde. This would take us too far. The above sketch of the history of the Mongol Empire and the Horde as a whole is only a reminder admirers of the Mongol system of government and mockers at the disorganization of our appange period of historical reality.[16] The appanage system, with all its defects further intensified by Oriental cruelty and faithlessness, existed also among the descendants of Jenghiz. The latter produced great personalities, Kublai, Batu, Bereke, Uzbek and Toktamish—just as the Russian descendants of Rurik had their Vladimir Monomakh, Andrei Bogolyubsky, Alexander Nevsky, Ivan III and others. But the historical results are known. The descendants of Rurik managed to cope with the tendencies of the appanage system and creat a strong system of government, a thing the descendants of Jenghiz were not able to do. There is, therefore, no basis on which the latter may be held up as examples to the former.

Let us now consider the direct relations between the Golden Horde and Russia.

The Golden Horde governed not only Russia but also Khorassan, the Caspian Steppes and Crimea, and its influence spread over Greater Bulgaria, the Uzbek steppes and originally the Balkan Peninsula. Besides this the Horde played its part in the lives of the Asiatic Mongol States. Thus the Horde was occupied with many affairs besides those of Russia. According to the investigations of Progessor Berezin,[17] the Golden Horde contained the following groups of population:

1. Princes, great, medium and lesser; 2. Ooloos and appanage princes; 3. Princes without appanages; 4. Commoner princes (of conquered peoples); 5. Beks; 6. Murzas; 7. Tarkhans; 8. Merchants; 9. Artisans; 10. Freedmen; 11. Cultivators; 12. Tenant-farmers.

---

15 Formally this date can be set at 1462, the commencement of the reign of Ivan III who mounted the throne without the approval of the Golden Horde and did not recognize it in his further dealings. In fact even his predecessor Vassili II did not count with the Horde in the second half of his reign, acting independently, for instance, in 1452 when he founded the Tartar appanage of Kasimov, dependent upon Moscow.

16 The same happened among other descendants of the sons of Jenghiz. For an account of the Ooloos of Jagatai *vide* Groom-Grzimailo, "Western Mongolia", II, pg. 510 *sqq*.

17 Berezin—"Outline", Works of the O.S.R.A.S., 1864, vol. VIII, ppg. 440, 460.

Besides these there existed the following military ranks: Princes or Beks (not princes) of tumens, thousands, hundreds, and tens; Bukauls; and Tamga Bukauls (bodyguards). Clerical ranks (Moslem) were as follow: Clerical judges, clerical lawyers, keepers of the regulations, preceptors, abbots and hermits (among them Imams and Sheikhs). Courtiers: stable-masters, falconers, panther-keepers, wolf-keepers, trappers, masters of ceremonies, stewards, gate-keepers, etc.

The civil ranks of the Golden Horde were as follows: 1. Noyons; 2. Darugas, 3. Chiefs (of a region or department); 4. Princes ruling a district or town; 5. Ambassadors; 6. Baskaks, tax-collectors; 7. Secretaries of the Court; 8. Scribes; 9. Customs officials; 10. Weighers; 11. Allotters of poll-taxes; 12. Heralds; 13. Architects; 14. Road-keepers; 15. Toll-gate keepers; 16. Bridge toll gatherers; 17. Boat toll gatherers; 18. Coast-guards; 19. Postmasters; 20. Bazaar inspectors; 21. Emissaries; 22. Messengers; 23. Collectors; 24. Plough tax collectors; 25. Managers; 26. Dragomen; 27. Princely scribes.

Generally, the character of administration within the Golden Horde was the same as that in the centre of the Mongol Empire. If the latter was described by Yeh-Liu-Ch'u-Ts'ai as "government from the saddle", this definition applied all the more to the state of affairs in the Golden Horde, which had no Yeh-Liu-Ch'u-Ts'ai or other administrators like him. The administration was remarkable for the same abuses, corruption and absence of justice as that of the Great Khanate. It was not for nothing that it was once said that justice in the Horde "was turned by a golden wheel of abuses" and not for nothing does our historian note that the Grand-Princely throne of Russia was the object of auctioning.

There existed in the Golden Horde a special department of Russian affairs, headed by a Daruga.[18] From time to time, also, a Baskak was appointed to one or another of the Russian cities to act as a supervisory organ, chiefly in the collection of tribute. The appearance of Baskaks and envoys, usually accompanied by armed Tartar detachments, was accompanied by violence, incendiarism and massacres of the peaceful population. These expeditions were regarded by the Russian people as the punishment of heaven, the scourge of God[19] bringing sinners to reason. As for systematic administration of Russia by the Tartars, there was none.

---

18 According to Mongol Chronicles Chak-Khan was appointed by Jenghiz-Khan after the battle of Kalka (1223) the first Daruga of Kiptchak and Huen Noyon the first Daruga of Oros (Rus.), v. Ts. Jamtsarano-Mongol Chronicles of the XVII c., 1936, p. 116 (in Russian).

19 As V. O. Kliuchevsky aptly remarks: "This scourge was most successfully used by the Grand Dukes of Moscow against their own relatives".

The Mongol-Tartars did not depose the Russian Princes or found their own dynasty in Russia as they did, for instance, in Persia. Neither did they have in Russia permanent viceroys or residents-general exercising definite functions, such as China later established in Mongolia (the Uliassutai Chiang-Chun and the Ambans). The Baskaks were appointed sporadically to different places and did not have definite administrative functions, confining their attention to the collection of tribute. They vanished from administrative practice very early, in the first century of the Tartar yoke. Administration remained in the hands of the Russian Princes, the Grand Prince taking charge of negotiations with the Horde. There were thus no established channels along which Mongol influence could flow.

Where then do those who contend that the Mongols exercised such a great influence on Russian principles of government discover concrete expressions of such influence?

They point out that the Russian Princes ruled subject to Mongol confirmation. This circumstance, however, did not change the previous administrative order.

Academician Platonov states: "The principles of succession to the Grand Prince's throne under the Tartars, during the first century of their rule (1240-1340), remained the same as before their coming, succession being hereditary with fairly common modifications and violations. The Grand Prince's title remained unchangingly in the house of Vsevolod of the Big Nest, in the line of his son Yaroslav. In the course of somewhat more than a century (1212-1328) fifteen Princes of four generations occupied the Grand Prince's throne, only three of them having seized the title illegally, over the heads of uncles or elder brothers. If we consider the pre-Tartar period in the so-called Kiev Russia, we shall see there the same order and the same violations. Evidently the Tartar overlordship changed nothing in the old system of succession, retaining only the right of sanctioning its operation. Moreover, it did not attach very much importance to even this right, and did not show too much anxiety to assert it, violations by various Princes going long unpunished. In the generations of the grandsons and great-grandsons of Vsevolod of the Big Nest a situation arose which revealed to the full the weakness of Tartar authority and influence. The appanage Princes were constantly at odds with the Grand Prince approved by the Tartars, and attempted jointly or separately to weaken him while. . . . the Tartars looked upon the quarrels of the Princes only as a source of profit and cynically told them that they would be Grand Princes if 'you give more tribute', i.e. if they paid more than their rivals. Knowing this the Princes bargained in the Horde, bidding one against the other".[20]

The Tartars tooks so little interest in the administration of Russia and watched it so remissly that they did not observe the strengthening of the Muscovite princedom. The only question which really interested them was a material one—the squeezing of greater resources from the rulers and population. This was why "the Grand Prince's throne was the object of auction with bidding and counter-bidding". This is why we meet so often with measures for the collection of tribute and various taxes and levies. This is why there are still preserved in the Russian language so many Mongol words pertaining to money and taxation. But this interest was not the interest of an enlightened government striving to better the economic and administrative situation of countries subject to it. It was the interest of predatory conquerors whose aim was to take from the vanquished (even though these had acquiesced in their conquest 50 years or a century before) as much as possible, and to take it by the crudest available methods and means.

The following elements of Mongol influence on the Russian system of government are also quoted.[21]

The Mongol government was based on the principle of the unconditional subordination of the individual to the collective—the tribe and through it the State. This Mongol idea is supposed to have served as a basis for the development, first in the Moscow and then in the St. Petersburg monarchy, of the universal service of the population to the government. This interpretation is erroneous.

During numberless campaings and hunts, especially in the XIIth and XIIIth centuries, the Mongols developed the principle of unconditional obedience to their military leaders who were usually also their tribal chiefs. This obedience turned in civil life into the despotism of one part of the population and the slavish servility of the other. The conception of the State and of service to the State was not, however, developed. The Mongols lived under clan and tribal conditions and their thinking was conditioned by tribal psychology. Higher they did not rise.[22] As a result neither their social system nor their ideas could have served as a foundation for the building of the Muscovite state, the social base of which was quite different. With us the clan and tribal order obtained much earlier (early chronicles talk of it as the original fact of our history), and by the time of the Mongol invasion had com-

20 "Lectures on Russian History", 6th. Ed., 1909, ppg. 107-109.

21 Among the new authors, Prof. G. V. Vernadsky gives a brief formulation in "A History of Russia", 1929, pg. 46 *sqq.*

22 The Empire of Jenghiz Khan too was built up on the clan and tribal principle and soon fell apart into appanages.

pletely disintegrated. It was succeeded (as a result of a process which began before the Tartars) by hereditary family property and prince's rule of the same character which later gave place to autocratic government of the public-law type. The impressing of all strata of the population into government service took place under the influence of internal social conditions (such an internal process cannot be borrowed from others) and began only under the Muscovite government, reaching the apex of its development in the Empire of Peter the Great.

Here again we see that the hypothesis of Mongol influence is based on a superficial analogy and must be discarded.

Older authors, such as Leontovich, were even more emphatic and stated that the system of servitude too was borrowed by us from the Mongols.[23] Their contemporary counterparts are more careful. They do not make such assertions, taking into account the evident impossibility of borrowing or developing from the ideas of others a social institution like the system of servitude, based on complex internal processes. But their more careful formulation is essentially the same as that of their predecessors. Both the institutions referred to above came later in time and were the product of internal social processes. These processes had close analogies in the West (not in the East), but were also not borrowed from it.

Of the same character is the assertion that the autocratic rule of the Muscovite Princes grew under direct Mongol influence on the model of the power of the Mongol Khans (the power of the Mongol Khan was destroyed, but reborn in the person of the Moscow Czar who took his place).

We know that in the European continental countries feudalism, under the influence of certain social conditions, gave way to absolute monarchy. The same is true of Russia where absolute monarchy came as a result of the strengthening of Moscow and the developing autocracy of her princes under the influence of internal processes, geographical, economic and political.[24] Simultaneously with the internal causative factors, external supplementary factors contributed to the basic process, perhaps accelerating it. Among these were the pressure of the Swedes and Teutonic Knights from the Northwest, of Lithuania from the West and the Tartars from the South.

Thus the Tartar influence was one of the indirect factors contributing to the establishment of autocracy in Russia, one among other

---

23 Op cit., 254.

24 Prof. Pavlov-Sylvansky draws an exhaustive analogy between ancient Russia and the West in his "Feudalism in Russia", and other works.

influences, internal and external. Contemporary observers did not perceive any direct Mongol influence or any internal connection with it. When the internal process of the formation of the autocracy ripened and took on definite form, an ideological basis for it was sought and found not in the East, in the disintegrating power of the Mongol Khan, but within, in Russia itself, in the ideals of Vladimir Monomakh, Vsevolod III and Alexander Nevsky.[25] From the West, from the failing power of the Byzantine Emperor, came the theory of Moscow, the third Rome.

Likewise totally incorrect is the third contention that the idea of the Prince as possessor of all the territory of the State was borrowed from the Mongols. At a certain stage of social development, where patriarchal hereditary relations are present, we find this idea among the most diverse peoples: in mediaeval England and Germany, in the Mohammedan world, among the Chinese, the Mongols and the Slavs. Most nations have long left this stage behind, only a few carrying it into the XXth century. In Russia we meet the idea before the Tartar invasion. Moreover, in the XIth century and even earlier, individual private property (church, ducal and private) began to appear, a circumstance which found its full expression in the Pskov Judicial Charter. The personal property of the Grand Prince gradually separated from the government domain; fiscal, treasury and Court property thus also came into being.

From this it may be seen that the development of Russia under Tartar rule proceeded contrary to this assertion.

It is further asserted that the tax system of the Moscow government was founded by, or under the influence of, the Mongols.

Before the Tartar invasion taxes were collected in Russia from each peasant courtyard (plough or smoke), i.e. from each piece of land cultivated by one head of a household. Consequently, the object of taxation was property. Taxes were levied on each parish or "verv" which later apportioned their payment among peasant households or ploughs. According to the majority of investigators, the Tartars introduced the poll-tax on a large scale, computing the entire poulation. To this was added a levy on trade (Tamga) and others, and a series of taxes in kind. Even if this is correct[26] we must still recognise that the

25 The old Russian chroniclers, states A. E. Presniakov, were right in their way when they represented Alexander Nevsky or Vsevolod III, and, in the distant past, Vladimir Monomakh, as the heralds of the tendency towards strong Grand-Ducal power. ("The Muscovite Kingdom", pg. 12).

26 Academician Diakonov doubts this, considering that the Tartars did not have the power or the means to take an universal census. He quotes the example of Novgorod, where, according to ancient chronicles, a census was taken of homesteads. ("Sketches", pg. 189). But the majority of our savants favour the poll tax hypothesis.

influence of the Mongol-Tartars on the Muscovite system of taxation was not great.

The system of taxation introduced by the Tartars cannot be considered as a financial reform carried out in the interests of more efficient administration, but only as a purely predatory measure having as its aim the squeezing of a maximum of material gain out of the population. The levies were of the crudest nature, the poor and the rich being taxed alike (e.g. a tithe of their total property, etc.). Futhermore, the collection of taxes was farmed out to "bessermens", whose abuses, carried out with the aid of Tartar detachments, gave rise to popular unrest as early as 1262 A.D. These troubles recurred in 1290, growing to the proportions of an insurrection which forced the Horde to entrust the future collection of tribute to the Russian Princes. The latter immediately abolished the crude poll tax and gradually returned to the old practice of property taxation by ploughs (towards the middle of the XV-th century). Thus, even before the establishment of the Moscow Czardom, our system of taxation was national, not borrowed, in character.

Finally, the establishment of the postal system in Russia is credited to the Mongols. This is not true. The postal organization for handling all varieties of mail was instituted in Russia only in the second half of the XVII-th century (1663 and years following[27]), on the western-European model. What is referred to is the matter of requisitions in kind—of the supplying by the local population of the means of transport for travelling officials (horses, carts, boats etc.). Such levies in kind existed in pre-Mongol Russia and were called "povoz", and organised in "stans" (stations). The requisitions made by the Tartars were much heavier, due to their greater demands for transportation, and the old terms "povoz" and "stan", were gradually supplanted by the Tartar "Yam". However, the Tartars changed nothing in the nature of these levies. They only increased the already heavy requisitions of transportation to which the people were subject and which then received a Tartar name.

It is also pointed out that the Muscovite hierarchy of administrative ranks (mestnichestvo) was of Mongol origin, having its roots in the Mongol system of clan seniority (Leontovich).[28] This analogy is superficial. It is true that the Mongols retained until the most recent times the aristocratic principle of clan seniority. The "Golden Clan" of Jenghiz Khan held in its hands the high places of State power and the nearest clansmen of the Great Khan ruled over the chief appanages.

27 Miliukov, "Outlines", vol. I, 1900, pg. 101. Vladimirsky-Budanov, "Outline of the History of Russian Law", 1909, ppg. 84, 208, 209.

28 v. Leontovich, "The Mongol-Oirat Regulations on Punishments", ppg. 248-275, 262.

Each of these clansmen could, in accordance with the degree of his relationship, claim a certain social standing. Next came the clans of the brothers of Jenghiz, and, a rung lower on the social ladder, those having no blood relationship to Jenghiz but descending from his Batirs (heroes) and tribal chiefs. At the same time the Muscovite system of local administration was in direct contradiction to the clain principle. Its basis was not hereditary but official (service) seniority, and Princes of the line of Rurik often held lower positions than some Boyar officials.[29]

Reference is also made to the system of Tarkhans (exemption from taxation and duties). This institution existed in Russia before Mongol times and took only its name from the Mongols, having previously been called "obelnichestvo" (obelni people, i.e. exampt from taxation and duties).

We may also note the alleged borrowing from the Mongols of the system of "prikazi" (public offices) the prototype of which is stated to have been the Mongol yamen. But the distance in time, the gradual formation of the prikaz in consequence of practical needs, and the doubtful familiarity of the Muscovite administrators with the organization of the Mongol yamen make this superficial analogy extremely unconvincing.

It may therefore be stated that Mongol Law did not in any way directly influence on Russian Law, either through the application of the Mongol Code in Russia or in the creation of a special Code.

The Mongol influence on government and administrative practice was likewise not great. The Horde confirmed the appointment of Grand Princes, but did not change previously existing institutions or meddle in the administration. The Tartar yoke was one of the contributory factors in the formation of the Russian autocracy and exercised a transient influence on the tax-system of princely Russia. It also had an indirect influence on the increase in the severity of punishments in administrative and criminal cases, as has already been stated above.

B. Mongol Law and Chinese Law.

After conquering China, the Mongols transferred to that country the capital of the Great Khanate and there founded the Mongol Yuan dynasty (1271-1368 A.D.) This dynasty promulgated legislation in China. The question naturally arises to what extent this legislation was influenced by Mongol law. Another question is whether, during this epoch, a special code was issued for Mongolia.

29 v. Vladimirsky-Budanov, "Outline of the History of Russian Law", ppg. 125 sqq.

Information exists that during the epoch of the Yuan dynasty five Codes were issued for China (for particulars see further). In literature dealing with the subject, the opinion has been expressed that the Yassa of Jenghiz Khan and Mongol law in general greatly influenced the legislation of the Yuan dynasty.[30] It is further stated in such literature that one of the Yuan Codes, the Yuan Tien Chang (1320 A.D.) was a Mongolian Statute, i.e. a special Code issued by the Yuan dynasty for Mongolia, and that it was itself a translation from the Mongol tongue and contained many references to the Yassa of Jenghiz Khan. This last opinion, which was expressed by the Russian Sinologue Professor Popov[31], was at first accepted by the writer who admitted its plausibility in his first work on the subject.[32] Further and more fundamental research, however, has resulted in the conviction that Professor Popov's point of view was erroneous and that another explanation[33] exists. The writer believes that the legislation of the Yuan dynasty, including the Yuan Tien Chang, was issued for China and represents the Chinese Law of the period. The influence of Mongol Law on this legislation was negligible. The legislation of the Yuan dynasty also affected (to some extent) Mongols resident in China, but did not apply to Mongolia. Let us here examine this problem and determine the relation between Mongol Law and the legislation of the Mongol (Yuan) dynasty.

In the official chronicle of the Yuan dynasty, Yuan Shih (元史), in the introduction to the history of criminal law (Book 102, section 50)[34] may be found the following: "In the beginning of the Yuan dynasty there was no prevailing law. All officials decided legal cases in accordance with the laws of the Chin dynasty which were very strict. When Shih Tzu (Kublai Khan) conquered and united the entire territory of the Sung dynasty, new laws were promulgated and published for universal guidance—the so-called 至元新格 "Chih Yuan Hsin Ke."

As is known, the central part of North China, including the city of Peking, was conquered by Jenghiz Khan in 1211-1215 A.D., and all North China (the territory of the Chin dynasty) was conquered by Khan Ogodai by 1234 A.D. The conquest of South China was completed by Kublai in the year 1280. From this we may gather that the quotation we have given from the Yuan Shih proves that prior to the promulgation by Kublai Khan of his "Chih Yuan Hsin Ke" (after

30 E.g. Mr. Hara-Davan, in his book," Jenghiz Khan as a Military Leader and His Heritage" (in Russian), p. 60 and others.

31 Proceedings of the Oriental Section of the Russian Archaeological Society, XVII, 4;0157.

32 "Customary Law of the Mongol Tribes", 1929, ppg. 23-24.

33 See the writer's work, "The Great Yassa of Jenghiz Khan" (in Russian), 1933, Chap. V.

34 *v.* the Author's work, "The Great Yassa of Jenghiz Khan" (in Russian), ppg. 64-65.

1280) the effective law in China was the Chinese Code of the Chin dynasty. Mr. Yang Hung-lieh, author of the two-volume "History of the Development of Chinese Law", states in his work that the "Chih Yuan Hsin Ke" was issued in the year 1291.[35] Consequently, we may take it that the Code of the Chin dynasty was effective in China until that year.

What was the nature of the law of the Chin dynasty? The Northern Chin was a foreign dynasty (Churchen) which ruled over North China after its conquest by the Churchen(Tartars) (1126-1234 A.D.). Information concerning the law effective during the rule of this dynasty may be found in the official dynastic chronicle, Chin Shih (金史).

In the chapter concerning criminal law (under the Chins) it is stated[36] that the new laws of the Chin dynasty were promulgated in the reign of "Tien Huai" (T'ai Tsung—the second Emperor) and extended in the reign of "Chang Lun" (Chang Tsung—the third Emperor). Originally old customs were followed, but "in the time of the second Emperor this situation changed somewhat and the laws of the Sung dynasty began to be applied." During the reign of Huang Tung (Emperor T'ai Tsung) all the old laws were rewritten and a new Code issued, incorporating in part the laws of the T'ang and Sung dynasties and called the "Huang Tung Ch'i". In the reign of T'ai Ho (Emperor Chang Tsung) laws were compiled consisting of the following 12 sections: 1) The application of laws; 2) The Imperial Court; 3) The system of administration; 4) Civil law; 5) Horse-breeding and the Treasury; 6) Acts of violence; 7) Theft; 8) Brawls; 9) Swindling; 10) Various crimes; 11) Search for criminals; and 12) Judicial procedure.[37]

A comparison of the table of contents given above with the contents of the Code of the T'ang dynasty (and also the Sung dynasty) is sufficient to convince one of their complete identity.[38] This identity, as well as the references in Chin Shih to to the application of T'ang and Sung laws during the Chin dynasty, leads to the following conclusions.

Even if at the beginning the influence of the Churchen conquerors operated to make the legal norms and customs applied in North

---

35 楊鴻烈 Yang Hung-lieh, 中國法律發達史 "History of the Development of Chinese Law", vol. II, pg. 682.

36 *v.* the writer's work, "The Great Yassa of Jenghiz Khan" (in Russian) pg. 64, where the chapter "Criminal Legislation" from the Chin chronicle (Chin Shih) is given in Russian translation.

37 The Code of the Sung dynasty was also divided into these 12 sections (Yang Hung-lieh, I, 556.)

38 We cannot compare the contents of the two Codes, as no copy of the Chin Code is available. Mr. Yang Hung-lieh states that the T'ang Code remained almost without change (*op. cit.* II, pg. 669.)

China under the Chin dynasty[39] somewhat different from Chinese law proper[40], the conquerors later came under the influence of the higher culture of China and applied purely Chinese law. This law continued to be applied by the Mongol conquerors until about the year 1291.

After 1291 the legislation of the Yuan dynasty was also based on the fundamentals of Chinese law which had already received clear expression in the T'ang Code. In some ways, also, the Yuan legislation represented the further development of these fundamentals. To clarify this assertion it is necessary to summarise briefly the Code of the T'ang dynasty.

This Code of the T'ang dynasty—T'ang-Liu-Shu-I consists of 30 books and 500 articles, and is divided into 12 sections as follows: (1) General principles (of the application of laws); (2) Guarding of the Imperial Court; (3) System of Administration; (4) Civil Affairs; (5) Horsebreeding and the Treasury; (6) Disregard of the Law; (7) Theft and robbery; (8) Brawls and quarrels; (9) Swindling and extortion; (10) Various crimes; (11) Search for criminals; (12) Decision of litigation.[41] In outline the contents of these twelve sections may be reduced to the following:

Part I—General Principles.

The Code opens with a scale of five punishments: (1) The lesser bamboo rod (flogging on the hands); (2) the greater bamboo rod (flogging on the buttocks); (3) Hard labour (as an alternative to confinement in gaol or near exile); (4) Exile; and (5) Death.

Then follows the recapitulation of the ten major crimes: Rebellion; Sabotage against the Emperor and the Imperial House; Coup d'Etat; Murder of elder relatives; Murder of three people and chopping to pieces; Disrespect for the Emperor; Disobedience to parents; Enmity to senior relatives; Immoral actions (with respect to spouses, teachers, friends, etc.); and Adultery with senior relatives.

Eight causes for mitigation of punishment are indicated as follows: for relatives of the Emperor, for aged persons, for wise persons, for able persons, for persons who have rendered great services, for senior officials, for persons who have served long and diligently, and for honourable persons.

---

39 Such juridical norms and customs are also referred to in Chin Shih.

40 Evidently this difference (due to the influence of the Churchens) was not great, since the Chin Shih states that the application of Sung laws only slightly changed the previous position.

41 If we consider that Section 6 deals primarily with military affairs, and Sections 7-12 deal with Criminal affairs, the contents of the T'ang Code may be divided into the following seven parts: (1) General principles; (2) Guarding the Imperial Court; (3) System of administration; (4) Civil Law; (5) Horsebreeding and the Treasury; (6) Military affairs; (7) Criminal affairs.

Part II—Guarding of the Imperial House.

It was forbidden to enter the Imperial Palace without good cause, to spend the night there without official permission, etc.

Part III—System of Administration.

Recommendation of unworthy persons for service was punished. To accept bribes was forbidden. It was forbidden to ask for the construction of a monument to one's self. If, upon the death of his parents, an official did not go into mourning, he was liable to exile at a distance of 3,000 li. If he made merry during the mourning period he was liable to 3 years of hard penal labour, etc.

IV—Civil Affairs.

Sons and grandsons were not permitted to live apart from the head of a family. The junior members of a family could not dispose of property. Marriages could not be contracted during the period of mourning for parents. The taking of a second wife was forbidden on pain of a penalty of a year's hard labour; the woman being exempt from punishment if she was deceived. The taking of a concubine was punished by two years' hard labour. Persons of the same family name were forbidden to enter into a contract of marriage. Civil officials were forbidden to marry the daughters of subordinates. Divorce in the absence of any of the seven good causes was punished by 100 strokes of the bamboo but if there were three counter-causes (mourning for parents, if the parties married when poor and then became rich, or if the wife had nowhere to go after divorce) divorce was forbidden generally on pain of 100 strokes of the bamboo and the leaving of the marriage contract in force. If the husband and wife did not love each other they could be divorced (by mutual consent). A slave could not marry the daughter of a free family. A marriage contract concluded in violation of the law, even if there were marriage brokers, was not valid.

The chief heir was the eldest son by the chief wife. If the chief wife was over 50 years of age and childless, the eldest son by a concubine could be appointed chief heir. Violation of this law was punished by a year's hard labour.

Ploughing of common land without official permission was punished by 30 strokes of the bamboo for every mu of land so ploughed. For the sale of common land as one's own the punishment was 50 strokes for each mu. Ploughing of another's family graveyard was punished by 100 strokes of the bamboo, etc.

V—Horse-breeding and the Treasury.

Horses were to be kept in good health and properly trained. A Treasurer did not have the right to hand over things and money, etc.

VI—Disregard of the Law.

For violation of the building regulations the punishment was 40 strokers of the bamboo. For manufacture of weapons without permission—a year and a half of hard labour; for informing the enemy of the despatch of troops—the death penalty; generals and officers retreating before their soldiers were likewise liable to the death penalty. Death was also the punishment for commanders badly defending a city or handing it over to the enemy.

VII—Theft and Robbery.

For rebellion against the government the offender and all members of his family over sixteen were put to death. Persons boasting of their intention to rebel against the government were liable to exile to a distance of 2,000 li. Attempting homicide was punished by 3 years of hard labour if the victim was unhurt, and by death (without decapitation) if the victim sustained any wound. For murder the penalty was death by decapitation. Poisoning was punished by death. Entering the courtyard of another at night without good cause was punished with 50 strokes of the bamboo. For theft from a temple and the theft of ritual accessories from the Imperial Palace the offender was exiled to a distance of 2500 li; for theft of imperial property he was put to death; for the theft of official documents the penalty was 3 years' imprisonment with hard labour; for theft from a tomb—death; for attempted theft—50 strokes of the bamboo; for the theft of one ch'i of money—60 strokes of the bamboo; for 10 ch'i by one degree higher; for 50 ch'i, a year's imprisonment with hard labour; for 500 ch'i, exile with hard labour.

A second theft was punished with exile to a distance of 2,000 li, a third theft with death. For theft among relatives the punishment was mitigated by one or two degrees, the inflicting of wounds being treated in the same way. For robberies where no money changed hands (attempted robbery) the penalty was 2 years' imprisonment with hard labour; where one ch'i of money changed hands—three years; 2 ch'i—a degree higher; for 100 ch'i accompanied by wounding of the victim of the robbery—death; for attempted armed robbery—exile to a distance of 3,000 li. Intentional arson and extortion were treated as robbery, etc.

VIII—Fights and Brawls.

For beating with the bare hands during a fight the offender was punished with 40 strokes of the bamboo; for tearing a square ts'un of hair from the head of another—80 strokes; if the victim bled from the nose or eyes the punishment was two degrees higher; for fights with arms—100 strokes; if one of the parties was wounded—2 years' imprisonment with hard labour. For fighting with senior relatives the penalty was one degree higher, etc.

IX—Swindling and Extortion.

Forging the Imperial seal was punished by death; forging the seal of the official authorities by exile to a distance of 2000 li; calling one's self an official without having any right to the title—a year's imprisonment with hard labour. Receiving goods under false pretences was punished by a year's imprisonment with hard labour; perjury by 70 strokes of the bamboo; erroneous translation into another language—by from 10 to 70 strokes; false notification of death by 100 strokes of the bamboo, etc.

X—Various Crimes.

The counterfeiting of money was punished by exile to a distance of 3000 li; the playing of musical instruments during periods of official mourning by 100 strokes of the bamboo; shooting in a private house by 40 strokes; gambling by 100 strokes; appearing in public in the nude by 20 strokes. The penalty for adultery was 1½ years' hard labour; for adultery with a married woman—2 years; for the adultery of a higher official with the wife or daughter of a subordinate the punishment was one degree higher; for adultery with a relative the punishment was also raised by one degree, the woman, however, going unpunished. For the falsification of weights and measures the penalty was 50 strokes of the bamboo; for starting a panic or spreading false rumours—50 strokes; for setting fire to dry twigs etc. in a field—50 strokes; for failing to help put out a fire—20 strokes, etc.

XI—Search for Criminals.

If a criminal was not arrested on the spot the authorities were obliged to arrest him within 30 days, failing which they were liable to a penalty one degree lower than that appertaining to the crime committed. If failure to detain the criminal or criminals arose from their resistance or large numbers the punishment to which the authorities were subject was reduced by 2 or 3 degrees. It was permitted to kill a criminal resisting arrest. A prisoner who resisted but was arrested was punished a degree higher, as was a criminal escaping from hard labour or exile.

XII—Decision of Litigations.

It was permitted to detain in gaol only those persons who were subject to arrest. Prisoners were to be provided with food, clothing and medicine. It was forbidden to apply torture to prisoners more than three times. Litigations were to be decided in accordance with petitions and no crime not contained in the petition could be tried in court. For wrongful decisions the judge was punished with 30 strokes of the bamboo and if the decision involved a death sentence, by a year's hard labour. Sentences of death were not executed after the onset of spring.[42] A pregnant woman could not be put to death.

We have summarised the Code of the T'ang dynasty in its essential parts. This Code gives expression to the fundamental institutions of Chinese law, such as the system of the Five Punishments, the separation of the ten major crimes, the general casuistry of crimes and severity of punishments, mourning, the permitting of real estate transactions, the prohibition against the seperation of junior members of families, the forbidding of marriages between persons bearing the same family name, the seven causes for divorce, the recognition of the rights of inheritance of the sons of concubines, and some others. These institutions received their further development in the succeeding dynasties—mainly the Sung, Chin and Yuan. The Sung Code recapitulated the main features of the T'ang Code, and the Code of the Chins, as we have already seen, repeated the features of the first two. Let us now consider the legislation of the Yuan dynasty.

In the Chronicle of the Yuan dynasty, the Yuan Shih[43], three Codes of law are mentioned: 至元新格 Chih Yuan Hsin Ko, i.e. the New Law of the Yuan Dynasty, promulgated during the reign of Kublai Khan about the year 1291 3) 風憲宏綱 Fang Hsien Hung Kang, i.e. the Collection of Disciplinary Laws, promulgated in the reign of Buyantu Khan or Jen Tsung about 1312 A.D., and 3) 大元通制 Ta Yuan T'ung Chih, i.e. General Laws of the Great Yuan Dynasty, promulgated in the reign of Shodi-Bala, the Emperor Yin Tsung in 1323 A.D. Besides these, there has been preserved another Code not mentioned in the Yuan Shih, the full designation of which is 大元聖政國朝典章 Ta Yuan Sheng Cheng Kuo Ch'ao Tien Chang (usually abbreviated to Yuan Tien Chang 元典章) or Collection of Laws of the Wise Dynasty of the Great Yuan. This Code had an extension, 至治條例 Chih Chi T'iao Li, i.e. Collection of Laws of the Era of Chih Chi. Mr. Yang Hung-lieh, in his "History of the Development of Chinese Law" (vol. II, pg. 685) speaks of a fifth Code, the Chi Cheng T'ia Ko, promulgated in 1334 by the Emperor Shun Ti, which contained 27 parts and was re-issued under the Ming dynasty. This Code has not reached us.

---

42 It was postponed until autumn.

43 *v.* Book 102, Section 50—History of the Criminal Law and the Preface.

The Yuan Shih recapitulates the essential contents of the legislation of the Yuan dynasty[44]. This legislation may be divided into the following 20 sections.[45].

(1) General principles (application of laws); (2) Guarding of the Imperial Palace; (3) System of Civil Administration; (4) Ritual Ceremonies; (5) Educational Affairs; (6) Affairs of Military Discipline; (7) Civil Affairs; (8) Products and Salt; (9) Major Crimes; (10) Adultery; (11) Theft; (12) Swindling; (13) Judicial Procedure; (15) Fights; (16) Prohibitions; (17) Various Crimes; (18) Search for Criminals; (19) Keeping of Criminals (treatment of criminals); (20) Alteration of Sentences.

We shall not here give this legislation in detail[46] as the three Codes recorded in Yuan Shih were not available to us, and will therefore briefly consider only the contents of the first and seventh parts.

Part I (General Principles) contains the following paragraphs: (a) The five punishments—the lesser bamboo rod and the greater bomboo, hard labour, exile and the death penalty; (b) The five degrees of mourning: 1st degree—3 years (a son for a father, a daughter-in-law for a father-in-law), 2nd degree—3 years, 1 year, 6 months, 5 months, and 3 months (a son for a mother, a daughter-in-law for her mother-in-law, etc.), 3rd degree—9 months, 4th degree—5 months, 5th degree —3 months; (c) The ten major Crimes: Rebellion, Sabotage in relation to the Emperor and the Imperial Court, Coup d'Etat, Murder of elder relatives, Murder of three or more persons and chopping to pieces, Disrespect to the Emperor, Disobedience to parents, unfriendly attitude to elder relatives, immoral treatment of spouse, teachers, friends, etc., adultery with elder relatives; (d) The eight applications of punishment (mitigation of punishment) for relatives of the Emperor, old friends, wise persons, able persons, for persons who have rendered meritorious service, old officials and persons who have given long and faithful service, and for honourable persons; (e) Ransom: Ransom from punishment was permitted to officials guilty of negligence, officials guilty of being abroad late at night, persons over 70 and under 15 years of age (from the bamboo), persons seriously ill and cripples.

---

44 See Books 102—105.

45 Twenty-one sections according to another reckoning.

46 It is described in greator detail in the Author's work, "The Great Yassa of Jenghiz Khan" (in Russian), *v.* pg. 47 *sqq.*

Part VII (Civil Affairs) contained, among others, the following provisions: When mortgaging or selling a plot of land or a house it was necessary to record the act with the proper authorities, and the buyer and seller were obliged to present to the authorities, at the proper time, a tax in kind (grain tax). Acts of mortgage and sale were to be signed by the head of the family, the other members of the family and the neighbours being first asked if they had any objections to the transaction. At redemption the mortgagor was forbidden, on pain of punishment, to demand an excessive price for the surrender of the pledge. All civil cases involving marriage and the sale of property were to be completed within the space of one year. It was forbidden to sell or pledge one's children.

The conclusion of marriage contracts involving children not yet born was forbidden. If a marriage contract was concluded and the prospective bridegroom was subsequently sentenced for some criminal act such as theft or robbery and punished with hard labour or exile, the marriage contract was dissolved. Marriage contracts were also dissolved in case of the adultery of the prospective bride. Betrothals concluded during periods of mourning were annulled and the marriage money confiscated. Elder brothers were forbidden to marry the wives of younger brothers, the penalty for such marriage being 107 strokes of the bamboo for men and 97 strokes for women, besides which the marriage contract was annulled. The sale of wives, concubines and sons was forbidden. Parties promising to deliver a bride and not fulfilling the promise were punished with 37 strokes, while those giving a promised bride to others were given 47 strokes. If, after 5 years had elapsed from the conclusion of the marriage contract, the bridgeroom still failed to marry the bride, she was permitted by the authorities to marry another. Adulterers and adultresses were not permitted to marry. Monks and priests were forbidden to marry on pain of 67 strokes of the bamboo. Officials who married prostitutes were punished. Mortgagors were not permitted to marry the daughters of mortgagees. Marriages between cousins were permitted within the same generation. Marriage to the concubine of one's father was punished by 100 strokes. Fugitive slaves received 77 strokes. A slave having relations with the wife or daughter of his master was put to death. A wife leaving her husband to join a nunnery was given 87 strokes and returned to her husband. The sale of a maiden into prositution was punished with 87 strokes and annulment of the marriage contract. Abortion was forbidden. Divorces were accomplished by being recorded in writing and attested by the fingerprints of the parties.

From the contents of the first and seventh parts we may see that the legislation of the Yuan dynasty was purely Chinese in character, reproducing the essential features of Chinese law as expressed in the T'ang Code (the system of punishments, right of real property, Chinese family relations etc.)

But, as we have noted above, besides the three Codes recorded in Yuan Shih and at present not available, there was another Code which has survived, the Yuan Tien Chang with its extension, the Chih Chi T'iao Li. It was this Code which Prof. Popov supposed to be a translation from the Mongol containing references to the Great Yassa of Jenghiz Khan. Professor Popov further advanced the hypothesis that it was issued specially for Mongolia.[47]

The Yuan Tien Chang is divided into 10 parts[48], 373 paragraphs and 2379 articles. The 10 parts are as follows: 1) Wise Givernment; 2) Wise Government (continued; 2) System of State Administration; 4) Control and Inspection; 5) Ministerial Rank; 6) Civil and Financial Affairs; 7) Ministry of Ceremonies; 8) Ministry of War; 9) Ministry of Criminal Affairs; and 10) Ministry of Public Works.

Part I—Wise Government.

This section contains first of all the edicts of the Yuan Emperors-from Kublai to the beginning of the reign of Shodi Bala inclusive. The most important of these are the Edicts of the Emperor Kublai on accession to the throne, on the selection of a capital (Peking), on the use of the Mongol language in the conduct of official business, and on the naming of the Yuan dynasty.[49] Then follow provisions for internal administrations: All must subordinate themselves to the central government; All must obey the laws. There are also directions on the selection of talented individuals, rural economy, and the loyalty and respectfulness of the population, etc.

Part II—Wise Government.

This section deals with the lightening of taxation, aid to victims of natural calamities, aid to widows and orphans, the acceleration of judicial procedure, ceremonies and rites.

Part III—System of State Administration.

---

47 Proceedings of the Eastern Section of the Russian Archaeological Society, vol. XVII, 4,0157.

48 In the opinion of its Editor, Mr. Shen Tian-pen (see Afterword, *v.* also Yang Hung-lieh, 11,684). Prof. Popov divides it into 6 basic sections and 4 additional ones. Strictly speaking, it may be said that there are 7 parts, as, according to Mr. Shen, the first four parts comprise one general section ("Wise Government" has two parts and the second of these parts has two sub-sections: "System of State Administration" and "Inspection and Control").

49 First Edict in 1260, a second in 1270, a third in 1269 and a fourth in 1271.

On the necessity of reports to the Emperor passing through the chief State Chancellery; on disciplinary regulations; on the acceleration of litigation; on the decision of litigation according to law.

Part IV.—Inspection and Control.

Regulations for the work of supervisory organs.

Part V—Ministry of Official Ranks.

Qualifications for the assumption of official posts; Selections for service; Succession in the official service; On the exile of officials; On military offices; On educational and other officials. Regulations for the appointment, transfer, and discharge of officials, the salaries and furloughs of officials (i.e. Service regulations.)

Part VI—Civil and Financial Affairs.

This section is divided as follows: 1) Salaries and wages; 2) Appointment and discharge of officials; 3) Population statistics, division of families and succession, abandoment of land; 4) Marriage law; 5) Land and houses—sale, mortgage, emphiteusis; 6) Law on the minting of coins; 7) Grain warehouses; 8) and 9) Taxes; 10) Agriculture and Silk-industry; 11) Requisitions; 12) Police; 13) Taxes on produce; 14) Debt obligations.

This section contained the following provisions of Civil Law.

Brothers were permitted to part and live separately but a son was obliged to live with his father. It was forbidden to adopt the son of another.

A marriage contract had to be drawn up in writing. The amount of the dowry was fixed. The marriage contract was to be executed with the consent of the head of the family. If the bridegroom's father was dead but his mother still lived, he had to obtain her consent. If the marriage did not take place within a certain period after the signing of the contract, the contract was annulled. A marriage contract between persons guilty of adultery was not valid. It was forbidden to conclude a marriage contract between persons bearing the same family name. Once concluded, the marriage contract was not to be broken without good cause. The parents of a dead son were forbidden to force his widow into another marriage. Officials did not have the right to marry the daughters of their subordinates. The widow of a high official was not permitted to remarry. A younger brother was forbidden to marry the widow of his older brother. If an elder brother married the widow of his younger brother, the marriage was dissolved. A nephew was forbidden to marry his aunt. It was forbidden to marry during periods of mourning.

After the death of a father, if there were no sons, the property went to the widow; but if there was a daughter the inheritance went to her. If there were several sons they shared the preperty equally. The sons of first and second wives enjoyed the same privileges. It was forbidden to divide the property before the funeral of the deceased father. If the deceased was a military man and had no sons, his property went to his nearest subordinates. If he was a civilian his property was divided among his brothers by the same mother and their sons.

It was forbidden to occupy the land of another by means of violence and threats. Empty land could be occupied and cultivated with the permission of the authorities, and after three years it became the property of the person occupying it who then began paying taxes for it. No one was permitted to own more than 100 mu of land. Officials were forbidden to acquire houses.

Before mortgaging or selling land it was necessary to obtain the consent first of the nearest relatives, then of distant relatives, and finally of close neighbours who might have objections. If such objections existed the deal could be annulled during the three days following its conclusion. If the formality of obtaining their consent was not complied with, relatives and neighbours could, within 100 days, buy over the sold or mortgaged property at the price at which it was sold or mortgaged. The purchase, sale and mortgage of land and houses could not be accomplished privately. When buying land or houses it was necessary to notify the proper authorities of the deal. The circumstances of the deal were then verified and the necessary documents issued, after which the new owner or mortgageor of the property paid the established tax. The authorities were compelled to keep a journal in which were entered the names of the buyer and seller, the location of the land or building concerned, the price paid, and the amount of the tax collected. At the end of each year a report was made to higher quarters. If these formalities were not complied with, the property was confiscated, half going to the treasury and half to the person denouncing the offenders.

Landlords were obliged, in case of necessity, to provide tenants cultivating their land with seed and grain at an interest of not more than 36 per cent per annum. The taking of interest higher than 36 per cent was strictly forbidden.

Loans secured by a man (*k'an t'ou ch'ien*) were strictly forbidden. The interest paid for any debt could not exceed the principal, irrespective of the period during which interest was paid. The junior members of a family were not permitted to borrow money, the lender and middleman in cases where they did so being punished in accordance with the law. It was forbidden to grant loans to the junior members of a family on the condition that payment be made after the death of their parents. It was forbidden to charge interest in excess of 3 per cent. (monthly). If interest higher than this limit, or compound interest, was charged, the principal of the debt was confiscated. Loans of grain were regulated by the customary usage in the village where they were made (local customs.)

The pledging of gold, silver and other articles (in pawnshops) was permitted for not more than two years.

Part VII—Ministry of Ceremonies.

Here we find provisions for congratulations to the Emperor on the occasion of his birthday, on the form of congratulations, on the uniforms of military and civil officials. Preparations for ritual ceremonies: Before the beginning of the ceremonies all the participants were to bathe, eat only vegetable food and live separately from their families. They were not permitted to visit the dead or the sick, make merry, pass sentence on criminals, or take part in any unclean affair. Memorial services for deceased Emperors were to be held at the graveside, in family shrines, at Temples of Heaven and Earth, on the Five Mountains, and in the Temple of Confucius. On the 1st and 15th of each month, regional and district officials were to hold services at the Temple of Confucius and tell the population of the life of the Sage.

The five degrees of mourning were as follows: 1st degree: 3 years (son for father, daughter-in-law for father-in-law); 2nd degree: 3 years, 1 year, 6 months, 5 months, 3 months; 3rd degree: 9 months; 4th degree: 5 months; 5th degree: 3 months. This section also dealt with educational affairs and rewards for services.

Part VIII—Ministry of War.

On the enlistment of soldiers; On officers; On the prohibition of requisitions among the population; On desertion from the army; On the illness of military officials; On uniforms; On military supplies; On arms; On military stations; On military transport; On hunts.

Part IX—Ministry of Criminal Affairs.

This part of the Code contains the following sections: 1) Five Punishments; 2) On Ransom (from punishment); 3) Implements of Torture; 4) On the System of Prisons; 5) On the Examination of Criminals; 6) On the Decision of Criminal Cases in the Courts; 7) The Ten Major Crimes; 8) On Various Homicides; 9) On Fights; 10) On Adultery; 11) On Bribery; 12) On Robbery and Theft; 13) On Swindling; 14) Judical Procedure; 15) Various Crimes; 16) Various Prohibitions.

The Five Punishments were as follows: Flogging on the palm with the lesser stick (ch'i); flogging on the buttocks with the greater stick (change); hard labour (t'u); exile (lu); and death (ssu) by decapitation or strangulation.

Ransom from punishment was permitted in the case of old persons over 70, of persons younger than 15 years of age, of cripples, and on account of illness and physical disability. In these cases the bamboo was not used and ransom was permitted at the rate of 1 kuan (1,000 cash) for each stroke of the bamboo.

The implements of torture were the chia (cangue)—a wooden board with a hole for the head, weighing from 10 to 25 pounds; the niu (stocks) a wooden board with holes for the hands; the s'o, an iron chain; liao ,fetters; and chang, the bamboo. It was forbidden to put a man to torture without good cause.

Prisons were divided into two categories; for major criminals and those committing light offences. The cases of persons imprisoned were to be tried speedily. In case of necessity it was permitted to release prisoners on bail. Prisons were to be kept clean, and prisoners given warm clothing and blankets in winter. Sick prisoners were to be given medical treatment.

The questioning of prisoners was conducted in public. The judge was to consider the replies of the accused in accordance with his own convictions.

Criminal cases were to be decided within half a year, and at the end of each half year a report had to be made to the higher authorities.

The ten major crimes, according to the Yuan Tien Chang, were as follows: Disobedience to parents; Enmity among brothers and sisters; Coup d'Etat; Crimes against the Emperor and the Imperial family; Rebellion; Killing of senior relatives; Immoral dealings; Incest; Especially ferocious murders; Disrespect to the Emperor and the Imperial family.

The forms of homicide treated in the Code were as follows: Premeditated murder was punished by death; intentional homicide—by death; homicide attendant upon robbery—by death; homicide during a fight—by death or 77 stroke of the bamboo, in consideration of the circumstances; accidental homicide—from 37 to 107 strokes of the bamboo and payment of funeral expenses; homicide during a practical joke—by a fine, replacement of damages or flogging with the bamboo according with the circumstances of the case; homicide as a result of carelessness—from 27 to 97 strokes of the bamboo according to the circumstances; the killing of a wife as a result of adultery—by 97 strokes of the bamboo; of a son-in-law—by exile; of an infant daughter—by 57 strokes of the bamboo; of a son while drunk—by 77 strokes; of a slave by 77 strokes; of a prostitute—107 strokes; of the killer's wife's lover—by 47 strokes. The killing of the raper of a wife and of a concubine who committed adultery were left unpunished.

Fights with bare hands in which no one was hurt were punished by 40 strokes of the bamboo; When anyone was wounded—by 60 strokes; wounding with a knife—by 2 year's hard labour and 77 strokes; wounding with other articles— by 47 strokes of the bamboo.

The raping of a married woman was punished by death; of an unmarried woman—by five years hard labour and 107 strokes of the bamboo; of a child—by death. Adultery by collusion between a married woman and a man was punished by 2 years of hard labour and 87 strokes of the bamboo; adultery with the aid of threats—by 107 strokes; for adultery with the connivance of the husband the latter was punished with 47 strokes of the bamboo, the adulterer with a year's hard labour and 70 strokes, and the woman with 47 strokes. Adultery between slaves was punished with 47 strokes of the bamboo.

Bribery was divided into two categories: with violation of the law and without violation of the law.

For armed robbery the punishment was 2 years hard labour and 87 strokes of the bamboo if no one was hurt. If money was taken the penalty was 3 years and 107 strokes. If the robber was unarmed he was punished with a year's hard labour and 67 strokes. The Code also treated of street robbery and robbery with arson.

For theft of over 10 kuan the penalty was a year's hard labour; for less than 10 kuan the punishment was left to the discretion of the judge. Second theft was punished by three years' hard labour, a third offence by exile. All thieves were branded on the hands. The violation of graves was punished by death.

Swindling: Calling one's self an official without any right to the title was punished by 2 years' hard labour and 77 strokes of the bamboo; forgery of documents concerning the transport of tea and salt—by death and confiscation of property; forgery of the seal of the Customs—by 87 strokes of the bamboo and confiscation of property.

The procedure with regard to litigations was fixed as follows: Anyone going to court had to first hand in a petition in writing, exceptions being made only in urgent cases. The judge was obliged to explain that to go to court was bad, and strive to reconcile the parties. The military authorities were not permitted to decide judicial cases. Questioning and the decisions of cases had to be carried out by the judges themselves and not by subordinate judicial officials. Plaintiffs had to apply to the court in the place of residence of the defendant. For false accusations the offender was given the same punishment as that which threatened the accused. In case of serious irregularities in any judicial case it was permitted to appeal to the supervisory chamber. It was forbidden to address petitions directly to higher courts, it being necessary to first try all cases in the local courts: before the district authorities, the prefectural authorities, the regional authorities, the provincial authorities, and the Ministry of Justice. Finally petition could be made to the Emperor. Complaints against officials, however, could be directly addressed to the higher courts. The ill and the aged were permitted to have attorneys to represent them in court.

Various Crimes: Irregular court decisions were punished by a decrease in salary amounting to 10 liang; if the irregularity resulted in the execution of a man, the punishment was demotion by one degree, 37 strokes of the bamboo, and a fine of 50 liang plus the victim's funeral expenses. Retarding the hearing of a case was punished by 37 strokes and a fine. The taking of a woman as security for a transaction was forbidden and if discovered, the transaction was annulled and the offenders punished. For the killing of horses and cows punishment was meted out in accordance with the proportions of the crime.

It was prohibited to gamble, sell poisonous drugs, foregather (in meetings) on the streets, and conceal weapons, etc. The punishment in each case was in accordance with the proportions of the offence.

Part X—Ministry of Public Works.

No one except the Emperor and the Imperial family had the right to use silk embroidered with dragons and phoenixes. There were also other provisions having to do with dress. In each town a city wall and a dyke to prevent floods were to be built, and trees were to be planted by the sides of all roads. Towns, villages and districts where river wharves existed were required to provide ferries for crossing passengers. The district authorities and postal stations were required to carry out repairs of service buildings annually. It was forbidden to requisition private houses.

Such is the outline of the contents of the Yuan Tien Chang.

An amendment of this Code, the Chih Chi T'iao Li was later issued, containing eight parts and 245 articles. The bulk of its contents consisted of edicts and orders issued during the two years of the era of Chih Chi (1321-1322 A. D.)

It is will hardly be necessary to prove that in the Yuan Tien Chang we have a typical body of Chinese Law. Both the general construction of the Code and the basic institutions of civil and criminal law which it contains are, generally speaking, identical with those contained in the "Ta Yuan T'ung Chih" and the Code of the T'ang dynasty. The evidence is convincing.

The wealth of the contents of the Code, demonstrating a higher level of cultural development than the Mongols had reached, the system of the Code, and, finally, the purely Chinese character of its basic institutions, leads us to the same conclusion. Such institutions as the traditional Chinese system of the Five Punishments (the lesser and greater bamboo, hard labour, exile, and death); the extremely detailed enumeration of crimes and severity of punishments; the special treatment of the ten major crimes; ransom; the severe punishment for adultery, and the violation of grave; branding; the system of instances connected with the Chinese system of central and local administration; and some others—and these are characteristic of Chinese criminal law. The five degrees of mourning, real estate transactions, the prohibition against the concluding of a marriage contract between persons not yet born, and between persons bearing the same family name, the prohibition of levira-tion, the prohibition against the marriage of adulterers, the prohibition against marrying even the concubine of one's father (to say nothing of a stepmother),—these are characteristic institutions of Chinese private law as distinct from that of the Mongols.

A comparison with the Code of the T'ang dynasty will convince us that the basic principles of the T'ang Code are here repeated. But it is necessary to note that the legislation of the Yuan dynasty is fuller and more developed than that of the T'angs.[50] This is not surprising. Between the two Codes a period of over 650 years had elapsed. Moreover it must be taken into account that during this interval at least two Codes were promulgated, that of the Sung dynasty in the X-th Century and of the Chin dynasty in the XII-th, both of which represented a further development of T'ang legislation.

No indications of the operation of the Yuang Tien Chang in Mongolia are available. It is true that the Code is a translation from the Mongol. But this is because the Emperor Kublai, in 1269 A.D., introduced the square Mongol character as the official language of the dynasty. All the documents of the period were first written in this character and then translated into Chinese and other tongues. Furthermore, as was recorded by the Archimandrite Palladius[51], there were two Chinese translations, one into the literary language and one into the vernacular which was more comprehensible to the Mongols. It was into this latter that the Yuan Tien Chang was translated.

---

50 The T'ang Code contained 500 articles, the Yuan Tien Chang had 2379. Prof. Escarra calls the Yuan Tien Chang a collection of administrative provisions (Le Droit Chinois, 1936, pg. 99), but, as is evident from the contents of the Code, it represented the usual type of Chinese code containing provisions of administrative, criminal and civil law, etc.

51 *v.* his preface to the Secret Chronicle of Jenghiz Khan. Works of the Russian Church Mission, IV.

All the legislation in the Code bears a Chinese character and the collection contains many provisions inapplicable in Mongolia. Thus, it provided for the right of property in land and houses (the latter of which were unknown to the Mongols) and transactions in real property—purchase and sale, mortgage, rent, emphiteusis etc., and regulated agriculture and sericulture, forbade leviration and marriage between persons of the same family name, and separation of children during the lifetime of their parents, and generally treated many features of life all of which were unknown among the Mongols of the period and some of which are unknown in Mongolia to this day.

As for the influence of the Yassa of Jenghiz Khan and Mongol Law generally on the Yuan Tien Chang, we cannot but admit that it was very slight. Prof. Popov, in his article. "The Yassa of Jenghiz Khan and the Code of the Yuan Dynasty—Yuan Ch'ao Tien Chang"[52], states that the Yuan Tien Chang contains three direct references to the Yassa of Jenghiz Khan, while the Archimandrite Palladius records one such reference (works of the R. Orth. Mission, IV, ftn. 536). When we remember that the Yuan Tien Chang contains 2379 articles, the reference made in three or four of them to the Yassa will only emphasise the insignificance of the latter's influence—all the more because these references did not affect the basic principles of Chinese Law.

We may here note the following analogous feature. Marco Polo wrote of courts among the Mongols as follows: "Judgment is carried out as follows: whoever steals even a little is punished for this by seven strokes of a stick, or seventeen, or twenty seven, or thirty seven, or forty seven, and so on until 307 is reached, increasing by ten each time depending upon what was stolen."[53] In the Yuan Shih where it treats of criminal legislation, and in the Yuan Tien Chang we constantly find provisions for such punishment: 27, 37, 47 and so on to 107 strokes of the bamboo. The question naturally arises. Have we here the influence of Chinese law on Mongol practice or the influence of Mongol custom on Chinese legislation?

If we consider that in the Code of the T'ang dynasty punishment with the bamboo is provided for in 20,30,40,50 100 strokes, in the Chin Code, Huang Tung Chi: by 60, 80, and 100 strokes, and that in the Codes of the succeeding Ming and Ta Ch'ing dynasties, 10, 20, 30 ...100 strokes were provided for, the supposition arises that the reckoning of blows of the bamboo under the Yuan dynasty in tens with the terminal digit seven was borrowed from the Mongols and represents the influence

52 Proceedings of the Oriental Section of the Russian Archaeological Society, v. XVII, issue 4.

53 Minaev's Edition, 91. In "The Travels of Marco Polo", by Komroff, 1926, ppg. 95-96 sqq. to 107.

of Mongol Law on that China. But such influence relates to minor questions and has no fundamental importance.

In this way we come to the conclusion that the legislation of the Yuan dynasty, including the Yuan Tien Chang, represents a body of Chinese Law. The influence upon this legislation of the Yassa of Jenghiz Khan and Mongol Law, in spite of statements to the contrary appearing in literature on the subject, was, generally speaking, very meagre.

That this Chinese legislation affected also the Mongols resident in China at the time may be seen from several directions and explanations contained in the Yuan Shih and the Yuan Tien Chang (e.g. Mongols and Chinese passing the first examination were obliged to study in government educational institutions; branding was not applied to Mongols and women; a Mongol killing a Chinese was impressed into military service and had to pay 50 liang for his victim's funeral expenses, etc.) But there is no indication or cause to think that this legislation also applied to Mongolia, the more because in China the Mongols enjoyed certain exemptions and exceptions under it, and it applied to them only partially. It may be seen from the Hsin Yuan Shih that for some crimes and in some civil cases the Mongols appeared before their own authorities, and in other cases, while they appeared before the ordinary courts, the presence of a representative of the Mongol authorities was required. Thus Mongol officials were tried before their own authorities. Cases involving marriage, debt obligations, fights etc. were also heard by the Mongol authorities. In the more serious criminal cases, however, such as those involving murder, robbery and the counterfeiting of money, Mongols were tried before the regular civil officials, but in the presence of representatives of the Mongol authorities (103, p. 13).

C. Mongol Law and the Law of Other Conquered Settled Peoples.

Our examination of the contents of the Codes of the Yuan dynasty has shown us that these also applied (partly) to Mongols. From the Hsin Yuan Shih it is clear that Mongols resident in China had to appear in some criminal and civil cases before the regular judicial organs (evidently on the basis of Chinese law)[54] though in the presence of representatives of the Mongol authorities, while in other cases they were tried by their own authorities (evidently according to Mongol law).

The same state of affairs was created in Egypt and Syria. The Egyptian Makrizi describes the situation as follows: "Egypt and Syria

54 As may be seen from some indications in the Yuan Tien Chang and Yuan Shih.

(under the Sultan Beibars)[55] were filled with Mongols and their customs spread everywhere. The terror before the name of Jenghiz and his successors was so strong that respect towards the Mongols themselves and fear of them entered into the flesh and blood of the inhabitants of Egypt. But since these Mongols had been brought up in Islam they united the dictates of their religion with their national customs. For instance they left to the Kazi-Kuzat all that was connected with religion, such as prayers, fasts, legitimate alms and pilgrimages to sacred spots, and all affairs concerning Wakufs (church lands) and orphans, judicial declisions concerning the marriage relation, etc. At the same time all that concerned the Mongols *personally* was regulated according to the laws of Jenghiz Khan and decided according to the provisions of the Yassa. For this purpose a special official was appointed."[56]

In Persia during the XIV-th century, the position was the same. As may be seen from the manuscript of Shemsu'l-Munshi quoted above, the investiture of the Emir Bayan as Chief Judge of Persia contained the following statement: "He is also entrusted with the Office of 'emir-i-yargu' to consider those cases between Mongols which *by their nature and fundamentals* pertain to it......" Here also, evidently, such of the Mongols' affairs as had connection with religion were in the hands of the ordinary authorities who decided them in accordance with the local laws, but all other affairs which were considered to pertain to the national customs of the Mongols were brought before special Mongol judges who decided them according to the Yassa of Jenghiz Khan and the legal customs of the Mongols ("according to the Yassa and Yassak", as the manuscript says).

Thus it may be seen that in the civilized countries conquered by the Mongols, where they settled among the conquered peoples, the Mongols were in some respects subject to the local laws and courts, but a series of cases preserved their own laws and tribunals (in the XIII-th and XIV-th centuries.)

But the Mongols did not impose their own laws on the civilized peoples they subdued. This was, of course, prevented by the difference between the cultures of the conquerors and conquered. The culture and law of the nomadic Mongols was fundamentally different from the culture and laws of settled agricultural peoples and the highly developed urban life of the trading and manufacturing countries. The culture and law of agricultural peoples is primarily based on the ownership and cultivation of land with their attendant institutions; and the culture and

55 Beibars I reigned in Egypt, 1260-1277 A.D. His troops repulsed the Mongol army. Beibars II reigned in 1309 A.D.

56 Berezin, Proceedings of the Oriental Section, R. Arch. Soc. VIII, 421.

law of trading and manufacturing states are based chiefly on trade, manufacturing and craftsmanship with the institutions arising from them. All these institutions, such as, for instance, the right to own real property, mortgage, rent in the former case and the trading and craft guilds with their rules and various trading transactions in the latter, were either totally absent or present in an embryonic state among the Mongol nomads. It was evident that the primitive law of the Mongols could not satisfy the needs of the more highly cultured agricultural and trading populations of Persia, Syria and Egypt (as well as China and Russia) and could not operate either entirely or essentially among them.

This circumstance, however, did not prevent the spreading of certain Mongol customs in the life of these peoples or the introduction of certain Mongol institutions into their systems of government. Constant contact with the Mongols under the rule of these conquerors could not but influence the customs and governmental forms of the subject peoples. But such influence, where it concerned jurisprudence, was not here exercised by means of the direct influence of Mongol law on the laws of the conquered countries (just as it was not so exercised in Russia). Such influence as existed was not direct and organic but indirect, making itself felt chiefly in the sphere of administrative practice. The local laws remained the essential legislation, being influenced to some extent by the Mongols only in the sphere of public law. This influence, however, worked no radical changes in the local law. With the passing of time the conquerors merged themselves with their subject peoples and the local laws absorbed Mongol law retaining only some vestiges of its influence.[57]

Thus we presume that Mongol law did not exercise great influence on the conquered settled peoples but only secondary effect.

The influence of Mongol law on the nomadic tribes of Asia and Eastern Europe, however, was much greater.

D. Mongol Law and the Law of the Nomadic Tribes of Asia and Eastern Europe.

The Great Yassa of Jenghiz Khan continued to retain its effectiveness among the Mongol, Turki, Tungus and other tribes after the disintegration of the Great Mongol Empire into separate Oolooses. Thus the Great Yassa was undoubtedly applied not only in the Ooloos of Ogodai and Tului (Mongolia and Djungaria with their subject tribes) but also in the Oolooses of Jagatai and Juchi (Central Asia and Eastern Europe).

57 Such Mongol vestiges in Persian law (with respect to some institutions and offices) were noted by Berezin in the work mentioned above. Academician Barthold also pointed out that some offices and institutions in Persia and Central Asia owed their origin to the Mongols, *v.* Brockhaus-Efron, vol. 76, pg. 843.

Jenghiz Khan himself attached great importance to the Great Yassa. We see from the Yassa (Fr. 26) that he entrusted his second son, the stern Jagatai, with special supervision of the observance of the Code. In his (verbal) Will he also prohibited any change in his Yassa: "You must not alter my Yassak after me."[58] As is known, Jagatai accused even his brother Ogodai of violating the Yassa, and he undoubtedly demanded with equal severity the observance of its provisions in his own appanage. In the State of Timur, or Tamerlane, (d. 1405) which arose in the end of the XIV-th century mainly from the ruins of the Ooloos of Jagatai, and consisted chiefly of the nomadic tribes of Central Asia and Eastern Europe, the provisions of the Great Yassa were likewise applied. Academician Barthold wrote in this connection: "The organization of the military and civil administration was governed almost entirely by the laws of Jenghiz Khan; later the religious authorities refused to recognize Timur as a faithful Moslem since he placed the laws of Jenghiz Khan above the prescriptions of religion."[59] Mr. Buvat also points out that Timur united the Shariat with the provisions of the Yassa. Crimes and offences relating to religion were judged by Cadis, while in civil cases the Yassa was applied.[60]

The well-known maxim of Batu, Khan of the Golden Horde, stated: "Anyone who violates the Yassa must lose his head." This maximum undoubtedly applied first of all to the his own Ooloos and pictures the state of affairs in the Golden Horde. The effectiveness of the Yassa in later periods may be judged from the references to it made in the Yarliks of the Khans of the Golden Horde to the Russian church (XIII-th and XIV-th centuries) which have been described above (in Chap. I).

However, the effectiveness of the Great Yassa did not extend beyond the XIV-th century and after this time remained only in individual cases. The disintegration of the Great Mongol Empire, the new conditions of life in which the Mongols and other nomadic tribes found themselves in the West, and the adoption of Mohammedanism (and Buddhism) all contributed to the decline of the Yassa's effectiveness.

Generally, the Great Yassa and the entire body of Mongol law were not only the effective law among many tribes subject to the Mongols, but also influenced the native laws of subject and neighbouring nomadic peoples. The traces of this influence have been preserved until the present time.

---

58 Rashid Ed-din, *op. cit.*, Works of the O.S. R.A.S., vol. XV, 97.

59 Barthold-*v.* Brockhaus-Efron, vol. 65, p. 196, also Hara-Daran, op. cit., 159-160.

60 Buvat—"L'Empire Mongol" (2-me phase), 1927, p. 67-69.

Here it is first of all necessary to mention the Buriats and Kalmucks. It is, of course possible to speak of the influence of Mongol law on Buriat and Kalmuck law. But the Buriats and Kalmucks were Mongol tribes having a common origin with the Mongols and, during their later history, living under similar conditions. The Kalmucks split away from the common Mongol root only in the XVII-th century and for long maintained contact with their native land. They brought with them to the Russian steppes not only the common Mongol legal customs but were guided in their legal life by the Mongol-Oirat Regulations of 1640. Their legal life consisted mainly of the adaptation of the provisions of these Regulations to changed conditions of life. The Buriats long ago (even before the XIII-th century) broke away from the main body of the Mongols. But they lived in a similar environment, maintaining connections with the latter, and entered into the composition of the Empire of Jenghiz Khan and also, evidently, into the great union of 44 Mongol tribes in the XVII-th century (the Regulations of 1640 mentioned the Bargu-Buriats). Later they maintained contact with Northern Mongolia and a number of clans and Otoks of Khalkha joined the Buriat tribes (e.g. the Selenga and Tunkinsk Buriats). Buriat law represents the further development of ancient Mongol customs in new conditions of life. Because of this, Buriat and Kalmuck law are here considered as a component part, a variety of Mongol law. Here we concern ourselves with the question of the influence of Mongol law, the law of the Mongol tribes, upon the law of the non-Mongol tribes of Asia.

As has already been stated above, the Mongols were not the only modern representatives of the nomadic clan-patriarchal organization in Asia. This organization forms the basis of the social and private life of many native Asiatic tribes to this day. Moreover, many of these tribes were once conquered by the Mongols and formed part of their nomadic Empire, and of the States into which the Empire split up. As a result of this they were subjected to Mongol influence, and it is interesting to investigate the effects of this influence on the laws of some of these non-Mongol tribes: the Tunguses, Yakuts, Kirghiz, Altais and Teleuts and others.

The well-known expert on Mongol law, Professor Leontovich,[61] expressed the opinion that Mongol law exercised great influence upon the laws of such Asiatic nomadic tribes as the Tunguses and Kirghiz,

61 Leontovich—"Mongol-Kalmuck Regulations on Punishments", 1879, pg. 238-9. "The existence among the Tunguses of the same type of tribal regulations as existed among the neighbouring Mongol tribes may be explained by their political dependence upon the later, from whom they, as subject tributaries, borrowed their tribal customs and regulations", *Ibid.* pg. 240. "It is undoubted that during the period of their subjection to the Mongols, the ancient Mongol regulations were effective among the Kirghiz, who were especially likely to adopt the order of things provided for by the Great Yassa of Jenghiz Khan (*Ibid.* 244).

but he did not produce any concrete proofs of his assertion, limiting himself to indicating and demonstrating the general similarity of the provisions of the laws of these tribes to provisions of Mongol law. Such treatment is not sufficient. Similarities in legal customs may arise from a common degree of cultural development, or they may represent independent developments from a common source. It is obvious that more concrete proofs are required.

The opinion of the writer on this point is as follows:

Of course Mongol law exercised its chief influence in the sphere of administration. Some of the nomadic tribes of Asia were destroyed by the Mongols. Others were forcibly subdued, while still others submitted of their own will. As a result, some of these tribes merged one with another, some were forced to change their territory, and others to change their chiefs and commanders, etc. Furthermore, all the nomadic tribes which entered the Mongol Empire were forced to submit to its State power and military-administrative organization (to enter the Tumens and Thousands of the Mongols, etc.),[62] as well as to observe the provisions of Mongol legislation. All this, however, had little effect upon the internal life of these nomads, which was chiefly regulated by local custom. At the same time, the customary law of the more unified and more cultured tribes inevitably influences the customs and law of less cultured tribes with which they may be in contact, or over which they rule. This fact is exemplified by the legal customs of the Mongol tribes. Although their common nomadic clan-patriarchal culture was the root causes of the identity or similarity of a whole series of institutions among the tribes named, it is nevertheless impossible to deny the direct influence of the law of the Mongol tribes upon the law of some other nomadic tribes of Asia.

A general comparison of the laws of the nomadic non-Mongol tribes of Asia with the law of the Mongol tribes reveals the similarity of many of their legal institutions and customs. But this similarity is not sufficient ground for conclusions concerning the inflence of one or another institution of one tribe upon those of another, or concerning the borrowing of legal customs between tribes. This general similarity may, in the first place, be explained by the general similarity of the culture of all of the above-named tribes. All of them: the Mongols, Buriats, Kalmucks, Tungus, Yakuts, Kirghiz, Altais and Teleuts are representatives of one and the same type of social organization: the nomadic clan-patriarchal organization. The similar legal institutions

62 We know from Rashid Ed-din that Jenghiz Khan organized his Tumens from separate large tribes under the command of their former (native) chiefs, or gave them new chiefs; but generally he left their internal organization untouched. In some cases, he built up mixed Tumens and thousands (*v. op. cit.*, XV. pg. 33. etc.)

had their origin in this similarity of culture, as, for example, the power of the clan chief, the absence (or the weak development) of the right of private ownership in immovables, and the use of land by clan unions chiefly for purposes of hunting and nomadic pastoral economy; the weak development of civil legal life., the patriarchate with the strong authority of the father—the lord of the household; polygamy; survivals of the purchase of wives in the form of the payment of Kalim; and several other institutions forming inevitable or usual attributes of this type of social organization. Consequently the influence of the stronger and the more cultured nomadic tribes on other nomadic tribes is to be sought not in the fundamental institutions of their similar culture, but amongst the less important and supplementary ones. But even in this case, given the resemblance of one or another set of customs, it is not always possible to speak of borrowing; it is possible that the occurrence of similar customs in the life of different tribes arises from their common origin or their common culture.

For instance, we saw above and we know that the Mongols encouraged certain altruistic deeds (the saving of human beings, animals and property from danger), and punished those who did not display such altruism for example when no help was rendered in times of danger from fire, water, wild beasts, etc. We meet this phenomenon in the Mongol—Oirat Regulations of 1640, in the Khalka Djirum, and in Buriat and Kalmuck law.[63] The same phenomenon could be observed amongst the Tunguses.

The customs of the Nerchinsk Tunguses (Art. 41)[64] contain the following regulation: "Anybody seeing anyone in fire or in water must immediately apply all his efforts and all the means at his disposal in order to free and save him. But should it be impossible to save him, then he must immediately notify the people near-by, no matter to which community they belong. Anyone who, seeing a man in such danger, makes no attempt to save him, will be beaten in accordance with law."

In both instances the phenomena are analogous, but it is difficult to speak here of borrowing. In both cases we see expressions of clan life and clan solidarity. The Tungus tribes, as well as the Mongol tribes, worked out measures for defence and increase in strength. The encouragement of altruistic deeds in the interests of the members of the clan and tribe was one such measure. Their school was the hunt and the campaign. In particular, amongst the Tungus, as among the Mongol tribes, beating of game was practiced and large hunts organized, and this was an excellent school for the development of the above qualities.

---

63 For further particulars, *v.* above page 223-225.

64 *v.* Samokvasov, "Collection of the Customary Laws of the Siberian Natives," 1876, ppg. 25-41.

Consequently, there are more grounds for speaking of the independent occurrence of analogous customs than for considering them as being borrowed: identical social reasons produced the same social results.

Let us take another example: Article 4 of the Ancient Code of the Hori Buriats (1781) and Art. 61 of the Steppe Code (of the Hori Buriats (1808) punished adultery with another's wife by flogging both the offenders and by taking a horse from the offender and giving it to the offended husband. We meet analogous provisions in Art. 6 of the Customs of the Nerchinsk Tunguses and in Art. 46 of the Customs of the Tunguses of the Department of Gantimurov,[65] both the parties guilty of adultery being punished with rods and the offender fined a horse in favour of the offended husband. This method of fining the offender a horse in favour of the offended husband did not arise from some common basis amongst the Buriats and the Tunguses, as in the first case, and was not met with amongst the other nomadic tribes.[66] It can be considered as borrowed. By whom and from whom? We suppose: by the Tunguses from the Buriats. From this it is possible to prove that the fine of a horse taken from the offender in favour of the husband in cases of adultery is an old Mongol custom. We meet this custom in the Ancient Tsaadjin Bichik (XVth. century) (Art. 3.) and in the customary law of Autonomous Mongolia. It is difficult to assume that the Tunguses of the XVth century, who were far away from Mongolia, especially from Western Mongolia, and who were weaker and less cultured than the Mongols, could, in this respect, influence the Ancient Tsaadjin Bichik and Mongol law in general. It is more natural to consider that ancient Mongol customs influenced Tungus law through the law of the Buriats.

Let us quote another example: To acquire wives by means of purchase was an ancient custom, and was connected with nomadic partiarchal culture. In a milder form this custom was practised among the nomadic tribes of Central Asia, e.g. in the payment of Kalim for the wife, a custom pertaining to all of the above-named tribes. Among the Buriats, however, a special form of marriage was developed (in deviation from the custom of paying Kalim)—the "Anda" marriage, or "mutual" marriage of the Southern Buriats (*cf.* St. C., 14, C. of Hor. B., VI, etc) or marriage "in exchange" of the Northern Buriats (C. of

---

65 *v.* The abovementioned Collection of Samokvasov, ppg. 25-41 and 43-66.

66 For example, among the Yakuts a man found guilty of adultery had, in addition to being flogged, to pay "dishonour" to the husband (a large property fine for the insult)—see Customs of the Yakuts, XVIII; among the Kirghiz the insulted husband received a maid from the offender and had the right to divorce his wife, but if he did not wish to do so, then both the offenders received corporal punishment (Customs of the Kirghiz—121).

For customs of the Yakuts see: Samokvasov, "Collection of the Customary Laws of the Siberian Natives", 1876, ppg. 199-243; *ibid*, The Customs of the Kirghiz ppg. 245-282.

Verkh. B., C. of Id. and other B., VI). Under this definition was understood the mutual marriage of two couples, from two families: a son of the first father with the daughter of the second, and a daughter of the first with the son of the second, i.e. a son and a daughter of one family with the son and the daughter of the second (son, grandson, nephew—daughter, granddaughter, niece, etc.). We meet this phenomeon also among the Tunguses. Art. 11, of "The Customs of the Tunguses of the Dept. of Gantimurov" reads: "It also happens that according to our faith the agreement can be concluded without payment of cattle, *in exchange,* when one takes from another a daughter for a son . . ." (cf. also supplement to the Customs of the Tunguses of the Dept. of Gantimurov, Par. 3). Thus the question arises as to what we have here: a borrowing or the independent occurrence of an analogous custom? Among the Buriats this custom was more developed and it was worked out fully in their juridical records. It was met with among the Southern and the Northern Buriats under different names. Among the Tunguses it was less developed and was met with only in the Customs of the Tunguses of the Dept. of Gantimurov, who were the neighbours of the Northern Buriats and among whom it bore the same name. Consequently this form of marriage was practised among the Buriats (Southern and Northern), while it was not to be met with in the customs of other nomadic tribes, except in the Dept. of Gantimurov, where these Tunguses lived next to the Northern Buriats and had constant intercourse with them, and among whom the above form of marriage had the same name as among the Northern Buriats. In view of the foregoing, we have to come to the conclusion that the Gantimurov Tunguses borrowed this form of marriage from the Northern Buriats.

We may notice such an influence of the customs of the stronger and more cultured Mongolian tribes on the customs of the less cultured Tungus tribes (the Tunguses of Nerchinsk and those of Gantimurov) in a whole succession of examples.

For example, Art. 40 of the Steppe Code embodies the regulation that a child of less than 8 years of age bears no responsibility for harm and damage inflicted by him, caused in the course of his games. "If a minor child should cause some grievance or damage in the course of his games, then if the child is less than 8 years of age such grievance or damage shall be left without consequences." (Art. 40 Steppe Code). We come across the same regulation in Art. 25 of the Customs of the Nerchinsk Tunguses. "If somebody's child, in the course of voluntary games, should cause damage or trouble, and if the said child should be less than 8 years of age, such damage or trouble shall be left unremedied" (Art. 25 of C. of Nerch. T.) Both these regulations are closely allied, and appear to repeat each other. Here we see that not only the age where there is no disposing capacity coincides, but also the same detail (reservation), viz., that the damage has to be caused in the course of the child's recreation. It is difficult to consider such coincidences as purely fortuitous. Evidently we are here dealing with borrowed customs.

The Steppe Code (Art. 48) and the Customs of the Nerchinsk Tunguses (Art. 29) respecting regulations of prescription are of the same nature.

"If there was an ancient debt due from someone and if there was a document respecting it, or witnesses, then it was necessary to recover it, even if 30 or 40 years had passed. But if there were no documents or witnesses, then such cases were to be decided within a priod of 15 years." (Steppe C., art. 48) "If someone has a debt due to him, even if 30 or 40 years have passed, but there is a written receipt and witnesses, when it can be recovered. But in case there is no letter or witnesses, there must be an investigation respecting it if more than 15 years have elapsed". (C. of Nerch. T., Art. 29) Even though the meaning of the end of the latter regulation is not quite clear, still there can be no doubt respecting the borrowing.

The Customs of the Hori Buriats: Chap. IX, Art. 13 embody provisions respecting found articles. If anyone found goods or money lost on the way, he had to notify the clan chief or the clansmen; if the owner was found, the finder received 1/10 of the value of the thing found; but if the owner was not found within a period of three years, the thing found became the property of the finder; if the finder concealed the fact of his finding, the article found had to be returned, and the finder was flogged, while the reward of 1/10 was given to the person proving the concealment.

The Customs of the Nerchinsk Tunguses, Art. 32, contain an analogous regulation, somewhat abbreviated: there is no indication of the three-year period. But here also the finder was entitled to 1/10 of the value of the thing found, and the concealment of the article found was also punished by corporal punishment and the person proving the concealment also received a reward of 1/10. Here, of course, it is impossible to establish a common basis of the 1/10 share reward for the finder[67] and the same reward to the person reporting the concealment. Here there is an evident borrowing of custom (with some omissions).

67 Amongst the Yakuts, the reward to the finder was sometimes as high as 1/4; amongst the Kirghiz—1/4 of the articles or 1/8 of the cattle, or what the owner gave (Cf. C. of Yakutz XVII, C. of Kir. Arts. 156, 157).

The Steppe Code, Art. 25., contained the following rule: If someone in possession of sharp-edged or pointed weapon rode on a horse, an ox, a waggon or a sled, and some person on foot asked the rider to take him along, and during the trip together the first suffered a bodily hurt or died, or the same occurred to his horse or ox, then 2/3 of all expenses were to be borne by the second, but if the second man died it was just his misfortune. But if the rider himself invited the pedestrian, and during their mutual travels the latter came to bodily harm, then the expenses were shared equally. We find an analogous provision in Art. 13 of the Customs of Nerchinsk Tunguses. Here also when the rider of the conveyance took along a pedestrian at the latter's request and received injuries or died, or his horse or ox died, then 2/3 of all the expenses had to be borne by the pedestrian; while if the latter died it was his own misfortune. If the rider himself invited the pedestrian and the latter received injuries, half the expenses had to be borne by the person inviting. The complete coincidence of the main regulations and their details indicate borrowing.

Of the same nature were art. 46 of the Steppe Code and art. 28 of the Customs of the Nerchinsk Tunguses. "If any man takes goods on credit against any security and names a term, and if at the designated time both of them will not be able to settle in accordance with the conditions previously laid down and shall apply to the court, then let all that there is be taken at the popular valuation and let him who has not paid his debt be severely punished with rods." (St. C., Art. 46). "If it so happen that anyone takes goods or any other thing for a definite period and after this period his debtor does not settle, and if the said case reaches the court, then let whatever he is found to possess be taken and given away at its real price, and also let him who has not paid his debt be flogged with rods." (C. of Nerch. Tung., Art. 28). The complete similiarity of these two provisions points to borrowing.

The Steppe Code, Art 33, contains the following provision "If a poor man takes away and eats the cattle of the rich man, without asking permission of the owner, and the latter finds this out and demands the cattle from the former, then the poor man may say that he ate the cattle because he was hungry and has nothing to return: 'What do you demand, that I should cut off my hands and feet and give them to you?' " If during the court investigation it is ascertained that the poor man who ate the cattle, previously showed it to the people and told them of the circumstances, he was punished by flogging and was forced to repay head for head. But if he ate the cattle without showing it to anyone, he was judged as a thief. An analogous regulation is to be found in the Customs of the Nerchinsk Tunguses, Art. 20. In this regulation the same concrete case was examined in the two possible variations (eating the cattle after notifying the community, or without doing so); and the same sanctions were applied as in Art. 33 of the Steppe Code. In the second regulation we even find the same phrase as in the first, when dealing with the cutting off of the hands and feet; but instead of the first person, the third person is used. The borrowing is evident.

The Customs of the Selenga Buriats, Art. 34., stated that when someone in a thieving manner shave wool off somebody else's cattle, the wool had to be returned and the culprit punished; in the event that a camel or some other animal was damaged through shearing, the culprit had to be reimbursed for the value of the animal and was to be punished as for stealing. We find an analogous provision in Art. 57 of the Customs of Tunguses of the Dept. of Gantimurov with the addition that if the sheared animal was a gravid she-camel, she was to be safe-guarded. It seems that we have here a borrowing of the original custom with the addition of a secondary detail.

Thus, we have presented about ten Buriat customs which we find repeated amongst the Tunguses. Moreover, we presented only such customs, in which not only the basic principles closely coincide, but also the secondary details. This, taken as a whole gives us the right to speak not of the coincidence of such customs, but of borrowings by the Tunguses from the more powerful and the more cultured Buriat clans. which influenced them greatly both through conquest and close neighbourhood.

But we have to stress that we have not, by far, made use of all the material at our disposal. For example, the regulations of Art. 69 of the Steppe Code and of Art. 52 of the Customs of the Gantimurov Tunguses (respecting giving cattle into another's herd) are analogous, as are Arts. 29 and 30 of the Customs of the Selenga Buriats and Art. 49 of the Customs of the Gantimurov Tunguses (on the finding of cattle which had been torn asunder by wolves); Art. 39 of the Steppe Code and Art. 24 of the Customs of the Nerchinsk Tunguses (on the giving up of a son to be brought up by somebody else); Art. 91 of the Steppe Code and Art. 67 of the Customs of the Gantimurov Tunguses (respecting giving up a daughter to be brought up by some body else); Art. 31 of the Steppe Code and Art. 18 of the Customs of the Nerchinsk Tunguses (respecting the adoption of a grandson); Art. 4 of the Hipp Toktogol of 1788, and Art. 9 of the C. of T. Gantimurov (on the death of a bridesroom before marriage); Art. 30 of the Steppe Code and Art. 17 of the Customs of the Nerchinsk Tunguses (on escheats): Arts 8, 9, 10 of the Ancient Code of 1781, Arts. 50, 51 of the Steppe Code; and Arts. 1, 2, 3, of the Ancient Customs of the Tunguses (XVIIIth century) on theft.

In the same way, we consider it necessary to mention that apart from the above, similar customs exist amongst the Buriats and the Tunguses, the origin of which amongst the Tunguses may be explained not only by borrowings from the Buriats but also by other causes, in particular by independent origin due to the similarity of cultures. Compare, for example, the provisions of Arts. 31, and 44 of the Customs of the Nerchinsk Tunguses, Art. 42, 50, and 81 of the Customs of the Gantimurov Tunguses with the analogous Arts. 63, 17, 52, 66 and 109 of the Horin Steppe Code of 1808.

Thus, on the basis of the material we have examined above, we come to the conclusion that the customs and law of the Mongol, and in particular the Buriat, tribes have to a considerable extent influenced the customs and law of the Tungus tribes, which were long subject to the Mongols and later lived in close neighbourhood with them and were under their influence.[68]

We shall now proceed to the Altais and the Teleuts. These Turki peoples were, for a considerable period of time, subject to the Western Mongols or Oirats and subsequently lived in close neighbourhood with them. Travellers (e.g. Potanin) who have described the customs of the Altais and Teleuts pointed to the similarity of the latter to those of the Mongols, and to the influence the Oirat customs had on them. At the present time we do not have at our disposal detailed materials pertaining to the customs of these tribes. But from the available information we can come to the conclusion that the influence of Oirat customs upon those of the Altais and Teleuts was undoubtedly present.[69]

Thus, for instance, there existed from of old among the Mongols, besides the division into thousands, hundreds and tens, also the division into forties (Docin) and scores (Horin). This division is referred to in the Mongol-Oirat Regulations of 1640, and the Russians came across it during their conquest of the Buriats in the XVIIth century. It was long retained by the Oirats and, as was pointed out by Academician Vladimirtzov, it passed from them to the Altais and Teleuts.[70] The Altais preserved this division into Töcün (forties) until the most recent times.

68 Of the great influence of Buriat culture on the Tunguses we may judge from the following data. According to the census of 1897, no less than 4,878 Transbaikal Tunguses (more than 15% of all the Tunguses in the Transbaikal region) spoke Buriat as their native tongue and knew no other language. Of the Buriats in the region, only two had Tungus as their native tongue (*v.* Serebrennikov, "The Buriats", 1925, pg. 13, note 2). After a consideration of such data it should be easy to understand the strong influence of Buriat culture and law on the culture and law of the Tungus tribes (and not *vice versa*).

69 *v.* the writer's article, "Some Characteristics of the Customary Law of the Altais and Teleuts", *Monitor of Chinese Law*, Harbin, 1931, No. 3.

70 "Social Organization of the Mongols", pg. 170, note 4.

Furthermore it is well known that the Mongols do not bury their dead deep in the ground but turn them over to Nature—as by placing the coffin in a field and either not burying it at all or covering it with a thin layer of earth; and also by suspending the bodies of the dead from trees or burning them. The Turki tribes, on the other hand, usually bury their dead. The Altais and Teleuts dispose of their dead in accordance with the Mongol Custom, i.e. they turn them over to Nature. Because of this the violation of graves was not considered a dire crime among the Mongols, and the same applied to the Altais and Teleuts.

Furthermore, among the Mongols marriage fell into three separate stages, having different juristic consequences and divided from each other by considerable periods of time. First came betrothal, which often took place while the bride and groom were still infants; then the agreement, when they had grown and the Kalim was paid; and the marriage itself (the marriage ceremony). Among the Altais and Teleuts also we find precisely the same procedure with respect to marriage: The betrothal (Kuda); the agreement (Yargashtik) and marriage (Ton), with each of these stages having the same significance as among the Mongols.[71] Some of their marriage customs and rituals, as described by Potanin and Efimova, bore a resemblance to those of the Western Mongols.[72]

Thus we come to the conclusion that the customs of the Altais and Teleuts were undoubtedly under the influence of those of the Mongols, and that possibly such influence was considerable.

With respect to the relation of the customs and laws of the Kirghiz to Mongol law, we may say in this connection that it is necessary to bear in mind the following circumstance: The Kirghiz are a big people, more numerous than the Mongols. There was a time when they formed part of the Empire of Jenghiz Khan,[73] and later one of its Western Oolooses (the Kipchak, or Golden Horde). After the fall of the latter they developed a historical existence independently of the Mongols.

The Kirghiz entered into the composition of the Kipchak Ooloos of the Mongols, or the Golden Horde, in which the Yassa of Jenghiz Khan was effective. After the disintegration of the Horde in the XVth century they continued their historical existence independently of the Mongols. Thus they retained the effectiveness of the Great Yassa and

71 *Cf.* Samokvasov, "Collection of Customary Laws", Pg. 2.

72 *v.* Potanin, "Outlines of Northwestern Mongolia", 1883, vol. IV; also the compendium, "Materials on the Marriage and Clan-Family Life of the Peoples of the U.S.S.R.", articles by Efimova and Dyrenkova.

73 The original submission of the Kirghiz to the Mongols was voluntary, but later they rebelled and were conquered and included in the Ooloos of Juchi. *v.* Rashid Ed-din, *op. cit.* XIV,131; XV,115, etc.

the severe ancient law of the Mongols, but did not come under the influence of the later tendency of this law to become milder (in the XVIth and XVIIth cent.). And indeed, the ancient laws of the Kirghiz (promulgated by Khan Tevka in the XVIIth century on the basis of ancient folk customs) was closest of all to the law of the Great Yassa, as was correctly noted by Professor Leontovich.[74] Thus we often meet here the application of the death penalty which was imposed for murder, robbery, theft, abduction of the wife of another, rape, mixed mariage, and adultery. Parents were not punished for killing their children, etc.[75] Of course, it is now impossible to determine the exact extent of the direct influence exercised by the Great Yassa on ancient Kirghiz law. But at the same time it is difficult to imagine that three centuries of subjection to the Mongols, a people of the same nomadic clan-patriarchal culture as themselves, could have failed to affect the law of the Kirghiz. Indeed, the provisions of old Kirghiz law recall those of the ancient law of the Mongols not only in their general (severe) character (as was already painted out by Leontovich) but also in the case of some separate provisions. Thus, according to old Kirghiz law (as distinct from the laws of other Asiatic nomadic tribes), a husband finding his wife in adultery had the right to kill her on the spot (Art. 9). Article 1 of the Great Yassa also provided for the death penalty for adultery, and if we take into account the spirit of ancient Mongol law, such punishment must have been imposed in cases of *flagrant delit* (this being confirmed by Plano Carpini, *op. cit.*, pg. 15). The old author Petis de la Croix (in his "Abbregé Chronologique de l'histoire Ottomane", 1768) quotes this fragment in the following version: "Adultery is punished by death. Persons guilty of this crime may be killed on the spot." This immediate killing of an adulterous wife taken *in flagrant delit* was preserved, apart from ancient Mongol law, only in old Kirghiz law. More than this, in the Customs of the Kirghiz of the XIXth century (Art. 123) the adultery of a single man with a maid was punished with death (if he refused to marry her).[76] No similar punishment was met with among the other Asiatic nomadic tribes, but the same penalty existed among the ancient Mongols (*v.* Fr. 1 of the Great Yassa; Plano Carpini, *op. cit.* pg. 15).

Death was the punishment for theft of a horse among the ancient Mongols, but it was replaced by payment of a ninefold fine by the thief

74 *v.* "Ancient Mongol-Kaluck Regulations on Punishments", 1879, 245.

75 For more details *v.* Levshin—Description of Kirghiz-Kaisak Hordes and Steppes, vol. III, pgs. 170-178. A French edition (1842) also exists.

76 The punishment for adultery with a married woman had already been changed in the XIXth century. The husband, in such cases, had the right to divorce the guilty wife and to receive a maid from the adulterer without paying Kalim for her. If, however, the husband did not want a divorce, the wife was subjected to corporal punishment (C. of Kir., art. 121).

(*cf.* Fr. 29 of the Great Yassa). According to ancient Kirghiz law theft was also punished by death or the payment of a fine of thrice nine times the value of the stolen property (*v.* Art. 2, 17) while for a smaller theft, as for instance the theft of a horse, the fine was 9 horses; and for thefts not exceeding the value of 1 horse the fine was 1 nine of cattle (C. of Kir., 133, 135, 149). Here the characteristic feature is not only the coincidence of the penalty—death, and the alternative payment of ransom, but also the reckoning of that ransom in nines or twenty-sevens.

Let us consider one more example:

As we have seen above, there existed among the Mongols from ancient times the custom of property fines in nines of cattle. We came across this institution already in the Yassa of Jenghiz Khan (v. Fr. 29). The punitive systems of the Mongol-Oirat Regulations of 1640 and the Khalkha Djirum were based on it. We also meet these institutions among the Kirghiz (*v.* Arts. 23, 28, 69, 131, 135, 141, 147, 149 and 189 of The Customs of the Kirghiz)—apparently under the influence of the Mongols. Naturally, we may suppose that among the Kirghiz the fine in nines of cattle was also an ancient (and independent) custom, just as it was among the Mongols. But in such a case the custom would have the character of a basic custom in the system of property punishments among the Kirghiz, or at least be on the same standing with the other customs. However, the basic customary unit of property fines amongst the Kirghiz was the "Koon" (100 horses, 2 servants, 2 camels, 2 suits of armour). A Koon or half a Koon was employed as the usual basic punishment; while fines by nines of cattle, or alternatively by units of 27 head of cattle were met with as additional punishment, where the Koon system was employed (v., for instance Arts. 23 & 28 of the Customs of the Kirghis)[77] and were applied alone only in the less important cases, when the punishment did not exceed 27 heads of cattle. This gives ground for the belief that the ancient basic institution of property fines among the Kirghiz was the Koon and not the fine by nines of cattle; and that the latter method was employed as an additional or supplementary punishment. The subordinate secondary position that fines by nines of cattle assumed among the Kirghiz forces us to consider that it was not an ancient national institution and was of later origin than the Koon. This gives ground for supposing that it originated from the times when the Kirghiz formed a part of the Mongol Oolooses in which property fines were imposed in nines of cattle.

77 Art. 23 states: "Whoever wounds another fatally before the judges or kills him must pay a full Koon; while to the judge, for disrespect to him, he must pay nine different animals including one camel".

Art. 28: "Whoever kills a judge must pay a full Koon, and besides this . . . . 8 different animals and one Kalmuck of the male sex."

The Kirghiz also borrowed from Mongols the *tamga*—brands put on the movable clan property.[78]

In respect to the Yakuts, it is necessary to bear in mind the following fact: the Yakuts inhabiting the Northern fringe of Central Asia in ancient times comprised a part of the Empire of the Mongols[79] and were forced to retreat from the South by the Mongol tribes approximately in the XIVth or XVth centuries, thenceforth having very little intercourse with the latter. However, some of the Yakuts regulations concerning theft, divorce and the payment of Kalim show common characteristics with the corresponding regulations of the Buriats.

Thus, art. 8 of the Ancient Code of the Hori Buriats (1781) provides that "for the theft of cattle, the so-called Yal is enforced, which rules that for each stolen head of cattle three more of the same kind, from 2 to 4 years old, must be given. Moreover, the culprit is liable to corporal punishment."[80]

According to the Customs of the Idinsk and Balagansk Buriats four head of cattle had to be given for each stolen head (supplemented by corporal punishment in case of second theft—C. of Bal & Id. B., V, 1), while third theft was punished by exile (*Ibid.*).

The Customs of the Yakuts contain analogous provisions. Thus anyone committing theft for the first time paid four similar animals for every head of cattle stolen, while if the stolen animal was recovered alive, he returned it and paid three others, also compensating the owner for any losses suffered; and thieves who had previously committed any evil actions were subjected to corporal punishment (C. of Yak., XVI, 3), for the second theft flogging was obligatory, and after the third theft the culprit was considered incorrigible and banished (*Ibid.*, 4). Not only the basic rule that cattle thieves were to be punished by fines in cattle (Yal) and the amount of the multiple fine were identical among both the Buriats and Yakuts, but also the supplementary details.

Furthermore, the Steppe Code of the Hori Buriats (art. 51) stated: "If anyone commit theft of goods or anything else and the stolen articles are not found, the thief must be forced to pay the actual value of the goods and be severely flogged with the knout." In the Customs of the Selenga Buriats (Chapter I, art. 5) we find the following provision in this connection: "If anyone steal anything from another and the theft be uncovered, the articles are to be returned in

78 *v.* Levshin. Description of the Kirghiz-Kaisak Hordes and Steppes, V. III, 1832, pg. 135.

79 In the Yakut sagas the name of their tzar Jenghiz is sometimes mentioned (Seroshevsky).

80 *v.* Riasanovsky-"Customary Law of the Mongol Tribes", 1929 pg. 157.

kind, but if the article has been used up let it be evaluated and let the cost be collected from the thief who is moreover to be dealt with in accordance with the first paragraph.[81] And if the owner of the article has borne any losses as a consequence of the theft, these are, in accordance with the circumstances and justice, to be collected from the thief."

Analogous provisions are found in Yakut law: "For money and things the thief pays not fourhold but the value of what was stolen, with the losses which as a result of his theft have been suffered by the owner of the stolen money and goods; besides this he is punished corporally by rods, irrespective of whether the amount stolen is small or great." (C. of Yak., XVI, 5).

From the data given one may see the close resemblance, almost identity, of the Buriat and Yakut provisions regarding theft which forces us to assumed that borrowing took place, borrowing by the Yakuts from the Buriats. This is confirmed by the fact that the Buriats were the more cultured and stronger tribe as well as by the following data. In the ancient law of the Tunguses (XVIIIth century) we find analogous provisions regarding theft, i.e. cattle thieves were obliged to pay fourfold for stolen cattle and were punished with rods, while a thief stealing other articles was obliged to return them or replace their value, being also punished with rods.[82] Thus we find the same provisions regarding theft among the Buriats, Tunguses and Yakuts. It is evident that they stemmed from one and the same source. The only such common source could be Mongol and, more particularly, Buriat law, in which the Yal was the basic and most widespread punishment, met with in the XVIIIth and XIXth centuries among both the Northern and the Southern Buriats. The Tunguses borrowed this custom (with other customs) from the Buriats (*v.* above) and it came to the Yakuts through their Tungus neighbours as well as directly from the Buriats.

Other provisions analogous among the Yakuts and Buriats are those relating to divorce. Here we meet the possibility of divorce by unilateral desire, not only of the husband but also of the wife, as well as analogous provisions governing the return of property. For instance, according to the Customs of the Selenga Buriats, if the divorce transpired as a result of the husband's reluctance to continue living with his wife, he had not the right to demand the return of his Kalim and was obliged to send away his wife "with good clothing and outfitting." (C. of Sel. B., 49). The same applied to divorce resulting from cruelty on the part of the husband (*Ibid.* 42). We find analogous provisions

81 Punishment by rods (*v.* art. 1) and, in case of inability to pay, compulsory service (art. 4).
82 Leontovich, *op. cit.*, pg. 142, arts. 1, 2.

among the Yakuts: "A husband leaving his wife without any cogent motive does not receive his Kalim but, on the contrary, gives her her dowry, clothing and apparel, ornaments and things; this right is also possessed by a wife leaving her husband as a result of cruel or bad treatment." (XIV, 5).

On the basis of the above, we reach the conclusion that the law of the Mongol tribes to a certain extent influenced not only the military-administrative organization of the Yakuts, but also their private and criminal law.

Thus, in briefly reviewing the foregoing, we must stress the following points:

The influence of the Mongols on the other nomadic tribes of Asia was in those times considerable in the military and administrative spheres. The influence of the Mongol tribes was also felt in the internal life of these peoples (their private and criminal law). But we must bear in mind that the influence of the customs and law of the Mongol tribes on the customs and law of some of the nomadic tribes of Asia (*e.g.* the Tunguses and the Altais) was considerable, while in the case of other tribes (*e.g.* the Kirghiz and Yakuts) it was apparently not so great but considerably less.

Further we may point to the resemblance of some of the customs of the Tartars of the province of Tomsk to the corresponding customs of the Mongols, *e.g.* marriage customs, the killing of horses at funerals, etc. (Samokvasov, *op. cit.*, ppg. 8-9) and also the resemblance between certain of the customs of the Ostyaks, Samoyeds and Voguls of the province of Tobolsk and some Mongol customs (such as the reckoning of relationship, customs relating to divorce, the giving of brides in return for labour service, etc.—Samokvasov, *op. cit.*, ppg. 19-20). The native tribes mentioned above were once part of the Ooloos of Juchi, and Mongol influence is quite possible. However, owing to the absence at the disposal of the Author of sufficient relevant material, it is not possible for him to state definitely that Mongol customs influenced those of the abovementioned native tribes and that the resemblance was not simply a result of parallel development.

Of course the examples here given do not exhaust the available material on this question. They represent only some surviving remnants of the once great influence of Mongol law upon the law of other nomadic peoples.

It has been stated above that in the opinion of Professor M. Kovalevsky the original model of the clan organization of these nomads is to be sought in Mongolia and Manchuria where it was most ancient, and that the clan organization of the Mongols was one of the most ancient and fundamental in Asia (see above, Chapter IV, ppg. 257, 258). Moreover, we have stated that the military-administrative organization of the Mongols connected with their clan organization reached its highest development in the Empire of Jenghiz Khan, was applied fully by Tamerlane, and left survivals which were until the most recent times evident among the Mongols, Buriats, Kalmucks, Altais and Teleuts. From the last sections of this chapter we have also seen that Mongol law found application not only in the Great Mongol Empire and the separate States into which this Empire disintegrated, but also in the State of Tamerlane, exercising, moreover, its chief influence on the laws of the nomadic tribes of Asia both in the past and in the present.

As a result of this, and on the basis of his study of the laws of the peoples of Eastern Asia, the Author has come to the conclusion that in this part of the continent there existed two fundamental systems of law: the system of Chinese law and the system of Mongol law. The first was a system of settled law created for an agricultural people. The second represented the law of a nation of cattle-breeders and hunters. Chinese law greatly influenced the laws of neighbouring settled peoples, for example in Korea, Japan, Annam, etc., and also, to a certain extent, the laws of some nomadic peoples. Mongol law, on the other hand, exercised its chief influence on the laws of the nomadic peoples which once formed part of the Empire of Jenghiz Khan and his successors and later of the Empire of Tamerlane, as well as on the law of the modern Buriats, Tunguses, Kirghiz, Altais, Kalmucks etc. Besides this, it had a certain influence on the laws of some settled peoples. The first system of law was richer in content, being the expression of a higher culture; the second was poorer in content, just as the culture of the nomads was poor. But it is necessary to recognize that these two systems of law were totally distinct and arose from different cultural bases: one from a settled agricultural way of life and the other from a nomadic pastoral economy. Just as China developed the fundamental institutions of settled agricultural law and culture in the Far East which later greatly influenced the culture and law of other, chiefly settled peoples, so the Mongols developed the fundamental institutions of nomadic pastoral culture and law, exercising great influence on the culture and law chiefly of the nomadic tribes of Asia.

APPENDIX.

COLLECTION OF THE LAWS OF KHALKHA "KHALKHA DJIRUM."[1]

"We worship the supreme Lama, our refuge and salvation, who concentrates (within himself) all the Buddhas of the ten lands; who is filled with the best omens; who nourishes with the seeds of the Teaching all living things; who has a pleasant voice and the heart of Bodhi which guides all things with impartial compassion!

"May the life of the High Lama, the crown of all living things, be everlasting as the diamond! May the Faith spread! May the lives of the charitable who exalt it be prolonged! May the State and Faith flourish! Let there not be heard even the name of evil things! Let the heart be tranquillised and good deeds multiply like a constantly running stream!

"After they had reported the matter to the dowager Khanna and she had given her consent, all the Noyons and Saits with Vachirai Tushetu Khan at their head[2] .... (gathered) on the Southern side of Burin-Khan mountain in the valley of the river Ibin-Gol, in the year of the Earthen Cow on the 28th day of the midsummer moon, on a good and favourable day, and did discuss (promulgate) the present Great Statute of the Three Hoshuns.[3]

Articles from the Great Statute of the Three Hoshuns.

(Published in the year of the Earthen Cow, 1709).

CHAPTER I.

ON THE MESSENGERS OF THE HUTUKHTU GEGEN.

Art. 1. Wherever the Hutukhtu Gegen may go let him have horses (carts-Ulaga) and victuals (Shigusu) without limitation, as was settled by the Seven Hoshuns some time ago.

In case of refusal of a cart and provisions, all the property (of the offender) shall be confiscated for the treasury (of the Gegen), and as for the offenders and their lives—let them remain at the disposal of their Noyon.

Art. 2. Should Noyons themselves refuse carts and provisions, let 300 head of cattle be taken from their personal herds.

---

1 In view of the fact that the Khalkha-Djirum has never been published, the Author considers it necessary to present to the readers a translation of some excerpts from the code, so that they may form some idea of its general aspect.

2 Here follows a long list of persons participating in the drafting of the code, which is omitted.

3 This is a translation of the preamble to the Great Statute of the Three Hoshuns of 1709 (Barun Kuren copy).

Should the Noyon turn out to be poor and his cattle not reach 100 in number, then let up to 100 cattle be taken from his subjects and given up, on the basis of 50 horses and 50 head of horned cattle—the age of all to be four years.

Should a Taidji or Tabunang refuse, let all his personal cattle be confiscated. But if he be poor and the number of his cattle not reach 50, let it be supplemented by the cattle of his son on the basis of 25 horses and 25 head of horned cattle—the age of all to be four years (Hidzalan).

Should anyone refuse cartage and provisions on the plea of absence, then they must be forced to take the oath—a Noyon for a Noyon, and for a Haratzu—one of the Saits by election.

Art. 3. Wherever a messenger of the Hutukhtu may go, he has 10 carts and 2 Shigusu (i.e. two sheep). However, out of respect for the words of the Gegen who said: "Do not kill any living thing, yet also do not remain hungry for the night", no animal should be killed on the pretext that it is needed as provision for a messenger travelling under the orders of the Gegen, yet also the messenger must not be left hungry for the night..

Should anyone refuse a cart or provisions, then (let him be fined) three nines (of cattle).

If the messenger is driving the Gegen's property (cattle) he can use them in the measure of necessity for himself and his baggage. If he uses them beyond this, let the messenger be fined three nines; and the extent of each nine is to be 4 Boda, and 5 sheep. At the head of the Boda (large cattle) must be a Hidzalan (four-year-old).

A runner (messenger, summons-server) has 2 carts. For the night the householder must give him food, at his own discretion and whatever is available. If he does not provide him with provisions then (let him be fined) 1 Hul (Kul or Hul, a leg or rump), the size of the Hul to be 1 Shidulen (i.e. three-year-old).

Should anyone refuse a cart and provisions—(he is to be fined) a five, the extent of the five to be 2 Shidulen (3-year-old) horses or horned cattle, and 3 Shidulen sheep.

If anyone refuse a cart and provisions to these two messengers, on the pretext that he does not have them, then the Daruga of the Otok is to be put to the oath.

Art. 3. If anyone drive horses away from the paddock of a messenger (Elchi), then, however many offenders there may be, let there be taken from each the horse on which he rode together with the saddle, and also:

If the offender be a Noyon, one five. Be he a commoner (Haratzu) let him be given 50 Tashurs (strokes of the knout).

If the horses they are riding turn out to belong to others, then the truth must be established by means of the oath and the proper (his own) horse taken from the offender.

Art. 5. If anyone, hearing of the approach of an Elchi, drive away his herds with the aim of avoiding (the levy), a three-year-old horse must be taken from each such owner.

The Aldangi (fine for neglect, a mistake or accidental misdeed) is to be delivered to the treasury of the Noyon to whose Elchi performance of the duty was avoided.

As concerns the compensation (Ideshi) to the messenger of an official, it is the same; as regards the Ideshi of a victimised messenger, this is at discretion of his master.

(Otherwise: "As concerns refusal of provisions .... etc.)

If people with the status of Tarkhan present as their own cattle which belong to people liable to the levy of cartage and thus unfairly defend them, then such Tarkhans must be fined a Hidzalan (four-year-old) horse; while a person concealing his herd in the herd of a Tarkhan is liable to the same punishment as that meted out for concealing one's cattle from a messenger.

If any man should say that he is an Elchi of the Gegen and thus use Ulaa (carts) and Shigusu (provisions) and if he should falsely invoke a Dzarlik (ukase), this is to be treated as equivalent to cases of refusal of carts and provisions during the journeyings of the Gegen himself.[4])

The Great Statute of 1728.

May the paths of the Supreme Lama, the concentration of all saviours, be firm!

He incessantly does good for the holy faith and living beings!

May the lives of the highly-placed connected with his teaching be prolonged!

May they bring happiness to all by their administration and righteous deeds!

May they spend days and nights in good deeds!

May all their deserving wishes fulfil themselves!

May they never hear the name of evil deeds!

And may happiness descend on all life spent in pure and proper well-doing!

---

4 The above is a translation of the first chapter of the record described above (on ppg. 57-58). under the number I.

In the year of the Earthen Monkey called "Kalika" ("Kalaya" in the MS.), on an auspicious day of the mid-autumn moon—Vachirai Batu Tushetu Khan, assistant to the commander of the troops of the left flank of the Khalkha Chiang Chun Wang, and other Djassaks (ruling princes) met at the Order of the Highest at the arrow (confluence) of the Orkhon and Tola and compiled the present Great Statute.

If any man commit theft (robbery), let all the thieves, whatever their number, be confined for one year (in a well), the earth being dug to a depth and width of 4 Aldans (1 Aldan = 2 metres) in each direction.

The wife, children yurt and cattle of the chief thief are all to be confiscated and given to the owner of the (stolen) cattle.

The lesser thieves are to be fined 3 nines of Boda each.

After the release of the thieves from the well they are each to be given 100 Tashur and forced to collect firewood for three years. . . . In cases of full confiscation (Talahu - to ruin) and fines, a portion of the thief's property is to be left him.

The composition of a nine shall be: 2 horses, 2 cows, 2 three-year-olds (of horned cattle) and 1 yearling calf (Biragu, Burun in Siberia).

From a thief condemned to full confiscation there shall be taken for court costs (Gargagu) 1 selected (animal) and 4 four-year-old horses.

For the Tushimels and Elchis there shall be reserved 1 five-year-old horse and 1 four-year-old.

From the amount due from an accused second thief (i.e. accomplice) of 3 nines of cattle there shall be reserved for court costs: 1 horse, 1 bull, 1 cow, 2 three-years-olds, and 1 Burun. Of them there shall be reserved for court costs proper—1 horse, 1 cow and 1 three-year-old; and 1 Burun shall be divided between themselves by the Tushimels and Elchis as a fee.

However many three-nines (27's) there may be, this rule must be followed with respect to each three-nines. And whatever the quantity of the fine (Yal) the Hoshun Elchi of the guilty (wrong) party must not receive more than 1 three-year-old.

If a man have insufficient (property) for (the payment of) the fine, it is necessary that the fine be paid by taking his wife and children into the accounting. And if the Noyon or kinsmen of the guilty one shall wish to ransom (substitute for) him, then the price shall be in accordance with the Old Statute.[5]).

---

5 The above is a translation from the record described on pg. 58 of the present work under the number V.

Articles of the Statute of 1709.

ON MARRIAGE AND INHERITANCE.

One more article: If a Noyon give a princess (Abai) in marriage to aTabunang who is already married to a princess, then from this Noyon shall be taken (he shall be forced to pay) Baa of 10 camels and 100 horses. And this Baa (voluntary fine) shall be taken (in favour of) the Administration.

Furthermore: If a ruling Noyon himself and in his own Hoshun give his princess in marriage to a Tabunang already married to a princess, then from the ruling Noyon shall be taken Baa of 15 camels and 150 horses. And this Baa is to be given to the Djassaks (ruling princes) participating in the compilation of this Statute of the Three Hoshuns. As for the Tabunang, he shall be fined 5 nines. And this cattle (taken as a fine) shall be given to the previous princess. She must return to her parents, taking away the dowry (Indji) which she brought with her.

One more article: If a princess shall herself, of her own will, marry a Tabunang married to a princess ("marry to a princess"—i.e. when the wife is living), then the second princess must be taken away and the Tabunang fined 5 nines. The cattle (taken as a fine) is to be delivered to the Administration. If his Djassak, knowing (this) beforehand, shall attempt to conceal it, let the ruling princes of the Three Hoshuns divided this cattle among themselves.

If a Tabunang abandon a princess, he must go away with only a whip in his hands; and the princess, having taken her dowry, must dispose of herself in her Hoshun. All the cattle and property confiscated from the Tabunang must be divided in half, and one half is to be taken to the Administration and the other given to the princess.

Furthermore: If anyone take himself to wife a woman of common degree (Haratzu) when he himself is married to a princess, let this woman be taken away and her commoner father be ruined (have all his property confiscated), while the Tabunang is to be given 80 strokes of the Tashur without (the alternative of) ransom. If a princess insulted in marriage shall leave a Tabunang (divorce him), then the commoner wife he takes afterwards shall be taken away and the rest of the fine (Yal) be as prescribed. As for the princess, having taken her dowry and her herds and Yurt, let her dispose of herself in her Hoshun.

Furthermore: If Noyons, among themselves, take from each other their respective betrothed brides, then the fine shall be 3 families (households—Eruké) of people and 300 Andzo. Of these three families one is to be taken by choice, but not from amongst officials, while the other families let the Noyon give at his discretion. The betrothed (bride) taken away is to be removed.

One more article: If within the limits of the Three Hoshuns a Noyon shall take the betrothed bride of a man of common degree (Haratzu), let him give him one camel and an unbetrothed maid from his Hoshun (to wife) by choice (of the man whose betrothed bride has been taken).

One more article: If a Novon go in to a princess (commit adultery) this is equivalent to violation of betrothal (i.e. the taking by a Noyon of the betrothed bride of another Noyon) between Noyons. If he have not sufficient for the Andzo, then let him himself be taken.

If a Noyon go in to the wife of a commoner, he shall be fined 50 Andzo.

If a man of common degree (Haratzu) go in to a princess, all his property shall be confiscated and he himself made a slave of a slave in the Hoshun. The position of Hatuns (Hatun—princess, the wife of a prince) and Abais (Abai—princess, the daughter of a prince) shall be the same.

Furthermore: If a man of common degree go in to the wife of another commoner, he is to be fined 300 Andzo with 30 rare things (Berké) at their head. If he has not sufficient (for the Andzo), he shall receive for each Boda 25 Tashurs, but the total number of strokes shall not exceed 100. The abduction of the wife or daughter of another (forcing her to run away) shall be considered equivalent to entering into carnal connection with the wife of another ("to going in to another's wife"). If anyone lay hold of the corner of a blanket—then 3 nines. If a woman crawls in to a man—3 nines.

Furthermore: If a Noyon, after the performance of the Horim (marriage feast) of his daughter, give her in marriage to another Tabunang, the fine shall be 55 Andzo with 5 rare things at their head. If the Horim has not yet been performed, he must return the cattle previously given.

Furthermore: If a Noyon give in marriage to another man the wife of a man of common degree who has had a Horim, then let him first inform the Noyon of that man who had the Horim. If he shall give her in marriage without warning, then she is to be returned to the original man having the Horim. If he does not return her, let him give Andzo of 100 animals (i.e. 100 head of cattle).

If anyone take to himself a maiden betrothed to another, having falsely declared to the Noyon that she was not betrothed, then she shall be taken away and given to her original betrothed (fiance). And half of the property and cattle of the liar shall be confiscated.

One more article: If a man of common degree (Haratzu) will betroth a princess who is the daughter of a man of Khan rank, then such betrothal shall only be recognized as valid if the betrothal gifts comprise: a white camel with a silver plate on its nose (Mongon Builatai), a white horse with a halter (trappings—Montzuk), a silver cup filled with wine (Araki) and a pearl without flaws (Subad Erdeni—a pearl of great price).

Furthermore: If Noyons shall betroth the daughters of Tabunangs, let such betrothals be considered valid when there are delivered: a silver cup, a pearl and wine. If these are absent, the betrothal must not be recognized.

Furthermore: If persons of common degree shall be betrothed among themselves, then let such betrothals be considered valid when there is (brought) wine and all the entrails of a sheep with the horns and hooves. And let it be recognized as valid when there are witnesses and the witnesses know this. But if there be no witnesses or should the witnesses not know it, it must not be recognized.

Generally: The terms of pregnancy of cattle given to a man giving a woman in betrothal: for camels—the last summar month, for mares—the last winter month, for cows—the last autumn month and for sheep—the mid-autumn month. In these months they may be considered pregnant (i.e. their pregnancy may be verified).

Generally: If anyone, having betrothed a woman and received the cattle due him (Kalim), will not give his daughter in marriage during many years, and a separation (annulment of the betrothal) comes about on the initiative of the father of the maid, then he must return all the cattle for one (the past) year, and of that cattle which he received two years before he must return a half with increase (i.e. with young for each animal—Holbogatai). If three years and more have passed he must return all the cattle with their increase.

If a betrothal is annulled (a couple is separated) at the instance of the father of the bridegroom, he must take (back) only the cattle which he has given. A year consists of 12 months.

One more article: If a betrothed bridegroom or a betrothed bride dies before the marriage, the cattle given is to be taken back.

One more article: If anybody takes a wife without giving cattle (Kalim), entering (the family of the bride's parents) in the capacity of a worker son-in-law, but later himself betrays (them) and leaves, then let him give (his wife and her parents) 10 Boda and 30 sheep. And if he himself does not wish to go but his Noyon demands him insistently, then he must give 8 Boda and 20 sheep, the children not being ransomed. When he himself has betrayed, sons follow their father, and if there be girls (daughters), then let him ransom each girl (daughter) for 2 Boda.

One more article: If a Noyon give in marriage the wife (widow) of a dead man, then let this woman divide her cattle between her sons, whatever their number, and her new husband equally according to the number of souls, and let her children go out to their service (i.e. separate themselves to become independent taxable units). But if (she marries) without the permission (mandate) of the Noyon, then let her go forth with (only) a whip (Tashur) in her hand.

Furthermore: Elder and younger Djige cannot be accused in relation to their own Nagatzu (i.e. elder and younger grandchildren could not be accused in relation to their maternal grandfather: i.e. they did not pay Yal). If the Nagatzu (maternal grandfather) be no longer living, they cannot be accused likewise before his elder and younger sons (i.e. their maternal uncles).

Furthermore: Presents given to a Naidji (tutor, protector of the family, patron, middleman, godfather of a young couple, arbitrator between husbend and wife, a Shaman or Lama undertaking to defend a child from evil), when he comes with a sheep and wine (i.e. with ritual offerings of food) for a visit shall not require a gift in return (are not later collected, do not represent a debt).

One more article: Generally, let Noyons, when they shall hand over the inheritance (Umchi—property) to their children, report this to the Gegen and the Khan and register it with their ruling princes so that it may be sealed. If it does not bear this note and a litigation or objection arise, then the words of the children or the statement that "it was so" or a document seen by no one must not be taken as proof. But in view of the fact that there is no distinction between children, the inheritance must be divided equally among them all with the exception of two: the generally known just and generally known unjust of the sons. If the own mother of the children who are parties to the litigation be still alive, then let her dispose ("let her know").

Furthermore: Generally, if a man of the rank of Khan himself bestow anything upon a man of common degree (Haratzu), or a man of common degree bestow anything upon a person of Khan rank, then this does not require any return. To say: "I took from an abandoned wife or from a household servant or slave" is punishable by a fine (Yalatai Byi).[6]

Regulations of 1746.

In the 11th year of the reign of Ch'ien Lung, on the 29th day of the last summer month, the following was sent from the Djisan (administration):

In the 11th year of the reign of Ch'ien Lung on the 12th day of the midsummer month, at a united session of the Seims in Urga with the participation of Jassaktu Khan, Setsen Khan, the President of the Seim—Ch'ing Wang Dechin-djab, the Ch'ing Wang Erintzin Dordji, the assistant of the Chiang Chun Shitzu, the assistant of the Chiang Chun Chun Wang, the assistant of the Chiang Chun Beile, the assistant of the Chiang Chun Gun and others, it was decided:

That any man committing robbery is, in accordance of the Old Statute of His Majesty (Degedu), to be executed (killed), and his Yurt, cattle, wife and children are all to be given to the owner of the (stolen) cattle.

That from an accomplice are to be taken 3 nines and given to the owner of the cattle, and he (the accomplice) is also to be given 100 Tashurs. Furthermore, if he shall not have sufficient cattle to pay the fine, then his Yurt, household utensils, cup, Tagan, etc. are to be taken in payment being equivalent to 1 nine, and if the man have children one child shall be equivalent to 1 nine and two children to 2 nines. But more than two children must not be given. If there are no children but only the husband and his wife, then she shall be given. If the man be unmarried, he himself shall be delivered up. If after having given his cattle and children and wife, some cattle will still be lacking to pay

6 The above is a translation from the record described on pg. 59 of the present work under the number VIII.

the fine, then in accordance with the Statute of His Majesty (the Sovereign's Statute) let him be given 25 blows of the Tashur for each head of cattle (Mal—cattle, animal), but not more than 100 blows altogether.

"If this is done, then thieves who misbehave will be taught better." Thus saying, they agreed and came to a decision as is noted separately. Furthermore, they agreed that in future, in all other affairs, they would be guided in all four Aimaks in the same measure.[7]

Regulations of 1724.

A provision written in the year of the Golden Dragon in the last spring month on the 7th day.

If any man shall seek a debt, then, if the creditor and debtor dwell in the neighbourhood of the Great Kuren, the litigation is to be dismissed if the loan was contracted without the permission of the Khan, the Shanzotba and the Wang (without declaration to the Khans, Shanzotbas and Wangs), and must be considered only if it was so declared. In villages (Kudöns) the suit must be dismissed if the parties, being of the same Somun or Otok and of noble or mean degree (Khan Haratzu) belonging to the Otok have failed to declare the loan to their Somun Taidji and Ooloos (settlement) Tzangin or to the Daruga (of their Otok). If the parties are from different Somuns and Otoks, then such suits concerning debts must be dismissed as have not been declared to the Dzarikchis (administrative officials) of both sides. Suits shall also be dismissed in the case of the loan being declared by only one party, so that the Daruga or Tzangin only of the plaintiff knows of it, and the Daruga or Tzangin of the defendant does not know.[8]

7 The above is a translation of the record described on pg. 59, under the number VI.

8 The above is a translation of the record described on pg. 60, under the number XVII.

THE STUDY OF MONGOL LAW (BIBLIOGRAPHY).

Works in the Russian Language.

Russia bordered, and the U.S.S.R. now borders, on Mongolia; and two large Mongol tribes, the Buriats and Kalmucks, are among the inhabitants of its territory. Because of this it is easy to understand why Russian scientists have for a very long time played an important part in the study of Mongolia and the Mongol tribes in its different branches, including the sphere of law.

As early as the second half of the XVIII-th century the Russian Academy of Sciences organized a series of scientific expeditions with the aim of studying Russia and the peoples inhabiting it. The scientists who participated in these expeditions gathered a great amount for scientific material, some of which later appeared in print. A part of this material was concerned with the description of the legal customs of the Mongol tribes living in Russia. In this connection the following works are of interest:

"Dnevnie zapiski doktora i Akademii Nauk adiunkta Ivana Lepekhina po raznym provinziam Rossiiskogo gosudarstva v 1768-1769 gg." Part I ("Journal of Dr. *Ivan Lepekhin,* Adjunct to the Academy of Sciences, on Various Provinces of the Russian State", Part I), St. Petersburg, 1771. Here may be found information concerning the clan organization and legal customs of the Stavropol and Astrakhan Kalmucks. *Georgi,* "Opisanie vsekh obitaiuschikh v Rossiiskom gosudarstve narodov. . .", IV ("Description of All the Peoples Inhabiting the Russian State", etc., Part IV), St. Petersburg 1776-1778. In this work and another in the German language (Beschreibung der Reise, etc., for which see further) a description of the organization and customs of the Buriats and Kalmucks may be found. *Pallas,* "Puteshestvia po raznym provinziam Rossiiskoi Imperii" (Travels in Various Provinces of the Russian Empire), 1773-1778 "Sobranie istoricheskikh svedenii o mongolskikh narodakh", (Collection of Historical Data on the Mongol Peoples); "S. P'burgski Vestnik" (St. Petersburg Herald), part I. These works contain valuable information on the life and law of the Mongol tribes.

In 1776, in the "Opyt trudov Volnogo Pusskogo Sobrania pri Moskovskom Univ-te", (Essay of Works of the Private Russian Society at Moscow University), part III, *Count Sheremetiev* published the first edition of the Mongol-Oirat Regulations of 1640 under the heading: "Perevod s prav mungalskikh i kalmytskikh narodov" (Translation from the Laws of the Mungal and Kalmuck Peoples). In the same year (1776), Academician Pallas published the German text of this Code as well as several fragments of the Ancient Tsaadjin Bichik (*v.* the German edition of the second mentioned work of Acad. Pallas, "Sammlungen Historischer Nachrichten," etc., for further particulars of which look below.)

Between the publication of the above-described pioneer works of Lepekhin, Georgi, Sheremetiev and Pallas and the present time, *i.e.* over a period of 150 years, there have appeared in Russian literature many books, outlines, sketches and articles dealing with the social organization of the Mongol tribes. The writer does not consider it necessary to enumerate the entire mass of this literature, and will here confine himself to mentioning some works of essential importance for the study of the legal records and customs of the Mongol tribes

Much light was cast upon the Mongols of the first period,[1] their life, morality and customs,by the works of the noted Sinologue, Father Palladius (Kafarov) who translated into the Russian language (from the Chinese) such records as the "Yuan Ch'ao Pi (Mi) Shih", ("Sokrovennoie skazanie o pokolenii Mongol", Secret Chronicle of the Generations of the Mongols), Works of the Members of the Russian Orthodox Mission in Peiping, 1866, vol. IV; the "Hsi Yu Tze", (Opisanie Puteshestvia (daosa Chan-Chuna) na Zapad", or "Description of the Journey (of the Taoist Chang Chun) to the West", in the same volume); "Putevie zapiski kitaitsa Dja-de-hoi vo vremia puteshestvia ego v Mongoliu v pervoi polovine XIII st." (Travel Notes of the Chinese, Cha Teh-hua at the Time of His Journey to Mongolia in the First Half of the XIIIth Century), Translation and notes printed in the Proceedings of the Siberian Section, of the Russ. Geogr. Society, 1867, vols. IX-X; "Shen Wu Tsin Chen Lu", or "Opisanie mnogikh pohodov sviaschennvoinstvuiuschego" (Description of the Many Campaigns of the Holy Warrior) (Jenghiz Khan), Translation, with introd. and notes, "Oriental Collection", 1877, vol. I; and "Kommentarii na puteshestvie Marko Polo po Severnomu Kitaiu" (Commentaries on Marco Polo's Travels in North China), pub. Russ. Geogr. Soc., 1902, vol. XXXIII, I.

Another famous Sinologist, Father *Hyacinth* (Bichurin) published "Istoria pervikh chetyrekh khanov iz doma Chingizova" (History of the First Four Khans of the House of Jenghiz), 1829; and "Sobrania svedennyi o narodakh obitaiuschikh v srednei Azii v drevnosti" (Collection of Information Concerning the Peoples Inhabiting Central Asia in Ancient Times), 1851.

---

1 Concerning periods in Mongol law, *v.* above pg. 197 *sqq.*

Acad. *Vasiliev* published "Istoria i drevnosti vostochnoi chasti Srednei Azii ot X do XIII veka" (History and Antiquities of the Eastern Part of Central Asia from the Xth to the XIIIth Centuries), a description of the Mongol, Tungus and Turki tribes containing, in particular, a translation of the "Meng Ta Pei Lu" (Notes on the Mongol-Tartars) ascribed to Men Hun, in the Works of the Oriental Section, Russ. Archaelogical Soc., 1859, part IV.

Prof. *Berezin* translated (from the Persian) and annotated the "Sbornik letopisei; istoria mongolov Rashid Ed-dina" (Collection of Chronicles, History of the Mongols by Rashid Ed-din): I. "Vvedenie —o turetskikh i mongolskikh plemenakh" (Introd., Concerning the Mongol and Turkish Tribes), Proceedings of the R. Arch. Soc., 1858, vol. XIV; 2. "Istoria Chingis-khana do vosshestvia ego na prestol" (History of Jenghiz Khan Before His Accession to the Throne), Works of the Oriental Section, R. Arch. Soc., part XIII; 3. "Istoria Chingiz-khana ot vosshestvia ego na prestol do konchiny" (History of Jenghiz Khan From His Accession to the Throne to His Death), *Ibid.* part XV, 1888. Among other information, the Maxims of Jenghiz Khan are most fully quoted in this work. Prof. Brezin was also responsible for "Ocherk vnutrennego ustroistva oloosa Djuchieva" (Outline of the Internal Organization of the Ooloos of Juchi), printed in the Works of the Or. Sec., R. Arch. Soc., 1864, part VIII, which contained the translation into Russian of fragments of the Great Yassa of Jenghiz Khan that have reached us from Persian and Arabic sources.

Patkanov published, "Istoria mongolov po armianskim istochnikam" (History of the Mongols According to Armenian Sources), Part I 1873; Part II 1874; and "Istoria Mongolov inoka Magakii" (History of the Mongols by the monk Mahakia), 1871.

We may note here the Russian translations of the works of the first travellers in the Great Mongol Empire: *Minayev*-Puteshestvia Marko-Polo" (Travels of *Marco Polo*), Proceedings of the R. Geogr. Soc., Section of Ethnography, 1902, vol. XXVI; *Plano Carpini,* "Istoria Mongolov" (History of the Mongols), trans by *Mahlein,* 1911; *Rubruquis,* "Puteshestvia v vostochnye strany" (Travels to Eastern Countries), trans. *Mahlein,* 1911. See also, Lama Galsan *Gomboev,* "O drevnikh mongolskikh obychaiakh i suieveriakh, opisannikh u Plano-Karpini" (On the Ancient Mongol Customs and Superstitions Described by Plano Carpini), Works of the Or. Sec., R. Arch. Soc., 1859, IV. This author indicated how many of the customs described still existed in the XIXth century.

Grigoriev—"O dostovernosti yarlykov dannykh khanami Zolotoi Ordy russkomu dukhovenstvu" (On the Authenticity of the Yarliks

Given by the Khans of the Golden Horde to the Russian Clergy), 1842. The text of the Yarliks is given.

Barthold—"Turkestan v epokhu mongolskogo nashestvia" (Turkestan in the Epoch of the Mongol Invasian), vol. II, 1900. An English edition (1928) of this work exists. Also, "Obrazovanie imperii Chingiz-khana" (Formation of the Empire of Jenghiz Khan), Proceedings, Or. Sec., R. Arch. Soc., 1896, vol. X.

Melioransky—"O Kudatku Bilige Chingiz-khana" (On the Kudatkou Bilig of Jenghiz Khan), Ibid., 1900, vol. XIII, 1st issue.

Vladimirtzov—"Chingiz-khan", 1918. An English edition (1930) of this work exists.

Hara-Davan—"Chingis Khan kak polkovodetz . . ." (Jenghiz Khan as a Military Leader and his Heritage), 1929. This book gives information concerning some ancient Mongol customs shall extant among the Kalmucks.

Riasanovsky—"Velikaya Yassa Chingiz-khana" (The Great Yassa of Jenghiz Khan), an outline, 1933.

The following works may be referred to the literature describing the social, and particularly the legal, organization of the Mongol tribes during the second period.

Besides the first edition of the Regulations of 1640, published by Sheremetiev in 1776 and already referred to, there are: the 2nd Edition of the "Ustav 1640 goda" (*Mongol-Oiral Regulations of* 1640), printed in the "Severny Arkhiv" (Northern Archive) and "Syn otechestva" (Son of the Fatherland) magazines, 1828, under the heading: "Zakony mungalskie i kalmytskie" (Mungal and Kalmuck Laws). For the 3rd edition of the Regulations of 1640, according to the Bentkovsky MS., see *Leontovich*—"Drevni Mongolo-kalmytski ili Oiratski Ustav Vzyskanii" (Ancient Mongol-Kalmuck or Oirat Regulations on Punishments), 1879. This work contains the Russian text of the Regulations and the first Decree of Khan Galdan, besides which it reprints the German text of Pallas. Prof. Leontovich supplemented his edition of the Regulations with an investigation into the origin and final fate of the Code, with particular reference to the records of the law of the Buriats and some other native peoples of Siberia. The fourth edition: *Golstounsky,* "Mongolo-oiratskie zakony 1640 g. . . ." (The Mongol-Oirat Laws of 1640, etc.), 1880 (containing the M.O. Regulations of 1640, the two supplementary decrees of Khan Galdan and the supplementary laws of Khan Donduk Dashi). A translation from the Kalmuck.

Jurists are much indebted to *Ts. T. Jamtsarano* who, besides his linguistic and ethnographic works, brought to light almost all the available information concerning the native law of the Khalkha Mongols and much material on Buriat law. Mr. Jamtsarano discovered, described, translated into the Russian language, and is now preparing for publication the Code of Northern Mongolia, the Khalkha Djirom. He is responsible for the discovery and collection of many records of Buriat law, among them such important documents as the Steppe Code of 1808, etc. See *Jamtsarano and Turunov,* "Khalkha Djirom", a description of the record in the Collection of the Irkutsk State University, 1923, 6th issue; Jamtsarano and Turunov, "Obozrenie pamiatnikov pisannogo prava Mongolskikh plemen" (Review of the Records of the Written Law of the Mongol Tribes), *Ibid.,* 1st issue.[2]

Among other works casting light on the position of law during the above mentioned period the following must be noted: *N. Popov*—"O pisanitsakh Minusinskogo kraia" (On the Inscriptions of the Minusinsk Region), Proceedings, Sib. Sec., R. Geogr. Soc., vol. III, issues 4-5; also by the same author, "O pamiatnikhakh tangutskogo i mongolskogo pisma v. Minusinskom kraie" (On the Monuments of Tangut and Mongol Writing in the Minusinsk Region)[3], *Ibid.,* vol. V, issues 3 and 4; *Kotvich*—"Russkie arkhivnye dokumenty po snosheniu c Oiratami v XVII i XVIII v. "(Documents in the Russian Archives Concerning Relations with the Oirats in the XVII and XVIII Centuries), Pub. by the Russian Academy of Sciences, 1919 (mentions the editions of the Regulations of 1640, etc.).

To the list of auxiliary works concerning the given period we may refer the following: *Meng Ku Yu Mu Tze,* or Notes on the Mongol Camping Grounds, transl. by *Popov; Pokotilov*—"Istoria Vostochnykh mongolov v period dinastii Min. 1368-1634, po kitaiskim istochnykam" (History of the Eastern Mongols in the Period of the Ming Dynasty, 1368-1634, According to Chinese Sources"), 1893; *Posdneev*—"Mongolskaya Letopis 'Erdeniin Erikhe', podlinni tekst s poiasneniami (1636-1736)" (The Mongol Chronicle, "Erdeniin Erikhe", Original Text with Elucidations, 1636-1736), 1883. These works contain information on the organization and life of the Mongols, as well as data concerning their laws and customs.

"Posolstvo iz Tobolska syna boyarskogo *Yudina* k Bushukhtu Ziungarskomu" (The Embassy from Tobolsk of the Boyar's Son, *Yudin,* to the Djungarian Bushukhtu" (Galdan Khan), in 1691, printed

---

2 The Mongolian Scientific Committee in Urga (Ulan Bator) also possesses manuscripts on the laws of the Mongol tribes.

3 Minusinsk is a district town of Yenisei province, in Eastern Siberia.

in "Sibirski Vestnik" (Siberian Messenger), 1821, vols. XV, XVI (from the manuscripts of Cherepanov).

Some interesting works refer to both the first and second periods:

Lama Galsan *Gombaev*—"Altan Tobchi (Zolotoie Skazanie)" (Altan Tobchi, the Golden Chronicle), a Mongol chronicle (from ancient times to *circa* 1627), translated. Proceedings of the R. Arch. Soc., 1858, XIV, II. *Gurland,* "Stepnoe zakonodatelstvo s drevneishikh vremen do XVII veka" (Steppe Legislation From the Most Ancient Times to the XVII-th Century), Proceedings of the Historical, Archaeological and Ethnographic Society at Kazan University, 1904, vol. XX, issues 4-5; *Grum-Grzimailo*-Western Mongolia and the Uriankhai Region, v. II, 1926. *Guins*—"Mongolskaia gosudarstvennost i pravo" (Mongol State Organization and Law), Vestnik Kitaia, 1931, 3; Acad. *Vladimirtzov,* "Obschestvenny stroi mongolov" (Social Organization of the Mongols), 1934.

In connection with the third period it is necessary to refer to the following works.

Timkovsky—"Puteshestvie v Kitai cherez Mongoliu v 1820 i 1821 gg." (A Journey to China Through Mongolia in 1820 and 1821). In this work, besides other particulars, there are data on the Mongolian Code of the Emperor of K'ang Hsi (vol. III, ppg. 222 and 343) which were repeated by Leontovich and after him by Dareste. This information has recently been confirmed by the discovery in Mongolia of the Mongolian Code of the Emperor K'ang Hsi (1696).

In 1828 Father *Hyacinth* (Bichurin) published his "Zapiski o Mongolii" (Notes on Mongolia) in 2 volumes which, besides much valuable data on the country, contained a translation of the Mongol Regulations (Code) of the Chinese Board of Foreign Relations of 1789. Besides this, he published in 1829 "Opisanie Djungarii i Vostochnogo Turkestana v drevnem i nyneshnem sostoianii" (Description of Djungaria and Eastern Turkestan in their Ancient and Present Condition), a translation from the Chinese; and "Istoricheskoie obozrenie Oiratov ili Kalmykov c XV stoletia do nastoiaschego vremeni" (Historical Account of the Oirats or Kalmucks from the XV-th Century to the Present Time), 1834. Both these works refer to both the second and third periods and deal with legal problems.

Lipovtzev—"Ulojenie Kitaiskoi Palaty Vneshnikh Snoshenii" (1815 g.) Regulations of the Chinese Board of Foreign Relations—(1815), a translation from the Manchu published in 1828.

Igumnov with additions by *Spassky*—"Obozrenie Mongolii" (Survey of Mongolia), "Sibirski Vestnik" (Siberian Messenger), 1819, vols. V and VI (containing *inter alia* a Russian translation of the fragments of the Ancient Tsaadjin Bichik).

To this period pertain many works by Russian travellers and investigators in which indications are given concerning the organization, life and legal customs of the Mongols.

Veselovsky—"Puteshestvie k Ziungarskomu Khun-Taidji Tseven--Rapthanu kapitana . . . Unkovskogo i putevoi jurnal ego na 1722-1724 g.g." (A Journey Made to the Djungarian Khun-Taidji, Tseven-Rapthan, by Captain . . . Unkovsky, And His Travel Journal for the Years 1722-1724), Proceedings R. Geogr. Soc., 1887, X, 2.

Father *Palladius*—"Dorojnie zametki na puti po Mongolii v 1847 i 1859 g.g." (Travel Notes on the Way Through Mongolia in 1847 and 1859), Notes of Russian Geogr. Soc., Dept. of General Geography, 1892, vol. XXII, 1.

Prjevalsky—"Mongolia i strana tangutov" (Mongolia and the Land of the Tanguts), 1875.

Potanin—"Ocherki severo-zapadnoi Mongolii" (Outlines of Northwestern Mongolia), 1881-83, vol. IV.

A. Posdneev—"Mongolia i Mongoly" (Mongolia and the Mongols) 1896 and 1898, vols. I, II, and especially vol. III of this work (description of the administrative structure of Mongolia), MS. only.

Vladimirtzov—"Otchet o komandirovke k Durbotam Kobdosskogo okruga" (Report of a Mission to the Durbots of the Kobdo Region), Proceedings of the Russ. Committee for the Study of Asia, 1909, No. 9.

An idea of the position of law in Mongolia in the first half of the fourth period, i.e. at the time of the socalled Autonomous Mongolia, may be gleaned from the following works:

Maisky—"Sovremennaia Mongolia" (Modern Mongolia), 1921; and *Kotvich*, "Kratki obzor istorii i sovremennogo politicheskogo polojenia Mongolii" (A Short Account of the History and Contemporary Position of Mongolia), 1914.

The writer will make bold here to mention his own works: *Riasanovsky*—"Obychnoe pravo mongolskikh plemen" (Customary Law of the Mongol Tribes), 1924; and "Mongolskoie pravo, preimuschestvenno obychnoe" (Mongol Law, with Special Reference to Customary Law), 1931. A historical account covering all the periods.

On the subject of Buriat law it is necessary to note the following works:

A.R.—"O zakonakh nekotorykh Sibirskikh inorodtzev" (On the Laws of Some Siberian Natives), "Sibirsky Vestnik", 1823, (containing fragments of the Steppe Code of the Buriats, 1781).

"Svod Stepnykh Zakonov" (Code of Steppe Laws) of the nomadic natives of Eastern Siberia, 1841. Draft.

Samokvasov—"Sbornik obychnogo prava Sibirskikh inorodtzev" (Collection of Customary Law of the Siberian Natives), 1876 (dealing with the customary law of the Tunguses, Northern and Southern Buriats, Yakuts, Kirghiz, etc.).

Hangalov—"Iuridicheskie obychai u Buriat" (Juridical Customs of the Buriats), "Etnograficheskoe Obozrenie" (Ethnographic Review), 1894,2.

Riasanovsky—"Obychnoie pravo Buriat" (Customary Law of the Buriats), 1921; also, "Dva pamiatnika obychnogo prava Mongolskikh plemen" (Two Records of the Customary Law of the Mongol Tribes), "Vestnik Mandjurii" (Manchurian Messenger), 1930, XI, (containing a decription of the Code of Steppe Laws.

It is necessary to note that in the above mentioned work by Leontovich (Ancient Mongol-Kalmuck or Oirat Regulations on Punishments, 1879) much attention was given to Buriat law; that the records of Buriat law form the main subject matter of the enumerated articles by Jamtsarano and Turunov; and that the second parts of Riasanovsky's "Obychnoie pravo mong. plemen", (Customary Law of the Mongol Tribes) 1924; and Mongolskoe Pravo, ("Mongol Law, with Special Reference to Customary Law"), 1931, are devoted to Buriat law.

The following works furnish auxiliary material on Buriat law.

"Buriaty ili bratskie" (The Buriats or Brats), from the MS. of *Langans,* with additions by *Spassky,* "Sibirski Vestnik", 1824, parts I and II.

Rayev—"Buriaty" (The Buriats), Journal of the Geogr. Soc., 1858, 9.

Schapov—"Buriatskaia ooloosnaia rodovaia obschina" (The Buriat Ooloos Clan Community), Proceedings of the Sib. Sec., R. Geogr. Soc., 1875, V, issues 3-4.

Jamtsarano—"O pravosoznanii u Buriat" (On the Legal Consciousness of the Buriats), "Sibirski Vestnik", 1906, 2.

Hangalov—"Zegete Aba, oblava na zverei u drevnikh Buriat" (Zegete-Aba, The Hunting of Beasts Among the Ancient Buriats), Proceedings, Sib. Sec., R. Geogr. Soc., 1888, vol. XIX, 3; *Klementz and Hangalov*—"Obschestvennie okhoty u severnykh Buriat" (Community Hunts Among the Northern Buriats), Materials on the Ethnography of Russia, 1910, vol. I. Both these investigators made an interesting attempt to reconstruct the social organization of the Buriats before the Russian conquest, in the period extending approximately from the XIII-th to the XVI-th centuries.

Krol—"Brachnoie pravo Mongolo-Buriat" (Marriage Law of the Mongol-Buriats), "Jurnal Ministerstva Iustizii" (Journal of the Ministry of Justice), 1900, 1.

Petri—"Brachnye normy severnykh buriat" (Marriage Provisions of the Northern Buriats), Collection of Irkutsk State Univ., VIII; "Elementy rodovoi sviazi u severnykh buriat" (Elements of Clan Relations Among the Northern Buriats), "Sibirskaia Jivaia Starina" (Siberian Living Antiquity), 1924, II.

Turunov—"Proshloie buriat-mongolskoi narodnosti" (Past History of the Buriat-Mongol Nation), 1922.

Bogdanov—"Ocherk istorii buriat-mongolskogo naroda" (Outline History of the Buriat-Mongol People), 1926.

As regards Kalmuck law, the basic work on the subject is Prof. *Leontovich's*, "Kalmytskoie pravo" (Kalmuck Law), 1880, in which the author reproduces the text of the Digest of Kalmuck Laws, 1822-1827, and gives a picture of the social organization of the Kalmucks.

Strakhov—"Nyneshneie sostoianie kalmytskogo naroda, s prisovokupleniem kalmytskikh zakonov i sudoustroistva" (The Present Condition of the Kalmuck People, With A Supplement Containing Kalmuck Laws and Court Organization), etc., 1810. An account of social organization, customs, the Regulations of 1640, judicial procedure etc.

In this connection we may remind the reader that Golstounsky's already mentioned "Mongol-Oirat Laws of 1640", reproduced the legislation of the Kalmuck Khan Donduk Dashi, and that in both the work of Riasanovsky mentioned above (1924 and 1931) the third part is devoted to Kalmuck law.

For auxiliary material (besides the already mentioned "Historical Outline of the Oirats and Kalmucks", 1834, by Father *Hyacinth*) the following works may be referred to:

Nefediev—"Podrobnye svedenia o voljskikh kalmykakh", (Detailed Data on the Volga Kalmucks), 1834.

N. Z—v—"Istoricheski obzor stavropolskikh kalmykov i neskolko dannykh o sovremennom ikh sostoianii "(Historical Outline of the Stavropol Kalmucks and Some Information Concerning Their Present Condition), "Otechestvennye Zapiski" (Fatherland Notes), 1844, vol. 35.

Kostenkov—"Statistichesko-hoziaistvennoie opisanie Kalmytskoi stepi" (Statistical and Economic Description of the Kalmuck Steppe), 1868.

Ochirov—"Astrakhanskie kalmyki i ikh sovremennoie ekonomicheskoie sostoianie" (The Astrakhan Kalmucks and Their Present Economic Condition), 1915.

Palmov—"Ocherk istorii kalmytskogo naroda za vremia ego prebyvania v predelakh Rossii" (Outline History of the Kalmuck People During Its Sojourn Within the Borders of Russia), 1922.

Works in Other Languages.[4]

The works in languages other than Russian devoted specially to the study of Mongol law are very few in number. Foreign scientists have given little attention to the questions of Mongol law but have produced a considerable body of works of a historical and descriptive character, some of which contain data on the life and customs of the Mongols. We shall mention the most significant of these.

De Sasy—"Chrestomathie arabe", 1828, II. (Contains fragments of the Great Yassa).

Hammer v. Purgstall—"Geschichte der Goldenen Horde in Kiptschak", 1840.

**Erdmann*—"Temudschin der Unerschutterliche", 1862.

Howorth—"History of the Mongols", 4 vols., 1876-1927. The three last mentioned works quote the legislation of Jenghiz Khan.

***Pallas*—"Sammlungen Historischer Nachrichten uber die Mongol-Volkerschaften", 1776-1801, 2. (Reproduces the text of the Regulations of 1640 and fragments of the Ancient Tsaadjin Bichik).

Von der Borg translated into German Father *Hyacinth's* "Notes on Mongolia", 1832.

Alinge—"Mongolische Gesetze", 1934 (Contains the text of the Great Yassa and the Ancient Tsaadjin Bichik, and the contents of the M.O. Regulations of 1640 and the Regulations (Code) of 1789).

**Riasanovsky*—"The Customary Law of the Mongol Tribes (Mongols, Buriats and Kalmucks)", 1929 (Containing the text or summaries of the contents of the records of Mongol law as well as a survey of the

4 An asterisk (*) marks the works of Russian scientists; two asterisks (**) the work of Russian scientists of foreign descent.

law of the Northern and Southern Buriats and the Kalmucks); "The Influence of Chinese Law Upon Mongolian Law"—in the "Chinese Polit. and Social Science Review", 1931, No. 3; "Mongol Law and Chinese Law in the Yuan Dynasty", *Ibid.*, 1936, 2: "The Code of Northern Mongolia—Khalkha-Djirom", *Ibid,* 1936, 3, The Influence of Ancient Mongol Culture and Law on Russian Culture and Law, *Ibid.* Jan., 1937; "Les monuments de droit Mongol"—"Bulletin trimestriel de la Société de Législation Comparée," 1932, No. 7-12.

***J. Schmidt* translated into German the work of *Sanang Setsen* under the title of "Geschichte der Ost-Mongolen und ihres Fursten-hauses (aus dem Mongolischen)", 1829.

Abel Remusat—"Nouveaux Melanges asiatiques", II, 1829.

Aboul Ghazi—"Histoires des Mongols et de Tatars", trans. Baron *Desmaisons,* 1874.

**Barthold*—"Turkestan in the Epoch of the Mongol Invasion", 1928; "Gingiz-Khan", article in the Enzikl. des Islams, I.

Bouvat—"L'empire Mongol", 1927.

Bretschneider—"Mediaeval Researches From Eastern Asiatic Sources", 1888, vol. II.

Chavannes—"Inscriptions et piece de chancellerie chinoises de l'epoque mongole", in "T'oung Pao", 1904, 1905, 1908.

Dareste—"Etude d'histoire du droit", (2-me serie), 1926.

***Georgi*—"Beschreibung aller Nationen der Russischen Reiches", etc., 1776-78; Bemerkungen einer Reise in Russischen Reich im Jahre 1772", 1775.

Klaproth—"Description de la Chine sous la regne de la dinastie Mongole, traduite de Persane de Rashid Ed-din", in "Journal As", 1833, XI.

Korostowetz—"Von Chingis Khan zur Sowjetrepublik", 1926.

**Lepekhin*—"Tagebuch der Reisen durch verschiedenen Provinzen des Russischen Reiches", 1774-1777.

d'Ohsson—"Histoire des Mongols depuis Tchingis-Khan jusqu'a Timour Beg ou Tamerlan", 1852.

*Father *Palladius*—"Deux traversees de la Mongolie 1847-1859", in "Bulletin de georgaphie historique et descriptive", 1884.

***Pallas*—"Reise durch verschiedene Provinzen des Russ. Reiches", 1771-1776.

Parker—"Mongolia After the Jenghizides and Before the Manchus", in "Jour. of the N. China Branch of the R. As. Soc.," V, XLIV, 1913.

Pelliot—"Mongols et la Papaute",—"Revue de l'Orient Chretien", vol. III, IV, 1924, "Notes sur le 'Turkestan' de M. W. Barthold" —"T'oung Pao", 1930, XXVII.

"The Travels of *Marco Polo*", by *Komroff*, 1928.

"Contemporaries of *Marco Polo*", by *Komroff*, 1928.

Quatremère—"Histoire des Mongols de la Perse par Rashid Eddin"—"Collection Oriental", vol. I, 1836.

Vladimirtzov—"The Life of Chingis Khan", 1930.

Waley—"The Travels of an Alchemist" (the monk Ch'ang Ch'un), 1931.

Valentin A. Riasanovsky: Bibliography

The Bibliography is divided into four Sections: I. Russian Law and Legal Procedure, II. Oriental Law, III. Russian History and Culture, and IV. Works in Preparation. The Sections are subdivided according to the type of publication (Books and Monographs, Articles), and the language in which the work was published. The following abbreviations are employed for the names of periodicals cited:

Bb—Bibliograficheskii bjulleten' (Harbin)
BdlSdLC—Bulletin de la Société de Législation Comparée
Bs—Bibliograficheskii sbornik (Harbin)
GB-M—Golos Burjat-Mongola (Chita)
IJuFvgKh—Izvestija Juridicheskogo Fakul'teta v g. Kharbine (Harbin)
Juo—Juridicheskoe obozrenie (Vladivostok)
NSaEQ—Nankai Social and Economic Quarterly
P—Pravo
TCSaPSR—The Chinese Social and Political Science Review
TIGU—Trudy Irkutskogo Gosudarstvennogo Universiteta (Irkutsk)
VA—Vestnik Azii (Harbin)
VIpISSSR—Vestnik Instituta po Izucheniju SSSR (Munich)
Vkp—Vestnik kitaiskogo prava (Harbin)
VM—Vestnik Man'chzhurii (Harbin)
Vp—Vestnik prava
Vpin—Vestnik prava i notariata
WLR—Washington Law Review
ZhMJu—Zhurnal Ministerstva Justitsii

I. Russian Law and Legal Procedure

A. Books and Monographs in Russian

1. *O posmertnom preemstve suprugov po russkomu pravu (Succession by Husband and Wife in Russian Law),* Nizhnii Novgorod: 1914, 220 pp.

2. *Vymorochnoe pravo (Escheat Law),* Nizhnii Novgorod: 1914, 75 pp.

3. *Granitsy nasledovanija (The Limits of Inheritance),* Jaroslavl': 1915, 28 pp.

4. *Preemstvo v linii voskhodjashchei po russkomu pravu (Succession along the Ascending Line in Russian Law),* Jaroslavl': 1916, 220 pp.

5. *Nasledovanie polnorodnykh, edinokrovnykh i edinoutrobnykh brat'ev i sester (Inheritance by Brothers and Sisters Fully and Not Fully Related by Blood),* Jaroslavl': 1916, 95 pp.

6. *Tolkovanie 1140 st. t. X ch. 1 (Interpretation of Art. 1140, Vol. X, Pt. 1),* Jaroslavl': 1917, 50 pp.

7. *Pravovoe polozhenie russkikh v zanjatykh Japoniei mestnostjakh Sakhalinskoi oblasti (The Legal Position of Russians in Areas of the Sakhalin Region Occupied by Japan),* Vladivostok: 1921, 58 pp.

8. *Lektsii po grazhdanskomu pravu (Lectures on Civil Law),* I-V.

Obshchaja chast' (General), I, ed. 1, Vladivostok: 1922, 92 pp.; ed. 2, Harbin: 1924, 85 pp.

Obshchaja chast' (General), II, ed. 1, Vladivostok: 1922, 99 pp.; ed. 2, Harbin: 1924, 113 pp.

Prava veshchnye, prava prisvoenija, prava na produkty dukhovnogo tvorchestva (Rights over Things, Rights of Appropriation, Rights over the Products of Creative Genius), III, Harbin: 1923, 101 pp.

Prava objazatel'stvennye (Obligations), IV, Harbin: 1924, 108 pp.

Prava semeinye i nasledstvennye (Family and Inheritance Law), V, Harbin: 1924, 82 pp.

9. *Edinstvo protsessa (The Unity of Procedure)*, Harbin: 1924, 57 pp.

B. Articles in Russian

1. "Kto javljaetsja sobstvennikom imushchestva, prodannogo s rassrochkoi platezha" ("Who Is the Owner of Property Sold on Installment Payments"), *Vpin*, 11, 1911.

2. "O prave negramotnykh byt' svideteljami pri sostavlenii dukhovnogo zaveshchanija" ("On the Right of Illiterates to Serve as Witnesses when a Will Is Drawn"), *Vpin*, 16-17, 1911.

3. "O dukhovnykh zaveshchanijakh, sovershaemykh russkimi poddannymi zagranitseju" ("On Wills Made by Russian Subjects Abroad"), *ZhMJu*, 3, 1912.

4. "Tolkovanie 1068 1 st. t. X ch. 1" ("Interpretation of Art. 1068 1, Vol. X, Pt. 1"), *P*, 13, 1913.

5. "O primenenii rumynskikh grazhdanskikh zakonov v Bessarabii" ("On the Application of Rumanian Civil Laws in Bessarabia"), *P*, 27, 1914.

6. "Osnovnaja sdelka, veksel' i st. 1521 t. X ch. 1" ("The Fundamental Transaction, the Promissory Note, and Art. 1521, Vol. X, Pt. 1"), *Vp*, 27, 1914.

7. "Obespechenie iska i ponuditel'noe ispolnenie po aktam" ("The Security of the Claim and the Compulsory Execution of the Acts"), *Vp*, 7, 1916.

8. "Edinstvo protsessa" ("The Unity of Procedure"), *TIGU*, I, 1920.

9. "Administrativnaja justitsija" ("Administrative Jurisprudence"), *Juo*, 1-2, 1921.

10. "Organizatsija suda v Sovetskoi Rossii" ("The Organization of Courts in Soviet Russia"), *Juo*, 3-4, 1922.

11. "Narodnyi Sud Sovetskoi Rossii" ("The Peoples' Court of Soviet Russia"), *Juo*, 8-9, 1922.

12. "Grazhdanskii Kodeks R.S.F.S.R." ("The Civil Code of the R.S.F.S.R."), *VM*, 3, 1925.

II. Oriental Law

A. Books and Monographs in Russian

1. *Obychnoe pravo burjat (Customary Law of the Buriats)*, Chita: 1921, 120 pp.

2. *Sovremennoe grazhdanskoe pravo Kitaja (Modern Civil Law of China)*, I-II, Harbin: 1926-1927, 196 pp., 107 pp.

3. *Osnovnye nachala zemel'nogo, gornogo i lesnogo prava Kitaja (The Fundamental Principles of the Land, Mining, and Forest Law of China)*, Harbin: 1928, 135 pp.

4. *Mongol'skoe pravo, preimushchestvenno obychnoe (Mongol Law, with Special Reference to Customary Law)*, Harbin: 1931, 306 + 42 pp.

5. *Javljaetsja li mongol'skoe pravo pravom obychnym? (Is Mongol Law Customary Law?)*, Harbin: 1932, 30 pp.

B. Articles in Russian

1. "O nauchnoi razrabotke i kodifikatsii burjatskogo obychnogo prava" ("On the Scholarly Investigation and Codification of Buriat Customary Law"), *GB-M,* 2(3), 1921.

2. "Obychnoe pravo mongol'skikh plemen: Ch. 1. Obychnoe pravo mongolov; Ch. 2. Obychnoe pravo burjat; Ch. 3. Obychnoe pravo kalmykov" ("Customary Law of the Mongol Tribes: Pt. 1. Customary Law of the Mongols; Pt. 2. Customary Law of the Buriats; Pt. 3. Customary Law of the Kalmuks"), *VA,* 51-52, 1923-1924.

3. "Pravootnoshenija po nedvizhimostjam v Kitae" ("Legal Relations on Immovables in China"), *IJuFvgKh,* I, 1925.

4. "Osnovnye instituty kitaiskogo grazhdanskogo prava" ("Fundamental Institutions of Chinese Civil Law"), *VM,* 5-6, 1926.

5. "Novoe kitaiskoe grazhdanskoe pravo" ("The New Chinese Civil Law"), *IJuFvgKh,* IV, 1927.

6. "Zemel'noe pravo Kitaja" ("Land Law of China"), *IJuFvgKh,* VI, 1928.

7. "Gornoe pravo Kitaja" ("Mining Law of China"), *IJuFvgKh,* VI, 1928.

8. "Lesnoe pravo Kitaja" ("Forest Law of China"), *IJuFvgKh,* VI, 1928.

9. "Kitaiskoe pravo, bibliografija" ("Chinese Law: Bibliography"), *IJuFvgKh,* VI, 1928.

10. "Mongol'skoe pravo i sravnitel'noe pravovedenie" ("Mongol Law and Comparative Jurisprudence"), *IJuFvgKh,* VII, 1929.

11. "Dva pamjatnika obychnogo prava mongol'skikh plemen" ("Two Monuments of the Customary Law of the Mongol Tribes"), *VM,* 11, 1929, 1, 1930.

12. "O primenenii iskovoi davnosti s obratnoi siloju po novomu kitaiskomu zakonodatel'stvu" ("On the Application of Prescription with Retroactive Effect in the New Chinese Legislation"), *Vkp,* 2, 1931.

13. "Nekotorye cherty obychnogo prava altaev i teleutov" ("Some Characteristics of the Customary Law of the Altais and the Teleuts"), *Vkp,* 3, 1931.

14. "Obzor pamjatnikov mongol'skogo prava" ("A Survey of the Monuments of Mongol Law"), *Bs,* I, 1932.

15. "Velikaja Jasa Chingiz-Khana" ("The Great Yassa of Genghiz-Khan"), *IJuFvgKh,* X, 1933.

C. Works Edited in Russian

1. *Proekt Grazhdanskogo Ulozhenija Kitaiskoi Respubliki (The Draft Civil Code of the Republic of China),* trans. from Chinese K. V. Uspenskii, I-II Harbin: 1927.

2. *Grazhdanskii Kodeks Kitaiskoi Respubliki (The Civil Code of the Republic of China),* trans. from Chinese Wang Tzen-jun, I-V, Harbin: 1931-1935.

D. Books and Monographs in English

1. *Fundamental Institutions of Chinese Civil Law,* Harbin: 1926, 74 pp.

2. *The Modern Civil Law of China,* I-II, Harbin: 1927-1928, 190 pp., 150 pp.

3. *Customary Law of the Mongol Tribes,* Harbin: 1929, 306 pp.

4. *Mongolian Law and Comparative Jurisprudence,* Harbin: 1933, 19 pp.

5. *Fundamental Principles of Mongol Law,* ed. 1, Tientsin: 1937, 338 pp.; ed. 2, Bloomington: 1965, 350 pp.

6. *Chinese Civil Law,* Tientsin: 1938, 310 pp.

7. *Customary Law of the Nomadic Tribes of Siberia,* Tientsin: 1938, 151 pp.; ed. 2, Bloomington (to be publ., 1965).

E. Articles in English

1. "Fundamental Institutions of Chinese Civil Law," *VM,* 5-6, 1926.
2. "Chinese Law—Bibliography", *Bb,* 8, 1928.
3. "The Influence of Chinese Law upon the Mongolian Law", *TCSaPSR,* XV, 3, 1931.
4. "Mongol Law and Chinese Law in the Yuan Dynasty", *TCSaPSR,* XX, 2, 1936.
5. "The Code of Northern Mongolia: Khalkha Djirom", *TCSaPSR,* XX, 3, 1936.
6. "Customary Law of the Kirghiz", *TCSaPSR,* XXI, 2, 1937.
7. "Customary Law of the Yakuts", *TCSaPSR,* XXI, 3, 1937.
8. "Customary Law of the Tunguses", *NSaEQ,* X, 2, 1937.
9. "Juristic Customs of the Voguls, Ostyaks and Samoyeds", *TCSaPSR,* XXI, 4, 1938.
10. "Conflicts of Different Laws (General Rules and Chinese Norms)", *TCSaPSR,* XXII, 2, 1938.
11. "Application and the Interpretation of the Norms of Law", *TCSaPSR,* XXII, 3, 1938.
12. "Mongol Law: A Concise Historical Survey", *WLR,* XXIII, 2, 1948.

F. Articles in French

1. "Les monuments de droit mongol", *BdlSdLC,* 7-12, 1932.
2. "Le droit mongol", *BdlSdLC,* 3, 1937.

G. Books and Monographs in Japanese

1. *Customary Law of the Mongol Tribes,* Harbin: 1929, 306 pp., trans. from English, 1934.
2. *Mongol'skoe pravo, preimushchestvenno obychnoe (Mongol Law, with Special Reference to Customary Law),* Harbin: 1931, 306 + 42 pp., trans. from Russian, 1935.

III. Russian History and Culture

A. Books and Monographs in Russian

1. *Ob izuchenii drevnei russkoi zhivopisi (On the Study of Ancient Russian Painting),* Harbin: 1934, 51 pp.; also in *IJuFvGKh,* XI, 1934.
2. *Osnovnye vidy drevnei russkoi zhivopisi (The Main Types of Ancient Russian Painting),* Harbin: 1935, 45 pp.
3. *Obzor russkoi kul'tury (Survey of Russian Culture),* I, New York: 1947, 639 pp.; II, 1, New York: 1947, 557 pp.; II, 2, New York: 1948, 213 pp.
4. *Razvitie russkoi nauchnoi mysli v XVIII-XX st. st. (nauki o prirode) (The Development of Russian Scientific Thought in the XVIII-XX Centuries: Natural Sciences),* New York: 1949, 136 pp.

B. Articles in Russian

1. "K voprosu o vlijanii mongol'skoi kul'tury i prava na russkuju kul'turu i pravo—Aktovaja rech' " ("On the Question of the Influence of Mongol Culture and Law on Russian Culture and Law—Commencement Address"), *IJuFvgKh,* IX, 1931.
2. "Iz istorii nauchnogo vostokovedenija v S.S.S.R." ("From the History of Oriental Studies in the U.S.S.R.,") *VIpISSR,* 3 (24), 1957; short English, French,

and German language summaries under slightly different titles also appear in *VIpISSSR,* 3 (24), 1957.

C. Articles in English

1. "The Influence of Ancient Mongol Culture and Law on Russian Culture and Law", *TCSaPSR,* XX, 4, 1937.

IV. Works in Preparation

A. Books and Monographs in Russian

1. *Rossica* (a collection of essays on mediaeval Russian history).

2. *Iz istorii nauki v S.S.S.R.: 1918-1963 (From the History of Science in the U.S.S.R.).*